S0-BAP-293

"Mr. Markham's book is notable . . . a well-balanced study of a man vastly bigger than his 5 feet 6 inches, who has been for generations one of the most fascinating of subjects for biography."

—BALTIMORE EVENING SUN

"A surprisingly sympathetic biography of one of the most fascinating men who ever strutted across the stage of history."

—NASHVILLE TENNESSEEAN

"A remarkable achievement. The story moves as fast as one of Bonaparte's campaigns and is told with the clarity of his dispatches."

—THE ECONOMIST

NAPOLEON

Felix Markham

A MENTOR BOOK

NEW AMERICAN LIBRARY

NEW YORK AND SCARBOROUGH, ONTARIO

MENTOR TRADEMARK REG. U.S. PAT. OFF. AND FOREIGN COUNTRIES
REGISTERED TRADEMARK—MARCA REGISTRADA
HECHO EN CHICAGO, U.S.A.

SIGNET, SIGNET CLASSIC, MENTOR, ONYX, PLUME, MERIDIAN AND
NAL BOOKS are published in the United States by
NAL PENGUIN INC.,
1633 Broadway, New York, New York 10019,
in Canada by The New American Library of Canada Limited,
81 Mack Avenue, Scarborough, Ontario M1L 1M8

   14   15   16   17   18   19   20   21   22

PRINTED IN THE UNITED STATES OF AMERICA

CONTENTS

PREFACE   *page* xi

1 CORSICAN BACKGROUND   15

2 THE TURN OF THE WHEEL   24

3 VICTORY IN ITALY   34

4 THE EASTERN ADVENTURE   55

5 BRUMAIRE AND MARENGO   68

6 FIRST CONSUL   88

7 THE NEW CHARLEMAGNE   103

8 AUSTERLITZ AND THE DEFEAT OF THE THIRD
   COALITION   120

9 THE NAPOLEONIC EMPIRE   131

10 THE CONTINENTAL SYSTEM   155

11 THE SPANISH ULCER   164

12 WAGRAM AND THE AWAKENING OF EUROPE   173

13 CATASTROPHE IN RUSSIA   185

14 LEIPZIG AND ABDICATION   200

15 THE HUNDRED DAYS AND WATERLOO   217

16 ST HELENA   236

17 THE NAPOLEONIC LEGEND   255

    APPENDICES   267

    BIBLIOGRAPHY   271

    GENEALOGICAL TABLE   284

    MAPS   285

    INDEX   290

ILLUSTRATIONS

1 The earliest known drawing of Napoleon from life, 1785 (*Photo: Bulloz, Paris*)

2 A medallion of 1832 by David d'Angers of Napoleon during the Italian campaigns of 1796–7 (*Photo: Giraudon, Paris*)

3 A drawing by Appiani in 1796, after the battle of Lodi (*by permission of Brera Gallery, Milan*)

4 The centre-piece of the celebrated but idealized picture by J. L. David of Napoleon crossing the Alps in the Marengo campaign, 1800 (*Photo: Giraudon, Paris*)

5 Portrait by Greuze of Napoleon in his official Consular uniform (*Photo: Giraudon, Paris*)

6 Portrait by Gérard, 1803 (*Photo: Bulloz, Paris*)

7 Gros depicts the First Consul at a military review (*Photo: Bulloz, Paris*)

8 The centre-piece of J. L. David's huge picture of the Coronation, 1804 (*Photo: Bulloz, Paris*)

9 Napoleon I in his Coronation robes, by Ingres (*Photo: Bulloz, Paris*)

10 A contemporary print of 1805 (*by permission of La Bibliothèque Nationale*)

11 Napoleon as Emperor of the French and Protector of the Confederation of the Rhine, 1806 (*Photo: Bulloz, Paris*)

12 On leaving Tilsit, 1807, Napoleon decorated with the Legion of Honour the bravest soldier of the Russian Imperial Guard; picture by Debret (*Photo: Giraudon, Paris*)

13 Napoleon greeting Queen Louise of Prussia at Königsberg, 1807; centre-piece of picture by Debret *(Photo: Giraudon, Paris)*

14 Napoleon in 1808; an unfinished portrait by J. L. David *(Photo: Giraudon, Paris)*

15 Napoleon in 1809; by R. Lefèvre *(Photo: Bulloz, Paris)*

16 Napoleon I, by Girodet *(Photo: Giraudon, Paris)*

17 Bust, from life, by Houdon *(Photo: Giraudon, Paris)*

18 Statue by Canova, now in the possession of the Duke of Wellington, at Apsley House, London *(by permission of the Victoria and Albert Museum)*

19 The plague of rats at Longwood was a favourite theme of caricaturists in the St Helena period *(Photo: Bulloz, Paris)*

20 A Gillray cartoon of 1808 *(by permission of the Mansell Collection)*

21 A Gillray cartoon of 1804 *(by permission of the Mansell Collection)*

22 A Gillray cartoon of 1805 *(by permission of the Mansell Collection)*

23 A German cartoon of 1813 *(Photo: Arthur L. Brinicombe, Exeter)*

24 Napoleon in the campaign of France, 1814; picture by Meissonier, 1864 *(Photo: Bulloz, Paris)*

25 Napoleon's farewell to the Old Guard at Fontainebleau, April 1814; contemporary print *(Photo: Jean-Pierre Vieil, Paris)*

26 Napoleon as Père la Violette; Bonapartist propaganda during the First Bourbon Restoration, April 1814–March 1815 *(Photo: Jean-Pierre Vieil, Paris)*

27 Napoleon lands at Antibes, March 1815 *(Photo: Bulloz, Paris)*

28 Napoleon wins over the 7th Infantry Regiment near Grenoble, March 1815 *(Photo: Bulloz, Paris)*

29 Napoleon's quarrel with the Governor of St Helena *(Photo: Bulloz, Paris)*

30 Napoleon dictates to Las Cases' son *(Photo: Jean-Pierre Vieil, Paris)*

31 Napoleon meets Jane and Betsy Balcombe *(Photo: Bulloz, Paris)*

32 Napoleon gardening at Longwood; by an unknown artist *(Photo: Giraudon, Paris)*

33 The funeral cortège of Napoleon at St Helena, 1821 *(Photo: Jean-Pierre Vieil, Paris)*

34 The 'Sankey' death-mask of Napoleon; see Appendix II *(by permission of the Bodleian Library)*

35 Napoleon lying in state on his death-bed; drawing by an English officer *(by permission of the 'Illustrated London News')*

36 Napoleon in captivity recalls his triumphs *(Photo: Jean-Pierre Vieil, Paris)*

37 The Duke of Reichstadt, dying in 1832, joins his father *(Photo: Jean-Pierre Vieil, Paris)*

38 Napoleon as the champion of the Catholic faith; an exotic expression of the legend and the martyrdom of St Helena *(Photo: Jean-Pierre Vieil, Paris)*

LINE MAPS

1 Lombardy 1796–7   286

2 The Russian Campaign   287

3 Europe under Napoleon 1812   288–9

4 The Waterloo Campaign   290

PREFACE

IT IS A BOLD undertaking for an historian, especially an English one, to embark on writing a new biography of Napoleon. The shades of the great Napoleonic historians of the past look over one's shoulder: in France, Thiers, Sorel, Vandal, Georges Lefebvre; in Germany, Fournier and Kircheisen; in Russia, Tarlé; in England, Holland Rose of Cambridge; from Oxford, Rosebery, Fisher, J. M. Thompson. In the Preface to his *Napoleon Bonaparte: his Rise and Fall* (1952), Thompson declared that 'there cannot be too many likenesses of a great man in the picture-gallery of history'. Let that in itself be my excuse.

Even since 1952, important new material on Napoleon has come to light, notably through the deciphering of the second and third volumes of General Bertrand's St. Helena diaries, the discovery in the Swedish Royal Archives of the Empress Marie-Louise's letters to Napoleon, and of her letters to her son, the Duke of Reichstadt, in the Montenuovo archives. Among recent secondary works Professor J. Godechot's *Institutions de la Révolution et de l'Empire*, and Professor F. Crouzet's *L'Économie Britannique et le Blocus Continental*, based on an exhaustive survey of the English official records, may be singled out as of first-rate importance.

It was, moreover, only in the third decade of this century that the letters of Napoleon to Marie-Louise, the memoirs of Caulaincourt, Duc de Vicence, and those of Queen Hortense appeared.

It therefore comes both as a shock and a challenge to find that, apart from Thompson's work and Tarlé's slighter *Bonaparte* of 1937, it is necessary to go back more than thirty years for a full-length biography of Napoleon by a professional historian: to Kircheisen (1927), to Holland Rose (1901), to Fournier (1886). The authoritative work of Professor G. Lefebvre, *Napoléon* in the series *Peuples et Civilisations* (1935), is a history of the Napoleonic period; that of Professor P. Geyl, *Napoleon—For and Against* (1944), is a penetrating analysis of the views of French historians of Napoleon.

My book is designed to be a biography of Napoleon: what he thought and did; not an account of everything that happened in the Napoleonic era. Yet it must be admitted at once that for nearly twenty years the career of Napoleon and the history of Europe were almost synonymous. I have tried to preserve the continuity and sweep of the narrative by introducing and explaining the forces in and against which Napoleon was operating—military, diplomatic, moral and economic —at the precise points at which they impinged on his career. For example, the reader will not, I hope, be surprised that Chapter Twelve on 'Wagram' opens with an analysis of the intellectual movement in Germany at the end of the eighteenth century; it is not irrelevant. The campaigns of 1796 and of Waterloo are analysed in some detail, because they are the most typical examples of Napoleon's strategy: otherwise I have aimed at keeping military narrative to the essential minimum.

The sources and the literature on Napoleon are so vast and mostly accessible in print that I have dispensed with detailed references and footnotes, and confined myself to a selected bibliography, arranged for each chapter, which may reduce it to manageable proportions both for the student and for the general reader.

I refrain from drawing analogies, which may be misleading, between Napoleon and the rulers and dictators of earlier or later times. But one thing can safely be said of him: as a man of action he remains unique in two respects. No man in this category before him can be known in such wealth of detail; no man after him has combined outstanding military genius as a leader in the field with a political career on a world scale.

I gratefully acknowledge the help which enabled me to start putting this book on paper in the summer of 1961: to Hertford College, Oxford, which allowed me leave of absence for a university term; to the Leverhulme Trustees who awarded me a research and travelling Fellowship; to the Rockefeller Foundation for their generous hospitality at the Villa Serbelloni.

At the neighbouring Villa Melzi, Duca Gallarati Scotti kindly showed me his unique collection of Napoleonic books and portraits including a drawing by Appiani of Napoleon after the battle of Lodi (Plate 3); I am most grateful to him for the opportunity to reproduce it. I thank Madame J. Wittouck for permission to quote in Chapter Thirteen from an unpublished letter from Maréchal Ney. Sir Wilfrid Le Gros Clark, Emeritus Professor of Human Anatomy in the University of Oxford, and his successor, Professor G. Harris, have given me invaluable help in sorting out the medical evidence concerning Napoleon's health.

Permission to quote extracts from the letters of Marie-Louise in *My Dearest Louise* by C. F. Palmstierna has kindly been given me by Methuen & Co.; and by Hamish Hamilton to quote extracts from the archives of Marie-Louise in *Napoleon's Son* by André Castelot.

I am also glad to acknowledge my indebtedness to Mr John Eldred Howard for permission to quote freely in chapters 1 to 6 from the translations contained in Volume 1 of his *"Letters and Documents of Napoleon"* published by the Cresset Press.

I must also express my gratitude for the help given me by the staff of the Bodleian Library in exploring the unpublished portions of the Curzon Collection; to Mrs Mary Denniston in checking my proof-reading; to Miss Catherine Northover, who typed the whole book, and dealt kindly and imperturbably with my hand-writing.

June 1963   F. M. H. M.

I

Corsican Background

NOTHING ANNOYED NAPOLEON MORE when he was Consul and Emperor than the name given to him by his enemies, 'the Corsican'. He did not attach much importance to his origins and lineage; he claimed to be a self-made man whose titles rested on his sword and on the votes of the French nation.

At St Helena he recalled that when his marriage to an Austrian Archduchess was being negotiated, the Emperor of Austria 'actually wished to publish a genealogy showing that my ancestors had reigned at Treviso. He did not want a *mésalliance*.' Napoleon would have nothing to do with it, and his reply was: 'Permit me to be the Rudolph of my dynasty.' When he was Emperor and one of his officers complained to him of his preference for promoting members of the *ancienne noblesse,* he replied: 'Am I after all a noble, I, a poor Corsican squire?' He was not ashamed of his origin and indeed he retained to the end of his life a sense of family loyalty and obligation which was a markedly Corsican trait; but when he came to power 'a foreign origin was an embarrassment which had to be hidden like bastardy'. Moreover, when he left Corsica for the last time in 1793, his early life which he was leaving behind seemed to be associated with nothing but poverty, hardship and defeat.

15

16 NAPOLEON

The importance of Napoleon's Corsican origin and background has often been exaggerated; but, viewed in retrospect, it combines certain factors which laid the foundations of his career. First of all, there was the influence of his mother in his childhood. At St Helena he reflected that 'I was very well brought up by my mother. I owe her a great deal. She instilled into me pride and taught me good sense.' He used to recount with a mixture of admiration and indignation how his mother gave him a birching for mimicking his grandmother. He might have added that it was his parents' friendship with de Marbeuf, the French Governor of Corsica, that gave him the chance of the best professional education for a military career. Thirdly, it was in the minute but complicated and hardhitting school of Corsican politics that he acquired his political apprenticeship.

Napoleon was born on August 15, 1769, at Ajaccio in Corsica; and it was not surprising that he was at first a sickly infant, as his mother had spent the last months of her pregnancy wandering about the mountains as a refugee. Three months earlier General Paoli, the champion of Corsican independence, had been finally defeated by the French.

For many years the Corsican struggle for independence had been a subject of romantic interest and speculation in Europe. In his *Contrat Social* (1762) Rousseau declared, 'I have a presentiment that one day this small island will astonish Europe.' Boswell visited the island in 1766 and his *Account of Corsica* (1768) gave wide publicity to Paoli. Boswell compared the Corsicans, in their character and conditions, to the Highlanders of Scotland, and wrote, 'Europe now turns her eyes upon them, and with astonishment sees them on the eve of emancipating themselves for ever from a foreign yoke, and becoming an independent nation.' In a society based on the clan, status was assessed by the solidarity of the family, and feuds were settled by private vengeance—the Corsican vendetta. Napoleon remarked that 'a Corsican would never think of abandoning his cousin'. Although he disapproved of the vendetta as a barbarous custom, there were at least two occasions in his career when he reverted to the vendetta concept—the execution of Enghien, and the bequest in his will to the man who had tried to assassinate Wellington.[1] When Paoli became an exile in England in 1769, he was naturally introduced by Boswell to

[1] See p. 112.

Dr Johnson, who greatly respected him. But sometimes the Doctor became bored, if perversely and unfairly, by Boswell's enthusiasm for Corsica. 'Sir, what is all this rout about the Corsicans? They have been at war with the Genoese for upwards of twenty years, and have never yet taken their fortified towns. They might have pulled the walls in pieces, and cracked the stones with their teeth in twenty years.'

In 1761 Paoli had expelled the Genoese, but in 1768 the French, having acquired by treaty the Genoese claims to Corsica, invaded in force. Napoleon's father, Carlo Buonaparte, was one of Paoli's lieutenants in the guerrilla resistance; and Napoleon was baptized with the name of a cousin who died fighting the French. If Carlo had followed Paoli into exile, Napoleon might have been brought up as an English subject. But he remained and made his peace with the French; in 1770 he was admitted as a member of the French *noblesse*.

The formal verification of his lineage showed that he came of a noble Florentine family, traceable as far back as the eleventh century, and resident in Corsica for two hundred years. Napoleon's mother, Marie-Letizia Ramolino, was the daughter of a civil engineer and niece of a canon of Ajaccio cathedral, whose family could equally claim a long lineage, being related to the distinguished family of Coll 'Alto, established in Lombary since the fourteenth century. Among a poor people, the possession of a few acres of property, a country farm and a town house in Ajaccio made the Buonapartes one of the leading families of Ajaccio. Napoleon's uncle, the Archdeacon of Ajaccio, used to boast that 'never had the Buonaparte family bought oil, wine or bread'. Napoleon recalled that 'we thought ourselves as good as the Bourbons: in the island we really were'. Married at the age of fourteen, Letizia bore thirteen children of whom eight survived infancy—Joseph, Napoleon, Lucien, Elisa, Louis, Pauline, Caroline, Jerome.

She was a young woman of striking beauty and force of character: Carlo was a man of considerable charm and culture if weak and extravagant. This handsome pair attracted the benevolent attention of Monsieur de Marbeuf. Their friendship became so close that it soon aroused gossip about Napoleon's parentage, as de Marbeuf was already in the island before Napoleon's birth. Napoleon himself discussed this possibility with his friend, the scientist Monge, when they were sailing back from Egypt. Given the Corsican attitude to family honour and adultery, it was inherently improbable. Moreover de Marbeuf was an elderly man of sixty-six and Letizia was in Corte, Paoli's stronghold, when Napoleon was conceived.

Through the influence of de Marbeuf, Carlo secured for Napoleon a place at Brienne, one of the twelve royal schools founded in 1776 by St Germain, Louis XVI's Minister of War, for the sons of nobles. In 1779 Napoleon, aged nine, arrived in France to begin his schooling; the first three months were spent in Autun, at the church school where his elder brother Joseph had been placed. In 1782 he was visited by his parents (when, as an English fellow-pupil records, his mother's beauty made a considerable impression), but he was not to see home till eight years later as a young man. In the meantime his father had died of cancer of the stomach in 1785.

It is, on the whole, exceptional for men of strong personality, destined to make their mark in the world, to be happy or successful schoolboys. Napoleon, when reminiscing about his schooldays, tended to exaggerate his hardships, solitude, and unpopularity; and the truth has been further obscured by letters and school reports of doubtful authenticity. To his teachers Napoleon certainly appeared a model and promising pupil, especially in mathematics. The work was hard—eight hours a day of lessons, predominantly in Latin and history. Napoleon remembered many of his teachers with gratitude, and later rewarded them with places and pensions.

To his school-fellows he was an obvious object for mild ragging because of his foreign accent and his passionate Corsican patriotism, though this did not prevent him from making a few close friends. His odd Corsican name 'Napoleone' was corrupted into the nickname of *Paille-au-Nez* (Strawnose). Was his pose of the persecuted Corsican patriot a form of defence against his foreign accent and poverty, or was it even a form of subconscious jealousy of his mother's friendship with his patron, de Marbeuf? His parents had, after all, thrown in their lot with the French, and a more ordinary boy would have conformed to the French background in which he found himself.

Even as a small child he was noted for his enthusiasm in organizing fierce and elaborate mock-battles. An English fellow-pupil of Napoleon recalled in 1797 the cold winter of 1783 when fierce battles raged among the snow fortifications designed by Napoleon.

The school inspector reported that Napoleon's aptitude for mathematics would make him suitable for the navy, but eventually it was decided that he should try for the artillery, where advancement by merit and mathematical skill was much more open than in the infantry. In 1784 he was nominated, in a patent signed by Louis XVI, to a place at the *École Militaire* in Paris.

This French Sandhurst had been founded in 1751, largely at the instance of Madame de Pompadour, to remedy the lamentable lack of education of gentlemen-cadets. It contained both paying pupils and King's scholars and, despite St Germain's reforms, it reflected the social standards of the *haute noblesse,* who affected to despise the poor scholars. Napoleon here encountered the 'cascade of disdain' which was one of the most important psychological causes of the Revolution. Laura Permon, later wife of General Junot, Duc d'Abrantès, whose mother was a friend of Letizia Buonaparte and befriended Napoleon in Paris, recollects that Napoleon ranted violently against the snobbery of the *École Militaire.* Napoleon said, 'We were fed and served magnificently', and as First Consul he made the *École Militaire* considerably more austere. But even before the Revolution its staff of teachers was of high quality.

Napoleon took the passing-out examination in one year, instead of the normal two or three years, and was placed forty-second in the national list. His performance was so good that he jumped the intermediate grades and was commissioned as Lieutenant to the *Régiment de la Fère* at Valence, together with his greatest friend de Mazis. When Napoleon and de Mazis visited the Permons to show off their new uniforms Napoleon looked so thin and small that Laura and her sister instantly gave him the nickname of 'Puss-in-Boots'. This was too much for Napoleon's sense of humour, and for many years Laura was greeted by Napoleon as 'little pest'. As a schoolboy Napoleon was certainly a youth with a considerable chip on his shoulder. Like so many of the products of the *École Militaire,* de Mazis emigrated during the Revolution. When he returned to Paris in 1802 under the amnesty for the *emigrés,* he was warmly welcomed by Napoleon; as Keeper of the Wardrobe he remained one of his court officials till the end of the Empire.

The artillery *Régiment de la Fère* had a reputation as one of the smartest and most efficient in the French army. The significance of the professional and practical training

Napoleon received there between 1785 and 1788, and at the artillery school of Auxonne, commanded by Maréchal du Teil, in the year 1788–9, will become apparent later at Toulon and in the Italian campaigns. Although he was the junior in rank at Auxonne, he was picked out by du Teil to write a report on experiments in the use of guns with explosive shells. Nevertheless there was plenty of time for leisure and general reading, and for the aristocratic officer corps of the *ancien régime* leave was on a lavish scale. Between 1786 and 1788 he was able to spend three-quarters of his time on leave in Corsica or Paris.

At Valence he lived in lodgings and was mothered by an admirable landlady, Mlle Bou. He also made friends with a family called Colombier; at St Helena he recalled his first flirtation with the daughter Caroline, 'It will scarcely be considered credible, perhaps, but our whole business consisted in eating cherries together.' This was more than a passing acquaintance; they kept up a correspondence, and Caroline, as Mme Bressieux, was a frequent visitor at the court of the Emperor, as a lady-in-waiting to Madame Mère. By the standards of the time Napoleon was an exceptionally chaste and bookish youth; and apart from a brief encounter with a young prostitute when he visited Paris in 1787, sex seems to have occupied little of his thoughts. At Brienne he had tried to reform one of his friends who had fallen a prey to homosexual temptations. His first leave in Corsica in 1786 and his visit to Paris in 1787 were largely taken up with complicated family business involving a mulberry plantation, for which the government had promised a subsidy.

Napoleon's posting to Auxonne (September 1788—September 1789) coincided with the outbreak of the Revolution: but his immediate contact with it was limited to the suppression of local food-riots. The regiment at Auxonne swallowed the oath of allegiance to the Nation in August 1789 without difficulty. The officers of the artillery corps, being of the *petite noblesse*, were less inclined to emigrate than their more aristocratic colleagues of the infantry. It is significant that during the Revolution the artillery corps lost one-third of its officers through emigration, compared with two-thirds in the infantry. At the battle of Valmy in September 1792 it was the artillery corps that was to ensure the survival of revolutionary France.

As at Brienne and Paris, Napoleon's heroes remained Rousseau and Paoli. For him the Revolution meant a great opportunity of freedom for Corsica. At Valence he had written: 'What sight shall I see in my own country? My compatriots in chains and fearfully kissing the hand that oppresses them?' In June 1789 he wrote a letter to General Paoli: 'You left the island, and the hope of happiness went with you; slavery was the price of our submission.'

When he returned to Corsica in September 1789 he found that the Revolution had hardly as yet touched the island. He at once took the lead in organizing a volunteer National Guard, distributing tricolour badges, and drawing up an Address to the National Assembly. When the Address reached Paris, the Assembly, on the motion of Mirabeau, decreed that Corsica should henceforth be part of France, and that Corsicans should have the full rights and liberties of French citizens. This was a triumph for the Buonapartist faction, and an important change in Napoleon's attitude to France; henceforth he was to take the French and Jacobin side in Corsican politics. Paoli returned from exile, and was acclaimed as the liberator and leader.

Napoleon was again at Valence in 1791, where he had been posted to the *Régiment de Grenoble*, with promotion to First Lieutenant. Here the news of Louis XVI's flight to Varennes turned him from a monarchist into a Republican. In September 1791, he again obtained leave, on the plea that his uncle, the Archdeacon, was dying. In January 1792, Narbonne, as Minister of War, sanctioned Napoleon's transfer from the regular army to the post of adjutant to a volunteer Corsican battalion.

Political unity in Corsica under the leadership of Paoli was already breaking down; Paoli and Pozzo di Borgo were taking the royalist and clerical side. Napoleon secured his election as second-in-command of a volunteer battalion by the kidnapping of his opponents. On Easter Sunday, 1792, the religious schism provoked riots in Ajaccio, in the course of which Napoleon's battalion fired on the citizens. Pozzo di Borgo, as Corsican deputy in the Legislative Assembly, denounced his actions. Moreover, Napoleon had ignored the army order that all regular officers should return to their regiments by April 1, 1792, and he had been struck off the army list. It was high time for him to visit Paris and restore his position with the authorities.

Napoleon was in Paris from the end of May to the middle of September 1792—the crucial period of the Prussian invasion, the fall of the monarchy, and the September Massacres. He wrote several times to his brothers, but the last letter is dated August 7. In Las Cases' *Mémorial de Ste-Hélène*, Napoleon gives an eyewitness account of the attack on the Tuileries on August 10. He judges that a resolute defence of the Tuileries would have won the day for the King. On July 23 he had written to Lucien, 'Those at the top are poor creatures. It must be admitted, when you see things at first hand, that the people are not worth the trouble taken in winning their favour. You know the history of Ajaccio; that of Paris is exactly the same; perhaps men are here even a little smaller, nastier, more slanderous and censorious. You have to see things close to realize that enthusiasm is but enthusiasm and that the French are an old nation without ties.' Shrewdness and cynicism were rapidly replacing Napoleon's youthful ideals.

The shortage of officers as a result of emigration was acute, and Napoleon had little difficulty in procuring reinstatement in the army, with a step in rank to Captain. He was also allowed to return to Corsica, on the plea that the royal school in Paris where his young sister Elisa was a pupil was being closed.

Encouraged by their success at Valmy, the Girondin government in Paris approved an expedition to seize the strategically important islands of Caprera and Maddalena near Sardinia. Four thousand 'patriot' troops were brought by the Fleet from Marseilles, but they combined so badly with the Corsican volunteers that the Corsicans had to be used in a separate attack on Maddalena, in January 1793. Napoleon was under the orders of a Paolist general, Cesari; and his first experience in the field ended in a complete fiasco. Napoleon's artillery had nearly won the day when the troops panicked and mutinied, and the expedition retreated in disorder. Napoleon sent an angry denunciation of his commander to the Minister of War.

When England entered the war against France at the beginning of 1793, suspicion of Paoli's pro-English sympathies and connexions was bound to come to a head. In February 1793, Saliceti, a Corsican friend of the Buonaparte family, was sent as Deputy of the Convention *en mission* to supervise Paoli and to put the Corsican forces under the command of the Army of Italy. These instructions were rapidly superseded by the news that the Convention had decreed the arrest of Paoli for treason—an action which had been precipitated by a wild denunciation of Paoli's 'despotism' by Lucien Buonaparte at a meeting of the Popular Society of Toulon.

Napoleon either knew nothing of Lucien's move, or at least regarded it as premature, as the Buonapartists were in no position to meet a show of force by the Paolist faction. Napoleon's first action was to write to the Convention, defending Paoli and pleading for conciliation. The Convention withdrew its decree, but it was too late to avert civil war in Corsica. Napoleon made an abortive attempt to seize the citadel of Ajaccio, and the whole family was forced into exile. A Paolist congress condemned the Buonaparte family to 'perpetual execration and infamy', and their property was pillaged.

Paoli delivered Corsica to the English, who occupied it till 1796, when Napoleon's conquest of North Italy made it untenable and the Buonaparte house in Ajaccio was restored for Madame Mère.

Meanwhile the family gathered in exile at Marseilles, dependent almost entirely on Napoleon's army pay. Napoleon was temporarily employed in organizing heated shot for the coastal batteries to fire at English ships.

In June 1793 Napoleon drew up a memorandum recommending that an expedition of five thousand men could easily recapture Corsica from Paoli: but in effect his connexion with Corsica and his Corsican allegiance were now at an end. The revolutionary war against Europe was fast moving into a critical phase, and it was to provide Napoleon with his first great opportunity.

2

The Turn of the Wheel

THE SUMMER OF 1793 brought upon France the most dangerous crisis of the Revolution. The Girondin faction, insanely optimistic about the efficacy of an ideological war, had declared that the Republic would assist 'all peoples who rise against their rulers'. They had provoked war with all Europe, including England, and then had shown themselves quite incompetent to wage it. Expelled from the Convention by the Montagnard faction, which was backed by the people of Paris, they had raised the provinces in revolt, and joined hands with the counter-revolutionary royalists. Two-thirds of the Departments of France were affected by civil war: Lyons joined the revolt, and at the end of August Toulon, the second most important naval base in France, welcomed the English and Spanish fleets. It was lucky for France that Pitt had sent the bulk of the English army to die of yellow fever in the West Indies. There were never more than two thousand English troops available at Toulon. Six thousand Austrian troops were promised but never arrived. The seven thousand Neapolitan and six thousand Spanish troops were unreliable, and the total force was insufficient to hold the approaches to the harbours indefinitely.

In July, Napoleon was ordered to join the Montagnard

force under General Carteaux which had been assembled to prevent the rebels of Marseilles joining hands with those of Lyons. Carteaux rapidly captured Avignon, Aix and Taras-con, and entered Marseilles. In the middle of August Napo-leon applied from Avignon for a post in the Army of the Rhine, and in the meantime published a political pamphlet *Le Souper de Beaucaire*. In the form of a dialogue, it de-nounced the folly of a fratricidal civil war and defended the Montagnard cause against the Girondins and the Royal-ists. 'Your success is the object of the prayers of all the notorious aristocrats.'

The style of this pamphlet shows a considerable advance on his earlier writings, notably the *Lettres sur la Corse* and the *Discours de Lyons* of 1791 (the latter being a prize essay for the Academy of Lyons which was placed fifteenth in the competition). These had been turgid, undistinguished, and feeble imitations of Rousseau, and he had not yet de-veloped the terse, natural, striking and individual style of his mature letters, bulletins and proclamations. At St Helena Napoleon said: 'At the age of twenty I sent to the Academy of Lyons various writings which I subsequently withdrew. When I read them I found that their author deserved to be whipped. What ridiculous things I said and how annoyed I would be if they were preserved!'

Carteaux's army, ten thousand strong but very short of ar-tillery, started to invest Toulon within a few days of captur-ing Marseilles. In the first two days of the siege the artillery commander was wounded, and Napoleon was brought in to replace him. Saliceti, the Deputy *en mission* attached to the army, reported to Paris that 'chance has helped us well; we have retained Captain Buonaparte, an experienced officer, who was on his way to the Army of Italy, and ordered him to replace Dommartin'. Napoleon saw that the key-point was Fort Éguillette which commanded the western prom-ontory between the inner and outer harbour; its capture would make both harbours untenable for the enemy fleet. He at once tried to seize the point, before the English in-stalled batteries, but he had too few guns and men. It was to be four months before Napoleon's plan could be successfully carried out.

Barras, the second Deputy sent specially to report on the situation, at one time despaired and recommended that the whole of Provence should be abandoned to the invader. But Napoleon had despatched his plan to Paris through Saliceti.

Carnot's directive endorsed this plan, and Napoleon, as secretary to the council of war at Toulon, drew up the operational orders. Carnot had already seen the point about Éguillette, though his military advisers in Paris had put up to him various and much inferior plans. Napoleon had asked for an artillery General to be appointed, to organize and concentrate the artillery resources: but the General appointed never arrived because his orders went astray. Dugommier, an experienced veteran of the Seven Years' War, was in command of the siege from November, 1793, and he brought with him du Teil, the bother of Napoleon's commander at Auxonne. They both approved Napoleon's handling of the artillery, and left him a fairly free hand.

On December 14 the decisive bombardment and assault began, and by December 18 Admiral Hood decided to evacuate and leave Toulon to its fate. In their sudden retirement the English succeeded in destroying only a part of the French fleet and installations. In the assault Napoleon received the only considerable wound of his military career—a thrust in the thigh from an English bayonet. On December 24 he wrote to the Ministry of War, 'I promised you brilliant successes, and, as you see, I have kept my word.'

Napoleon never held a rank higher than that of acting Lieutenant-Colonel throughout the siege, but immediately after it he was promoted Brigadier-General. He chose as his aides Marmont and Junot, who had become his close friends during the siege. The Deputies and Generals naturally claimed the credit for the success at Toulon, and only briefly mentioned Napoleon's part. But the men on the spot had no doubt about his worth, and the importance of the part he had played in the operations. Du Teil wrote to the Minister of War, 'Words fail me to describe Bonaparte's merits. He has plenty of knowledge, and as much intelligence and courage: and that is no more than a first sketch of the virtues of a most rare officer.' Augustin, the brother of Maximilien Robespierre, described him as 'an artillery officer of transcendent merit'. Napoleon had been helped by an incredible run of luck: the facts that Dommartin, the artillery officer, was wounded and out of action; that no artillery General was available; that Saliceti, the Deputy, was a Corsican and an old friend; that Dugommier and du Teil recognized his professional competence. But he had made the most of the opportunities offered him.

With the fall of the Hébertists and the Dantonists in the

spring of 1794, Maximilien Robespierre was reaching the peak of his power in Paris. Augustin was a devoted follower of his brother, but he was far less involved in political squabbles and ideology, and he spent his time as an energetic and effective Deputy *en mission* in the South. In the period of the Directory (1795–9) Napoleon had nothing but contempt for the Jacobin politicians, but at St Helena, no doubt influenced by his recollection of Augustin Robespierre, he paid tribute to the *Représentants aux Armées* of 1793–4. 'It was the *Représentants* who made the success of the armies.' Augustin was impressed by Napoleon's ability, and under his patronage, Napoleon became in effect the operational planner for the Army of Italy. He was responsible for the planning of the successful attack on the port of Oneglia and on Saorgio (April 1794). At the end of June Augustin Robespierre took with him to Paris a memorandum by Napoleon on the future operations of the Army of Italy which strikingly foreshadows his campaign of 1796, and reveals his developing military genius.

'It is the same with strategy as with the siege of fortresses; concentrate fire on a single point; when the breach is made the equilibrium is broken; all the rest becomes useless and the fortress is taken.

'It is Germany that must be overwhelmed; when that is done Spain and Italy will fall of themselves. The attack must therefore be concentrated and not dispersed. An offensive in Piedmont will stir up Poland and encourage the Grand Turk.

'If we obtain a big success, we can in the succeeding campaigns attack Germany through Lombardy, the Tessin and the County of Tyrol, while our Rhine armies strike at the heart.'

But the sudden fall of Robespierre in the political crisis of Thermidor (July 1794) left Napoleon in a very dangerous position. He had been Augustin Robespierre's 'planner', and under pressure from Paris the Deputies Saliceti and Albitte arrested him on August 9. After a fortnight's investigation he was released and Saliceti reported to Paris that he was cleared of suspicion in any Robespierrist political intrigue. If he had been nearer to Paris, and in the hands of any Deputy less favourable to him than Saliceti, he might well have gone to the guillotine.

Napoleon resumed his staff work for the Army of Italy under Saliceti, and was responsible for the planning of the

neat victory over the Piedmontese at Dego (September 1794).
Dumerbion, the commander, reported to the Committee of
Public Safety that: 'It is to the ability of the General of artillery that I owe the clever combinations which have secured
our success.' Napoleon now advised that a landing in Corsica
would be a 'walk-over'; he was no longer interested in Corsica
for its own sake, but it was clear to the men on the spot,
and to Carnot, that it must be denied to the English fleet
as a base from which the supply lines of the Army of Italy
could be strangled. Napoleon was with the Toulon fleet when
it put to sea in March 1795, but it was so roughly handled
by the English that the project of a landing in Corsica had to
be abandoned.

The wheel of fortune again seemed to turn against Napoleon, as he was informed that he had been posted to command an infantry brigade in the civil war in La Vendée. To an
artillery expert this was an insult, and it might well have
been the grave of his reputation. The Government in Paris
appears to have become suspicious of English influence in
Corsica, and decided to transfer Corsican officers from the
Army of Italy. On arriving in Paris with Marmont and Junot
he staved off his departure for La Vendée on the plea of
illness, and the faithful Junot kept him going with remit-
tances of money from his family. However, Doulcet de Pontécoulant, a member of the Committee of Public Safety, was
interested in his plans for the Army of Italy, and got him appointed temporarily to the Topographical Bureau of the Committee. In July 1795 Napoleon wrote a memorandum which
concluded prophetically, 'Controlling Lombardy as far as
Mantua, the Army would find all that was necessary to re-
equip itself and would be able to mount the gorges of Trent,
cross the Adige and reach the Tyrol, while the Army of the
Rhine passed into Bavaria and also entered the Tyrol.'

On August 20, 1795, Napoleon wrote to his brother Joseph,
'If I ask for it, I shall be sent by the Government to Turkey
as a General of artillery with a good salary and a flattering
ambassadorial title to organize the artillery of the Grand
Turk.' But on September 5 he reported to Joseph that 'the
Committee has decided that it is impossible for me to leave
France while the war lasts. I am to be reposted in the artillery and shall probably continue to work for the Committee.' The War Office clerks were unable to keep pace with
these developments; on September 15 the War Office issued
three separate orders; one striking him off the list of Generals

in employment, the second sending him to Turkey, the third putting him under the orders of General Bonaparte, in charge of the military mission to Turkey.

Napoleon's thoughts of Turkey were receding into the background, as a new political crisis in Paris was blowing up. In August he had told Joseph, 'Things are quiet here, but storms may be brewing; the primary assemblies meet in a few days.' The people of France were being asked to vote on the establishment of a new constitution, that of the Year III, with an executive Directory of five, and two legislative councils, the Elders and the Five Hundred.

The National Convention had sat since October 1792, and the Committee of Public Safety had governed France dictatorially since October 1793. It had saved France in the crisis of the invasion, but its name was associated with terror and civil war, and the Thermidorian reaction after the fall of Robespierre had brought not only a demand for a return to constitutional government, but a considerable revival of royalism, particularly in Paris. The regicides and revolutionaries were determined that they would run no risk of a royalist or counter-revolutionary majority at the polls: the Convention had therefore passed the 'Decree of the Two-Thirds', providing that if two-thirds of the members of the Convention were not elected to the Councils under the new constitution, the remainder were to be co-opted. The royalists, entrenched in the Paris electoral Sections and the National Guard, reacted violently and prepared for yet another Parisian insurrection to impose the will of Paris on France.

Napoleon was by this time well known to the members of the Committee of Public Safety and particularly to Barras, who had been at Toulon, and had also organized the anti-Robespierrist forces in Thermidor (1794). On October 6 (14 *Vendémiaire*), 1795, Napoleon wrote laconically to Joseph, 'The Convention appointed Barras to command the armed forces of the Government: the Committees chose me as second-in-command. We disposed our troops. The enemy attacked us at the Tuileries. We killed a large number of them. They killed thirty of our men, and wounded sixty. We have disarmed the Sections, and all is quiet.' It was the cavalry Captain Murat who had been sent to secure the all-important cannon, which provided Napoleon's 'whiff of grape-shot'. At St Helena Napoleon explained: 'I made the troops fire ball at first because to a mob who are ignorant of firearms, it is the worst possible policy to start out by firing blanks. For the populace, hearing a great noise, are a little frightened after the first discharge but, looking around them and seeing nobody killed or wounded, they pluck up their spirits, begin immediately to despise you, become twice as insolent, and rush on fearlessly, and it becomes necessary to kill ten times the number that would have been killed if ball had been used in the first place.' Napoleon was immediately rewarded for his part in the *Vendémiaire* crisis by promotion to the rank of Major-General: and shortly afterwards he succeeded Barras as commander of the Army of the Interior.

Even when his prospects were very uncertain before *Vendémiaire* he had written to Joseph, 'If I stay here, I may take it into my head to marry.' He added later, 'I badly want a home.' Joseph had married Julie Clary, the daughter of a rich Marseilles merchant, and her younger sister, Desirée, was attracted to Napoleon. His departure for Paris, and the attitude of her father, who thought not unreasonably that one Corsican and one Buonaparte in the family was enough, did not allow this affair to mature. Desirée later married General Bernadotte and became Queen of Sweden. Napoleon even proposed marriage to Madame Permon, who had been a friend of his father's, and whose daughter Laura was later to marry his friend, General Junot. Mme Permon merely laughed, and pointed out that she was old enough to be his mother. If Napoleon was contemplating a *mariage de convenance*, he was also being affected by the atmosphere of feminine seduction and sensuality which, never absent from Paris, was heightened by the relief from the shadow of the guillotine. In July 1795 he had described this atmosphere to Joseph: 'The ladies are everywhere . . . and the men are mad about them, think of nothing else and live only for and through them. A woman needs six months in Paris to know what is her due and her empire.' Through Barras he had been introduced to the salon of Madame Tallien, his mistress, and the reigning beauty of Thermidorian society; also in this circle was Joséphine de Beauharnais, a former mistress of Barras.

At St Helena, Napoleon recalled his first meeting with Josephine; 'I was certainly not insensible to feminine charms, but I had never till then been spoilt by women. My character rendered me naturally timid in their company. Madame de Beauharnais was the first woman who gave me any degree of confidence.' At the age of thirty-two her beauty was already fading, but she had the elegance of an *ancien régime* aristocrat, and a fascinatingly feminine personality which was not only to soften the brashness of Napoleon's imperial court but to leave a lasting image of grace in the memory of the French people. Of the aristocratic French family Tascher de la Pagerie of Martinique, she was the widow of the Vicomte de Beauharnais who had been a liberal member of the National Assembly and a republican General in 1793. He had been arrested and executed at the height of the Terror in 1794: Josephine only escaped the guillotine through the fall of Robespierre.

Hortense, the daughter of Josephine, tells in her memoirs how Napoleon's attention was drawn to Josephine. After the rising of *Vendémiaire* the citizens of Paris were ordered to surrender arms to the authorities. Josephine sent her son Eugène, aged 14, to ask that she might keep her husband's sword. Napoleon was impressed by Eugène's charm, and granted the request. Josephine called on the General to express her thanks, and their acquaintance did not end there. Before the close of the year Josephine was Napoleon's mistress.

Why this liaison should have turned into a marriage is less obvious. Napoleon's early letters to Josephine certainly show that he was passionately in love for the first time in his life. 'You have taken my soul; you are the one thought of my life,' he writes in April 1796. At the end of his life Napoleon hinted that he had been influenced by the mistaken impression that Josephine possessed a substantial fortune. On her side there was the need for security and the feeling of being swept up by an irresistible force. They were married on March 9, 1796, and parted after only two days by Napoleon's appointment to command the Army of Italy. It was not in Josephine's nature to be able to reciprocate a grand passion: and her cynically nonchalant infidelities were soon to quench Napoleon's romantic love. After some stormy passages, it was replaced by a mutual affection, tolerance, and *camaraderie*. At St Helena, Napoleon admitted: 'Josephine told lies practically all the time, but with elegance. I can say that she was the woman whom I have loved the most.' But this early disillusionment may have been costly. Madame de Rémusat, who judged him severely as Emperor, thought that 'he might have been a better man if he had been more and better loved'.

Barras was now one of the Directors, and there was naturally gossip that Napoleon owed his appointment to the

Army of Italy to favouritism. But La Revellière, one of the Directors by no means friendly to Barras, says in his memoirs that the appointment was made unanimously by the Directors on straightforward military grounds. With the peace of Basle (1795) Prussia and Spain had dropped out of the war: the Directory were now free to consider a forward policy in Italy. Napoleon had a proved record of achievement: he was the acknowledged expert and advocate of an Italian offensive, and he continued after *Vendémiaire* to press his plans on the Directory. After an Austrian counteroffensive in the summer of 1795, Schérer, the commander of the Army of Italy, had been reinforced. After winning the battle of Loano in November 1795, his campaign had been brought to a standstill. On January 19, 1796, Napoleon pointed out that 'If the Army of Italy lets February slip by without doing anything as it has let January, the Italian campaign will be entirely fruitless.'

Schérer now asked to be relieved of his command, unless his army was brought up to a strength of sixty thousand men. The Directory lost patience with him, and decided to let Napoleon have his chance. No doubt they had no great expectations from this appointment: and it hardly seems credible that a young man of twenty-six should be given an independent army command. But it must be remembered that the Revolution had already given youth its chance: Augustin Robespierre and St Just, for instance, were front rank politicians before they were thirty. The emigration and the guillotine had produced in the army a desperate shortage of professionally trained officers capable of commanding above the divisional level. If he survived the guillotine or the hazards of battle, a man with Napoleon's qualifications was not unlikely to get high command at an unusually early age.

One of the first of the Napoleonic myths is the picture of the young, small, insignificant General being greeted with derision by the veteran officers of the Army of Italy. In fact, he was known to them through his staff work for the Army in 1794–5, and even the Piedmontese commander was aware of his reputation as 'a brilliant theorist and strategist'. Yet he was young and untried as a commander in the field. Masséna recalled his first meeting with Napoleon: 'They imagined from the way he carried about his wife's portrait, and showed it to everyone, and still more from his extreme youth, that he owed his appointment to yet another bit of intrigue.' 'But in a minute or two he put on his General's hat and seemed two feet taller.' General Augereau went about saying, 'I can't understand why this little b . . . has so frightened me.' Napoleon reported, in more conventional language, to the Directory the day after he assumed command: 'I have been received by the Army with signs of pleasure and the confidence owed to one who was known to have merited your trust.' Henceforth he was to sign his name 'Bonaparte' instead of the Italian 'Buonaparte'.

3

Victory in Italy

WITH THE ITALIAN CAMPAIGNS Napoleon steps on to the stage as a figure of European importance. A dozen victories in as many months were announced in dramatic and highly-coloured bulletins: 'to lie like a bulletin' became a proverb under the Empire. Valmy and Jemappes had been a shock to the old Europe: but the battles of the Revolution had so far been mainly defensive. Now there was revealed a new kind of offensive warfare such as had not been seen in Europe for centuries. Was it, as public opinion assumed and was encouraged to think, simply due to the personality of the commander and to the *élan* of the republican soldiers? To military historians it appears rather as the logical culmination of a series of developments, material and intellectual, in the conditions of warfare.

First in importance was the increase in the fire-power of weapons. An improved flintlock musket with bayonet had appeared about 1720, and the standard French model of 1777 remained unchanged till 1840. The rifled musket of the late eighteenth-century was suitable for sharpshooters and skirmishers, but it was too expensive to produce and too slow in its rate of fire to supersede the smooth-bore musket for general use. In 1763, Gribeauval was commissioned by

Louis XV's minister the Duc de Choiseul to reform the French artillery. He made use of Belidor's recent discovery in ballistics that the weight of the powder-charge could be reduced without lessening the range. The gun-barrels and carriages could thus be made much lighter. Gribeauval was able to produce twelve- or twenty-four-pounder calibres for field-guns, hitherto only possible for siege guns; though eight- or twelve-pounders remained the normal calibres. Gribeauval's field-guns were the best in Europe, and remained unchanged till 1825; within the limits of smooth-bore, muzzle-loading guns they were elegant, light and simple in design. Napoleon asked Marmont, his artillery expert, to design yet lighter guns in 1802, but the renewal of war interrupted this project.

England and, to a lesser extent, France, were leading Europe in scientific and industrial development in the second half of the eighteenth century—in fact, France, with far less coal, had a higher production of iron.[1] Valmy was the biggest artillery battle yet known: twenty thousand rounds were expended. Scientists like Monge were called in to help with the emergency expansion of war production in 1793, and France produced seven thousand cannon in 1793. Napoleon was, in fact, the first commander who was in a position to use artillery fire lavishly. The development of metalled roads in the late eighteenth century increased mobility. Maréchal de Broglie in 1760 was the first commander to form and manoeuvre an army in units of the division, which allowed much greater flexibility. Even with commanders of genius like Marlborough, set-piece battles of the old style did not often materialize, as it was easy for the enemy to avoid giving battle. Frederick the Great's army, on the other hand, was already old-fashioned in its composition; he fought with a drill and formation inherited from his father, and his successes were due to tactical genius on the battlefield rather than to any innovations in strategy or tactics.

As so often happens in military history, humiliating defeat in the Seven Years' War had a stimulating effect on the French Army. With the encouragement of the Minister Choiseul, and later St Germain, new ideas were discussed about strategy, tactics, and *matériel,* with an emphasis on a mobile, offensive strategy. In 1778 du Teil, the brother of Napoleon's commander at the artillery school of Auxonne,

[1] See p. 160.

wrote a treatise on *L'Usage de l'artillerie nouvelle dans la guerre de campagne*. He worked out the combined use of artillery and infantry, and stressed particularly the importance of using artillery in mass at the decisive point. Artillery experts were agreed that to be effective, guns must be massed, in order to compensate for the inaccuracy and slow rate of fire. Bourcet, who was adviser to de Broglie in 1759–60 and Director of the Staff College at Grenoble, wrote a treatise on *Principes de la guerre des montagnes*. It developed the implications of movement in divisional formations; divisions should disperse to move, and concentrate to fight. They should therefore move at a distance of not more than two days' march apart. Strategic plans should be flexible, 'with several branches', enabling the line of operations to be changed.

In 1772 Guibert, whose father had been chief-of-staff to de Broglie, wrote his *Essai Général de Tactique,* which was widely read and discussed. Though some of his ideas were toned down and obscured in his later work, the *Défense de la Guerre Moderne* of 1779, he predicts a new era of wars of manoeuvre. Everything must be sacrificed to mobility: the complicated battle-formations of the eighteenth century were no longer necessary. The army must be freed from clumsy baggage trains: 'war must feed on war'. Two of his predictions are particularly striking. 'It would be easy to have invincible armies in a State in which the subjects were citizens,' he declared. Criticizing the politicians and Generals of his own day, he wrote: 'Among men like these let there arise—there cannot but arise—some vast genius. He will lay hands, so to speak, on the knowledge of all the community, will create or perfect the political system, put himself at the head of the machine and give the impulse of its movement.'

The comparative merits of line and column, *l'ordre mince* and *l'ordre profond*, as battle formations were hotly debated. Much of this controversy was academic, but there was a vital principle at stake—whether infantry should be regarded as a weapon of mass and shock, relying on the bayonet, or a weapon of fire-power. Maréchal de Saxe in his *Rêveries*, written in 1732, gave some valuable lessons about mobility; he anticipated Napoleon when he said 'the whole secret of manoeuvres and of combats lies in the legs'. The French ordinance of 1776 was largely a copy of Prussian drill and tactics, but as a result of the large-scale invasion manoeuvres of 1778 in the American War of Independence,

Guibert strongly advocated an *ordre mixte*, in a flexible combination of line or column according to circumstances. This
was adopted in the ordinance of 1791 which had to take into
account the new National Guard militia formed in 1789.
The volunteers manoeuvred efficiently at Jemappes with this
drill, and it was not substantially changed, even in the
1802–4 period when the *Grande Armée* was being inten-
sively trained.

The tactics of the Peninsular War, and of Waterloo, have
tended to produce an exaggerated antithesis between the
'thin red line' of the English infantry and the massed column
attack of the French. Ney's massed columns at Waterloo
were exceptional, and a poor example of French tactics.
Normally the French in the revolutionary and Napoleonic
period used column formation for approach and changed to
line for the actual attack: but it appears that at the battle of
Maida in 1806 and frequently in the Peninsular War battles,
they were taken unawares by the English method of concealing their infantry behind a rising crest of ground, and were
caught by the English volleys before they could open out
their columns. Napoleon explained at St Helena that this
again happened at Waterloo. Napoleon himself seldom inter-
fered in the tactical handling of infantry, which varied according to the skill of his Marshals and Generals, because he
had to keep his attention for the general handling of the battle. But one of his first orders to the Army of Italy was to
confirm the use of the *ordre mixte*. He, of all people, was
aware of the importance of fire-power. At St Helena he said:
'It is with artillery that war is made.' 'The invention of
powder has changed the nature of war: missile weapons are
now become the principal ones: it is by fire and not by shock
that battles are decided today.'

It has already been noted that the weapons used in the
revolutionary and Napoleonic wars were designed before
1789. There followed a stable period in military technology
which gave the greatest scope and weight to Napoleon's genius
in strategy, organization and leadership. Was this stagnation
due to military conservatism? It is true that Napoleon made
no attempt to develop military observation balloons which
had first been used at the battle of Fleurus (1794) and then
abandoned by the French War Office in 1798. He also
showed little interest in Fulton's submarine and steamboat.

Yet the revolutionary leaders and Napoleon can hardly be
accused of lack of interest in science and scientists, despite

the notorious comment at the trial of the great chemist
Lavoisier that 'the Republic has no need of scientists'. The
Committee of Public Safety offered prizes for war inventions, experimented with explosive shells, built the first
semaphore telegraph from Paris to Lille (a system developed
by Napoleon all over Europe) and applied the hydrogen balloon to military use. Napoleon was proud of his membership
of the *Institut* and was intimately associated with scientists
such as Monge, Laplace, Chaptal. The limiting factor in the
development of military technology seems rather to have
been in the field of metallurgy, where the break-through,
which was to produce steam propulsion and the breech load-
ing, rifled cannon and gun, was not to come until at least a
decade after Waterloo. It is significant that great difficulty
had been found in boring cylinders of sufficient precision
even for Watt's low-pressure steam-engines. The English car-
ronade guns were first used in the American War of Independence. Congreve's rocket batteries were certainly an innovation and were in action at the battles of Leipzig and
Waterloo; but the Duke of Wellington considered that they
were more likely to hit his own troops than the enemy.

It is thus clear that, by the outbreak of the Revolution, the
staff of the French Army already possessed a coherent doctrine of offensive strategy and tactics. The spirit of the Enlightenment, with its questioning of tradition and its scientific
curiosity, had paved the way for a revolution, not only in the
political but also in the military sphere. Two conditions were
still wanting before it could be applied in practice; a commander with the training, intellectual grasp and practical
genius to carry it out, and the kind of army which was to be
his instrument.

The royal army, despite its intellectual vitality, suffered
from the internal rot which destroyed the *ancien régime*.
The rift between the officer corps monopolised by the
noblesse and the non-commissioned officers and men destroyed its discipline and solidarity. The emigration of officers amounted to a mass strike against the Revolution, and
the *émigré* army at Coblenz openly boasted that the army
of the Revolution would be helpless without its officers. A
long period of garrison duty in peace-time exposed the army
to intensive revolutionary propaganda; at the outbreak of the
war in 1792 whole regiments broke and murdered their officers. The volunteers raised in 1791, largely from the National
Guard militia, were good material but took time to train. The

volunteers of 1792 and 1793 were less good; they were in fact largely conscripts, as the Departments had to make up their quotas by compulsion.

When national conscription was decreed in July 1793, and Carnot took charge of its mobilization, the republican army was gradually forged into a powerful weapon. The principle of the amalgam, the fusion of regular and conscript battalions into the new unit of the *demi-brigade*, which was long delayed on ideological grounds, restored cohesion to the army. In the meantime vigorous young officers had risen from the ranks; many of Napoleon's future Marshals and Generals began their careers in this way. By the end of 1794 the Republic had armies totalling eight hundred thousand men in the field: and the industrial mobilization required to equip and sustain these armies was as remarkable a feat as the mobilization of manpower.

The republican army now realized Guibert's dream of a citizen-army; it could be called upon for exceptional exertions and sacrifices, and it could be relied on to disperse for foraging without desertions. It was freed from the cumbersome supply trains and the deadening discipline of the professional dynastic armies. The Army of Italy had been seasoned by four years' campaigning. It had a high proportion of regulars and early volunteers, and, although it was badly fed and clothed, its morale and discipline were relatively high.

How much did Napoleon's strategy and tactics owe to his predecessors? It is known that he took Guibert's and Bourcet's writings with him to Italy; he also sent to Paris for the account of Maillebois' campaign in Piedmont in 1748. It would not be far wrong to say that Napoleon's Italian campaigns were Guibert and Bourcet in action. Their influence was a great deal more important than Napoleon's general reading of Plutarch, Caesar, and Frederick the Great. In discussing the principles of strategy at St Helena, Napoleon asserted, 'I have fought sixty battles, and I have learnt nothing which I did not know in the beginning.'

To explain the origins of Napoleonic strategy is not, of course, to belittle his genius. As he said at St Helena, 'Everything is in the execution.' The planning which preceded a battle was an intense and painful process. 'I am like a woman in labour.' At St Helena he pointed out, 'Few people realize the strength of mind required to conduct, with a full realization of its consequences, one of these great battles on which depends the fate of an army, a nation, the possession of a throne. Consequently one rarely finds Generals who are keen to give battle. . . .' 'I consider myself the boldest of Generals.' The earlier Generals of the Revolution were unable to apply the new theories successfully; they tended to disperse their divisions too widely, and failed to concentrate them at the decisive point. Jomini, who was one of Napoleon's staff officers, describes in his *Précis de l'Art de Guerre* (1838) how Napoleon 'decided in a moment the number of marches necessary for each of his columns to arrive at the desired point by a certain day'.

It follows from the flexible nature of this new war of movement that Napoleonic strategy can, least of all, be reduced to a formula or a system. Jomini and Clausewitz tried to draw general conclusions from the Napoleonic experience, but they never succeeded in seizing the subtlety of Napoleonic warfare, and they often produced dangerously misleading conclusions. Clausewitz did, however, recognize that strategy cannot be reduced to a 'system'. 'What genius does must be the best of all rules.' Napoleon at St Helena ridiculed 'maxims' of war. 'Of what use is a maxim which can never be put into practice and even if put into practice without understanding would cause the loss of the army?'

It is for this reason that, while Napoleon's Italian campaigns contain in essence all the subsequent campaigns, no two Napoleonic battles are alike. The most that can be said is that Napoleon's favourite strategical manoeuvres fell into two patterns—first, the classic flanking attack on the enemy's rear and communications, exemplified by the Marengo campaign, Ulm, Jena, Friedland, Smolensk (where it failed to come off), Montmirail; secondly, the attack on the centre of an enemy dispersed on a wide front, so as to defeat him successively in detail. This is the strategy of his first campaign in Piedmont, and also of his last campaign of Waterloo.

On arriving at Nice on March 27, 1796, Napoleon was first concerned with questions of commissariat and discipline. Berthier was his chief-of-staff (and was to remain so till 1814). The invaluable Saliceti, his old Corsican friend and patron, was the civil commissary to the Army; by raising a loan from Genoa, he considerably eased the Army's supply position. But Napoleon had to report to the Directory on March 28 that 'one battalion has mutinied on the ground that it had neither boots nor pay'. On April 6 he wrote, 'The army is in frightening penury. . . . Misery has led to in-

discipline, and without discipline there can be no victory.'
Even after the first victories, he writes on April 24, 'the
hungry soldiers are committing excesses that make one blush
to be human. The capture of Ceva and Mondovi may give us
the means to put this right, and I am going to make some
terrible examples. I will restore order or I will give up the
command of these brigands.' His first Order of the Day
(March 29) said that he was 'satisfied with the bearing of
the troops, their devotion to the Republic and the strong
will to victory which they showed him'. The 'Proclamation'
which reads, 'I will lead you into the most fertile plains in
the world. Rich provinces and great cities will be in your
power. There you will find honour, glory and wealth,' was,
in fact, dictated by Napoleon at St Helena and inserted in his
Correspondence and Memoirs.

The Directory were well aware that there was no love
lost between the Piedmontese and the Austrians. Under
pressure the Piedmontese would come to terms with France,
and the Austrians would sacrifice the Piedmontese to protect Lombardy. Napoleon's plan of campaign was intended
to exploit the weakness of the alliance: he hoped to separate
their forces, knock Piedmont out of the war as quickly as
possible, and then deal with the Austrians. On April 6
Napoleon reported to the Directory that the Piedmontese
had forty-five thousand men and the Austrians thirty-seven
thousand, against forty-five thousand French. But in fact the
significant figures are those of the troops available for active
operations in the field. When Napoleon arrived, the field
divisions of the Army of Italy amounted to thirty thousand
men out of a total strength of nearly sixty thousand. By
combing the rear formations Napoleon was able to bring
his striking force up to thirty-eight thousand men. Against
these the Austrians could bring to bear in the field no more
than thirty thousand and the Piedmontese only twelve thousand.

The opening moves of the campaign were made by the
Austrians, and they were to be fatal against an opponent
of Napoleon's speed and decision. Before Napoleon arrived
at Nice, Schérer had moved a small force on Voltri to put
pressure on the Genoese. Beaulieu, the Austrian commander,
interpreted this move to mean that the main theatre of
operations would be on the Riviera coast. He therefore sent
considerable forces to capture Voltri, and in doing so
moved too far south from his Piedmontese allies. Na-

poleon was given exactly the opening he wanted, and attacked the Austrian right wing in the mountains. In the actions at Montenotte, Millesimo and Dego (April 12–16, 1796) the Austrians had six thousand casualties and Beaulieu was so shaken that he fell back on his base at Alessandria. This left Napoleon free to turn on the Piedmontese, who were broken in the battles of San Michele, Ceva, and Mondovi (April 19–23), on which day Colli, the Piedmontese commander, proposed an armistice. Napoleon's timing and deployment had ensured that in each of these battles the French had a superiority of numbers.

The armistice signed at Cherasco on April 28 gave Napoleon control of the fortresses and line of communication with Lombardy, and he turned immediately to the pursuit of Beaulieu. He wrote to the Directory, 'Tomorrow I shall march against Beaulieu, force him to cross the Po, cross myself immediately after and seize the whole of Lombardy: within a month I hope to be on the mountains of the Tyrol, in touch with the Army of the Rhine, and to carry the war in concert into Bavaria. . . . As to the conditions of peace, you can dictate whatever you see fit, since the principal fortresses are in my power.' Napoleon's hopes of cutting off Beaulieu south of the river Po were disappointed; but by crossing the river at Piacenza on May 7 he threatened Beaulieu's line of retreat. The Austrians were forced to retreat towards Mantua, and on May 10 the French forced the bridge of Lodi on the river Adda, defeating the Austrian rearguard. On May 14, Napoleon entered Milan.

Lodi was a dramatic, but not a decisive battle. Napoleon was in the thick of the fighting, placing the guns, but it was only later legend which depicted him leading the column across the bridge. In his despatch, he mentions Berthier, Masséna and Lannes as rallying the head of the column. But Lodi remained in his mind as a psychological landmark in his career. At St Helena he recalled that 'it was only on the evening after Lodi that I realized I was a superior being and conceived the ambition of performing great things, which hitherto had filled my thoughts only as a fantastic dream'. Probably he was beginning to realize the hold which unbroken victory was giving him over his troops, and the demands he could make on them when he had their confidence. It was about this time that he acquired the nickname among the troops of 'Le Petit Caporal': it began with a unit which, as a joke, awarded him a promotion from the ranks after each victory. Even more important was the idea growing in his mind that victory was giving him the whip-hand in his dealings with the Directory. But the taste of victory was soured by his anxiety at the lack of news from Josephine. The letters he wrote to her at this time reflect his inner turmoil and stress. 'Ah! this evening if I do not get a letter from you, I shall be desperate. Think of me, or tell me with contempt that you do not love me, and then perhaps I shall find some peace of mind.'

The news that peace had been concluded with Piedmont assured him that his line of communications was secure, but he was now told by Saliceti, the *commissaire,* that the Directory proposed to divide the command in Italy: Kellermann was to command in Lombardy, while Napoleon was to move south to secure, and plunder, Genoa, Leghorn, Rome, and Naples. Napoleon countered this snub by a veiled threat of resignation. 'In the present situation of the Republic in Italy, it is essential that you have a General in whom you have complete confidence. If it is not I, I shall not complain but shall deport myself with ever more zeal to earn your regard in whatever post you may place me.' The Directory drew back, and postponed their decision about dividing the command. Napoleon had taken the first and most significant step in asserting his independence from the political control of Paris.

The Directory's plans for Italy were strictly limited; they intended to plunder it, and hold it as a counter to exchange for the Rhine frontier in peace negotiations with Austria. On May 9 Napoleon wrote to the Directory, 'I repeat my request for a few reputable artists to take charge of the choice and transport of the fine things we shall think fit to send to Paris.' Milan, Parma, and Modena were required to make contributions; on May 22 he reports that 'you can now count on 6 to 8 millions in gold or silver ingots or jewels, which are at your disposal in Genoa'. By July 1796, Italy had already provided sixty millions of francs. Already in May Napoleon was able to give his troops half their pay in silver instead of paper *assignats;* a welcome novelty which attached them more firmly to their commander. Through political and financial weakness, the Directory were rapidly losing control over their Generals. Gone were the days of 1793 and 1794 when the Committee of Public Safety through the powerful *Représentants aux armées* could supervise and dismiss their Generals at will. The *Représentants aux armées* had already

been replaced by the *Commissaires aux armées* of lesser
status and powers. Saliceti was sent to look after Leghorn
and Corsica in June 1796, and was replaced by the less
competent Garrau. By the end of the year the Directory were
forced to suppress the office of *commissaire* under pressure
from Napoleon and the Generals of the Army of the Rhine.
Faced with a political threat, from the left in the form of
Babeuf's *Conspiration des Égaux* and from the right in the
crisis which was to culminate in the *coup d'etat* of Fructidor
the following year, the Directory were forced to depend
more and more on the support of the Armies of the Rhine
and Italy where republican feeling was still strong.

If the organized plunder of Italy gave Napoleon the whip-
hand in his relations with the Directory, it generated a
potentially dangerous situation for him in Italy itself. On
the surface Italy appeared indolent and apathetic, stunned by
the rapidity of the French conquests. But underneath there
were dangerous fires: and Napoleon realized that his small
army could not afford to be faced with an actively hostile
populace. Already in May there had been an ugly popular
rising in Pavia, which had to be severely crushed. How far
was Napoleon to rely on a pro-French Jacobin party, with the
risk that it would provoke a counter-revolutionary clerical
fanaticism? He had to feel his way, and learn rapidly how
to deal with delicate political problems. Throughout the
Italian campaigns, his mind had to be applied as much to
political as to military problems.

Napoleon's grasp of the grand strategy of the war, which
he had shown in his memoranda as far back as 1794, did
not desert him. He was now anxious about the Austrian
reaction to the loss of Lombardy. He wrote to the French
Minister in Switzerland on May 20, 'Can the Emperor weaken
his Rhine frontier to reinforce that in Italy? What troops
could he still send into the Tyrol? Please let me know what
information you have about this and send agents to all parts
so that you can instruct me precisely what forces could be
sent into Italy.' He well knew that his dream of an advance
through the Tyrol towards Vienna could only be realized
if Moreau and Jourdan on the Rhine took the offensive:
otherwise the Austrians, with their interior lines of communication, could heavily reinforce their army now concentrated in Mantua. On June 8 he wrote to General Clarke,
in charge of the Topographical Bureau in Paris, 'I see only
one way of avoiding being beaten in the autumn: that is

to arrange matters so that we are not obliged to march into the south of Italy. According to all the information reaching us, the Emperor is sending many troops to his Italian army. We wait impatiently for news from the Rhine.'

With no news from Moreau and under pressure from the Directory to exploit the riches of Florence, Rome and Naples, Napoleon had to take the risk of a quick southern expedition before tackling Mantua. This diversion was completed in the course of July; two divisions had to be used to occupy Bologna and Ferrara, and Tuscany. The threat of invasion was sufficient to force the Papacy, Tuscany, and Naples to sign agreements and to pay cash. For the remaining months of the campaign of 1796, the governing factor was the frustration of Moreau's offensive on the Rhine by the skill of the Archduke Charles. This put Napoleon on the defensive and exposed him to repeated and dangerous counter-attacks by the Austrians through the Alpine passes.

At the end of May, Napoleon had resumed his advance against Beaulieu, and forced him to retire into the mountains, leaving a strong garrison in the fortress of Mantua, protected by its lakes and marshes. The ensuing battles centred in the area of the quadrilateral fortresses—Peschiera, Verona, Mantua and Legnago—which were again to figure prominently in the campaigns of 1848 and 1859. There is no coincidence in this, because the narrow gap between the southern tip of Lake Garda, where the foothills of the Alps begin, and Mantua, protected by its marshes and lagoons, is the natural gateway to Lombardy and the bastion of the defence of Venetia and the Tyrol. The capture of Mantua was not for Napoleon the prime objective: more important in his strategy was the fact that the area of the quadrilateral commanded the exits from the Brenner and some of the lesser passes from the Alps.

The Austrians mounted no less than four successive counter-offensives, culminating respectively in the French victories of Castiglione (August), Bassano (September), Arcola (November) and Rivoli (January 1797). At the end of July, Wurmser, who had replaced Beaulieu, advanced from the mountains with an army of forty-seven thousand men, divided into three columns, his centre on either side of Lake Garda, his right on Lake Iseo, and his left further east on the line of Bassano and Verona. Napoleon had forty-five thousand men in the field, of whom ten thousand were tied up in the siege of Mantua. The initiative lay with the Austrians, and Napoleon was fighting his first defensive campaign. He had moments of doubt, of uncertainty, and even of fumbling, but his strategic insight, backed by the fighting qualities of his officers and men, carried him through. When the Austrian right wing threatened Brescia, his base and line of communications, and Wurmser's centre drove back Masséna's division, Napoleon realized that he must concentrate (*réunir*) all his forces in a central position, at the cost of abandoning the siege of Mantua and sacrificing his siege-train. He ordered concentration on the line of the Chiesa river, south-east of Brescia.

On the other hand, Wurmser wasted time in reinforcing Mantua, and fought the campaign without managing to bring his left-wing column into action at all. The French counter-attacked at Castiglione and Lonato (August 1–3) and Wurmser moved west to support his right wing. He was caught by Napoleon at Castiglione on August 5 before his left wing could come up, and was forced to fight with twenty-one thousand men against the French twenty-seven thousand. While Wurmser over-extended his line to join hands with his right-wing column, Napoleon was routing his left wing, and the victory was completed by a rupture of the centre of Wurmser's front. The battle exemplifies Napoleon's comment made at St Helena, in his *Précis des Guerres de Frederic II*, that 'the best and most economical means of ensuring victory is to effect on the enemy front by a vigorous attack a local disorganization sufficient to entail the disorganization of the whole front'. It was at Castiglione also that Napoleon first used artillery massed in two big batteries; and Marmont used the horse artillery with great boldness.

Napoleon now wrote to Moreau (August 31) that he had hopes of resuming his advance into the Tyrol, and joining hands with the Army of the Rhine. Wurmser was regrouping well to the east on the river Brenta, and by occupying Trent Napoleon could take Wurmser in the rear if he tried to advance and relieve Mantua. On September 4, Napoleon defeated an Austrian detachment at Rovereto and captured Trent. On September 8, he took Wurmser's army in the rear at Bassano. To avoid envelopment, Wurmser had to retreat westward away from his base, and to take refuge in Mantua. But, at the end of October, the Archduke Charles' success against Moreau encouraged the Austrians to make another attempt to defeat Napoleon and raise the siege of Mantua. Alvinzy, the new Austrian commander, assembled nineteen thousand men on the Brenner and twenty-eight thousand men on the Brenta.

This third phase, the campaign of Arcola, was the most dangerous for Napoleon. The few reinforcements he had received had not yet kept pace with wastage: and his troops were nearing exhaustion. The forced marches accomplished by Napoleon's troops in the summer heat of Lombardy were astonishing: Augereau's division once covered seventy miles in two days. On November 12, Napoleon sustained a definite defeat at the hands of Alvinzy on the heights of Caldiero outside Verona. The following day he wrote despondently to the Directory, 'Perhaps we are on the eve of losing Italy. None of the expected help has arrived. I despair of being able to avoid raising the siege of Mantua, which would have been ours within a week. . . . In a few days we will make a last effort. If fortune smiles, Mantua will be taken and with it Italy.'

Napoleon realized that desperate measures must be taken before the Austrian column from the Brenner forced the Rivoli position, which was being held by one French division, and joined up with Alvinzy. He decided on a daring flank march to cross the Adige south of Verona, and attack Alvinzy's rear communications. He failed to achieve complete surprise, because unexpectedly he encountered a strong Croat detachment defending the village and bridge of Arcola. It was only after three days of heavy and costly fighting in a terrain of marsh and dykes that Alvinzy decided to retire on the Brenta. In his report to the Directory (November 19) Napoleon describes how, at Arcola, 'in vain did the Generals, knowing the importance of time, rush to the front to force our columns to cross the little bridge . . ., we had to cross this bridge or make a detour of several leagues which would have nullified our whole operation. I went up myself and asked the soldiers if they were still the victors of Lodi; my presence had an effect that decided us to attempt the crossing once more.' But he adds that 'we had to give up the idea of taking the village by frontal assault'. The Polish officer Sulkowski, who was aide to Napoleon, described in a letter how Napoleon raised the standard on the bridge of Arcola, and condemned the cowardice of the troops for not responding. Such appears to be the truth of the scene at Arcola, which became a favourite and romanticized theme for painters.

The campaign of Arcola was costly, and won by the nar-

rowest margin. Louis, Napoleon's younger brother, now on
Napoleon's staff, wrote despondently that 'the troops are no
longer the same, and shout loudly for peace'. The Directory,
depressed by the situation on the Rhine and the resistance
of Mantua, were inclined to offer peace to Austria, and sent
General Clarke to report on the situation. When they met,
Napoleon had no difficulty in persuading Clarke that the
prospects of taking Mantua were now good, and Clarke reported optimistically to Paris. Vienna showed no signs of
offering favourable terms, and Alvinzy was mounting yet
another counter-offensive, putting his faith once more in a
three-pronged advance. The main column was to advance from
the Brenner on to Rivoli, while diversionary attacks were to
come from Bassano and Padua.

Waiting at Verona, Napoleon had to determine where the
main attack was coming. Joubert with ten thousand men at
Rivoli was being attacked in force and late on January 13
Napoleon decided to ignore the most easterly threat, and concentrate on Rivoli. Alvinzy had twenty-eight thousand men
in his advance from Trent, and essayed a complicated out-
flanking manoeuvre to envelop Joubert's division, thereby
separating his infantry from his artillery. By January 15,
Napoleon had concentrated twenty-three thousand men on
the plateau of Rivoli with forty guns. Alvinzy's flank and rear
attacks caused some anxiety, but they were too dispersed to
be effective, and his separate columns were crushed in detail,
with the loss of fifteen thousand men. Napoleon did not stay
to see the rout of Alvinzy completed at Rivoli, but rushed
back to deal with the Austrian force advancing from Padua
to Mantua. On January 16 this force was surrounded at
La Favorita outside Mantua and forced to surrender. Napoleon reported to the Directory on January 17, 'In three
or four days, therefore, the Emperor's fifth army has been
entirely destroyed. We have taken twenty-three thousand
prisoners.' At the beginning of February 1797, Mantua capitulated.

The spectacular success of the Rivoli campaign persuaded
the Directory to switch forces from the Rhine to the Army
of Italy. By March Napoleon had received two fresh divisions.
He could advance either over the Brenner pass into the
Tyrol, or over the river Tagliamento towards Trieste. When
he found that the Archduke Charles, who had replaced
Alvinzy, was concentrating his forces to the east in Friuli,
he chose the Trieste route, leaving Joubert to advance on the

Brenner. By the end of March he had reached Klagenfurt against weakening Austrian resistance. Joubert had reached Brixen and was ready to join Napoleon in the valley of the Drave. But again the inactivity of Moreau on the Rhine caused him anxiety. He had learned to respect the Austrian powers of recuperation: and if Moreau failed to pin down sufficient Austrian forces, Joubert's flank might be exposed. Napoleon was a long way from his base, and there were disquieting risings against the French in the Venetian territories on his lines of communication. On March 31 he offered the Archduke Charles an armistice, and pending a reply, pushed on to Leoben (less than a hundred miles from Vienna). The Archduke Charles had already advised against further resistance: and after a week of sparring with the Austrian envoys Napoleon signed preliminaries of peace at Leoben on April 18, 1797. To his chagrin he learned only later that Moreau had crossed the Rhine two days after the agreement had been signed at Leoben. As he said later, 'I was playing *vingt-et-un* and I stopped at twenty.'

How did it come about that Napoleon was able to sign on his own authority, not only an armistice but peace terms, and that the definitive peace of Campo Formio was delayed for a further six months? The answer to this question requires an analysis not only of the political situation in Italy but in France as well, and the general diplomatic scene in Europe. By force of circumstances and his own personality Napoleon had become, in the year 1797, the hub of French and of European politics. In the summer an Austrian envoy sent by the Austrian Chancellor, Thugut, to Paris, reported that 'only Bonaparte can make peace, and he can do it on any terms he wants'. By May, Napoleon had taken up residence in semi-royal state at the palace of Mombello outside Milan, where he was joined at last by Josephine. Miot de Melito describes him at Mombello. 'He was no longer the General of a triumphant Republic, but a conqueror on his own account, imposing his laws on the vanquished.'

Apart from their feeling that 'the Roman religion will always be an irreconcilable enemy to the Republic', the Directory had no wish to republicanize Italy, because it might make it more difficult to exchange the conquered territories with Austria. They instructed Napoleon on October 18, 1796, 'that you will take care that France is not committed to any guarantee, so that she can reserve for herself the widest possible liberty to make peace with the Emperor if things

turn out badly'. There is no reason to suppose that Napoleon
had at this time any plan for the political settlement of Italy
which differed in principle from that of the Directory. But
his prime concern was the security and supply of the Army:
and for this purpose he had to offer some encouragement
to the pro-French party without provoking counter-revolutionary fanaticism.

In May 1796, Napoleon had suppressed the Austrian ma-
chinery of government for Lombardy. A provisional administration was formed, consisting of a Congress of State
and municipal councils, under the control of French military
agents. Napoleon had reported to the Directory that 'Milan
is very eager for liberty: there is a club of eight hundred
members, all business men or lawyers'. At the end of September he told the Senate of Bologna that 'the time has come for
Italy to take her place with honour among the nations.
Lombardy, Bologna, Modena, Reggio, Ferrara, perhaps the
Romagna, if it shows itself worthy, will one day astonish
Europe and re-create the great days of Italy.'

Having struck the note of the *Risorgimento,* he encouraged
a meeting in October of a hundred deputies from Modena,
Ferrara, Reggio and Bologna, which decreed the formation
of an 'Italian legion', and the setting up of a united Cispadane
Republic, to be confirmed by an elected Assembly in December. At the end of the year Napoleon explained to the
Directory that 'the Cispadane republics are divided into three
parties: (1) the friends of their former government, (2) the
partisans of an independent but rather aristocratic constitution, (3) the partisans of the French constitution and of
pure democracy. I repress the first, I support the second,
and moderate the third. I do so because the second is the
party of the rich landowners and priests, who in the long
run will end by winning the support of the mass of the
people which it is essential to rally around the French party.'

After Rivoli, Napoleon turned south to settle accounts with
the Papacy. The Pope had refused to conclude a treaty, still
pinning his hopes on an Austrian victory. By the time
Napoleon's forces reached Ancona on February 10, the Pope
was ready to come to terms, and on February 19 Napoleon
despatched to the Directory the Treaty of Tolentino, by
which the Pope ceded Bologna, Ferrara and the Romagna
and paid an indemnity of thirty millions. He explained to
the Directory that his failure to enter Rome and depose the
Pope was due to the danger of Neapolitan intervention and

the pressing need for him to return to his Army. He added that 'in my opinion Rome, once deprived of Bologna, Ferrara and the Romagna and of the thirty millions we are taking, can no longer exist: the archaic machine will break down of its own accord'. At the same time he wrote to the Pope, 'The French Republic will be, I hope, among the truest friends of Rome.' It would be an exaggeration to say that the Treaty of Tolentino foreshadowed the Concordat: but Napoleon was already aware from his experience in Italy of the danger of arousing religious fanaticism.

But Napoleon was disappointed by the results of the elections in the Cispadane Republic. On May 1, 1797, he reported that, 'Their choice has been very bad: priests have influenced all the electors. In the villages they dictate the lists and control all the elections. However, in conformity with your orders and the treaties, I shall start by joining Lombardy and the Cispadane under a single provisional government. Thereafter I shall take steps in harmony with their customs to enlighten opinion and lessen the influence of the priests.'

The constitution of the new Cisalpine Republic, incorporating the Cispadane Republic and some of the mainland territories of Venice, was drafted under Napoleon's eye. It followed closely the constitution of the Directory in France —a Directory of five and two legislative Councils. In order to avoid any electoral mistakes, Napoleon himself nominated the members of the executive and the legislatures. It was true that they were good appointments, including nobles of great insight like Serbelloni and Visconti. The same course was followed with Genoa, when the murder of pro-French democrats provided the means of intervention (May 1797). The new Ligurian Republic was to have an executive of twelve Senators and a Doge, elected by two legislative chambers.

These constitutional arrangements aroused no protests from Paris, possibly because the Directory was now absorbed in the constitutional crisis at home. Napoleon himself did not have much confidence in their future. He wrote to Talleyrand in October 1797, 'You do not know the Italian people. They are not worth the lives of forty thousand Frenchmen. Since I came to Italy I have received no help from this nation's love of liberty and equality, or at least such help has been negligible. Here are the facts: whatever is good to say in proclamations and printed speeches is romantic fiction.' His

cynical realism was confirmed only too soon in 1798 when
attempts to 'revolutionize' Italy ended in the sudden collapse
of French rule. In August he had told the Directory that
'the islands of Corfu, Zante, and Cephalonia are more important for us than the whole of Italy. If we were forced
to choose, I believe it would be better to restore Italy to
the Emperor and keep the four islands, which are a source
of wealth and prosperity for our trade.' These remarks are
probably coloured by his disquiet and self-justification concerning the squalid transactions over Venice: and at the same
time he was striving hard to provide the Cisalpine Republic
with a sound administration. Napoleon's later policy in Italy
was to exhibit the same cynicism and the same realism.

In the meantime, the Austrian Government was in no
hurry to ratify the preliminaries of Leoben. Everything depended on the outcome of the political crisis in Paris. No
sooner had the leftwing conspiracy of Babeuf been crushed
than the elections of May 1797 to the legislative Councils
gave a majority to the moderates. Barthélemy, their representative, entered the Directory, and General Pichegru, as
President of the Five Hundred, was intriguing for a royalist
restoration. A moderate government in Paris and a restoration of the monarchy might lead to a moderate and even
durable peace: England was feeling the strain, and even Pitt
was prepared to negotiate. Spain had gone over to the French
side in August 1796, and the English fleet had withdrawn
from the Mediterranean. Ireland was ripe for rebellion, and
Hoche's Bantry Bay expedition had only narrowly failed.
Faced with the Spithead and Nore mutinies and a financial
crisis, Pitt sent Malmesbury to Lille to negotiate with Talleyrand, the new French Foreign Minister.

Napoleon had little doubt about the side he should back.
Apart from the republican sentiment in his army which was
still strong, a monarchical restoration would block his own
ambitions. At Mombello he hardly troubled to keep this
secret from his intimates. He said to Miot de Melito, 'Do
you believe that I triumph in Italy for the Carnots, Barras,
et cetera? I do not want peace. A party is in favour of the
Bourbons. I wish to undermine the Republican Party, but
only for my own profit and not that of the ancient dynasty.'

Only a military *coup d'état* could now save the three ex-
Jacobin Directors, Barras, Reubell, and la Revellière, from
Carnot, Barthélemy, and the Councils. They first looked to
Hoche, from the Army of the Rhine, but the plan to make

him Minister of War was exposed in the Councils. On July 14, Napoleon issued a proclamation to the Army of Italy, 'Mountains separate us from France: but were it necessary in order to uphold the Constitution, to defend liberty, to protect the Government and the Republicans, then you would cross them with the speed of the eagle.' This hint was followed by the arrival of General Augereau in Paris as Napoleon's agent. On September 4, 1797 (18 *Fructidor*), Augereau surrounded the Tuileries with troops, and invaded the Councils; under the threat of force the arrest of Barthélemy and Carnot was decreed, and the election of two hundred deputies quashed. The peace negotiations at Lille were broken off at the end of September, and the Austrian Government at last realized that they must settle peace terms with Napoleon.

The published terms of the preliminaries of Leoben merely provided that Austria should cede Belgium: but secret articles involved the partition of Venetian territories to compensate Austria for the loss of Belgium and Lombardy. Napoleon was not unaware that Austria coveted Venice, and that this bait would be the quickest way of making a settlement. Austria, as the champion of legitimacy, would, however, insist on leaving to France the dirty work of overthrowing the Venetian Republic. This was not difficult to procure as tension had been rising in the mainland towns of the Republic—Brescia, Bergamo, Verona—which had been fought over in the past year. On April 17, there was a massacre of the French by the populace in Verona. An ultimatum from Napoleon panicked the Doge into accepting a democratic constitution and government, which at once called in French troops. Napoleon was now in a position to use, not merely part, but the whole of the Venetian territories as a bargaining counter to improve the terms which he had rather hastily accepted at Leoben.

At Udine the treaty with Austria, formally known as Campo Formio, was signed on October 18, 1797. Austria ceded Belgium, and recognized the Cisalpine Republic, now including Bologna, Modena, Ferrara and the Romagna. Of the Venetian territories, France took the Ionian islands and Venetian Albania; Austria received the mainland territories up to the river Adige, Venice itself, Istria and Dalmatia. In a secret article of the treaty, Austria agreed to support the French claim to the left bank of the Rhine at a Congress to be held at Rastadt, while France was to help Austria

to obtain Salzburg and the Breisgau. It was a brilliant but
unstable settlement for France. Her original war aims com-
prising the 'natural frontiers'—the Alps, the Rhine, and the
Pyrenees—had been diverted by Napoleon's Italian annexations. The partition of Venice was not only a moral blot
on the peace settlement, but left Austria a foothold in Italy,
which could only lead to further war.

4

The Eastern Adventure

AT THE TIME OF the Peace of Campo Formio, Napoleon
was already an extraordinary man; his genius had been formed
and tested in action. It is too early to attempt to analyse
the character of the mature Napoleon, but certain elements
in his nature are already apparent. His professional training
as an officer was the foundation of his success: but from the
start it is clear that he was as much interested in political
and literary as in military matters. The romantic sensibility
which is so marked in his early writings and letters did not
survive his association with Josephine: it was killed by her
incapacity either to respond to his passion or to bear him
children. Henceforth the women in his life were to be no
more than distractions or instruments of his policy.

But the romantic element in his nature was to be not so
much extinguished as transmuted into a romantic ambition,
into dreams of a career which should outdo all the heroes
of history. He wrote to General Lauriston in 1804: 'Death
is nothing, but to live defeated and inglorious is to die
daily.' The carefully calculated and limited ambition of a
Frederick the Great was no longer enough for Napoleon.
The urge to dominate, to dare, to play for the highest stakes
was as instinctive to him and as irresistible as the urge of

the mountaineer to climb Everest. This element of the ir-
rational, the unlimited, the daemonic is as fundamental to
the nature of Napoleon as it is to the character of Mozart's
Don Giovanni. Without it the career of Napoleon is un-
intelligible. When he visited Rousseau's tomb he remarked:
'The future will tell us whether it would not have been better if neither I nor Rousseau had ever lived.' He wrote to
his brother Joseph shortly before his coronation in 1804,
'I am destined to change the face of the world; at any
rate this is my belief.' At St Helena he said: 'What a ro-
mance my life has been.' Moscow, the Hundred Days and
St Helena seem as implicit in his personality as Austerlitz
and the Grand Empire. One of his Ministers, Molé, commented: 'It is strange that though Napoleon's common sense
amounted to genius, he never could see where the possible
left off. . . . He was much less concerned to leave behind
him a "race" or dynasty than a name which should have no
equal and glory that could not be surpassed.'

Napoleon was not of the generation which made the Revolution, but he was a product of the revolutionary age—a
time when the mould of tradition and custom was broken,
and nothing seemed impossible in the face of reason, energy
and will. In his youth he had been influenced by the two
most potent forces of the eighteenth century—the scientific
rationalism of the Enlightenment and the romantic sensibility of Rousseau.

In his rise to power, the sweep and vigour of his imagination were perfectly matched and balanced by the lucidity
and precision of his intelligence. Such a dazzling combination of qualities was difficult to resist, especially for the men
of his own age who had been brought up under the same
influences. Many of them surrendered their lives and their
souls. When Junot's father wrote suspiciously to his son
shortly after the siege of Toulon: 'Who is this unknown
General Bonaparte?' Junot replied: 'He is the sort of man
of whom nature is sparing and who only appears on earth
at intervals of centuries.'

At Mombello in 1797, the idea of seizing supreme power
in France had already entered his mind. So also had the
idea of an Egyptian expedition, a result of his preoccupation with Venice, gateway of the East. On August 16, 1797,
he wrote to the Directory: 'The time is not far distant when
we shall feel that, in order truly to destroy England, we must
occupy Egypt. The approaching death of the vast Ottoman

Empire obliges us to think in good time of taking steps to preserve our trade in the Levant.' Napoleon had read Raynal's *Histoire des Deux Indes* (1780) and Volney's *Considérations sur la guerre actuelle des Turcs* (1788) in which he wrote: 'Only one thing can indemnify France . . . the possession of Egypt. Through Egypt we shall reach India, we shall re-establish the old route through Suez and cause the route by the Cape of Good Hope to be abandoned.'

Magallon, the former French consul in Egypt, had urged an attack on India by way of Egypt as early as 1795, and Talleyrand was interested in his scheme. It was possible, in Talleyrand's opinion, to keep Turkey friendly, on the ground that France was driving out the Mameluke usurpers as the ally and protector of Turkey. On September 13, 1797, Napoleon wrote to Talleyrand: 'We could leave here with twenty-five thousand men, escorted by eight or ten ships of the line or Venetian frigates and take it. Why should we not occupy Malta? The inhabitants, of whom there are more than one hundred thousand, are very well disposed to us and thoroughly disgusted with their knights, who are dying of hunger. I have purposely had all their possessions in Italy confiscated. With the island of St Pierre, which the King of Sardinia has ceded to us, Malta, Corfu, et cetera, we shall be masters of the whole Mediterranean.'

Napoleon had two secret agents in Malta and was well informed. The Grand Master of the Order of St John was de Rohan, and the majority of the knights were French; the abolition of feudal dues and the nationalization of ecclesiastical property in the French Revolution had already wrecked the finances of the Order and of the individual knights.

In November 1797, Napoleon was informed that he had been appointed commander of the 'Army of England': but that, before returning to France, he was to attend the Congress of Rastadt as principal French delegate. By the end of the month agreement in principle had been reached at the Congress, and Napoleon returned to Paris. His reply to the formal welcome by the Directory ended with a mysterious phrase: 'When the happiness of the French people is founded on the best organic laws, the whole of Europe will become free.' Was this a hint of a further *coup d'état*?

If so, it was not followed up: Napoleon decided that 'the pear was not yet ripe'. He avoided public appearances and military display. More probably, Napoleon wished to dis-

sociate himself from the discredit of the Fructidor *coup*.
He wore civilian dress, cultivated the company of scientists
and writers, and was rewarded by election as a member of
the *Institut*. He was acutely aware of the danger to his
career of an anti-climax after Italy, which would be not
unwelcome to the Directory. 'In Paris, nothing is remembered for long. If I remain doing nothing for long, I am
lost.' The project for the invasion of England might well be
a snare. Mallet du Pan, the *émigré* publicist, reported that
'Bonaparte can rest assured that half of those who applauded
him would willingly have smothered him under his triumphal
laurels.'

Yet he had fifty thousand troops at his disposal and the
pick of the officers: on paper he had nearly fifty warships
to escort them. It was only after careful inspection of the
Channel ports that he advised against the project at the
end of February 1798. He pointed out that the naval preparations were hopelessly in arrears: most of the warships were
not fitted out, and were without crews. A concentrated and
costly drive to prepare the fleet might make the invasion
feasible in 1798, but if that were not possible, 'then any
expedition against England should in fact be abandoned,
though the appearance of it should be kept up'. 'Whatever
efforts we may make we shall not attain naval supremacy
for several years. To carry out a descent on England without
mastery of the sea would be the boldest and most difficult
operation ever undertaken.' He concludes by suggesting an
expedition 'into the Levant which would threaten the commerce of India'.

At the same time Talleyrand (probably in collusion with
Napoleon) was urging on the Directory the alternative Mediterranean project, and the Minister of Marine confirmed Napoleon's gloomy report on the northern naval preparations.
When Napoleon presented an estimate of the requirements
for Egypt on March 5, the Directory had in fact been won
over. They were persuaded that the Mediterranean project
would be much less costly; Napoleon asked only for twenty-
five thousand men, and the Toulon fleet was in being and
ready. Napoleon's arguments against the invasion project were
eminently sound in their appreciation of command of the
sea; why did not he (and the Government) see that English
naval supremacy made an Egyptian expedition equally haz-
ardous? It is easy to be wise after the event, but in 1798
it appeared unlikely that the English would appear in the

Mediterranean in force, after their withdrawal in 1796. With Malta and Corfu in French hands, the English would have hardly a foothold in the Mediterranean. The secret of the expedition was well kept, and even when the preparations were known, Ireland, the Channel or Portugal seemed more likely. The English agent at Leghorn reported on April 16 that the Toulon expedition was destined for Alexandria, but the Admiralty remained sceptical. Of the English Ministers, only Dundas guessed correctly at this stage, and ordered reinforcements to India. Pitt's decision to send a strong force into the Mediterranean, instead of merely blocking the exit, was in the circumstances a courageous one.

When the expedition sailed from Toulon on May 19, it was considerably larger than the estimates Napoleon had given to the Directory in March. There were over thirty-five thousand troops, nearly four hundred transports, and an escort of thirteen ships of the line. In addition, there were over a hundred and fifty experts, including the distinguished scientists Monge, Berthollet, and Fourier—the cream of the *Institut* and the *École Polytechnique,* a complete *encyclopédie vivante,* equipped with libraries and instruments. The incursion of these savants caused considerable astonishment, jealousy and some bad manners among the military. During the voyage Napoleon held long conversations with his *Institut.* Junot, Napoleon's aide-de-camp, was found to be snoring during one of these sessions, and when woken up, exclaimed 'General, it is all the fault of this confounded *Institut* of yours: it puts everyone to sleep, yourself included.' Napoleon had paid particular attention to the recruitment of these experts, with the agreement of the Government; and it leaves no doubt that the expedition was intended from the start as the foundation of a permanent colony. Whether there was a further thought at the back of Napoleon's mind, that he might overrun the East with all the resources of European science at his disposal, remains a question-mark, as the opportunity never developed. But there is an air of grandiose fantasy about the whole expedition; not since the Crusades had such an armada appeared in the Mediterranean.

It was a miracle that such an unwieldly convoy escaped being cut to pieces by Nelson's squadron. Nelson was off Toulon by May 17, but Napoleon's departure on the 19th took him by surprise. The strong wind which carried the French fleet rapidly south past the east coast of Corsica,

became a fierce gale further west, which damaged Nelson's
ships so severely that he had to put in to Sardinia for re-
pairs. It was not till June 7 that Troubridge's squadron joined
Nelson and brought his force up to thirteen battleships.
On June 15 he wrote to the Admiralty: 'If the French pass
Sicily, I think they intend to seize Alexandria.' On the 18th
he heard that the French were headed for Malta.

But Napoleon had captured Malta on June 12. His information about the internal weakness of the Knights of St John
had been correct. The immensely powerful fortifications of
Valetta, with fifteen hundred guns, were surrendered after a
token resistance of a day. The whole garrison seems to have
numbered less than a thousand men; the Maltese were indifferent or hostile to their rulers, and some of the French
knights refused to fight against their compatriots. De Rohan's
successor as Grand Master, the Prussian Hompesch, was de-
featist and had taken no steps to prepare the defences. It
was a sad anticlimax to the great days of the Order of St
John in the sixteenth century, when they held Malta for a
year against the flower of the Turkish Janissaries.

Napoleon stayed only a week in Malta to provision the
fleet, but in that time he organized a complete military and
civil administration for the islands. The Grand Master and
the Knights were pensioned off, and exiled. Their property
and that of many of the monasteries was confiscated: and
Napoleon seized all the bullion and precious metal in the
treasury and the churches. Nobility and slavery were abolished: all Maltese were to have the rights and duties of
French citizens. He even found time to reorganize the University and to arrange for sixty Maltese youths to be educated in France. He left behind three thousand troops as a
garrison under a military governor, and sailed straight for
Alexandria, revealing for the first time to his army that
Egypt was their destination. 'Soldiers! You are going to undertake a conquest whose effects on civilization and the
commerce of the world will be incalculable. You will strike
the greatest and most painful stroke possible against England
until you can deal her final deathblow.'

Meanwhile Nelson, having heard of the fall of Malta,
sailed for Alexandria and arrived there two days before
Napoleon. With no sign of the French, he returned to Sicily
to revictual; at last he got definite news off Greece, and
returned to Alexandria on July 31. The French army had
disembarked, but Nelson caught the fleet in Aboukir Bay

and annihilated it (Battle of the Nile, August 1, 1798). Only
two battleships out of thirteen escaped destruction. Admiral
Brueys had assumed that by anchoring his ships close to
the shallows and shifting his guns to the seaward side, he
would be able to offset the English superiority in manoeuvre,
and stave off an attack. The daring and seamanship of Nelson
and his captains enabled them to slip in between the French
ships and the shallows, and attack from both sides.

Napoleon was already at Cairo when he heard of the disaster at Aboukir. He had captured Alexandria by assault on
July 2 within a few hours of landing; and, knowing that
Nelson's fleet had been there only a few days before, he
rapidly completed the disembarkation of the whole army.
Leaving Kléber with six thousand men at Alexandria, he set
out for Cairo with twenty-five thousand men. It was a fortnight of terrible desert marches: foraging for food and water
was a desperate business in the face of hostile Bedouin.
But Napoleon's strategy was to seize the capital, and dis-
organize resistance by rapidity and surprise. On July 21 he
came up to the Mameluke camp at Embabeh (Battle of the
Pyramids). Six thousand of the superb Mameluke cavalry,
supported by a rabble of twelve thousand infantry, desperately strove to break the French squares: but the French
grapeshot and musketry made it a massacre as complete as
Kitchener's victory at Omdurman a century later. The French
lost only thirty men killed in action. On July 24, Napoleon
entered Cairo.

It was not till the middle of August that he received
news of the destruction of the fleet. He concealed his anxie-
ties, and quelled the misgivings of his officers who were already disillusioned by the squalor of Egypt. From the moment
of landing Napoleon proclaimed the policy already envisaged
in his Instructions for the expedition drawn up in April.
The Army were warned on June 28 to show respect for the
Mohammedan religion and to refrain from pillage and rape.
'You will find here customs different from those of Europe:
you must get used to them.' To the Egyptians, he presented
himself as the ally of the Sultan and of Islam, freeing Egypt
from the tyranny of the Mameluke usurpers.

In his proclamation of July 2 at Alexandria he said, 'Peoples of Egypt, you will be told that I have come to destroy
your religion: do not believe it! Answer that I have come
to restore your rights and punish the usurpers, and that,
more than the Mamelukes, I respect God, his Prophet and

the Koran. . . . Is it not we who have been through the
centuries the friends of the Sultan (may God grant his de-
sires) and the enemies of his enemies?' A *Diwan* of nine
Egyptians was nominated for the administration of Cairo:
similar *Diwans* were set up in the provinces. Finally a General *Diwan* of notables from the whole of Egypt was summoned in October 1798 for consultation, to which two
French *commissaires* were attached.

Such an approach to a form of national representation was
a complete innovation in Egypt. The fact that the two *commissaires* appointed were Monge and Berthollet, the eminent scientists, shows that Napoleon took this body seriously,
and important questions of internal administration were referred to it. In Egypt Napoleon was acting as an independent
ruler, and the functioning of the General *Diwan* is a
significant anticipation of Napoleon's administrative concep-
tions which were to mature in the Council of State of the
Consulate. He strove to obtain from the *muftis* of the Mosque
of El Azhar, the great Moslem university, a *fetwa* or declaration that the faithful could properly swear allegiance to his
régime. 'To obtain from these religious notabilities a declaration in favour of the French would be a moral victory
which would complete the victory of the Pyramids.' The
muftis countered by suggesting that Napoleon and his army
should be converted to Islam. These prolonged theological
discussions gave rise to the rumour that Napoleon was seriously contemplating conversion. General Menou actually did
so, and married a Moslem wife. After a great deal of hag-
gling, Napoleon did obtain a *fetwa*, confirmed from Mecca,
that the French were allies of Islam, and were exempt from
the rules of circumcision and abstention from alcohol. At
the same time he took care to write to the Sherif of Mecca,
as well as the Bey of Tripoli and the Pashas of Acre and
Aleppo, to reassure them of his intentions as the 'friend of
Islam'. He took part officially in the celebrations of the
birthday of Mahomet.

Napoleon's propaganda could not, however, persuade the
Egyptians that the French were not infidel invaders, though
in the short run it had a negative value in allaying panic
and lulling fanatical passions. Napoleon was unlikely to forget that the basis of his security was force and fear. He
wrote to General Menou at the end of July, 'We have had
to treat them gently so far so as to destroy the reputation
for brutality which preceded us: but today we must adopt

the tone necessary to make these people obey, and, for them, to obey is to fear. . . .' Uncertainty about the strength of the French and the permanence of their conquest was the greatest danger.

The naval disaster at Aboukir produced no immediate re-action in Alexandria, but anti-French propaganda could in-filtrate from several sources—from the English blockading squadron left by Nelson and from the Mameluke Beys who had taken refuge in Upper Egypt and Syria, and from Con-stantinople itself. Napoleon sent several messages to the Di-rectory to confirm whether Talleyrand had gone to negotiate at Constantinople. In fact Talleyrand had excused himself from going and the envoy nominated in his place had not even started. As soon as the news of Aboukir reached Con-stantinople, the Turks declared war on France on September 9, and this was soon known in Cairo. Unrest was growing as the French imposed forced loans and new-fangled taxes, in a hurried attempt to replace the bullion which had all gone to the bottom in the French flagship *L'Orient*. On October 21 a major rising, headed by the fanatics of the University of El Azhar, took place in Cairo: it took two days to crush, at the cost of two hundred and fifty French and seven hundred Egyptian dead. Napoleon dealt with it by a com-bination of speedy ruthlessness and politic conciliation so that the *Diwan-Général* could be restored to its functions by December. Many of the French complained that Napoleon had been too lenient. But a network of forts was quickly built to dominate Cairo.

Meanwhile Napoleon's corps of experts had not been idle. At the beginning of August Napoleon had founded the In-stitute of Egypt, under the presidency of Monge, with its own buildings, libraries and laboratories in Cairo. Most of the in-struments and books, as well as the technical equipment of the Army, had been lost with the fleet. But Conté, head of the balloon corps, rapidly improvised workshops for the manufacture of every kind of instrument. A printing press (hitherto unknown in Egypt) produced two newspapers. A geographical survey of Egypt was at once put in hand. Hy-giene in a strange climate and the control of unfamiliar dis-eases was an immediate necessity for the health of the Army: the setting up of military hospitals was followed by the foundation of a civilian native hospital. The architects and archaeologists brought back drawings of Thebes, Luxor, Karnak. In July 1799 the Institute discussed a report on the

Rosetta stone, which later enabled Champollion to decipher Egyptian hieroglyphics; this session marked the birth of Egyptology. Napoleon himself led a party of scientists to inspect the remains of the ancient Suez Canal, which was later surveyed. In 1832 the Saint-Simonians took up the Suez Canal project which was finally realized by de Lesseps. The achievements of the Institute of Egypt are enshrined in the magnificent *Description de l'Égypte,* published between 1809–28.

Napoleon's original intention had been to return to Europe after a few months, having launched the new colony. The situation in France and in Europe was so unstable that a political or military crisis, or both, might soon arise from which he could not afford to be absent. The Battle of the Nile had completely altered his situation, and he could get no news from Europe. On December 17 he wrote to the Directory that no couriers had got through since July. 'There are a few concentrations of Turkish forces in Syria: I would have gone to have an argument with them if seven days of desert did not separate us. . . . We await news of France and Europe: that is a great need for our souls, for if the national glory had need of us we should be inconsolable at not being there.' But on February 10 he wrote that a Frenchman had arrived in a Venetian ship. As Austria had not yet entered the war, he proposed to march into Syria, with the object of forestalling a Turkish attack, and 'using the two months of winter left to me in making the whole of the coast friendly through war and negotiation.' 'If during March the report of Citizen Hamelin is confirmed, and France is in arms against the kings, I shall return home.' There was another motive which he did not mention; his troops were being demoralized by *cafard*, induced by the boredom and squalor of Cairo, despite his efforts to provide them with European cafés and entertainment.

He took only thirteen thousand men with him into Syria: Desaix was sent with five thousand men into Upper Egypt, and five thousand were left in Cairo. The idea that in Syria he 'missed his destiny' and that it was an abortive prelude to the conquest of the East was a product of Napoleon's imagination in retrospect, when he liked to recall that Egypt was the 'finest time of his life, because it was the most ideal'. It is true that he wrote to Tippoo Sahib of Mysore in January 1799, announcing that 'he had arrived on the coasts of the Red Sea with an innumerable and invincible army, filled with the desire to deliver you from the iron yoke of England'. But he made no promises, and his intention was probably to try to stiffen resistance to the English in India. Whatever dreams he may have had for a conquest of the East, or a return to Europe by way of Constantinople, were dispelled by Nelson's victory at the Battle of the Nile. It is clear that at the time he regarded the Syrian campaign as a strictly limited sideshow. It would have been a different matter if Europe had remained quiet, and he had been able to receive a flow of reinforcements. In July 1797, Arthur Wellesley, the future Duke of Wellington, had written from India about the dangerous possibilities of French infiltration. 'As long as the French have an establishment [in Mauritius], Great Britain cannot call herself safe in India. They will come here to seek service in the Armies of the Native princes, and all Frenchmen in such a situation are equally dangerous. They would shortly discipline their numerous armies in the new mode which they have adopted in Europe, than which nothing can be more formidable to the small body of fighting men of which the Company's armies in general consist.'

The capture of Jaffa by assault on March 7, 1799, was disgraced by Napoleon's order to shoot three thousand prisoners. Normally a humane commander, he was driven by military necessity: already he had neither the food nor the escorts to provide for prisoners. It must be admitted that the rules of war were rather different in the East. The commander of Jaffa cut off the head of Napoleon's envoy who had been sent to parley with him. Jaffa had fallen so quickly that Napoleon underestimated the difficulty of taking Acre. The first assault, without siege artillery, failed and he was held up for two months. The factors which turned the scale at Acre were Sir Sidney Smith and his naval squadron which cut Napoleon's sea communications and were able to strengthen the garrison with naval artillery and experts, among whom, ironically, was the French émigré, Phélipeaux, who had been a fellow cadet of Napoleon. During the siege Napoleon hurried south to win a quick and decisive victory over a Turkish relieving force at Mount Tabor (April 16).

The decision to abandon the siege of Acre (May 17) was a blow to Napoleon's prestige, but militarily it was not very important. Its capture would have cost more men than he could afford, and the plague which had broken out in the town would have been even more fatal to his army. The summer months were likely to bring a seaborne invasion of

Egypt from Turkey. Moreover he had received despatches from the Directory informing him that Russia and Turkey had declared war on France, and that a Russian army had invaded Italy. To the hardships of the retreat were added the horrors of plague. Napoleon was subsequently accused of ordering lethal doses of opium for the sick. The truth appears to be that Napoleon suggested this form of euthanasia for the victims who could not be transported, but that he dropped the suggestion when his surgeons opposed it. They could not accuse him of callousness, because he had already tried to allay panic by visiting and even touching the plague victims in hospital.

It is probable that Napoleon's army was reduced by nearly half when it returned to Cairo. At the end of June Napoleon asked the Directory for six thousand reinforcements; otherwise his effective force would be reduced to twelve thousand by the next year. On July 15 Napoleon heard, as he expected, that the Turkish seaborne invasion had arrived; they had landed at Aboukir Bay. Within three days Napoleon had concentrated ten thousand men at Alexandria, and attacked. The Turks were nearly two to one, but they were annihilated, and their commander was captured (July 25, 1799). On August 2, in the course of negotiations about the exchange of prisoners, Sir Sidney Smith sent to Napoleon newspapers for the month of June 1799. From them he learned that Italy had been lost and Jourdan had been defeated on the Rhine. He made up his mind forthwith to return to Europe, and ordered two frigates and two smaller vessels to be prepared in the greatest secrecy. On August 24 he sailed, accompanied by a handful of Generals and scientists. Kléber, to whom he handed over the command, and the Army, were only informed in writing after he had left. Naturally there was a good deal of indignation in the Army at Napoleon's 'flight' and 'desertion'. Kléber was particularly bitter against Napoleon. He wrote to Desaix that 'there is no doubt: Bonaparte had sacrificed this country a long time before his departure. But he needed an occasion for flight, and he has fled in order to escape the catastrophe of its surrender.'

At the time this was unfair and untrue. The secrecy of his departure was essential: it offered the best, perhaps the only chance of getting through the English blockade. In his Instructions to Kléber, Napoleon says, 'The arrival of our Brest squadron at Toulon and of the Spanish squadron at

Cartagena leaves no doubt as to the possibility of transporting to Egypt the muskets, sabres, pistols and shot of which you and I have an exact list, together with enough recruits to make good the losses of two campaigns. . . . You can appreciate how important the possession of Egypt is for France.' He authorizes Kléber, if he has received no help by the following May and if there were serious losses from plague, to make peace with Turkey, even at the cost of the evacuation of Egypt. But he must try to delay negotiations until a general peace.

Napoleon had guessed from the fleet movements that the Directory were trying to get in touch with Egypt. He did not know that the Directory, under heavy fire of criticism for locking up the flower of the French Army in Egypt, had decided to write off the colony and evacuate the army. Admiral Bruix took the Brest fleet to Toulon but got no further, waiting in vain for his Spanish ally. Napoleon's reference to 'a general peace' in his letter to Kléber indicates his reading of the general strategic picture. The key to the retention of Egypt was success in Europe; and he could be best employed in turning the tide in Europe. This was the correct strategical conclusion in the circumstances, and it had been understood between him and the Directory from the start of the Egyptian expedition. A General with the customary reactions of military honour and obedience would, no doubt, have remained at his post in the absence of specific orders to the contrary. It is already clear that Napoleon was not the sort of man to be swayed by such sentiments. Through the fog of uncertainty, the baffling scarcity of news, he guessed that the fate of France, and of his own career, were at stake. If he were not too late, if he were not caught by the English cruisers, the moment was at hand which would bring him to supreme power or to the guillotine.

5

Brumaire and Marengo

THE NEWS OF NAPOLEON'S victory over the Turks at Aboukir
arrived in Paris on October 5, 1799; it was followed on
October 13 by the news that he had landed at St Raphaël, in
Provence. The skilful navigation of Admiral Ganteaume,
aided by unfailing luck, had brought him to France in six
weeks, and only once, near Corsica, was an English sail
sighted. Strong northwesterly winds enabled them to hug the
African coast, then a strong south-easter brought them
quickly to Corsica. For five days they were kept by contrary winds in Ajaccio, and Napoleon fretted with impa-
tience: 'I shall arrive too late.'

All the way to Paris he was received with popular enthusiasm and acclaim. At first sight this seems surprising;
but the timing of Napoleon's victory over the Turks had
been a godsend. It had wiped out the dismal impression
made by the Syrian campaign, and to Frenchmen Napoleon
was still the man of Campo Formio, whose name meant
'victory and peace'. Napoleon's first meeting with the Directors was awkward and frosty; in their minds, but unspoken,
was the thought that Napoleon might be arrested for deserting his army. It is true that Napoleon had now seen the
Government's letter of September authorizing him to return

to France, but only with his army. General Bernadotte, now
Minister of War, suggested that Napoleon should be arrested for desertion and evasion of the regulations for
quarantine against plague. But in the face of public opinion,
the Directors did not dare even to discuss it officially.

By the end of 1799 the credit of the Directors and the
Councils was in inverse proportion to the pomposity of their
official costumes; the Directors wore hats with plumes three
feet high, the Elders and the Five Hundred swathed themselves in Roman togas. Since the *coup d'état* of *Fructidor*
and the Peace of Campo Formio the situation, both internally
and externally, had gravely deteriorated. Nelson's victory at
the Nile had started a chain-reaction of events leading to
the formation of the Second Coalition against the Republic.
First Turkey, and then Naples, stimulated by the pressure of
Nelson and the Hamiltons, had declared war.

Tsar Paul of Russia was incensed by the capture of
Malta, where he had been intriguing with the Knights for his
election as Grand Master of the Order, and by the appearance of France in the Eastern Mediterranean as a com-
petitor in the partition of the Turkish Empire. One of the
Knights, Litta, had gone to St Petersburg in 1789 and became the Empress Catherine's lover; he was also friendly with
Paul. The Tsar's disordered mind had conceived the fantastic
idea that the Order, with its tradition of chivalry, should become the spearhead of the counter-attack against the Revolution. In January 1797 he established a Russian priory of
the Order, and made the Prince of Condé, fighting leader
of the French *émigrés*, its Prior. In November 1798 the
Russian priory proclaimed the deposition of the exiled Grand
Master Hompesch, and elected Tsar Paul in his place.
By March 1799 both Russia and Austria were in the war.

Napoleon's firm but cautious policy in Italy had been abandoned by the Directory for a more reckless policy of 'rev-
olutionizing' both Italy and Switzerland, and intensifying
the financial exploitation. Pope Pius VI had been expelled
from Rome, and a Roman Republic set up, with the support of a pro-French Jacobin minority. Masséna's governorship
in Rome had been disgraced by the most blatant corruption, and a mutiny of his troops. General Championnet had
little difficulty in beating Ferdinand's Neapolitan army
which had rashly tried to march on Rome; Ferdinand had
to retire to Sicily, and the Parthenopean Republic was proclaimed in Naples. But the *lazzaroni* of Naples and the

Calabrian peasants were fanatically hostile to the anti-
clerical French, and Cardinal Ruffo's counter-revolutionary
crusade in Calabria provoked a guerrilla civil war which
foreshadowed the horrors of the Peninsula. The Parthenopean Republic foundered in a welter of bloody reprisals,
and the French Army had to abandon Naples and Rome.

In April 1799 an Austro-Russian army under General
Suvorov had occupied Milan and on August 15 Joubert,
the new commander of the Army of Italy, was defeated
and killed at Novi. Jourdan's Army of the Danube had
been defeated by the Archduke Charles at Stockach in
March. Not only was there a threat of an invasion of
southern France but an Anglo-Russian force had landed in
Holland. It is true that the military situation had been to
some extent stabilized since Napoleon's arrival in France,
and that the Second Coalition was much more fragile than it
appeared. Masséna had beaten the Russians at Zürich on
September 26 and Brune had forced the Duke of York's
expeditionary force in Holland to re-embark (October 18).

The government of the Directory was in no condition to
withstand such shocks. It is not easy to give a fair judgment on this period of French government. The glories of
the Consulate, and the Napoleonic myth, have tempted many
historians to exaggerate the contrast between the incompetence and corruption of the Directory and the achievements of the succeeding régime. Barras is conspicuous because he was the one Director who remained permanently
in office from 1795 to 1799: an able man, he was corrupt,
cynical, and prematurely exhausted by dissipation. Others
like Carnot (ejected in *Fructidor* 1797), Reubell, Merlin,
François de Neufchateau were competent and hard-working,
if not outstanding political figures.

But, whatever their intentions, they were the prisoners of
a defective system. Power was strictly divided between
the executive Directory of five and the legislative Councils;
though the Directory were elected by the Councils, the provisions for renewal of the Directory and the Councils ensured that the majority of the Directory never reflected the
political attitude of the Councils. Friction could only be
overcome by an unconstitutional purge, and the first example of this method in *Fructidor* 1797, had undermined
confidence in the morality and permanence of the régime.
As a result of the elections of May (*Floréal*) 1798, over
a hundred deputies elected were excluded as being too

Jacobin and 'anarchist'. In the course of 1799 Sieyès, Gohier, General Moulins and Ducos entered the Directory. With the exception of Sieyès, these were all nonentities: but Sieyès was one of the fathers of the Revolution, a leading member of the States-General and the National Assembly of 1789, who had survived the Terror by judicious withdrawal into obscurity. He was a moderate, with his own dogmatic ideas of constitutional reform. The elections to the Councils in May (*Prairial*) 1799 produced a further swing to the left, reflecting the military reverses.

The second great handicap of the Directory was financial weakness. They had inherited from the Convention a fearful legacy of debt and inflation. The paper money of the Revolution, the *assignat*, was down to one per cent of its value by 1797. The Directory performed a valuable service, which was to benefit the Consulate, by repudiating the debt and *assignats*, and returning to a metallic currency; but the new *mandats territoriaux*—government bonds issued on the security of the nationalized lands of the Church and the *émigrés*—soon depreciated. The efforts made by the Directory to collect the land tax, the main direct tax created by the Revolution, and to introduce new indirect taxes were frustrated by the lack of control of the central government over the locally elected departmental authorities. When the occupied territories and their financial contributions were lost, the situation became desperate. The deficit on the budget for 1799 amounted to four hundred million francs. The armies could no longer be paid, and deserters swelled the bands of brigands which infested whole areas of France. The *chouannerie* of the west, the civil war of La Vendée, had flared up again.

The royalist cause had been discredited by Louis XVIII's Declaration of Verona in 1795 in which he offered no guarantee for the maintenance of the revolutionary settlement. But moderates such as Sieyès were meditating a reform of the Constitution which would strengthen the executive power. Sieyès was looking round for a General to play the part which Augereau had filled in the days of *Fructidor*. Joubert had been appointed to the Army of Italy with this end in view, and when he was killed, Moreau was approached, but proved to be elusive and hesitant. When he heard of Napoleon's arrival in Provence, he told Sieyès, 'There is your man, he will make your *coup d'état* better than I.'

Bernadotte was linked with Jourdan, the victor of Fleurus in 1794, and the Jacobins in the Council of Five Hundred. They were thinking in terms of a return to the dictatorship and terror of the Committee of Public Safety of 1793. They passed a law of hostages, authorizing the imprisonment of the relatives of *émigrés*, which recalled the days of the Terror, and an income tax which alarmed the financiers and the bourgeoisie. On September 14, a motion to declare *'la patrie en danger'* (which implied a suspension of the Constitution and a dictatorship) was narrowly defeated in the Council of Five Hundred. Napoleon might well have been faced on his return with a Committee of Public Safety headed by Bernadotte. But as Marbot, who served under him, later noted in his memoirs, 'Bernadotte conceals beneath his bold gestures and words a great deal of indecision, even timidity in his decisions.' Sieyès and the moderates struck back; Bernadotte was dismissed from the Ministry of War, and they succeeded in carrying the elections of the Presidents of the Elders and of the Five Hundred. The new President of the Five Hundred was Napoleon's brother Lucien. There was therefore no need for Napoleon to take the initiative when he arrived in Paris. Lucien, Talleyrand (now out of office and intriguing for a change of government) and Roederer, an influential journalist, were there to bring him abreast of events. He had only to wait for each faction in turn to sound him out.

But he was at first preoccupied with a domestic crisis. He had come back from Egypt determined to divorce Josephine. Soon after his arrival in Egypt he had been convinced of Josephine's adultery with the handsome young hussar, Charles; even worse, in his eyes, was the fact that they were both notoriously making money with the help of corrupt army contractors. On July 25, 1798, Napoleon had written to his brother Joseph, 'I have great private unhappiness; the veil has at last fallen from my eyes. . . . It is a sad state to be in to have all one's thoughts centred in the heart of one person. . . . Good-bye, my only friend. I have never wronged you. You owe me that at least, whatever my heart may have desired; you understand?'

The last sentence is mysterious, but it implies that Napoleon was regretting that he had not married Desirée Clary instead of Josephine. The suggestion is that he had not pressed the engagement because of her father's opposition which would have embarrassed his son-in-law Joseph.

However, Napoleon had consoled himself with the company of Madame Fourès, wife of a lieutenant, who had somehow managed to follow her husband to Egypt. She was a charming and sprightly blonde known to her friends as Bellilote and to the troops of the Army of Egypt as 'Cleopatra'.

When Josephine heard the news of Napoleon's arrival in Provence, she desperately set off to meet him, but missed him *en route*. When she arrived at their house in Paris, Napoleon at first refused to see her; but after a night of anguish for both of them, he capitulated to the sound of her voice, and the entreaties of her children, Eugène and Hortense. The reconciliation was permanent, though their marriage had become one of convenience and tolerance. Napoleon agreed not to see Madame Fourès again; Josephine never again risked her position by a love affair, and she was unable to protest effectively against Napoleon's numerous but transitory *affaires*.

Napoleon soon saw that he would have to work with Sieyès, though he disliked him personally as a metaphysical windbag. He at first thought of being elected as Director, but the politicians soon made it clear to him that the rule requiring Directors to be at least forty years old could not be waived. Barras, his old patron, would have liked to get him out of the way by offering him the command of the Army of Italy; Napoleon kept him at arm's length, knowing that he was corrupt, despised and isolated. The Jacobin Generals, Bernadotte, Jourdan and Augereau, would have offered him a military dictatorship to get him on their side. But the Jacobin politics were even more distasteful to him than Sieyès'; and he had no intention of becoming a prisoner of the military, or of an unpopular faction.

Napoleon and Sieyès finally met on November 1 (10 *Brumaire*) after Talleyrand and Lucien had acted as intermediaries. Napoleon made it clear to Sieyès that he had no intention of acting simply as Sieyès' 'sword'; there must be a provisional government of three Consuls—Sieyès, Ducos, and Napoleon. Sieyès was taken aback; he had feared that Napoleon's 'sword would be too long' but he had no other General to fall back on. Which of the two would, in the event, be the horse and which the rider? If Sieyès still hoped that the politicians could use Napoleon and then discard him, Napoleon was determined that the outcome would be precisely the reverse.

Napoleon had already been three weeks in Paris and it was

time to act, or the moment would pass. It was typical of Napoleon's luck that he had arrived in Paris at the precise moment when a seizure of power was possible; either sooner or later public opinion might not have supported it. But as Napoleon remarked at St Helena, of great men, 'Is it because they are lucky that they become great? No, but being great, they have been able to master luck.' The preparations for the *coup d'état* were hasty, vague and ill-co-ordinated—largely because Sieyès and Napoleon were each concealing their hand from the other. Compared with Louis Napoleon's elaborately prepared *coup* of December 1851, it was an improvised and bungled affair, not improved by Napoleon's own interventions.

Napoleon accepted, with mental reservations, Sieyès' plan to induce the Elders to vote, as they had the legal power to do, that the Councils should move to St Cloud, where they could be surrounded by troops and undisturbed by popular manifestations. Napoleon was to be appointed to the command of the Paris garrison. On paper, the whole operation should go through smoothly and legally. The Generals, apart from Bernadotte, Jourdan and Augereau, would follow Napoleon. Sebastiani, a Corsican and comrade of Napoleon in the Italian campaigns, and Murat, would command the two key regiments. Sieyès and Ducos could manage the Directors and the Elders; Lucien was President of the Five Hundred. Fouché, as Minister of Police, would hold the ring. Roederer, the journalist, had arranged on Napoleon's behalf for the secret printing of proclamations and manifestos.

On November 9 (18 *Brumaire*) the Elders voted without difficulty that the Councils should meet the following day at St Cloud, and that Napoleon should be invested with the command 'to ensure the safety of the national representation'. At this point Sieyès began to lose control of the situation. He had intended to limit Napoleon's command to the troops of the line, and to keep control of the guards of the Directory and the Councils. Napoleon calmly altered the draft decree to give himself command of both. Talleyrand and Admiral Bruix obtained from Barras his resignation as Director, and when Gohier and General Moulins refused to resign, they were kept under guard in the Luxembourg. Napoleon further disconcerted Sieyès by appearing at the session of the Elders accompanied by a throng of Generals, and by haranguing the crowd outside with a violent denunciation of the incompetence of the Directory. 'I left you with conquests and now the enemy invades our frontiers.' On the first day, Napoleon had stolen the initiative from Sieyès, but at the cost of increasing the hazards of the following day.

The weak point in Sieyès' plan was the day's delay in the meeting of the Councils at St Cloud, and the further delay in preparing the rooms in which they were to meet. The Jacobins of the Five Hundred were now alerted and enraged by Napoleon's military display in Paris; and they had time to concert their opposition. Sieyès had already warned Napoleon of the danger from the Jacobin deputies, and now proposed that forty of them should be arrested. Napoleon rejected this suggestion, saying, 'I do not fear such feeble enemies.' He had already assured himself that Bernadotte would take the safe course of remaining in Paris and awaiting the outcome of the St Cloud session. When Bourrienne, Napoleon's secretary, drove out to St Cloud the following morning, he remarked to his companion as they passed the scene of Louis XVI's execution, 'My friend, tomorrow we shall sleep at the Luxembourg, or we shall finish here.'

Owing to the delay in preparing the halls, the Councils did not meet till after midday. Both sessions opened in stormy mood with the opposition on the offensive. In the Elders, they complained that members had not been sent a summons to the extraordinary session: they demanded an explanation from the Directors of the reasons for summoning it. When they were told that the Directors had resigned, they concluded their session by sending a message to the Five Hundred inviting them, according to the rules of the Constitution, to draw up a list of nominations for a new Directory. In the Five Hundred, Lucien as President was unable to prevent a motion that all members should individually swear an oath to maintain the Constitution; this procedure would take an hour. By 3.30 pm Napoleon was losing patience, and determined on a personal intervention. Augereau and Jourdan, hearing of the attitude of the Councils, had arrived from Paris to bargain with him: he rebuffed them. Napoleon suddenly appeared, with his aides-de-camp, in the hall of the Elders, just as they were rising from their formal session. He harangued them in a long, discursive, badly delivered speech, which was interrupted by the opposition. Finally, he made the mistake of turning to his aides and making a direct appeal to the military. 'If there is talk of declaring me *hors la loi*, I shall appeal to you, my brave companions in arms. Remember that I march accompanied by the god of victory and the god of fortune.' Nothing could have made a worse impression, and Bourrienne tugged him out of the hall, saying, 'General, you don't know what you are saying.'

As he went out, he received a message from Fouché and from Talleyrand in Paris that there was no time to lose, and that the affair must be brought to a head. Napoleon resolved to appear before the Five Hundred in a final attempt to cut through the parliamentary deadlock. He suddenly interrupted the debate of the Five Hundred on the resignation of the Directors, and advanced alone into the hall. Before he could speak, he was surrounded by angry deputies who shook him and beat him with their fists. He was rescued, half fainting, by four grenadiers. The news of this scene incensed the troops of the line, and both Murat and Sieyès now advised him to send in the troops. Napoleon was still reluctant to resort to open illegality, but when cries of *hors la loi* (the dread words which had precipitated the downfall of Robespierre) were heard from the hall of the Five Hundred, he decided on a direct appeal to the guards of the Councils, who were still hesitant. He sent for Lucien, and called for a horse. Lucien had resisted all demands to put the vote of *hors la loi,* and when he left the tribune, no formal procedure could be followed.

The two brothers appeared together before the guards of the Councils. Lucien spoke first, and his appeal, as President of the Five Hundred, was ingenious and decisive. 'The President of the Council of Five Hundred declares to you that the great majority of the Council is, at this moment, terrorized by certain deputies armed with daggers.' He added that these 'bold brigands' were 'doubtless in the pay of England'. Taking his cue, Napoleon embroidered this theme: 'I went to speak to them, and they answered me with daggers.' Napoleon's face was now bleeding where he had scratched himself in his nervous excitement; officers spread the rumour through the ranks that there had been an attempt to assassinate Napoleon in the Council of Five Hundred. The scruples of the guards were now overcome, and Murat led a column of grenadiers into the hall of the Five Hundred. No blood was shed as the deputies fled at the sight of fixed bayonets, many of them climbing out of the windows. At 7 pm the Elders at last decreed the nomination of a provisional executive of three Consuls—Sieyès, Ducos, and Napoleon. By 9 pm Lucien had collected a rump of the Five Hundred—not more than a hundred in all—to ratify the decision of the Elders. A further decree provided that two commissions of twenty-five deputies each from the two Councils should consult with the Consuls on the form of the new Constitution.

On returning to Paris, Napoleon dictated a manifesto in which he referred not only to 'daggers' but 'firearms'. The vitally important part played by Lucien was ignored. It is obvious that without Lucien's unfailing presence of mind the day would have been lost; and there were moments when it seemed that Napoleon would be abandoned by his supporters, and outlawed. He had taken great risks to preserve a semblance of legality, and he had succeeded, but only just succeeded, in avoiding a military *coup d'etat*. The final appeal had been made to the guards of the Councils, on the plea of protecting the Councils from a minority of 'assassins'. He had not resorted to the ultimate weapon, the troops of the Paris garrison. His own part in the day was not one he could be proud of. His appearances had been ineffective and ill-judged, and he had been met with violent hostility by the politicians. He admitted afterwards that he had struck the wrong note, and lost his head. His dislike and fear of political assemblies, already strong after witnessing the scenes of the Revolution, became a positive obsession after the day at St Cloud.

Napoleon had been named only third on the list of Consuls, and his position was still uncertain and precarious. On the other hand, it was clear that he had more support from the man in the street: Paris had remained perfectly quiet. This sprang, however, more from anger against the Directory and Councils than from enthusiasm for Napoleon personally. In the event, the bungled day at St Cloud had one important but unforeseen result—the disappearance of the Councils as well as the Directory. If it had gone more smoothly, the Councils would have remained in being as a check to the Consuls. Sieyès later remarked, 'I made the 18th *Brumaire,* but not the 19th.'

Miot de Melito wrote in his memoirs, 'We are struck, above all, with the small share taken by Bonaparte in the events of a day which founded his power.' This may be true of 19 *Brumaire,* but it is not true of 20 *Brumaire* and the following days. In fact *Brumaire* comprises two distinct *coups d'état*—the first of which is the victory of Sieyès and the party of the Brumairians over the Jacobins on 18 and 19 *Brumaire*, and the second of which, in the month following and ending in the promulgation of the Constitution of the Year VIII, is the victory of Napoleon over Sieyès and the Brumairians. The second is the more important because it produced a form of government quite different from the Directory. This was not intended or foreseen by the Brumairians; they did not want a radical change in the distribution of power between the executive and the legislature, but only a change of emphasis. It was brought about by Napoleon's willpower, persistence and resourcefulness, backed by his hold on public opinion.

In the month's discussion between the provisional Councils and the legislative committees, which followed *Brumaire*, Sieyès unfolded his constitutional plan. He described its principle as 'authority from above, confidence from below'.

In theory, universal suffrage was to be applied for the first time; the constitutions of 1791 and 1795 imposed property qualifications on voters, while the democratic constitution of 1793 was never implemented. In effect it meant that the functions of the electorate were to be limited to drawing up local and national lists of 'notabilities'. The electors in each commune would make a list of one-tenth of their number, who would be eligible for communal offices: one-tenth of the communal list formed the departmental list, of which again one-tenth formed the national list, eligible for the central Government. From this restricted national list, a Senate would nominate a Tribunate to discuss legislation, and a Legislature to vote on it. The Tribunate could discuss but not vote, the Legislature could vote but not discuss. A 'Grand Elector' nominated for life, but subject to deposition by the Senate, would appoint, at will, two Consuls, one for foreign and one for internal affairs, each with his separate administration. They were to be assisted by a Council of State. Central and local government officials, including Prefects of departments and mayors of communes, would be appointed by the Consuls from the lists of 'notabilities'.

Some of these ideas were not new. Sieyès had suggested a Tribunate in 1795; Consuls and Prefects had appeared in the constitution of the Roman Republic in 1798. Sieyès' plan was an ingenious scheme for emasculating democracy, entrenching the Brumairians in the Legislature, and so distributing the executive power as to ensure against a dictatorship. If it had ever been realized it would probably have resulted in complete governmental paralysis. He evidently hoped to shelve Napoleon by giving him the honorific but powerless office of Grand Elector. Napoleon made no objection to Sieyès' proposals for the electoral system, but he reacted violently to his scheme for the executive power. He ridiculed the idea of the Grand Elector as 'a fatted pig'. Daunou, one of the Brumairians, then submitted a draft which restored the three Consuls but gave them an equal vote, made the First Consul incapable of commanding the army or of re-election, and rejected Sieyès' list of notabilities in favour of direct election. The final debates on the draft constitution ended in a complete victory for Napoleon. The Consuls were now to hold office for ten years and be re-eligible: the position of the Second and Third Consuls was to be 'consultative', and their inferiority was marked by the fact that their salary was to be one-third of that of the First Consul.

It was intended that the three Consuls should be elected by the legislative committee by secret ballot. Napoleon, at the last minute, outmanoeuvred the Brumairians by proposing that Sieyès should nominate them: he was thus forced to return the compliment by nominating Napoleon's candidates, Cambacérès, an ex-regicide, and Lebrun, an ex-royalist. Napoleon feared that in a secret ballot Daunou might be put in as Third Consul. In compensation, Sieyès' list of notabilities was restored, and he himself was given the Presidency of the Senate with the right to nominate nearly one-third of the members: he further accepted the grant of a national estate which effectively destroyed his political reputation.

Napoleon also insisted that the Constitution should be promulgated as quickly as possible and submitted to plebiscite, without waiting to fill in the details. As Napoleon said later, 'A Constitution should be short—and obscure.' In their proclamation to the nation announcing the new Constitution, the Consuls made the bold claim, 'Citizens, the revolution is established on the principles with which it began. It is complete.' The plebiscite completed in February 1800 gave three million votes in favour, with fifteen hundred dissenting. As the list of notabilities was not ready till a year later, all officials were simply nominated by the First Consul, and the members of the Tribunate and Legislature by the Senate. As provisional Consul Napoleon had tactfully suggested that the Consuls should take the chair in rota-

tion; but even before he was installed as First Consul under
the new Constitution of the Year VIII, he was taking the
initiative as head of the Government.

From the start, his aim was to form a truly national Government; he wished not only to be independent of factions,
but to abolish them. His choice of Cambacérès and Lebrun as
Second and Third Consuls was a symbol of this policy. He
vetoed Sieyès' proposal, based on the precedent of
Fructidor, that a number of the opposition, including General Jourdan, should be deported to Guiana. Proscription of
the opponents at St Cloud was limited to a short period of
house arrest in a few cases. The law of hostages and the
special income tax on the rich were immediately revoked.
Josephine and Talleyrand used their aristocratic connections
to rally the *noblesse* to the new régime.

Napoleon hoped that the Vendéan war could be brought
to an end by a judicious mixture of conciliation and force.
In his Proclamation to the Western Departments of December 28, 1799, he pointed out that the law of hostages had
been repealed, and guaranteed freedom of worship. 'The first
magistrates of the Republic . . . do not wish to employ force
until they have exhausted the resources of persuasion and
justice.' In the early months of 1800 he had secret but
fruitless interviews with Hyde de Neuville, d'Andigné, and
Cadoudal, the royalist leaders. At the same time General
Brune was appointed to speed up military action in the west.

Finance was the most immediately pressing problem.
Dubois-Crancé, the Minister of War under the Directory, who
was replaced by Berthier, had to admit that the pay and
supply of the Armies were at a complete standstill. The
bankers were asked to advance twelve millions to the Government, but, even after the abolition of the special income
tax, they were still doubtful about the stability of the new
régime. They would only offer three millions, and the
organization of a national lottery. Napoleon arrested Ouvrard, the leading war contractor, and forced him to dis-
gorge some of his profits. With the proceeds he founded a
new private bank, the Bank of France, to assist the Government. But his most important and successful action in
this field was to persuade Gaudin, a distinguished Treasury
official of the *ancien régime,* to become Minister of Finance.
Collectors of taxes were now required to make a deposit in
advance of the estimated yield of the taxes, and by the end of
1800 the tax returns were up to date.

This could not have been achieved without the fundamental reform of local government, embodied in the law of February 1800. In suppressing the *intendants* and provinces of the *ancien régime* and creating the new unit of the Department, the Revolution had given excessive local autonomy to the elected Departmental and district Councils. The central Government was powerless to enforce an efficient collection of taxes. The Committee of Public Safety had temporarily restored centralized control, but this had lapsed with the Committee in 1795. The Directory had tried to set up a centralized administration for the assessment and collection of taxes, but it was not strong enough to overcome local autonomy. Now, with the new law, Napoleon turned Sieyès' conception of a departmental Prefect into something much more powerful and efficient than the *intendant* of the *ancien régime*. The cantons of the Directory were suppressed; there were now only to be the Departments, *arrondissements,* and communes. The Prefects of Departments, Sub-Prefects of *arrondissements,* and Mayors of Communes were to be appointed by the First Consul (on the recommendation of the Minister of the Interior) and their councils were also to be nominated, and purely consultative. The tax system was to be entirely in the hands of paid officials. As de Tocqueville pointed out in his *Ancien Régime et la Révolution,* the Prefect was the Bourbon *intendant* writ large. The rapid development of the semaphore signal telegraph since 1794 increased the dependence of the Prefect on Paris.

The choice of the new Prefects was mainly the work of Lucien Bonaparte, who succeeded Laplace as Minister of the Interior in January 1800. Laplace, the scientist, had been appointed during the provisional Consulate as a compliment to Napoleon's old friends of the *Institut,* but he was lacking in drive, and Lucien's services in *Brumaire* had to be rewarded with an important post. Most of Lucien's nominations were confirmed by Napoleon, and they were nearly all moderate men of the Revolution; they included, on the one hand, Jean-Bon St André, a former member of the Committee of Public Safety, and, on the other, Mounier, leader of the constitutional royalists in the States-General. On March 5, writing to General Brune about his interview with Cadoudal, Napoleon said, 'Here everything goes from good to better. The Prefects are going to their posts, and I hope that in a month France will at last be an organized State.'

As with the Prefects, Napoleon took over Sieyès' conception of a Council of State and transformed it. Sieyès had thought of it as an independent body for the drafting of legislation. Napoleon made it a body of experts, appointed by the Consuls, and used it as his main instrument for the making of policy. From the start, he tried to attract the ablest men, regardless of their past politics. 'I have composed my Council of State of ex-members of the Constituent Assembly, of moderates, *feuillants*, royalists, Jacobins. I am national: I like honest men of all colours.' Stendhal wrote, from personal experience as a civil servant, that Napoleon 'assembled in the Council of State fifty of the least stupid Frenchmen'. Napoleon said of the ex-revolutionaries, 'There were good workmen among them: the trouble was that they all wanted to be architects.' Towards the end of the Empire, Napoleon commented on the vigour and ability of the men of the Revolution, and wondered how they were to be replaced. The eminent scientist, Chaptal, who succeeded Lucien Bonaparte as Minister of the Interior in 1801, and was a severe critic of Napoleon in his later years, said of the Consulate in his memoirs, 'Bonaparte conceived the idea of uniting and amalgamating everything. He put in the same committee, side by side, men who had been opposed in character and opinions for the last ten years, men who detested each other, men who had proscribed each other. It was in this way that Bonaparte assembled all the talents in every sphere and fused all the factions. The history of the Revolution became as remote for us as that of the Greeks and Romans.' Many of them, including the Secretary-General, Locré (who had been Secretary to the Council of Elders), served right through the Consulate and Empire.

In the Council of State, Napoleon regarded himself as *en famille*, encouraged free discussion and even violent debate. It was divided into five main sections—War, Navy, Finance, Legislation, and Interior. As early as January 12, 1800, he decreed that the sections should meet on stated days of the month at 9.30 pm in the Tuileries. The Council of State was, at least under the Consulate, an approximation to the collective mind of a Cabinet. Napoleon took care to allow no collective responsibility to the Ministers, and he regarded the Council of State as a useful check on bureaucracy. He took over from the Directory the office of Secretary of State, and

appointed Maret, a good executive with no ideas of his own.
The Secretary of State kept a central registry, and co-
ordinated the work of the Ministries. Napoleon multiplied the
number of Ministries, and never allowed more than informal
meetings of Ministers, preferring to work with them individually.

The administrative institutions of the Consulate were thus
set up and in working order within a few months of
Brumaire. France was already beginning to feel the impulse
of a unified will and a controlling mind working at top
speed—often eighteen hours in a day. But the results would
take some time to show, and Napoleon had yet to prove
that he was a statesman as well as a successful General.
Would the Consulate be, as the royalists hoped, a prelude
to a restoration of the monarchy, and would Napoleon be
content with the role of General Monk? Or would the politicians entrenched in the legislature be too strong for him?
Napoleon knew that the French people had silently voted
him into power, because he alone seemed capable of giving
them peace with honour. As always throughout his career,
the key to his political problems lay in victory in the field.

On December 25, 1799, Napoleon had written personally to
George III and to the Emperor Francis, offering peace negotiations. But in February 1800 he made it clear to Austria,
through Talleyrand, that France would negotiate only on the
basis of the settlement of Campo Formio. The Second Coalition was still in such a strong position that peace overtures
on these terms could only be intended for French public
opinion. In February 1800, he ordered Admiral Bruix to
proceed to the Mediterranean and, with the Spanish squadron,
lift the blockade of Malta, and send a fast convoy to supply
the Army of Egypt. On January 25, he told Berthier to
prepare, in the greatest secrecy, for the formation of a Reserve Army centred on Dijon.

This central position would keep the enemy guessing; a
concentration of troops there could be used either for defence against invasion, or reinforcement of the Army of
the Rhine or the Army of Italy. Masséna, commanding the
remnants of the Army of Italy, was being hard pressed in
Piedmont by the Austrian General Mélas, with an army
twice as large. On March 1, Napoleon ordered pack mules
to be purchased and sledges for guns to be constructed. His
strategic design was gradually unfolded in despatches to

Moreau, commanding on the Rhine, to Berthier, commanding the Reserve Army, and to Masséna. While Moreau attacked across the Rhine, Masséna was to keep Mélas in play in Piedmont, while the Reserve Army penetrated the Alpine passes to take Mélas in the rear. It was a bold but practicable plan, involving the movement of comparatively large forces over difficult country. Though Suvorov had crossed the St Gotthard in winter only the year before, in his Bulletins after the event Napoleon tried to give the impression that the crossing of the Alps was unparalleled since Hannibal.

Napoleon saw the whole front from Genoa to the Danube as one; as he told Berthier on April 9, the Reserve Army was to 'form the centre of the great line of operations, whose right is at Genoa, and whose left is on the Danube'. It was to be, on a strategic scale, the penetration of the enemy's centre which he had achieved on a tactical scale at the battle of Castiglione. The Austrians assumed that, with sixty thousand men tied in the Vendéan war, and Anglo–Russian forces threatening landings from the Channel Islands, the Reserve Army would not amount to more than a division of raw conscripts for the reinforcement of Masséna. In fact, by the end of April, forty thousand men had been concentrated at Dijon, though a high proportion of them were new conscripts, and a further corps of not less than ten thousand was to be detached from the Army of the Rhine to enter Lombardy through the St Gotthard pass. Mélas continued to play Napoleon's game by attacking Masséna, who reported at the end of April that he was blockaded in Genoa, with provisions for only one month. Pitt now missed a great opportunity of making a landing in force behind the enemy lines. If Genoa had fallen earlier, Napoleon's whole strategy for the campaign of 1800 would have been disrupted.

Napoleon told Berthier to push through the Great and Little St Bernard passes to Aosta and Ivrea. As First Consul, he could not assume command in the field, but he was determined to join the Reserve Army as soon as the operations became active. He reached Geneva on May 9, 1800, and Aosta on the 21st, having crossed the Great St Bernard, and stayed three nights at the monastery on the pass. He was worried by the delay in taking the fort of Bardo commanding the narrow valley south of Aosta, which was holding up the passage of the artillery. On May 4, he had written to Berthier, 'It could happen (1) that Masséna capitulates and

evacuates Genoa, without being taken prisoner, and takes up
the Borghetto line or some other, (2) that he is overwhelmed
in Genoa. In either case you will see that General Mélas
needs only eight days to move from Genoa to Aosta, and
if he were to arrive before you had crossed with more than
twenty thousand men, it would give him immense advantages
in disputing your entry into Italy.' The Bardo fort was not
captured till the beginning of June: but enough guns were
passed through under cover of darkness or over a mountain
détour. Only weak Austrian forces were met, and by May
26 Napoleon was established at Ivrea with thirty thousand
men. The following day he wrote to the Consuls, 'Here
we are at last, in the heart of Italy: in ten days' time a
great many things will have been settled. Everything goes
well, I shall be in Paris before the end of Prairial (i.e. in
three weeks' time).'

His optimism reflects the fact that his main strategic plan
had been realized. Mélas was still in Piedmont, lured by
the prospect of capturing Genoa, while Napoleon was about
to seize his lines of communication and bases in Lombardy.
It did not now matter whether Genoa capitulated in the
near future, and it seems that it was at Ivrea that Napoleon
abandoned the less decisive objective of relieving Genoa for
the much greater prospect of catching the whole of Mélas'
army. He entered Milan on June 2, where he waited for
Moncey's corps, coming from the St Gotthard and Como,
to join up with him. On June 8, he learned from intercepted
despatches that Masséna had surrendered Genoa (but not
his army) on June 4, and Napoleon hastened his advance
to the west. On June 9 an Austrian corps was defeated
at Montebello. The decisive battle with Mélas' whole army
came on June 14, 1800, at Marengo.

There is a significant gap in Napoleon's correspondence
between 5 am on June 13, when Napoleon ordered Lannes
to 'attack and overthrow whatever is in front of you', and
the Bulletin of June 15, which is Napoleon's edited version
of the battle. In it, he admits that at one point 'the battle
appeared lost', but he conveys the impression that the sudden
reversal and rout of the Austrians was his own premeditated plan. The real facts, still disputed by military historians, have to be reconstructed without the evidence of
written orders. It seems that, through faulty information, he
had assumed that the bridges over the Bormida were destroyed, and, in his anxiety to trap the Austrians, he had

sent two divisions under Desaix to the south, and one under Lapoype to the north. In fact, Mélas acted in a way which Napoleon had come to regard as quite out of character for an Austrian General. He kept his army compactly massed, and advanced from Alessandria over the Bormida bridges, which were intact, and Napoleon found himself faced in the open plain by an army of thirty thousand men with ninety-two guns, to which he could only oppose twenty-two thousand men and fifteen guns.

The dispersed divisions were recalled, but only Desaix with one division was able to reach the battlefield by 4 pm: by this time the French were overrun, in confusion and retreating. Eyewitnesses recall Napoleon at the side of the road, flicking his riding whip in nervous tension, and trying to rally the troops by saying, 'Courage! The reserves are coming.'

Napoleon, Desaix and Marmont held a hasty conference to arrange a counter-attack with Desaix's fresh division. Somehow Marmont managed to assemble eighteen guns which, with the musketry fire from Desaix's division, took the advancing Austrians by surprise. Kellermann's charge with the heavy cavalry completed their confusion. They lost three thousand men in the counter-attack and their headquarters were overrun. Mélas was so shaken by his unexpected defeat that he signed an armistice next day which obliged him to evacuate Lombardy and retire to Mantua.

Desaix had been killed instantly, leading the counter-attack. He had only joined headquarters a few days before, having just arrived from Egypt. Napoleon told Roederer in Paris afterwards that Desaix had a presentiment of death on that day, saying 'The bullets no longer recognize me.' Napoleon was accused of doing less than justice to Desaix's part in the victory of Marengo in his Bulletin, and furthermore of attributing to him the impossible statement, 'Go tell the First Consul that I die regretting not having done enough to live in posterity.' More authentic than the Bulletin was Napoleon's hasty letter to the Consuls on June 15 in which he said, 'I am in the deepest sorrow at the death of the man I loved and esteemed the most.' Napoleon thought that Desaix, if he had lived, would have been the 'foremost General of the French army'.

At Marengo Napoleon certainly stretched his method of warfare to the limit, and he was lucky to bring it off. But equally he would have been unlucky, having already won the campaign strategically, to lose it by a momentary tactical error; and the criticism that Napoleon was saved from defeat by Desaix's initiative ignores Napoleon's methods. It can be seen from the analysis of his 1796 campaign that the hazards and fluidity of battle were inherent in his method of dispersion and concentration with self-contained divisions. At Rivoli he had caught the enemy off balance by the unexpected arrival of a fresh division; so also he did at Marengo, but only just in time. At Marengo the rawness of some of his troops was offset by the quality of his officers, including many of his well-tried team from the Italian and Egyptian campaigns—such as Desaix, Lannes, Murat, Marmont. As he said at St Helena, 'There is a moment in every battle in which the least manoeuvre is decisive and gives superiority, as one drop of water causes overflow.'

6

First Consul

A DEFEAT AT MARENGO might not have been militarily fatal; only half of Napoleon's forces were engaged, and he was always at his best in a tight spot. But politically it might have been disastrous: the spectacular and risky strategy of the Marengo campaign had been devised for political reasons. The first courier from the battlefield announced a defeat, but when the victory was known in Paris, the funds gained seven points. Hyde de Neuville, the royalist agent, wrote that 'Marengo was the baptism of the personal power of Napoleon'. Napoleon had assured his consular colleagues that he would be away from Paris for as short a time as possible; all three of them were worried by the intrigues of the opposition.

The politicians, predominantly the party of the Brumairians, controlled the legislative bodies, and they still hoped to use them to check the executive power. Daunou, one of the prominent Brumairians, had been elected President of the Tribunate, and opposition had already appeared over the local government law, and the powers of the Prefects. If Napoleon were defeated or killed, the way would be open for a monarchy or a new form of Directory. During Napoleon's absence from Paris, Sieyès' group and Madame de

Staël's salon at Auteuil gossiped, intrigued, and discussed possible successors to Napoleon, such as Carnot, Moreau, the Duc d'Orléans. Generals such as Bernadotte, who were jealous of Napoleon's success, might also become a focus of intrigue.

These speculations were dissipated by the news of Marengo, but it was only by gradual steps that Napoleon's personal power and personal policy were established. He compromised and played for time until his political and administrative achievements could speak for themselves. By 1802 peace with Austria and England, and peace with the Pope through the Concordat, had given him such overwhelming prestige with the nation that he could afford to eliminate a political *fronde* which had no popular backing.

Marengo by itself did not bring Austria to terms. Napoleon issued one of his propaganda appeals to the Emperor to make peace, but Austria was bound to England by treaty and subsidies at least until the following year. The Emperor was prepared to open preliminary negotiations with English participation at Lunéville, but Napoleon did not relax the pressure on Austria. Fighting continued in Italy and on the Danube, with the French armies on the offensive, and finally Moreau's decisive victory over the Archduke Charles at Hohenlinden (December 1800) forced Austria to sign a separate peace at Lunéville (February 1801). The French gains at Campo Formio were restored and increased in some respects. The Habsburg Duke of Tuscany was displaced to make room for the pro-French Duke of Parma, and Austria recognized the French possession of Belgium and Luxembourg.

The Second Coalition had now completely disintegrated. After the failure of the Anglo-Russian landings in Holland, Tsar Paul had withdrawn his armies in disgust, and Napoleon took the opportunity to work on his resentment against his allies. He returned Russian prisoners unconditionally and suggested that the Tsar, now elected Grand Master of the Order of St John by the exiled Knights, might have Malta. When Malta capitulated to the English in September 1800, the Tsar turned right round, and revived the Armed Neutrality of the Northern Powers against England.

In January 1801, he sent an envoy to Paris, and talked of an expedition against India through Central Asia. Napoleon wrote to his brother Joseph, French plenipotentiary at the Lunéville Conference, 'The Russian attitude is very

hostile towards England. You will easily see that we must
not be over-hasty, for peace with the Emperor is nothing
compared with an alliance that would master England and
keep Egypt for us.' These hopes were dashed by the assassination of Tsar Paul, and the collapse of the Armed
Neutrality after Nelson's attack on Copenhagen (March–
April 1801).

Nevertheless, Pitt had come to the conclusion that England
must negotiate for peace. There was no further chance of
action on the Continent. England was war-weary, and the
Armed Neutrality had caused a panic on the wheat-market,
which sent the price from a norm of 60s.–70s. up to 150s.
a quarter. Pitt was able to resign on the issue of Catholic
emancipation, and leave the peace-making to a stop-gap Ministry under Addington. As early as March 1801, the French
agent in London for the exchange of prisoners, Otto, received the first English peace-feelers. It took another year
to reach agreement in the definitive Peace of Amiens (March
1802), mainly because Napoleon was reluctant to give up
Egypt until the last hope had gone.

Kléber had signed an agreement with Sir Sidney Smith
to evacuate Egypt in February 1800, but both Governments
had repudiated it. Kléber defeated another Turkish invasion
and recaptured Cairo, but was assassinated in June 1800,
leaving only the less competent General Menou as his successor. Napoleon eventually prodded Admiral Ganteaume
into putting to sea in January 1801, but he fared no better
than Admiral Bruix's relief expedition in 1799, and had to
take refuge in Toulon. Menou was defeated by General
Abercromby in March 1801, and signed a capitulation. Napoleon still, however, hoped that Egypt might be kept by
diplomatic bargaining, and he persuaded the Spanish Government, with the help of French troops, to occupy Portugal,
to put pressure on the English. In the end Napoleon was
forced to recognize that, without Malta, Egypt was cut off
and lost to France.

In the final Peace, which differed little from the Preliminaries signed in London in October 1801, England was to
return Egypt to Turkey, and Malta to the Knights, and the
Cape of Good Hope to Holland. Of her colonial conquests,
England was to keep only Ceylon and Trinidad. France was
to evacuate Naples, and the independence of Portugal and
the Ionian Islands was to be guaranteed. In laying the Treaty
before the Legislature, Napoleon announced: 'Many years

will now pass for us without victories, without triumphs, without those great negotiations that decide the destiny of states.'

Peace with the Church was one of the corner-stones of Napoleon's policy from the beginning of the Consulate. He had seen the force of religious feeling and the dangers of religious strife in Corsica, in Italy and in Egypt. The fiasco of the Roman Republic in 1798 was in marked contrast with his own careful handling of the Pope in the Treaty of Tolentino in 1797. The Revolution had conspicuously failed in its religious policy. The Constituent Assembly had nationalized the lands of the Church in 1789, and its reorganization of the Church—in the Civil Constitution of the Clergy in 1791—had provoked a religious schism, by making the bishops and clergy not only salaried, but elected officials.

The Assembly had not been hostile to Catholicism as such and their aim was to create a national church by pushing Gallican principles to extreme lengths. Even the Catholic monarchies had become used in the eighteenth century to ignoring the Pope. In 1774 Pope Clement XIV had been forced to suppress the Jesuits under pressure from Spain, and the Habsburg Joseph II had pursued an openly anti-clerical policy. A majority of bishops advised the Pope to accept the Civil Constitution, but he was forced to condemn the principle of popular election as uncanonical. A minority of bishops and a majority of clergy accepted the Constitution; the remainder became non-jurors and *émigrés*, suspected of counter-revolutionary activities. The Convention had ended by persecuting non-jurors, Constitutional priests, and Catholicism as such, and had provoked a religious war in Brittany and La Vendée. The Hébertist *enragés* in Paris indulged in such antics as the Feast of Reason, where an actress impersonated the Goddess of Reason in Notre Dame. At Bourges, the municipality decreed that the cathedral should be demolished but fortunately did nothing about it.

Robespierre, before Napoleon, had realized the political dangers of religious strife, and his introduction of the 'Cult of the Supreme Being' was one attempt, which satisfied no one but himself, to find a formula of compromise and toleration. After his fall, the official policy was complete separation of Church and State, and toleration of individual sects. The Director, La Revellière, fostered his own sect of Theophilanthropy, while the Catholics were alternately harried or encouraged according to the political situation. La Vendée remained a running sore.

Napoleon, brought up like most of his contemporaries, in the tradition of Voltaire and the Enlightenment, was an agnostic; but unlike them he was much more realist and less ideological. In negotiating with the Pope for a Concordat, he could expect to be opposed by most of the politicians and the Generals. It is true that religious scepticism was no longer the undisputed, fashionable doctrine, even in intellectual circles. The religious revival which showed itself openly with the publication of Chateaubriand's *Génie du Christianisme* in 1802, and was to reach its zenith under the Restoration, was already challenging the scepticism of the Enlightenment. Bonald, de Maistre, Chateaubriand and Fontanes were leading a movement of thought which traced the anarchy of the Revolution to the undermining of religious faith and authority. The *émigrés* had already abandoned the scepticism of their youth and returned to religious orthodoxy.

More important to Napoleon were the reports of his Prefects which showed that the mass of peasantry were unaffected by the revolutionary propaganda and remained attached to their altars and their priests. The political advantages of a Concordat would be great. In France, it would dissociate Catholicism from royalism, pacify La Vendée, and reassure the bourgeois and peasants who had bought the nationalized lands of the Church. Abroad, it would strengthen French influence in the Catholic countries of Italy, Belgium and the Rhine provinces. A settlement based on Protestantism, a small minority, and on the schismatic constitutional church would bring none of these advantages. Napoleon argued that 'Fifty *émigré* bishops in English pay are the present leaders of the French clergy. Their influence must be destroyed, and for this I must have the authority of the Pope.'

Pius VI had died in exile at Valence in France in 1799, and the new Pope, Pius VII, formerly Cardinal Chiaramonte, a Benedictine monk, was regarded as a 'Jacobin' by the Italian bishops, as he had co-operated, when Bishop of Imola, with the French administration of the Cispadane Republic. Napoleon's address to the clergy of Milan in the cathedral on June 5, 1800, before Marengo, was an astonishingly frank announcement of his attitude and intentions. 'It is my firm intention that the Christian, Catholic, and Roman religion shall be preserved in its entirety, that it shall be publicly performed, and that it shall enjoy this public exercise with as full, extensive, and inviolable freedom as at the time when I came for the first time into these happy lands. All the changes which then occurred, particularly as to discipline, took place against my wishes and my way of thought.' 'No society can exist without morality; there is no good morality without religion. It is religion alone, therefore, that gives to the State a firm and durable support. . . . Do not let the manner in which the late Pope was treated inspire any fear in you: Pius VI owed his misfortunes in part to the intrigues of those in whom he placed his confidence, in part to the cruel policy of the Directory. As soon as I am able to confer with the new Pope, I hope to have the happiness of removing every obstacle which will hinder complete reconciliation between France and the head of the Church.' Immediately after Marengo, Napoleon asked the Bishop of Vercelli to convey to Pius VII his desire to negotiate a Concordat.

It was not until a year later, in July 1801, that agreement was reached after long and hard bargaining. The Concordat recognized the Roman Catholic religion as 'the religion of the great majority of the citizens' (not, as the Pope hoped, as the 'established' or 'dominant' religion). 'Its worship shall be public, so long as it conforms to such police regulations as are required by public peace.' The schism between the 'constitutional' and the non-juror clergy was to be ended by the resignation of all existing bishops, including the *émigré* bishops, and the appointment of a new episcopate. The right of the First Consul to nominate, and of the Pope to institute bishops was recognized. The French Government undertook to pay the salaries of bishops and clergy, thus securing the implicit recognition that the nationalization of the Church lands during the Revolution was irrevocable. The Pope had fought hard, but in vain, to get endowment rather than salary, and he refused to renounce outright the Church lands.

When it came to applying the Concordat, the schism was not completely healed. Thirty-eight of the ninety-three non-juror bishops refused to resign or recognize the Concordat, and some of them maintained dwindling congregations known as the *Petite Église*. The Pope refused institution to twelve former 'constitutional' bishops, nominated by Napoleon. There were complaints that some of the new bishops expelled and persecuted former 'constitutional' clergy. The Pope considered that the way in which the Concordat was passed into law in France was a breach of faith and he never ceased to

protest against it. Without consulting the Pope, Napoleon
presented it to the Legislature as a part of a general 'Law
of Public Worship' which regulated Protestantism and other
sects, and the Organic Articles which it contained reasserted
extreme Gallican principles, and subjected the Catholic
religion to minute governmental and police regulation.

Napoleon did not foresee that the financial and administrative dependence on the State which he demanded from the
Concordat would foster an ultramontane movement in the
Church as the inevitable reaction to such dependence. The
germ of the future conflict between Emperor and Pope already lay in the Concordat. In fairness to Napoleon it must
be recognized that he was fighting almost a lone battle for
approval of the Concordat. Pius VII himself recognized this,
and even after his long quarrel with Napoleon under the
Empire, never ceased to acknowledge his gratitude for the
'restoration of the altars'. On his side, the Pope had to suffer
a good deal of abuse from diehard Catholics.

The political opposition in the Legislature rose to its
height in the debates on the Corcordat. The law had to be
withdrawn after the first discussion, and it was finally passed
only after the Peace of Amiens had given Napoleon overwhelming popular support, and after the renewal of one-
third of the Tribunate had enabled him to remove the
most active members of the opposition. At the official *Te
Deum* to celebrate the Concordat the Generals signified their
displeasure by forcibly turning the priests out of their seats
in Notre Dame, and General Delmas annoyed Napoleon by
commenting at the reception that evening at the Tuileries: 'A
fine monkish show. It only lacked the presence of the hundred
thousand men who gave their lives to end all that.'

The institution of the Legion of Honour (May 1802) was also
the personal policy of Napoleon, which provoked strong
opposition both in the Council of State and the Legislature.
It tampered with the revolutionary philosophy of equality at
one of its most sensitive spots. The orders of chivalry of
the monarchy—the St Esprit, St Michel and St Louis—had
been allowed to remain until 1793 when the Convention
abolished them as relics of privilege. Occasional 'civic crowns'
were awarded by decree. The Directory had shelved the problem of instituting some form of national recognition for outstanding services. As a military leader, Napoleon understood
the force of the sentiment of honour and individual glory. As

General and First Consul, he had awarded 'swords of honour' and formed the Consular Guard as a *corps d'élite*.

In 1802, he brought forward a comprehensive scheme for a 'Legion of Honour'. There were to be sixteen cohorts, and the different ranks, including 'grand officer', 'commander', 'knight', were to be granted varying life pensions. The first Consul would preside at a Grand Council, nominated by himself, to select the members, who would be civilian as well as military. In this way Napoleon would draw into his own hands the main source of patronage. His immediate aim was, in fact, to nullify the effect of the electoral list of 'notabilities', incorporated into the Constitution of the Year VIII, and prepared in 1801 under the patronage of Sieyès.

When Thibaudeau, an ex-revolutionary, objected in the Council of State that decorations were 'baubles', Napoleon replied, 'You are pleased to call them "baubles": well, it is with "baubles" that mankind is governed.' In conversation, he revealed more of his motives. 'The French are unable to desire anything seriously, except, perhaps, equality. Even so, they would gladly renounce it if everyone could entertain the hope of rising to the top. Equality in the sense that everyone will be master—there you have the secret of all your vanities. What must be done, therefore, is to give everybody the hope of being able to rise.' In 1815 he summed it up in the famous phrase 'My motto has always been: a career open to all talents, without distinction of birth.' The project only passed the Tribunate and the Legislature by small majorities. Under the Consulate and Empire forty-eight thousand members were nominated, including fourteen hundred civilians. The Romans produced a typically ferocious *pasquinade* on the Legion of Honour, which reads:

> 'In fierce old times they balanced loss
> By hanging thieves upon a cross.
> But our humaner age believes
> In hanging crosses on the thieves.'

On the other hand, Napoleon's personal contribution to the making of the Civil Code, issued in 1804, and renamed the *Code Napoléon* in 1807, was much less. In undertaking this work the Council of State was bringing to fulfilment a project which had been discussed from the beginning of the Revolution. The ideal of *fraternité*, the unity of the French nation, urgently required a codification of law. In 1789

there were no less than 366 local Codes in force, and the
law of southern France, the Languedoc, was based on fundamentally different principles from that of the north. In the
south, property rights were based on Roman law, embodied
in the Code of Justinian; in the north, on Teutonic customary
law. A confused debris of feudal and canon law and royal
ordinance further complicated the situation. The Revolution
had brought about a drastic upheaval in the system of
property in France, by sweeping away feudal rights and
redistributing a vast amount of land through the nationalization and sale of the lands of the Church and of the *émigrés*.
There could be no confidence or stability in the revolutionary
land settlement until the new situation was defined. In 1792
the Convention had appointed a drafting committee which
rapidly produced a plan for a Code in 779 Articles. In
1796 this plan was modified into one of 1,104 Articles. In
all, five drafts were before the Council of State when it
started its work in 1800.

The Council had to decide what was to be the basis of the
new system. Was it to be abstract natural law, ignoring the
traditions and prejudices of the past, or a choice between the
existing codes—Roman law of the south, customary law of
the north, or feudal inheritance? In the drafting committee,
Berlier and Thibaudeau, ex-revolutionaries, supported customary and natural law; Tronchet and Portalis, two eminent
jurists of the *ancien régime,* supported Roman law, generally
with the backing of Napoleon and Cambacérès. The Code
became a compromise between the different principles, reflecting the changing trend of opinion since 1789.

The draft produced by the Convention in 1793 represented
the rationalist, philosophic influence at its height. It was hostile to Roman law which enforced the despotic authority of
the father and gave freedom to dispose of property by bequest: and it favoured customary law as more liberal, because
it limited parental authority and safeguarded the division of
inheritance in the family. It recognized the equality of the
sexes, civil marriage, divorce on grounds of incompatibility,
adoption, inheritance by illegitimate children if recognized
by the parents, and equal division of property among the
heirs. From 1795 onwards, the drafts show a reaction in
favour of Roman law, and away from the rationalism of
the Enlightenment. In the final draft of 2,287 Articles produced by the Council of State, the reaction to Roman law
was still more marked. Paternal authority and the subjection

of married women and children were restored. Grounds for divorce were severely restricted, and adulterous wives could even be imprisoned at the will of their husbands. The recognition of illegitimate children was discouraged. Equal division of property among the heirs was modified by the right of the testator to bequeath up to a quarter of his property away from the family.

These provisions reflect, in part, a deliberate and necessary reaction against the moral laxity of the period of the Directory, when the social order had broken down under the strain of war, terror, and inflation; and partly the personal influence of Napoleon, with his strong sense of family and his dislike of feminine influence in politics and society. He maintained in discussion that 'the husband must possess the absolute power and right to say to his wife: "Madam, you shall not go out, you shall not go to the theatre, you shall not receive such and such a person: for the children you will bear shall be mine".'

On the other hand he defended divorce on grounds other than adultery. 'While the stability of marriages serves the interests of social morality, those interests perhaps also demand the separation of a husband and wife who cannot live together and whose union, if prolonged, is often likely to dissipate the common patrimony, break up the family, and result in desertion of the children. To allow such ties to continue is an offence against the sanctity of marriage.' The Code also confirmed the revolutionary principles of the rights of individual property, as desired by the middle class who had made, and benefited from, the Revolution.

The French legal historian Esmein says of Napoleon's contribution that 'interesting as his observations occasionally are, he cannot be considered as a serious collaborator in the great work'. Substantially it is the work of the professional jurists, and probably it would have been much the same without his interventions. But he presided at thirty-six of the eighty-four sessions of the Council of State devoted to the Code. He was the driving force which pushed through a long delayed project. Thibaudeau, a reluctant admirer of Napoleon, admits that 'there was originality and depth in his lightest word'.

On the initiative of Napoleon, the Council of State had also set up in 1801–2 committees to draft a Criminal Code, a Commercial Code, a Rural Code, and a Code of Civil Procedure. These codes were not ready until the middle years of the Empire, and it will be convenient to discuss them as part of the institutions of the Empire rather than of the Consulate. This also applies to the educational, financial, and economic institutions which did not mature till later.

By 1802 Napoleon had proved himself to be a statesman, with a mind and will and policy of his own, as well as a General. The Napoleonic régime has often been labelled as a military dictatorship. This is surely a misleading use of words. It is only necessary to consider what would have happened if some General other than Napoleon had carried out the *coup d'état*. As a military dictator he would not have lasted six months; he would either have been elbowed out of the way by the politicians, or played the part of General Monk as a prelude to a monarchical restoration. Napoleon insisted, and with justification, that 'I do not govern in the capacity of General but by virtue of the civil qualities which in the eyes of the nation qualify me for the Government. If the nation did not hold this opinion the Government would not last. I knew what I was doing when, as army commander, I styled myself "Member of the Institute".' The success of the Consulate was in direct proportion to Napoleon's success in making his Government both civilian and national, and attracting to it the ablest administrators, regardless of their past.

One of the most interesting and original creations of the Napoleonic régime, which dates from a decree of 1803, is that of the *auditeurs* attached to the Council of State. These were promising young men from the ranks of the old *noblesse* and the higher *bourgeoisie*, chosen by nomination and an interview by three Counsellors of State, to be trained as higher civil servants. They worked with the committees of the Council of State and attended the full sessions of the Council as observers. Napoleon often encouraged them to speak in full Council, and was pleased when they showed ability and independence of mind. From the original sixteen appointed in 1803 they grew to sixty in 1809, and over three hundred in 1811. A decree of January 1813 required candidates to have a university degree. Despite the hasty expansion after 1810, selection seems to have remained free from favouritism and based on merit. Henry Beyle, better known as the novelist Stendhal, was appointed *auditeur* in 1810. He was certainly able, but hardly the best or a typical example, because he had the eccentricity of a literary genius. Forty-two of the *auditeurs* became Prefects under the Empire; others were employed on special missions reporting personally to Napoleon, or as administrators of occupied territories. Their favoured position created considerable jealousy among the bureaucracy and the military, but Napoleon usually supported his *auditeurs*.

Fain, Napoleon's secretary in the later years, says that Napoleon's intention was to counteract the crudity of a military or a bureaucratic administration. It seems that in this respect Napoleon was at least fifty years ahead of his time in his conception of a trained higher civil service. He told Las Cases at St. Helena in 1816 that 'having finished their education and reached the right age, the *auditeurs* would one fine day have filled all the posts of the Empire.' He claimed to have created 'the most compact Government with the most rapid circulation and the most energetic movement which ever existed'. He boasted that 'there is no conquest which I could not undertake because with the help of my soldiers and my *auditeurs* I could conquer and rule the whole world'.

The Generals, on the other hand, were cosseted but kept firmly out of Government, except for the few who also proved their worth as administrators. Only six of them served on the Council of State. Napoleon knew that their intrigues against him were largely due to jealousy, and that few of them were likely to be dangerous. The more republican Generals, especially from the Army of the Rhine, were conveniently shipped off to the reconquest of San Domingo, headed by General Leclerc, who was apt to give himself airs because he had married Napoleon's sister, Pauline. Moreau never got beyond a feeble, rather spiteful factiousness: Bernadotte, commanding a corps in Brittany, actually went so far as to have an anti-Napoleonic manifesto secretly printed, but, when the plot was discovered, he managed to shuffle off the blame on to his chief of staff.

It is, at first sight, odd that Napoleon showed himself to be surprisingly tolerant of opposition in private discussion but morbidly sensitive to public opposition. He maintained that 'there is a great difference between free discussion in a country whose institutions are long established and the opposition in a country that is still unsettled'. In a conversation with his brother Joseph in 1803 he said, 'I haven't been able to understand yet what good there is in an opposition. Whatever it may say, its only result is to diminish the prestige of authority in the eyes of the people.' His favourite term of

abuse for his political opponents was 'ideologist' or 'meta-
physician'. Of the Tribunate he declared, 'We have a dozen
or fifteen metaphysicians who ought to be thrown into a
pond.' As early as January 1800, a decree suppressed sixty of
the seventy-three political journals in Paris. Many of these
journals had been cheap and highly scurrilous. The *Moniteur* contained mostly Government propaganda, with many
of the political articles written by Napoleon himself. Napoleon said, 'If the press is not bridled, I shall not remain
three days in power.' Bourrienne, Napoleon's secretary under
the Consulate, recalls that he used to read the newspapers,
beginning with the *Moniteur*, to Napoleon while he was
shaving. 'Skip it, skip it,' Napoleon used to say about the
French newspapers. 'I know what is in them. They only say
what I tell them to.'

On December 24, 1800, a considerable number of people
were killed or wounded by an explosive machine hidden in a
cart in the Rue Niçaise on the route from the Tuileries to
the Opéra, where Napoleon was due to attend a performance
of Haydn's oratorio *The Creation*. Napoleon and Josephine
escaped the explosion by seconds; it is said that they owed
their lives to the fact that Napoleon insisted on employing a
coachman, who was usually drunk and always drove too fast,
because he had been with him at Marengo. Napoleon used
this outrage to dispose of the disaffected Jacobins, some of
whom had been arrested a few days before. He persuaded
the Senate to decree the deportation of a hundred and thirty
Jacobins. He overruled Fouché, who produced strong evidence that the plot was the work of Georges Cadoudal, the
Vendéan royalist. After Marengo, the royalists had had to
abandon their hopes that Napoleon would restore the monarchy. When Louis XVIII wrote personally to Napoleon, he
was curtly rebuffed. Napoleon replied, 'You must not expect
to return to France: it would mean marching over a hundred
thousand corpses.'

Napoleon next struck at the Tribunate. Under the Constitution, one-fifth of the membership was due for renewal in
1802, but the procedure had been left undefined. Napoleon
used the Senate to nominate the retiring members, and in this
way twenty of the most prominent members of the opposition were removed. The Tribunate was then induced to divide
itself into three sections—legislation, internal affairs, and
finance—and its debates ceased to be of interest. In 1803
the section of the Institute devoted to the moral and political

sciences was suppressed: Madame de Staël's salon was dispersed, when she was forbidden to live in Paris.

Napoleon's popularity in the country rose to its height with the conclusion of the Concordat and the peace treaties, and he used the opportunity to amend the Constitution. The Senate proposed that Napoleon's term as First Consul should be extended for a further ten years, but Napoleon took it out of their hands by drafting in the Council of State a plebiscite which asked the electorate to vote on a life-tenure of the Consulate. The official returns showed three and a half million in favour, with eight thousand dissenting, including Carnot and a considerable number of Army voters.

Once the Life Consulate had been voted, Napoleon induced the Senate to make important modifications to the Constitution by the procedure of *senatus-consultum* (August 4, 1802). All three Consuls were now to hold office for life, but the First Consul nominated the other two, and he could nominate his successor. A new Privy Council, limited to eleven members, was set up which could draft *senatus-consulta*, and sanction treaties and declarations of war. The powers of the Senate were increased, but at the same time its independence was undermined. It could revise the Constitution, and dissolve the Tribunate and Legislature. But the First Consul was to preside in the Senate, and he could nominate new Senators. He could also grant *Sénatoreries*— national estates—to one-third of the Senators: and could appoint Senators to administrative posts. At the same time Napoleon finally got rid of Sieyès' list of notabilities by changing the electoral system. Local assemblies, elected by universal suffrage, were to nominate departmental electoral Colleges. But only the most highly taxed citizens were eligible for the Colleges and they held their positions for life. The First Consul nominated the President of the Electoral College and up to twenty members. It was these exclusive bodies that were to nominate to the Senate, the Legislature, and a Tribunate reduced to fifty members.

With the constitution of the Life Consulate Napoleon held power far more absolute than any Bourbon monarch, the more so because all the independent corporations of the *ancien régime*, such as the *Parlements*, had been removed by the Revolution. Thibaudeau wrote to Napoleon warning him of the implications of the Life Consulate. 'It is not a light thing to give the death-blow to the Republic: you kill the Revolution at the same time. All the feudal institutions will surround your throne. Probably you will not wish it so; they will come in spite of you, and you will end by submitting to them.'

It does not seem that the mass of Frenchmen shared these apprehensions. The Consulate had secured the main social and material gains of the Revolution, which, at any rate in the short run, were more important to them than the aim of political liberty. *Liberté, egalité, fraternité* stood for the three facets of the Revolution, which had been not one, but three simultaneous Revolutions—political, social, and administrative. *Egalité* and *fraternité*, in the destruction of privilege and the realization of national unity, were tangible gains, whereas *liberté* seemed to have foundered. In this sense Napoleon's claim that he represented the Revolution is intelligible. Moreover, an authoritarian element is present in the revolutionary philosophy from the beginning. Did not many of the philosophers look to an enlightened despot to carry out their reforms? Did not Voltaire deplore Louis XVI's restoration of the *Parlements* at the beginning of his reign? Did not Rousseau declare in his *Contrat Social* that a Legislator was needed to 'enlighten the General Will'? Did not Robespierre justify the dictatorship of the Committee of Public Safety on precisely these grounds? In 1802 Napoleon seemed to be the most dazzling embodiment of the enlightened despot in action.

If Napoleon had known of Mirabeau's secret correspondence with the Court in 1790, he would have agreed with his arguments. Mirabeau repeatedly urged the King to lead the Revolution by abandoning the privileged orders and modernizing the State; by so doing, he predicted, the monarchy, far from being incompatible with the Revolution, would emerge stronger than before. Mirabeau and Napoleon were the two great realists among the doctrinaires of the Revolution.

In 1802 Mirabeau's prediction had been realized. Napoleon, like Mirabeau, saw no contradiction between monarchy and the Revolution. The fall of the Bourbon monarchy had been due to the feebleness of Louis XVI and the 'vanity' of the bourgeoisie. If the Bourbons had failed to rise to the occasion, it was an opportunity for Napoleon to 'pick a crown out of the gutter' and establish a 'fourth dynasty' of France, based on the social changes of the Revolution.

7

The New Charlemagne

WHEN THE CONCLUSION of the Treaty of Amiens was in sight, Napoleon gave orders for the route from Calais to Paris to be put in order, as a rush of English tourists was expected. Charles James Fox was among the more distinguished visitors. He had several conversations with Napoleon, which disturbed some of his illusions about Napoleon's character and intentions on which he had based his opposition to Pitt's war policy. Even before the Preliminaries of London were confirmed by the treaty, public opinion in England was turning against the peace. Malmesbury commented: 'Peace in a week, war in a month.'

Hopes in the City of London that the treaty would be followed by a revival of the free trade commercial treaty of 1786 were soon dashed, when Napoleon made it clear that he intended to exclude English manufactured goods from the whole coastline under his control. He had inherited this policy from the Convention and the Directory, and he was now in a position to make it more effective and far-reaching. The eminent scientist, Chaptal, who had succeeded Lucien Bonaparte as Minister of the Interior, and Coquebert de Montbret, the French commercial agent in London, argued in favour of a return to the free trade treaty, with safeguards for the protection of French industry. But the civil servants and industrialists were solidly hostile; the 1786 treaty had hit the French textile industry severely, and was associated with the outbreak of the Revolution. In this debate there could be little doubt which side Napoleon would back. His immediate pre-occupations were financial stability and the shortage of bullion, which would require a policy of cutting down imports and encouraging exports. He was keenly interested in pioneers like Richard Lenoir, who were developing mechanization in the textile industry.

After an initial boom, English exports began to decline at the end of 1802, as Napoleon's policy of prohibition was continued and extended to new areas. The French purchase of Louisiana from Spain and the expedition to San Domingo aroused fears of a new French colonial empire and renewed competition in colonial trade. Even more alarming to English public opinion was the expansion of France in Europe, because it involved not only the political balance of power but the markets of English exports.

As a gesture to Russia and England, Napoleon withdrew French troops from Naples and the Papal States, but he found excuses to delay the evacuation of Holland, annexed Piedmont and Elba to France, and occupied Parma (August to October 1802). Internal disputes in Switzerland enabled him to impose a federal constitution by an Act of Mediation (February 1803), followed by a defensive alliance. Napoleon had learned the importance of the Alpine passes from his Italian campaigns, and he was determined to control them, and build strategic roads, to ensure his communications with Lombardy. The Cisalpine Republic had been transformed in 1802 into the Italian Republic, with Napoleon as its President. The Treaty of Lunéville entailed a reshuffle of German territory, to compensate the German princes who had been dispossessed by the cession of the left bank of the Rhine to France. Much to the mortification of the Austrian and Russian Governments, the German princes looked to Paris and to Talleyrand, as Foreign Minister, for these arrangements. By the Imperial Recess of February 1803, many of the ecclesiastical principalities and free cities were suppressed and annexed by Prussia, Bavaria, Baden, Würtemberg, and Hesse-Cassel. Austria had lost control of the Rhineland and south German states, which now looked towards France.

Peace, or what is called in modern parlance the 'cold war', was certainly proving advantageous to Napoleon. Not merely the preponderance of Louis XIV, but the empire of Charlemagne seemed to be emerging of itself from the ruins of dynastic feudalism. Napoleon was in no hurry to break with England because it would cut short his colonial schemes, and he well knew that it would be years before the French fleet could be built up to parity with the English. In conversation with Decrès, his Minister of Marine, he said, 'It will take us at least ten years; after that time, with the help of Spain and Holland, we may perhaps hope to challenge the power of Great Britain with some chance of success.'

In London it was assumed that the Peace of Amiens implied the *status quo* in Europe. This was a poor case to argue as the *status quo* was guaranteed not by the Peace of Amiens but by the Peace of Lunéville, to which England was not a party. By now Pitt was convinced that a renewal of war was inevitable and less dangerous than 'the experimental peace'. He advised that Malta should be held as compensation for the French gains in Europe since Amiens.

When Lord Whitworth was appointed ambassador to Paris in September 1802, he was instructed to say nothing about the evacuation of Malta. In October Hawkesbury, the Foreign Secretary, sounded Russia about an alliance to resist French aggression. Then, in January 1803, an official report in the *Moniteur* on General Sebastiani's visit to Egypt quoted him as saying that 'six thousand men would suffice to reconquer Egypt'. It seems that Napoleon's motive in releasing this provocative statement was to put pressure on England to fulfil the Treaty by evacuating Malta. Whitworth had already sent alarming reports that Napoleon intended to reconquer Egypt, and the Cabinet seized on the Sebastiani report as an excuse to declare that Malta would be retained until the *status quo* of 1801 was restored.

On March 13 there was a violent scene between Napoleon and Whitworth in the presence of the other ambassadors. Was this deliberately staged in order to force a rupture? It seems unlikely, as Whitworth reported shortly afterwards that 'it is certain that the First Consul has no desire to go to war'. An immediate renewal of war would sacrifice his main fleet, which was covering the San Domingo expedition, and the naval force which he had dispatched under Decaen to the Indian Ocean. Nevertheless, the English Cabinet stiffened their demands—Malta for ten years, Lampedusa permanently, and the evacuation of French troops from Holland and Switzerland. Napoleon countered the English ultimatum by a proposal of Russian mediation, which was refused, and Whitworth left Paris on May 12, 1803.

Napoleon was probably telling the truth about the scene with Whitworth when he admitted to his stepdaughter, Hortense (as recorded in her memoirs), that 'Talleyrand told me something which put me in a temper, and this great gawk of an ambassador came and put himself in front of my nose.' The personality of Whitworth was not calculated to improve Napoleon's temper: proud and stiff, he was the embodiment of everything that Napoleon was wont to describe as the 'English oligarchy'. Some of Whitworth's prejudices led him into ludicrous judgments. He described Napoleon as a 'duplicate of Tsar Paul' and opined that France was 'ripe for revolt'.

Napoleon himself made the mistake of reading translations of English newspapers, including the gutter press, which was of unparalleled irresponsibility and scurrilousness. Even the *Morning Post* referred to his Corsican ancestry in the following terms: 'An indefinable being, half-African, half-European, a Mediterranean mulatto.' When Napoleon protested through his ambassador about these attacks, he was met by arguments about the liberty of the press. These replies struck Napoleon, with his views about the relations of Government and press, as hypocritical evasion; indeed to a considerable extent they were, as much of the press was subsidized by the Government.

Intelligent men like Fox and Canning were capable of more enlightened judgment. Canning wrote in 1803, 'I am not a panegyrist of Bonaparte, but I cannot close my eyes to the superiority of his talent, to the dazzling ascendancy of his genius.' Unfortunately Napoleon had formed a mental picture of the English which he had inherited from the days of the Revolution. The famous remark about a 'nation of shopkeepers' (which was not his own, but coined by his former leader, General Paoli) hardly sums up his views. He thought rather of a proud and ruthless oligarchy keeping down a proletariat who were ready to welcome French principles of equality. He was genuinely shocked by the savage and antiquated methods of discipline, such as flogging, in the English armed forces, which had been discarded in the French army since the Revolution. A frugal man himself, he was fascinated by the English standards of alcoholic consumption, and the 'drunkenness' of the English upper classes was a theme he frequently discussed at St Helena. His misconceptions of the nature of English government and society will emerge more clearly in discussion of the policy of the Continental System.[1]

This sad lack of communication and these mutual misunderstandings reflected and aggravated the underlying causes of conflict. The responsibility for the rupture of the Peace of Amiens has been endlessly argued. Technically the English Government were in the wrong, and broke the terms of the Treaty by refusing to evacuate Malta. Their refusal to accept Russian mediation created a bad impression. Castlereagh wrote that 'it will be difficult to convince the world that we do not fight solely for Malta'. The great French historian Albert Sorel argued that England was never really prepared to leave France in possession of Belgium; on that assumption Napoleon can be represented as waging a series of defensive wars against England, since he was bound as 'heir of the Revolution' to maintain the 'natural frontiers'. 'In reality,' wrote Sorel, 'seven hundred years of the history of England continued the struggle with seven hundred years of the history of France.'

This is surely a dangerously determinist view of history. It is clear that both at Lille in 1797 and at Amiens in 1801 England was prepared to recognize the French possession of the natural frontiers, provided that French expansion went no further. What was impossible for any English government to accept was a complete overthrow of the balance of power in Europe and a French hegemony of the Continent: just as similar threats from Philip II of Spain, from Louis XIV, from the Germany of William II and from Hitler had to be resisted. It was a matter of life and death, because a power which dominated the Continent could organize the shipbuilding resources of Europe and challenge English sea-power, the basis of her existence.

Economic historians have also argued that Napoleon was unable to dispense with war, because the problems of demobilization would have been insuperable. It is true that unemployed Generals would have been difficult to manage, and that the continual drain of conscription and war had eased the pressure of a growing population in France and reversed the trend of low wages for the working class before the Revolution. But bearing in mind Napoleon's immense prestige in 1802 and the deep-seated desire of the French

[1] See Chapter Ten.

people for repose after the upheavals of the Revolution, the task would not have been impossible. At St Helena Napoleon maintained that this was his intention: 'At Amiens I believed, in perfectly good faith, that my future and that of France was fixed. I was going to devote myself solely to the administration of France, and I believe that I should have performed miracles. I would have made the moral conquest of Europe, as I was on the point of achieving it by force of arms.'

Everything in Napoleon's previous career and his character makes this remark ring false. As the French historian Albert Vandal correctly and succinctly sums it up, 'It is impossible to say if the task was beyond the capacity of his genius; it was certainly beyond the capacity of his character.' It would have needed immense restraint to halt the expansion of France at this point; a restraint which was totally out of tune with Napoleon's character and ambition. France, *la grande nation*, was the largest and best organized state in Europe, with its twenty-eight millions of homogeneous population, bursting with the dynamism released by the Revolution, and now wholly responsive to Napoleon's will. Napoleon's real thought at this time is revealed by his remark, 'Between old monarchies and a young republic the spirit of hostility must always exist. In the existing situation every treaty of peace means to me no more than a brief armistice: and I believe that, while I fill my present office, my destiny is to be fighting almost continually.' It is perhaps not without significance that Napoleon's study in Malmaison, his country house in the Consular period, is designed to look like a tent.

In 1803 the French people had little idea to what heights of glory and to what depths of abasement Napoleon was to lead them. At first the war resumed on familiar and inconclusive lines, as neither side could really get to grips while England was supreme at sea and Napoleon on land. To the news that the English had seized French ships before the expiry of the ultimatum Napoleon retaliated not only by seizing English ships but by interning at Verdun English civilians of military age found on French territory. By the standards of eighteenth century warfare this was regarded as an unheard-of barbarity. More damaging was the rapid occupation of Hanover. The threat of invasion was remounted, and gradually developed on a much vaster scale. As soon as war was in sight, Napoleon had ordered two flotillas to be organized in the Channel ports.

Indirectly, the first important result of the war was the proclamation of the hereditary French Empire in the dynasty of the Bonapartes (May 1804). This step was the logical culmination of the Life Consulate not only because it accorded with Napoleon's ambition, but because it safeguarded the gains of the Revolution. The regicides, the bourgeoisie, and the peasants who now enjoyed the nationalized lands of the Church and the *émigrés* could never feel safe so long as the survival of the régime depended solely on Napoleon's life. If he were assassinated or killed in battle, they were threatened with a return to Jacobin anarchy or a Bourbon restoration. Roederer recounts in his memoirs a conversation with Napoleon as early as August 1800, in which he urged upon Napoleon a hereditary succession as the only possible solution.

Napoleon found the question at this stage embarrassing, especially as Roederer was a close friend of his brother Joseph. He did not relish the idea of Joseph or any of his brothers as his heir, and he wished to be free to nominate or adopt his successor. It was a long time before he could bring himself to contemplate a divorce from Josephine for dynastic reasons: indeed it was not until 1807 that the birth of a bastard son, later known as the Comte Léon, convinced him that it was not he, but Josephine who had been the sterile partner in their marriage. When his brother Lucien launched a pamphlet in November 1800 entitled *Parallel between Caesar, Cromwell, Monk, and Bonaparte,* which hinted at the hereditary solution, he was disavowed and forced to exchange the Ministry of the Interior for the Embassy in Madrid. It was only after a son, Napoléon-Charles, was born to Louis and his stepdaughter Hortense in October 1802 that Napoleon could look forward to adopting the infant Napoléon-Charles as his heir.

It was the renewal of plots against his life that hastened on the hereditary Empire. Stimulated partly by Whitworth's misleading reports of the fragility of the Consular régime, the English Government refurbished the weapon of a royalist fifth column in France. The redoubtable Chouan royalist, Georges Cadoudal, had put up to English officials, before the Peace of Amiens, a plan for 'kidnapping' the First Consul. This plan was adjourned by the Peace but the English Government continued to subsidize Cadoudal and his Chouans,

despite Napoleon's protests, and with the renewal of war it
received the backing of the Comte d'Artois.

Cadoudal and his men were landed in the Pas de Calais,
under Admiralty orders, by Captain Wright in August 1803.
Meanwhile an ex-Jacobin, Mehée de la Touche, arrived in
London with a plan to combine the Jacobin and royalist opposition to Napoleon, and to arrange a meeting between the
exiled General Pichegru and General Moreau. Moreau told
Pichegru, when they met, that he would have nothing to do
with Cadoudal or the royalists, although he would be glad to
see Bonaparte removed. It is possible, but it cannot now be
proved, that Mehée de la Touche was a double agent when
he went to London; but he certainly became so when he revealed the plot to Fouché on his return to France. Fouché
was only too glad to report this information to Napoleon, as
his Ministry of Police had been suppressed during the Peace,
and he was anxious to show that he was indispensable. Napoleon was now aware that Cadoudal and Pichegru were in
France and in touch with Moreau, and that a Bourbon prince
was expected to follow. He could only guess at the ramifica-
tions of the plot, but his experience during the Marengo
campaign had shown him that there were plenty of men
round him who would throw France into chaos if he were
murdered. He was not in the habit of taking elaborate security precautions, and a constant threat of assassination,
backed by the machinations of the English, wore down his
nerves and provoked him to violent retaliation.

In February 1804 it was announced that Moreau had been
arrested: this was quickly followed by the news of the arrest
of Pichegru, Cadoudal and about twenty other royalist exiles
who were secretly in Paris. The arrest of Moreau caused con-
sternation, but that of Pichegru and Cadoudal rallied opinion
to the Government as it provided clear proof that there was
a royalist plot. Pichegru died in prison, probably by suicide,
before he could be brought to trial; Moreau's sentence of two
years' imprisonment was commuted to exile. Cadoudal and
nineteen other conspirators were condemned to death; of
these, eight members of the *noblesse* were reprieved and sent
to prison.

But the identity of the Bourbon prince involved remained
an enigma: General Savary, head of the *gendarmerie d'élite*,
spent a whole month watching the Channel ports in a vain
attempt to catch the Comte d'Artois. Fouché, primed by
Mehée de la Touche, now drew attention to the presence of

the Duc d'Enghien, grandson of the Prince de Condé who had led the corps of *émigrés* in the Prussian invasion of France in the Valmy campaign of 1792, at Ettenheim in Baden, a few miles across the Rhine from Strasbourg. Mehée de la Touche, in his capacity as a double agent, was able to confer with Drake, the English agent in Munich, who confided to him that in the event of a Continental war Enghien was to lead an *émigré* force into Alsace. When the police reported that the exiled French General Dumouriez and an English Colonel Smith were with Enghien, Napoleon jumped to the conclusion that he must be the Bourbon prince awaited by Cadoudal, and ordered that he should be seized, even at the cost of violating the territory of Baden.

When Enghien was hustled to Paris, and his papers were examined by Napoleon, it was clear that Dumouriez had been confused with a harmless exile, the Marquis de Thuméry, and Colonel Smith with a German called Schmidt. There was no evidence of any connection with the Cadoudal plot. Nevertheless Napoleon was determined that Enghien must be executed without delay. A meeting of the Privy Council decreed that he should be tried by a military commission to be nominated by Murat, as Governor of Paris. Despite their subsequent denials, it seems certain that Talleyrand and Fouché advised in favour of execution; only Cambacérès, the Second Consul, opposed. At 1 am on March 21, 1804, Enghien appeared before the commission in the prison of Vincennes; and by 2.30 am he had been shot by a firing-squad. Savary was present to overawe the military judges; and Enghien's appeal for an interview with Napoleon was ignored.

This judicial murder did immense moral harm to the reputation which Napoleon had enjoyed during the Consulate as the hero-statesman. With a prophetic gesture Beethoven struck out the dedication of his *Eroica* Symphony to Napoleon when he heard the news of the execution of Enghien and the proclamation of the Empire. He flew into a rage and exclaimed, 'So he is also nothing more than an ordinary man? Now he will trample on the rights of mankind and indulge only his own ambition; from now on he will make himself superior to all others and become a tyrant.' It is true that in France only Chateaubriand had the courage to resign his official post on this issue, and that only the Russian Court formally protested; the Duke of Baden was too frightened to do so. The Russian protest was rebuffed with a tactless reference by Talleyrand to the assassination of Tsar Paul. Presumably Napoleon had already concluded that Russia would in any case join England as soon as she had the opportunity.

It cannot be maintained that the execution of Enghien was necessary to confirm the fact of the assassination conspiracy; this had been amply demonstrated by the arrest of Pichegru and Cadoudal, and French public opinion veered sharply against the Government on the news of Enghien's death. Napoleon must have known as soon as he saw Enghien's papers that a mistake had been made, and that he was neither guilty nor dangerous; yet he deliberately cut himself off from any calmer reconsideration. He refused to listen to Josephine's entreaties, 'You wish to see me murdered.' In the will dictated on his deathbed he wrote, 'I had the Duc d'Enghien arrested and tried because it was necessary to do so for the safety, interests, and the honour of the French people, at a time when the Comte d'Artois openly admitted that he had sixty paid assassins in Paris. In like circumstances, I should do so again.'

Mme de Rémusat, who, as the wife of Napoleon's court chamberlain, was close to Napoleon and Josephine, probably comes near to the truth when she concludes that it was a deliberate act of statecraft, once Napoleon had become convinced that it was the price he must pay to assure the exrevolutionaries; by shedding Bourbon blood he became their accomplice as a regicide, and the way to a restoration of the monarchy was irrevocably closed. He told Miot de Melito, 'Nor do I regret having acted as I did towards the Duc d'Enghien. Only thus would I remove all doubts as to my real intention, and destroy the hopes of the Bourbonists.' Moreover it cannot be denied that this terrible example had one concrete effect; royalist plots against Napoleon's life were not resumed. Lastly, Napoleon would, at any rate subconsciously, have in his mind the code of the Corsican vendetta, by which an attack by one member of a clan (the Comte d'Artois) could be avenged by the death of another member of the clan (Duc d'Enghien).

It is significant that Louis XVIII refused, under the Restoration, to allow any inquiry into the death of Enghien. The complicity of the Comte d'Artois and of English officials in the Cadoudal plot would have proved too embarrassing. The English historian, Holland Rose, writing at the beginning of the twentieth century, comments, 'But when all

is said the British Government must stand accused of one of
the most heinous of crimes.' When Charles James Fox talked
with Napoleon in 1802, he was shocked and indignant when
Napoleon alleged that Pitt and Windham had been concerned in plots against his life. When Fox became Foreign
Secretary in 1806, he at once showed the door to a stranger
who offered to assassinate Napoleon, and reported the fact
to Talleyrand. But the origins of the Cadoudal plot show
that Napoleon's allegations were not altogether unfounded.
Napoleon never succeeded in gaining moral acceptance by the
European Powers as a legitimate ruler. The Napoleonic wars
continued to be, like the Revolutionary war, the wars of the
sixteenth century and the Second World War, an ideological
conflict. In the minds of his opponents a code of conduct
prevailed which they would never have presumed to apply to
a legitimate monarch.

In his prison Cadoudal remarked, 'We have done more
than we hoped to do; we meant to give France a King, and
we have given her an Emperor.' On April 23, the Tribunate,
now thoroughly tamed, voted in favour of the principle of
heredity. By a *senatus-consultum* of May 18, 1804, it was
declared, subject to ratification by plebiscite, that 'the Government of the Republic is entrusted to a hereditary Emperor'.
In the absence of a son or an adopted son, Joseph was to be
Napoleon's heir.

The Pope's acceptance of Napoleon's proposal that he
should travel to Paris and assist in the Coronation at
Notre Dame on December 2, 1804, threw the ultra-royalists
into transports of rage. The Pope even agreed that after the
anointing, Napoleon should crown himself. De Maistre wrote
that 'the crimes of an Alexander VI are less revolting than
this hideous apostasy on the part of his feeble successor';
and Gentz described it as 'the Revolution legitimized and
even sanctified'.

Napoleon's brothers Lucien and Jerome were absent from
the Coronation, being in disgrace for contracting marriages
of which Napoleon did not approve: so also was his mother,
now given the title of *Altesse Impériale Madame-Mère*,
who was visiting Lucien in Rome. Nevertheless she was
painted into the huge picture of the Coronation by J. L.
David. Napoleon took the trouble to summon his old nurse
from Corsica to attend the Coronation: and before the ceremony he whispered to Joseph, 'If only our father could see us
now.'

It has been questioned whether Napoleon ever seriously intended to invade with the 'Army of England' concentrated at
the camp of Boulogne. Both Metternich and Miot de Melito
record that Napoleon told them afterwards that the Boulogne
camp was a ruse, and that the army was always intended for
use on the Continent. 'In order to amass such forces in time
of peace I required a pretext: the invasion was a blind.' But
this was said after the event, to explain away the failure of
the invasion. It is impossible to believe that the amount of
effort put into the invasion flotillas was simply intended as a
deception. At its peak the flotilla project aimed at the
construction of nearly two thousand boats of all kinds to
transport nearly a hundred thousand men and their equipment. Probably the 'Army of England' was concentrated for a
dual purpose: even if the invasion failed to come off, it could
be trained to a pitch of perfection for a rapid switch against
the Continental Powers. But it is doubtful whether Napoleon ever seriously contemplated a crossing of the Channel
by the flotillas without temporary command of the Channel
by the battle-fleet. At any rate it was soon shown that only
a proportion of the flotillas could get out of the ports at each
tide, and in the meantime they would be at the mercy of the
English warships.

In the spring of 1804, Napoleon issued detailed instructions
to Admiral Latouche-Tréville, commander of the Toulon
squadron, for a combined operation of the fleet with the
flotilla. He was to elude Nelson's blockade in the Mediterranean, join Villeneuve's Rochefort squadron, and enter the
Channel. 'Let us be masters of the Straits for six hours,
and we shall be masters of the world.' Latouche-Tréville, the
best of the French admirals, died in August 1804, and for
some months the plan was shelved.

The entry of Spain into the war in December 1804 altered
the prospects; Pitt had forestalled a Spanish declaration of
war by seizing the Spanish treasure convoy. The French
ambassador in Madrid reported optimistically that Spain
could have thirty ships of the line ready in a few months.
Napoleon now conceived his grand design in which Villeneuve, now commanding at Toulon, should sail for Martinique, after picking up a Spanish squadron, and there meet
Ganteaume with the combined Brest, Rochefort, and Ferrol
squadrons. Having thus forced the English fleets to disperse
in defence of the West Indies, Villeneuve would return with

temporary command of the Channel, to cover the crossing of the flotilla.

Villeneuve sailed at the end of March 1805, and succeeded in eluding Nelson, who was obsessed by the threat to Sicily, Malta, and Egypt. Nelson did not know for certain till April 18 that Villeneuve had passed through the straits of Gibraltar. By the middle of May Villeneuve was at Martinique, with Nelson hard on his heels, favoured by a fast passage. Ganteaume had failed to break the blockade, and Villeneuve was now instructed to return to Ferrol, if Ganteaume had not joined him within forty days. Nelson was able to send a fast ship to inform the Admiralty of Villeneuve's departure from the West Indies. Calder's squadron off Ushant was ordered to intercept and prevent Villeneuve from entering Ferrol. After an indecisive clash with Calder, Villeneuve took refuge in Corunna. By July 18 Nelson was back at Gibraltar but, finding that Villeneuve had not re-entered the Mediterranean, he moved north to join Calder.

Napoleon's plan had started well, but he had failed to disperse the English fleet. Admiral Middleton, Lord Barham, who had succeeded Henry Dundas, Lord Melville, as First Lord of the Admiralty, had applied imperturbably and unerringly the principle of concentration of force. Napoleon now thought that Nelson had returned to the Mediterranean. On July 16 he instructed Villeneuve to join Ganteaume at Brest, but gave him discretion to retire to Cadiz 'in case of an unforeseen event.' By August 14, Villeneuve was at sea again, but on sighting five ships of the line he turned south to Cadiz. By the irony of fate, the ships he had sighted were not the vanguard of the English fleet but Allemand's Rochefort squadron.

Napoleon had been waiting at Boulogne ready to embark the Army. As late as August 23 he wrote to Talleyrand: 'There is still time—I am master of England.' But Admiral Decrès, his Minister of Marine, who had never believed in the possibility of dispersing the English fleet, begged him not to order Villeneuve north to certain destruction. On August 24, Napoleon dictated to Berthier the orders for the *Grande Armée* to break up the camp at Boulogne and march for the Danube.

The invasion had been foiled by Barham's correct naval strategy and by Pitt's organization of the third Continental coalition against France. Nelson's overwhelming victory at Trafalgar on October 21, 1805, ensured that a direct naval threat to England was eliminated for years, possibly for a generation.

Once the English fleets had concentrated, it was fatal for Villeneuve to allow himself to be blockaded in Cadiz: he should have made for Toulon as soon as possible. By the end of September Nelson was off Cadiz with thirty ships of the line against the Franco-Spanish fleet of thirty-three; his only fear was that Villeneuve could not be tempted to come out, and he kept his main force well out to sea to conceal his strength. Villeneuve was in a desperate state of mind; harried by Napoleon on one side, and Nelson on the other, acutely conscious of the inferiority of his fleet in seamanship, gunnery, and tactics, and knowing that he was about to be superseded in his command. Finally he received instructions to sail for Naples 'at all costs' to counter the Anglo-Russian expeditionary force which was threatening the flank of the Grand Army.

When Villeneuve emerged from Cadiz on October 21, and sighted Nelson's fleet of twenty-seven ships of the line, he tried to turn about and re-enter Cadiz, thus throwing his line into confusion even before the start of the battle. Nelson had thought out his battle tactics before he left England for his last campaign. 'Rodney broke the line in one point; I shall break it in two.' With further reinforcements, he would have aimed at a three-column instead of a two-column attack. It was to be a battle of annihilation, a Nile victory on a greater scale. 'I shan't be satisfied with less than twenty ships.' His plan had been thoroughly explained in conferences with his captains, only eight of whom had previously served with Nelson.

The result of the battle was never in doubt; Nelson and Collingwood led the two columns which broke the enemy line and crushed the centre and rear. No historian can sum it up better than the simple entry in the log of the *Victory:* 'Partial firing continued until 4.30, when a victory having been reported to the Rt. Hon. Lord Viscount Nelson, K.B., he died of his wound.' Eighteen French and Spanish ships were sunk or surrendered; no English ship was lost in the battle. Four French ships of the vanguard escaped, but were later captured. Ten got back to Cadiz but only three could be made fit for action. Villeneuve himself was captured and, when released on exchange, committed suicide *en route* to Paris. Although the allied ships fought with courage and persistence the discrepancy in casualties was enormous. In the English fleet, 450 were killed and 1,200 wounded; in the allied fleet, 4,000 were killed and 2,500 wounded. Including prisoners and losses in the storm which followed the battle, the total allied casualties amounted to 14,000 men.

These figures are startling, and require explanation. Trafalgar was not only the crowning example of Nelson's genius, but the crushing proof of English naval superiority in tactics, seamanship, and gunnery. Napoleon had been aware, both in 1797 and 1802, of this superiority, but he could not bring himself to face the logical consequence—that only by years of patient rehabilitation could the French Navy regain parity. At St Helena Napoleon complained that 'there is a specialization in this profession which blocked all my ideas. They always returned to the point that one could not be a good seaman unless one was brought up to it from the cradle.'

In the American War of Independence the French fleet had fought the English on equal terms: and it remained ironically true that in the Revolutionary and Napoleonic wars the best designed ships in the English navy were those which had been captured from the French. France had a corps of scientific naval architects, while England relied on craftsmen. But the Revolution had dealt a fatal blow to the personnel of the French navy; the losses of trained and experienced officers through execution and emigration were irreplaceable. Their corps of seamen-gunners was disbanded. Such training and experience could not be improvised. The English naval strategy of continuous, close blockade deprived the French navy of any adequate training in seamanship and gunnery.

The English navy had some glaring defects of organization. A rigid system of promotion often gave command to elderly and incompetent admirals, but it was offset by a discriminating use of patronage which gave brilliant younger officers like Nelson their chance. Nelson might never have got high command but for the patronage of his uncle, who was Comptroller of the Navy, and of Lord St Vincent. Even so, Nelson's rank was never higher than Vice-Admiral, and he would have had to live until 1844 to become Admiral of the Fleet. Discipline and conditions of life on the lower deck were savage: recruitment, pay and provisioning were chaotic, and had produced the dangerous crisis of the naval mutinies of 1797. Some Admirals made enormous fortunes amounting to £200,000 through prize money, while scraps of it filtered to the lower deck. Under the system of pressing, a proportion of the crews were not even English subjects: in the *Victory* at Trafalgar there were seventy foreigners—including one Frenchman. The regulations excluding women from the lower deck when ships were on operational service were laxly enforced, and there were women helping to serve the guns at Trafalgar.

But these defects were outweighed by the benefits of hard and continuous experience at sea. Throughout the Revolutionary and Napoleonic Wars, the Royal Navy lost nearly 350 ships through accidents; 254 were wrecked, 75 foundered, 15 were destroyed by fire or blew up. Not one capital ship was sunk by enemy action; 5 were captured, of which 3 were subsequently retaken. On the other hand, the Royal Navy sank or captured 115 capital ships. The standard of seamanship and gunnery and signalling thus painfully acquired allowed the development of the tactics of breaking the line, first used by Rodney at the Battle of the Saints in 1782, and brought to perfection by Nelson at Trafalgar.

Up to this time naval battles were fought in line, and were rarely decisive. Nelson's battles of annihilation were the counterpart at sea of the Napoleonic battle. The tactics of attacking in column instead of in line not only isolated a portion of the enemy fleet but ensured the maximum effect of the fire-power available. Everything depended on the initial double-shotted broadside, fired through the stern and down the whole length of the enemy ship, as the English ship broke through the line. One such broadside was capable of killing two hundred and fifty men. The short-range carronades cast by Roebuck's Carron ironworks in Scotland were particularly destructive, and the heavy oak-splinters struck from the hull were as lethal as the solid shot. 'In this war,' wrote Napoleon, 'the English have been the first to use carronades, and everywhere they have done us great damage.'

While English gunnery concentrated on the hulls (a tradition which goes back to the Armada campaign) French gunnery concentrated on the masts and rigging, which caused fewer casualties. Moreover the English crews were trained to lie down until they were ready to fire. Nevertheless the English ships at Trafalgar suffered heavy punishment in the approach to the enemy line, and if they had been dismasted Nelson's tactics might have been foiled. It was only because Nelson had accurately assessed the dis-

cipline and training of his own men and the weakness of
the enemy gunnery that he could use such daring and decisive tactics. Villeneuve was well aware of these contrasts.
Shortly before Trafalgar he wrote, 'We have obsolete naval
tactics; we only know how to manoeuvre in line, which is
what the enemy wants.' But he well knew that the diver-
gence of English and French naval evolution since 1789
deprived him of any answer.

Napoleon did not acknowledge that the verdict of Trafalgar was final. He was lured into Spain in 1808 partly
by the hope of regenerating the Spanish navy. Canning's
decision to seize the Danish fleet in 1807 shows that the
English Government took seriously the revival of a challenge to English naval superiority. Napoleon constantly
prodded his leading naval architect, Forfait, for new designs
—heavily armed frigates, smaller ships of the line capable
of carrying ninety-six guns. In 1807 Napoleon had only
35 ships of the line; by 1812 he hoped to have 102, and
to be in a position to renew the invasion project. But
by this time the English naval lead could not be over-
taken; in 1813 Napoleon still had only 71 ships of line,
against 235 in the Royal Navy.

8

Austerlitz and the Defeat of the Third Coalition

NELSON HAD WRITTEN to the Queen of the Two Sicilies in the early summer of 1805 that 'Never perhaps was Europe more critically situated than at this moment, and never was the probability of universal monarchy more nearly being realized than in the person of the Corsican. Would to God these great powers reflected that the boldest measures are the safest.' Much was to happen before the Continental Powers were forced to adopt Nelson's clear-cut attitude. Between 1802 and 1807 they were suspicious as much of each other as of Napoleon, and it was only Napoleon's repeated encroachments that galvanized them into some semblance of concerted action.

Under Frederick William III Prussia, spineless and selfish, persisted in the neutrality which she had pursued since the Peace of Basle in 1795. Napoleon was able to keep her in play with the bait of acquiring Hanover, and a hegemony in north Germany. Austria's exhaustion after her long struggle against revolutionary France showed itself in the form of a dangerous currency inflation. She was in no mood for further struggle, and preoccupied with the consolidation of the Habsburg dynastic territories amid the debris of the Holy Roman Empire; in 1804 Francis assumed the title of Emperor of Austria. In Vienna there was suspicion of Russia's interest in Poland and Central Europe. The young Tsar Alexander's strange mixture of idealism, vanity and tortured guilt, arising from the circumstances of his father's assassination, made Russian policy unpredictable. Throughout his reign it was to waver between a western policy of rivalry with Napoleon as the arbiter of Europe and an eastern policy of isolation and partition of Turkey.

At the beginning of his reign Alexander's closest advisers were the anglophil chancellor Woronzoff, whose brother was ambassador in London, and the Polish Prince Czartoryski, who was working for the restoration of a united Poland under Russian auspices. He also was anglophil, rejecting a Franco-Russian *entente* as fatal to his Polish plans. Alexander was affronted by Napoleon's occupation of Hanover and his increasing influence over the princes of western and southern Germany. Russian apprehension of French designs on the Turkish Empire was revived by the publication of Sebastiani's report on Egypt, and the French reoccupation of Naples after the renewal of war with England. Napoleon had demanded the recall of Markov, the Russian ambassador in Paris, because of his anti-French intrigues, and the exchange of offensive notes on the Enghien affair completed the diplomatic rupture. Czartoryski became Russian Foreign Minister in 1804, and persuaded Alexander to send a mission to London to concert measures with Pitt. Austria and Prussia signed conventions with Russia in 1804 but these were precautionary and contingent on further French aggression in the Near East.

It was Napoleon's decision to turn the Italian Republic into a hereditary kingdom that crystallized the Third Coalition against France. Napoleon's Coronation in Milan (May 1805) as *'Rex totius Italiae'* and the annexation of Genoa to France were a breach of the Treaty of Lunéville, and seemed to Francis to portend the exclusion of Austria from Italy. Napoleon tried to mollify the Austrian Emperor by explaining that he only assumed the crown temporarily because his brothers Joseph and Louis had both refused it. But his real motive seems to have been the need to strengthen his hold on north Italy; there were rumours that Melzi, the Vice-President of the Italian Republic, dissatisfied with the lack of progress towards Italian autonomy, was secretly in negotiation with Austria. Napoleon could now rely on Eugène Beauharnais, his stepson, as an efficient and loyal Viceroy.

In April 1805, the Anglo-Russian Convention was signed in St Petersburg. The object of the alliance was stated to be the liberation of the territories acquired by Napoleon since the Peace of Amiens. A secret article contained a further aim, if the war was successful: the Netherlands were to be united to an independent Holland and Genoa given to a restored Kingdom of Piedmont. In August 1805 Austria adhered to the Anglo–Russian Convention. Napoleon secured alliances with Bavaria, Würtemberg and Baden; he offered Prussia an alliance and Hanover, but she preferred a waiting game of neutrality.

The allies acted on the assumption that Italy would, as before, be the main theatre of war. While eighty thousand men were assigned to the Archduke Charles in Venetia and the Tyrol, General Mack in Germany had only sixty thousand men, to be joined later by the Russian advance guard. Ferdinand, King of the Two Sicilies, did not dare to join the allies openly until after Trafalgar, and the Anglo-Russian expeditionary force of twenty thousand men did not land in Naples till the middle of November. In the meantime Napoleon had withdrawn his troops from Naples by agreement with Ferdinand, and was able to concentrate forty-two thousand men under Masséna to hold northern Italy. The most that can be said is that the allied effort in Italy tied up French forces, but Italy proved to be a sideshow, and the allied command fatally underrated the weight and speed of Napoleon's advance into south Germany. Mack's calculation was that Napoleon could not put more than seventy thousand men across the Rhine, and that he could not reach the Danube in less than eighty days. He therefore invaded Bavaria on September 11, 1805. In fact, Napoleon's first columns had left Boulogne on August 26, and by the end of September he was across the Rhine with 190,000 men. Reckoning that Prussia would not move, at least until the allies showed signs of winning the campaign, he had also summoned southward Bernadotte's corps of occupation in Hanover. Before he was even aware of the danger, Mack was cut off and surrounded at Ulm. He was forced to capitulate with fifty thousand men on October 20. Kutusov, now in command of the Austro–Russian forces, skilfully eluded Napoleon's pursuit, badly mauling one of the divisions of Mortier's corps, but at the cost of abandoning Vienna, which Napoleon entered on November 14.

Having failed to force a decisive battle with Kutusov,

Napoleon's position was now unfavourable, and might soon become critical. Kutusov had received reinforcements which brought his army up to ninety thousand men, and the Archduke Charles was withdrawing towards Laibach after an indecisive clash with Masséna at Caldiero on the line of the Adige. Napoleon's striking-force, reduced by wastage and the lengthening line of communications, was already inferior; if Prussia now took advantage of the situation, he would be in great danger. In hastening Bernadotte's march to the south, he had ordered him to march through Anspach, which was Prussian territory. This affront inclined Frederick William towards the Prussian war party, and Tsar Alexander, arriving in Berlin at the end of October, persuaded him to sign the Convention of Potsdam (November 3) which committed him to armed mediation with one hundred and eighty thousand men. But Frederick William still refused to burn his boats, fearing that Napoleon might forestall him by making a separate peace with Austria. He therefore insisted on sending Haugwitz to Napoleon's headquarters with an ultimatum which was dated to expire only on December 15. Haugwitz did not reach Vienna to negotiate with Talleyrand until the beginning of December.

Napoleon did not need the Haugwitz mission to tell him of the danger of Prussian intervention. He was now using every military and diplomatic manoeuvre to forestall it by tempting Tsar Alexander into risking a decisive battle. Kutusov was too wily to be hoodwinked by such manoeuvres, but Alexander had now arrived and was in command. His aide-de-camp Prince Dolgorouki had an interview with Napoleon on November 30 and reported that Napoleon was weak and hesitant, and could be defeated. Napoleon now confirmed this impression by moving as if to retreat, and on the morning of December 2, 1805, the allied army advanced on Austerlitz, stretching out their line to bar the line of retreat of the French right wing. As soon as Napoleon saw that the centre of the allied position, the heights of Pratzen, had been unduly weakened by this deployment, he sent in a powerful thrust to seize the heights, and cut the allied army in two. The day ended in the most decisive of all Napoleon's victories, reflecting the fact that the Grand Army which fought at Austerlitz was the most formidable and highly-trained instrument which he was ever to command.

In the 1805 campaign Napoleon was commanding much larger forces and operating on a much vaster scale than

in any of his previous campaigns; but, despite some confusion and fumbling in the rapid movement of such large
forces, he had demonstrated that his strategic and tactical
grasp was equal to war on this new scale. With seventy-
three thousand men against eighty-seven thousand men, he
inflicted on the allies a loss in killed, wounded and prisoners
of twenty-seven thousand: the French casualties did not
exceed eight thousand. The wreck of the Austro–Russian
army was disorganized and demoralized. Alexander, shaken
and humiliated, thought only of retreat to Russia and
agreed to the Emperor Francis' request for an armistice and
a separate peace. By the Peace of Pressburg, signed on
December 27, Austria lost Venetia, Istria, Dalmatia, the
Tyrol, and Vorarlberg, in exchange for Salzburg. By recognizing Bavaria, Würtemberg, and Baden as independent
kingdoms, she lost her last foothold in Germany as well
as Italy. As soon as the news of Austerlitz arrived in Vienna,
Haugwitz hastened to sign the treaty of Schönbrunn with
France, by which Prussia annexed Hanover, in exchange
for Anspach and Neuchâtel.

Having ruined the Third Coalition in 1805 by her selfish
neutrality, Prussia proceeded in 1806 to commit suicide by
taking on Napoleon single-handed. Napoleon had no wish to
fight Prussia, and preferred an alliance with her, provided
she was prepared to enter into his system of vassal states;
on these terms she would be allowed to lead a confederation
of North Germany. The French army remained in southern
Germany after Austerlitz, and in July 1806 sixteen German
princes attached themselves to Napoleon as Protector of the
Confederation of the Rhine. They undertook not only to
provide quarters for the French Army, but to provide contingents amounting to sixty thousand men. But Prussia was
driven desperate by the fear that England and Russia would
now come to terms with Napoleon. This would mean the
loss of Hanover, the prize for which Federick William had
abased himself in the eye of Europe and the Prussian war
party. In February 1806, he had suffered the further humili-
tion of accepting a treaty with Napoleon which obliged him
to surrender part of the Duchy of Cleves, and to close his
ports to the English.

With the death of Pitt in January 1806, Fox gained
office and was disposed to make another effort at appease-
ment. In June 1806 Lord Yarmouth was sent to Paris to

negotiate: shortly afterwards the Russian envoy, Oubril, also arrived. On July 20 Oubril signed the preliminaries of a treaty by which Ferdinand would be given the Balearic Islands in compensation for the loss of Naples and Sicily. Russia would keep the Ionian Islands and have a free hand in the Balkans: Napoleon would undertake to withdraw his troops from Germany.

In December 1805, Napoleon had proclaimed that 'The dynasty of Naples has ceased to reign.' Masséna reoccupied Naples, and the Anglo–Russian forces withdrew to Sicily and Corfu. Ferdinand and his Queen, Maria Carolina, took refuge at Palermo under the protection of the English troops occupying Sicily. In March 1806, Napoleon gave the crown of Naples to his brother, Joseph. In July General Stuart invaded Calabria from Sicily with five thousand men, and at Maida crushingly defeated in a few minutes a French force of six thousand men under General Reynier by well-timed infantry fire-power. Stuart withdrew his force but a formidable guerrilla resistance developed in Calabria, often led by priests, and Masséna was committed to a savage and costly repression which tied up forty thousand French troops in southern Italy. The tactics of the battle of Maida and the guerrilla war foreshadowed the course of the Peninsular War in Spain, but Napoleon was to show himself to be blind to the warning that had been given him.

The proposal to hand Sicily over to the French alarmed Yarmouth and the English Government, as Sicily was vital to the provisioning of Malta. But for a moment it looked as if Napoleon had successfully played off Russia against England. Faced with Oubril's signature of the peace terms, Yarmouth was forced to put forward conditions, acceptable to Napoleon, which recognized Joseph as King of the Two Sicilies, with compensation for Ferdinand in the Balearics, and the restoration of Hanover to England, together with the retention of Malta and the Cape of Good Hope.

But the diplomatic situation suddenly changed. Yarmouth secretly informed the Prussian Government that peace would mean the return of Hanover to England; this prospect finally drove Frederick William into the arms of the war party in Berlin. In turn, the change in the Prussian attitude encouraged the Tsar to refuse ratification of Oubril's treaty. Yarmouth was recalled and replaced by Lauderdale, armed with stiffer peace terms. As late as August 17, 1806, Napoleon had given orders for the Grand Army to withdraw from

Germany: they were cancelled on September 3, and Napoleon was already at his headquarters at Bamberg (where he was favourably impressed by his first hearing of Mozart's opera *Don Giovanni*) when he received the Prussian ultimatum on October 7. A week later, the Prussian Army was virtually destroyed.

With their Russian and Saxon allies, the Prussians could count on a total of a quarter of a million troops, and their striking force in October of 130,000 men was equal to that of the French. Napoleon had never yet had to fight the Prussians, and it was still thought that the army of Frederick the Great would be more than a match for him. But none of the developments in strategy, organization, and tactics which had produced the Napoleonic warfare of rapid movement had yet affected the Prussian Army. They had not even adopted the flexible organization of divisions and army corps. Their leading military theorist, Bülow, who published his *Geist des Neueren Kriegssystems* in 1799, devoted himself to reducing the rigid Frederician tactics to arid geometrical propositions. Battles like Marengo and Austerlitz left him completely baffled. With a high proportion of foreign mercenaries, the Prussian Army was tied to a rigid discipline and enormous, slow-moving supply trains. The Generals were elderly, and the officers were Junker nobles, whose lack of education was only equalled by their narrow conceit. With an army of this type pitted against Napoleon and the Grand Army, the result could only be a foregone conclusion. But the rashness of the Prussians in refusing to wait for Russian support made it quicker and easier for Napoleon.

They advanced into Thuringia in three columns, with the vague aim of threatening the French line of communications across the Rhine. Napoleon had concentrated his main force round Nuremberg, leaving the Rhine lightly held. As soon as he learned of the Prussian advance from the Elbe, he moved swiftly north-east to cut the Prussian line of communications. Too late, the Prussians retreated northwards, and on October 14, 1806, the opposing armies clashed at Jena and Auerstädt. Napoleon, with fifty-six thousand men, reinforced by midday up to a total of ninety thousand, assumed that he was facing the main Prussian force: in fact, it was Hohenlohe's secondary detachment of no more than forty thousand, and they were routed by 6 pm. Davout with twenty-six thousand men at Auerstädt re-

sisted and finally routed the main Prussian army. Bernadotte, with unaccountable inertia, failed to bring up his
army corps in time for either battle. The Prussians had already lost forty-five thousand men killed, wounded, or
prisoners, and practically all their artillery.

The disintegration of the Prussian Army was completed by
Murat's relentless cavalry pursuit. By October 25 the French
were in Berlin, and by the middle of November Frederick
William had taken refuge in Königsberg and most of the
Prussian fortresses had surrendered. Frederick William had
sued for peace soon after Jena and had agreed to Napoleon's terms on November 6. But Napoleon had changed
his mind when he entered Berlin. He was enraged by the
evidence which fell into his hands of Frederick William's
double diplomacy in the course of the past year, and it now
became clear that Russia was preparing to fight him in
Poland. He now preferred to occupy Prussia as a base of
operations and a hostage, pending a general peace.

Many of the Poles were won over by Napoleon's hints of
a restoration of independence for Poland, and he was able to
raise a Polish contingent of thirty thousand men. He also
decreed a levy of eighty thousand conscripts from France,
to be ready by the spring of 1807. The first clash with the
Russians came at Pultusk (December 27); fought in the mud
of a Polish winter, it was indecisive. The conditions were
so terrible that even veteran soldiers of the Grand Army
were unable to carry on, and committed suicide. The Grand
Army, now much reduced by wastage and miserably supplied, had to be dispersed into winter quarters, while Napoleon prepared for a summer campaign.

The Russian commander, Bennigsen, now tried a surprise
attack on the scattered French forces, and his manoeuvres led
to the battle of Eylau, fought in a snowstorm (February 8,
1807). Napoleon with sixty thousand men attacked eighty
thousand Russians and Prussians. It was a costly and purely
nominal victory for Napoleon. Augereau's corps panicked
and was nearly wiped out; the Russian counter-attacks were
barely surmounted, and they retired in good order. Writing
to Josephine, Napoleon admitted that it was 'a very stiff—
very bloody battle', but his official estimate of the French
casualties was eight thousand. In fact they were of the order
of eighteen thousand, not much less than the Russians.

As in the winter of 1805 before Austerlitz, Napoleon was
now in a precarious position, with the danger of Austria mo

bilizing on his flank. He was saved, as before, by the disunity of the allies, and the speed of his reorganization. For the summer campaign of 1807, the size of the Grand Army was substantially larger than in 1806, though considerably diluted by new conscripts. Austria was still too shaken by Austerlitz to intervene effectively, and her offer of mediation in March 1807 only enabled Napoleon to gain time until he was in a position to rebuff it in May. Napoleon reopened negotiations with Prussia for a separate peace, which alarmed the Tsar. He hurried to Memel and persuaded Frederick William to confirm the alliance by the Convention of Bartenstein (April 23, 1807). But the failure of the Russians to relieve Danzig, which fell on May 24, led to recriminations.

The Tsar was also increasingly irritated and discouraged by the attitude of England. Since the death of Fox in September 1806, the Coalition Government had become increasingly isolationist and preoccupied with opening up new markets in South America. They had tied up considerable forces in two abortive expeditions to Buenos Aires. Napoleon was also able to exploit Ango–Russian commitments in the Near and Middle East. Russia was now at war both with Turkey and Persia, and Napoleon received envoys from both countries at the Polish castle of Finkenstein. In February 1807, Admiral Duckworth's attempt to force the Dardanelles and compel the Porte to declare war on France had ended in a humiliating withdrawal: the force which he landed in Egypt in April fared no better, being besieged in Alexandria.

In March 1807, England was distracted by a change of government and a general election. The new Portland government, which included Liverpool, Perceval, Castlereagh and Canning, found that no more than twelve thousand men of the regular army were available for action on the Continent. It was not till the end of April 1807 that they resumed relations with Prussia, which had been broken off by the Prussian occupation of Hanover in 1805. The new English ambassador to Russia, Leveson-Gower, was only appointed in May, and when he met the Tsar early in June, Alexander complained bitterly of the delay in sending English forces to the Continent. 'Why do you not send your militia?' he exclaimed. A strong peace party was already forming in the Russian camp round the Tsar's brother, Constantine. With all these tensions and setbacks, it is not surprising that the allies were unable to withstand the shock of a further decisive military defeat.

At the opening of the summer campaign, Murat's rashness led to an initial French repulse at Heilsberg (June 10) but on June 14, 1807, Bennigsen allowed himself to be caught and crushed by Napoleon at Friedland. Assuming that he had only a French advance guard to deal with, Bennigsen moved his whole army across the river Alle, ignoring the fact that in case of retreat there were only one or two bridges, which would throw his army into chaos. At the start of the day, Marshal Lannes, with a bare ten thousand men, skilfully held off Bennigsen's forty-six thousand with a screen of skirmishers, while urgent messages were sent to Napoleon at his headquarters at Eylau.

Arriving with the main body of his forces, Napoleon at once saw the possibilities presented by the bottleneck of the bridges and town of Friedland, although thirty thousand of his army were still too dispersed to take part in the battle. He rested his troops till 5.30 pm and then ordered Ney, on the right wing, to start the attack by pushing the Russian left, not towards the river, but towards the town of Friedland. The town and bridges were set on fire by the French artillery, and the Russians, crowded into a narrow space with their backs to the river, were slaughtered where they stood. The battle was over by 11 pm, with twenty-five thousand Russian casualties. It was the anniversary of Marengo and Napoleon wrote triumphantly to Paris that 'this battle is as decisive as Austerlitz, Marengo, and Jena'.

On the advice of his Generals, Alexander at once sued for an armistice. In prolonged talks with Napoleon on a raft in the river Niemen, he fell under the spell of Napoleon's personality, and was converted to a complete diplomatic revolution. Napoleon unfolded to Alexander a grandiose design of partnership and partition of the Continent into western and eastern spheres of influence, which would leave Russia free to deal with Finland, Sweden, and Turkey, and force England to make peace.

By the published Treaty of Tilsit, Prussia lost both her western and her Polish provinces, recognizing both a new Kingdom of Westphalia under Napoleon's youngest brother, Jerome, and a Grand Duchy of Warsaw under the King of Saxony. Prussia was to remain occupied pending the payment of war indemnities. Russia lost only the Ionian islands; but in the secret clauses Alexander undertook to declare war on England and close his ports if England refused his mediation. Denmark, Sweden, and Portugal were also to be coerced into closing their ports to the English. If Turkey refused to make peace with Russia, the Franco–Russian allies would reduce the Turkish empire in Europe to the area of Rumelia and Constantinople.

9

The Napoleonic Empire

AT THE END OF 1807 the Napoleonic empire stood in its most brilliant and imposing form, before the Spanish entanglement and the quarrel with the Pope revealed the cracks in its structure. It is time to take a closer look at the Empire and its ruler.

It was after Tilsit that Napoleon took the final step in the establishment of an imperial nobility. In 1804, six Imperial Dignitaries (Grand Elector, Arch-Chancellor, Arch-Treasurer *et cetera*) were appointed, and the Grand Officers, including the new Marshals of the Empire. In 1806 hereditary fiefs in the Italian territories were allotted to certain soldiers and civilians, for example, Pontecorvo to Bernadotte, Benevento to Talleyrand. But the creation of Marshal Lefebvre as Duke of Danzig was the first occasion on which a title was endowed with a grant of lands within the French Empire; and it was followed in 1808 by the establishment of a complete hierarchy—Prince, Duke, Count, Baron and Knight. The rank of Marquis was omitted as savouring too much of the *ancien régime*. These titles were to be hereditary if supported by an income adequate to the rank, and the endowments attached to the title were to be inalienable. In 1830, 440 of these endowments, known as *majorats*, sur-

vived. Such an open breach with the principle of equality had
to be made with care; and Lefebvre had been chosen deliberately because he was a staunch Republican veteran, and
his wife was a former washer-woman. When the new Duchess
paid her first visit to the Tuileries, she startled the usher
who announced her by poking him in the ribs and saying,
'That will impress you, my lad.'

The appearance of an imperial nobility was not merely the
ostentation of a *parvenu* monarch: no part of Napoleon's
policy was more deeply considered or more carefully prepared. At St Helena he dictated a memorandum in which he
explained his motives. 'In establishing a hereditary nobility,
Napoleon had three aims, (1) to reconcile France with Europe, (2) to reconcile the old France with the new, (3) to
wipe out in Europe the remnants of feudalism by associating
the idea of nobility with that of public service and dissociat-
ing it from any feudal concept.' To former Jacobins who
criticized his policy he protested that 'I do not hurt the
principle of equality by giving titles to certain men without
respect of birth, which is now an exploded notion.' 'You
ought to rejoice for here is the old *noblesse* finally annihilated.' After the proclamation of the Empire in 1804 and
still more after the Austrian marriage in 1810 more and more
of the old *noblesse* rallied to the new Court. Many of them
accepted imperial titles, but, as Napoleon pointed out at St
Helena, none of them was given a rank as high as that of a
Duke, unless, like Caulaincourt, they had earned it by service
to the State. Napoleon considered that lavish rewards to his
Generals were part of the price he had to pay to keep them
out of politics, to identify their fortunes with his own and
to raise the lax standards of financial probity which had
prevailed under the Directory. He wrote to Joseph in 1808,
'My intention is to make the Generals so rich that I shall
never hear of them dishonouring by cupidity the most noble
profession, and attract the contempt of the soldiers.' In the
long run it was a policy which defeated itself. The extrava-
gance which Napoleon encouraged in his followers was
morally corrupting, and in the final *débâcle* of the Empire,
they thought more of preserving their lives and their fortunes
than of fighting to the last gasp for their benefactor. It is
ironical that it was Lefebvre who blurted out the feelings of
the Generals at Napoleon's fall in 1814. 'Did he believe that
when we have titles, honours and lands, we will kill ourselves
for his sake?'

Napoleon was obsessed by the problem of giving tradition and legitimacy to his throne and dynasty. It was for this reason that he attached an excessive, even naïve, importance to the Austrian marriage alliance. He even took to the ridiculous habit of referring to Louis XVI as *'mon oncle'*. Stendhal in his *Life of Napoleon* remarks that 'Napoleon had the defect of all *Parvenus*, that of having too great an opinion of the class into which he had risen'. He was shocked and incensed when the Republican General Malet attempted a *coup d'état* in November 1812, by announcing that Napoleon had been killed in Russia; none of his Ministers thought of the obvious course of proclaiming his son, the King of Rome, as Napoleon II. Frochot, the Prefect of the Seine Department, remarked after the event, 'One always forgets that damned King of Rome.'

With the help of court officials of the *ancien régime*, much of the etiquette of the Bourbon monarchy was revived. The public ceremonial of the Imperial Court outshone in magnificence (and boredom) the court of Louis XVI. Napoleon held that 'sovereigns must always be on show'. 'Kingship is an actor's part.' But as a foreign visitor Princess Dolgorouki had the impression that here was 'a power, but not a court'. At the same time, Napoleon was on guard against a revival of the Versailles system which, by its isolation, artificiality and petticoat influence, had sapped the Bourbon monarchy. He told Mme de Rémusat that 'he would have no women ruling at his court: they had injured Henry IV and Louis XIV'. Neither Josephine, still less Marie-Louise, nor any of his mistresses were allowed any political influence.

His harsh treatment of Madame de Staël was largely due to her pretensions as a *femme politique*. At first sight it seems surprising that Napoleon made no attempt to win her over to his side. As the daughter of Necker, the Swiss banker who had been Louis XVI's Finance Minister in 1789, she was immensely rich and had powerful connections, including Napoleon's brothers Joseph and Lucien and Generals Bernadotte and Junot, and she was a writer of European reputation. Germaine de Staël had been only too willing to set her cap at the hero and conqueror of Italy. In 1797 she had tried to corner him in the privacy of his bathroom when she called at his house in Rue Chantereine. In 1797 she wrote of Napoleon as 'that intrepid warrior, the most profound thinker, the most extraordinary genius in history'. She greeted the *coup d'état* of Brumaire with enthusiasm and her father wrote to her ironically: 'I congratulate you on the happiness you find in his glory.'

But to Napoleon the Neckers stood for everything that was in his eyes most detestable and dangerous. They were steeped in the ideology which had caused the chaos of the Revolution; and Germaine de Staël was a nymphomaniac man-eater who flaunted her love affairs in public, defying the decorum and discipline of family life which Napoleon aimed to restore. When Napoleon met Necker on his way to Marengo, he described him as 'a dull, bloated pedant'. Napoleon therefore met Germaine's advances with an emphatic snub. At a dinner party given by Talleyrand in 1797, she asked him, 'Who is the greatest woman, alive or dead?' Napoleon replied, 'The one who has had the most children.' Germaine's lover, Benjamin Constant, was the leader of the opposition in the Tribunate, and Napoleon strongly suspected that she was involved in Bernadotte's abortive conspiracy in 1802. After 1803 she was forbidden to reside in Paris. Napoleon complained that 'her house at Coppet [near Geneva] became a veritable arsenal against me'.

In December 1808, her son Auguste de Staël, was sent to plead with Napoleon to revoke her exile from Paris. At the mention of Monsieur Necker Napoleon burst out, 'Your grandfather was an ideologist, a madman, a senile maniac.' However, he pinched Auguste's ear as a mark of favour and told him, 'Far from offending me, your frankness pleases me. I like a son who pleads his mother's cause. She is much to be pitied, indeed! Except for Paris, all Europe is her prison. Your mother would promise miracles but she won't be able to keep from talking politics.'

Napoleon's 'persecution' of Germaine de Staël turned to her advantage: it made her the leader of the intellectual opposition to Napoleon throughout Europe. The long feud between them has a certain piquant irony, because their affinity of temperament is as striking as their antipathy. In both of them the ideas of the Enlightenment were uneasily at war with the emotions of the Romantic Movement. Both had genius, and both were supreme egoists who thought that genius and pursuit of glory put them above the ordinary rules.

Napoleon made a sharp distinction between public ceremonial and private life of his household, which remained simple, laborious, and even bourgeois. He refused offers from former members of Louis XVI's *Garde du Corps* to reconstitute a personal bodyguard, and he would have nothing to do with the nonsense of the formal *levées* of the Bourbon court. He paid little attention to the fickle opinions of Parisian society. In 1814 he wrote to his brother Joseph, 'I have never sought the praise of the Parisians. I am not an opera star.' It was only the opinions of the 'well-off peasant' that were worth considering. At the same time he took great care of the food supply and employment of the Parisian working class. 'I fear insurrections caused by a shortage of bread— more than a battle against 200,000 men.' Internal security, even at the Tuileries in the centre of Paris, was reduced to the minimum: a few soldiers on patrol, his valet, Constant, and his Mameluke Roustam, who slept outside his bedroom door. In 1806 he gave Joseph, as the new King of Naples, some advice about security precautions. 'Never appoint a single commander of the Guard, and never unlock your door at night to anybody but your personal valet or aide.'

The thirty-two volumes of Napoleon's correspondence are the monument to his industry. It is estimated that he dictated about eighty thousand letters and orders during the fifteen years of his rule—an average of fifteen a day. (His handwriting was so illegible that he frequently could not read it himself.) His normal routine was to rise at 7 am, to read reports (including the intercepted correspondence from his *cabinet-noir* and reports from his private agents) and to dictate letters till 9 am, when he received his physician, Corvisart, and his Ministers in private audience. Ordinarily he wore either the simple green uniform of the *chasseurs à cheval* of the Guard, or the royal blue of the *grenadiers à pied*. Murat, who was such a dandy that Napoleon once accused him of appearing on the battlefield dressed like a circus-master, told Napoleon that his clothes were unfashionable, but made little impression. Napoleon's tailor constantly complained that he spent too little on clothes. He rarely spent more than a quarter of an hour at meals, and always drank an indifferent Chambertin. When Augereau was invited to try the Emperor's wine, he unkindly remarked, 'I have tasted better.' The rest of the day would be spent at his desk or in conference, and he was usually in bed by 10 pm, though he would sometimes rise and resume work in the small hours. There were evenings when he would stroll incognito through the streets of Paris in civilian dress, accompanied only by General Duroc.

One of the more remarkable sights in the Tuileries, which only Fain, Napoleon's secretary (the successor in turn of

Bourrienne and Méneval) was able to witness, must have
been that of Napoleon and his map expert, Commandant
Bacler de l'Albe, crawling over large-scale maps and occasionally emitting sharp cries of pain as they bumped heads.
One of Napoleon's ministers, Mollien, affirms that 'In the
midst of his camp and during military operations, he wished
not only to govern, but to administer France by himself, and
he succeeded.' One of his Prefects writes that 'the Emperor
exercised the miracle of his real presence upon his servants,
however far they might be away from him'. When Napoleon
accused one of his civil servants of sleeping in his office, he
replied 'What a hope! You torment us all too much for that.'
Napoleon himself said 'What will they say of me when I am
gone? They will say "Ouf!"' '

The question of Napoleon's health and constitution, so
often debated, has recently been re-examined by a medical
expert.[1] The legend that Napoleon had an abnormally slow
pulse, that he could do without sleep, may be dismissed. On
the contrary, Marmont, his aide, says that he needed a lot of
sleep, but could defer it at will. He could make up for lost
sleep even during the course of a battle. In the Italian and
Egyptian campaigns he was suffering from the after-effects
of a skin disease, caught from an infection during the
siege of Toulon. He was cured of this during the Consulate
by the expert treatment of Corvisart and began to put on
weight, despite vigorous riding and his abstemious habits
of eating. The truth seems to be that Napoleon's powers of
work were due to highly-strung nervous vitality and willpower rather than to any exceptional physique.

In the end this expenditure of nervous energy had to be
paid for in a premature ageing. Even before 1805 there were
two occasions when he suffered a nervous crisis, due to
overstrain, which simulated epilepsy. Napoleon himself
recognized even after Austerlitz that he would not be fit for
more than a few more years of Napoleonic warfare: but in
fact he went on too long. Chaptal noted that 'after his return
from Moscow those who saw him noticed a great change in
his physical and mental constitution'. It was difficult to
recognize in this ageing and corpulent man, often drowsy,
the slim, taut, energetic figure of the First Consul. On the day
of the battle of Borodino he was suffering from a violent
cold and bladder trouble. After the battle of Dresden he

[1] See Appendix I.

was immobilized by an upset stomach: throughout the Waterloo campaign he had not the stamina to keep things moving at his accustomed speed. General Thiébault saw him at the Tuileries just before he left for the Waterloo campaign. "I never took my eyes from Napoleon, and the more I studied him the less could I succeed in seeing him as he had been in the days of his strength and greatness. . . . Everything about him seemed to have lost its nature and to be broken up: the ordinary pallor of his skin was replaced by a strongly pronounced greenish tinge which struck me.'

Napoleon professed to hold very decided theories about the art of ruling which he frequently expounded to his brothers —absolute unity of power, constant supervision, and fear. 'Abroad and at home I reign only through the fear I inspire.' He told his brother Louis, King of Holland, that 'a prince who, in the first year of his reign, is considered to be kind is a prince who is mocked at in his second year.' He would have agreed with Thomas Hobbes, the author of *Leviathan*, that 'Generosity is too rarely found to be presumed on, especially in the pursuers of Wealth, Command, or Sensual Pleasure, which are the greatest part of Mankind. The Passion to be reckoned on is Fear.' He said at St Helena: 'Men must be very bad to be as bad as I think they are.' 'In this crowd of men I have made into Kings, there is not one who is grateful, not one who has a heart, not one who loves me.' He told Bourrienne, 'Friendship is only a word, I care for nobody.' He told Fain, his secretary, that his anger was often a calculated scene, to inspire fear. 'Otherwise they would come and bite me in the hand.' Masséna told Lady Bessborough, a visitor to France after Napoleon's fall in 1814, that Napoleon 'never loved anybody in his life—women, men, children—nobody but himself. He was passionate in his ambition, hard as iron in everything else.' This was not a very generous judgment coming from a man who had been made Prince and Duke by Napoleon, and allowed to accumulate a fortune of forty million francs.

If Napoleon thought that he was living up to this image of a gloomy, cold blooded man and inaccessible tyrant, he deceived himself. He was a far too complex, vivid, talkative and gregarious personality to sustain it. Napoleon said of himself, 'There are in me two distinct men: the man of head and the man of heart.' Josephine remarked that 'One would judge him better if he did not resist sentiment which he regards as weakness.' Few of those who met Napoleon failed to find him fascinating as well as formidable. Caulaincourt, who, as Grand Equerry and Foreign Minister, was his close companion for ten years, says that 'the Emperor's feelings were expressed through every pore. When he chose, nobody could be more fascinating.' It must be conceded that Caulaincourt was an impartial observer; Napoleon himself told him, 'I know you don't like me, but you always tell me the truth.'

When Napoleon went on board the *Bellerophon* in 1815, fat, middle-aged and totally defeated, he captivated the officers and crew within two days, to such an extent that the Admiralty took alarm. 'Damn the fellow,' said Admiral Lord Keith, "if he had obtained an interview with His Royal Highness, in half an hour they would have been the best of friends in England.' Captain Maitland, of the *Bellerophon*, records apologetically, 'It may appear surprising that a possibility could exist of a British officer being prejudiced in favour of one who had caused so many calamities to his country; but to such an extent did he possess the power of pleasing, that there are few people who could have sat at the same table with him for nearly a month, as I did, without feeling a sensation of pity, allied perhaps to regret, that a man possessed of so many fascinating qualities, and who had held so high a station in life, should be reduced to the situation in which I saw him.'

Although he was a relatively small man, not more than 5 feet 6 inches in height, Napoleon's physical presence could not fail to be striking. His secretary, Méneval, says that 'his head and bust were in no way inferior to the most beautiful bust which antiquity has bequeathed to us'. Madame de Rémusat, who wrote a hostile *Memoir* under the Restoration, uses the same terms. 'His forehead, the setting of his eye, the line of his nose, are all beautiful, and remind one of an antique medallion.' Chateaubriand says of his first meeting with Napoleon, 'His smile was beautiful and gentle; his eyes were admirable, particularly on account of the way in which they were set beneath his forehead and framed in his eyebrows.' Eye-witnesses and idealized portraits may exaggerate, but the evidence of the few authentic death-masks which exist is conclusive.[1] Owing to the emaciation of his last illness, the face which appears in the death-mask is the fine drawn face of the First Consul, not the grosser Emperor, and it is a face of classic—one might almost say

[1] See Appendix II.

poetic—beauty. Add to this physical endowment a mind of extreme lucidity and quickness, and the effect would be overwhelming.

Napoleon was a voracious reader, even on campaign, when he had his travelling library. Apart from historical works he particularly admired Corneille and Racine. He was often at the theatre, and was very friendly with Talma, the great tragic actor. His interest in the tragic drama was chiefly in the analysis of human motive. 'I would like to be my posterity, and to see what a poet such as Corneille would make of my thoughts, feelings and sayings.' His partiality for the inferior poetry in Macpherson's *Ossian* seems odd, but it was probably the theme of heroic thirst for glory that attracted him. He told Lady Malcolm, the wife of Admiral Malcolm, at St Helena that 'I have often been accused of having my head clouded by *Ossian.*' The beginning of romanticism in literature, as in Chateaubriand and de Staël, repelled him by its wildness, and he would have preferred to revive the classical tradition. He had long outgrown his youthful passion for Rouseau, but when he re-read the *Nouvelle Héloïse* at St Helena he admitted that 'it was a work full of fire, moving, disquieting'. He enjoyed music of the Italian school, and would hum snatches from Rousseau's opera *Le Dévin du Village.* But his attitude to art and literature were political; he wanted to make them vehicles of propaganda. Literature and the the theatre were not so much stifled by Napoleon's oppression as smothered by official encouragement and direction.

Napoleon did not shine at polite small talk, but, given a concrete theme, his conversation could reach a high level. Metternich wrote in 1820, 'What at first struck me most was the remarkable perspicuity and grand simplicity of his mind and its processes. Conversation with him always had a charm for me, difficult to define. Seizing the essential point of subjects, stripping them of useless accessories, developing his thought and never ceasing to elaborate it till he had made it perfectly clear and conclusive, always finding the fitting word for the thing, or inventing one where the image of language had not created it, his conversation was ever full of interest. Yet he did not fail to listen to the remarks and objections addressed to him. He accepted them, questioned them or opposed them, without losing the tone or overstepping the bounds of a business conversation; and I have never felt the least difficulty in saying to him what I believed to be the truth, even when it was not likely to please him.'

Napoleon was not without a sense of humour, sometimes capricious. Poor Ste-Croix, who was already a General of Brigade when he was killed in Spain at the age of twenty-eight, was always addressed by Napoleon as Mademoiselle Ste-Croix, because he was so pretty. Monsieur de Turenne, who succeeded Rémusat as Chamberlain, was given the nickname by Napoleon (for reasons best known to himself) of 'milord Kincester', because of his anglomania. When accosted by a lunatic who announced that he was in love with the Empress, Napoleon replied, 'You should choose someone else to confide in.' In 1812 when Napoleon was returning alone with Caulaincourt from the Moscow campaign, he took it into his head to tease Caulaincourt with the prospect of being captured by the Prussians, and exhibited in an iron cage in London. They drove for miles convulsed with laughter at the absurd picture elaborated by Napoleon. One night at Vienna, before the battle of Wagram, Napoleon demanded the cold chicken which was always provided as a late supper. When it appeared, Napoleon complained, 'Since when has a chicken been born with one leg and one wing? I see that I am expected to live off the scraps left me by my servants.' The Mameluke who had been tempted to eat the Emperor's chicken had his ears severely pinched.

Napoleon gets surprisingly high marks from his personal servants—his aides, his secretaries, and his valets. In their experience he was naturally kind and considerate; if he got in a rage, it was quickly over, and he usually made amends. He once wrote to Decrès, his Minister of Marine: 'I regret that you should have lost your temper with me; but in a word, when once the anger is over, nothing remains; I hope, therefore, that you feel no ill-will towards me.' He had the 'art of increasing devotion towards him by a familiarity which possessed the knack of behaving towards his inferiors as if they were his equals'.

The charm which Napoleon could turn on at will was used unscrupulously to fortify his mastery over men's minds. He told Caulaincourt, 'When I need someone I am not squeamish, I would kiss his arse.' His surest touch was, of course, with his soldiers. A record of victory and professional skill is the first requisite for a commander in gaining the confidence of his soldiers; but to this Napoleon added an uncanny insight into the psychology of the soldier. As he said, 'The military are a freemasonry: and I am its Grand Master.' His constant

reviews, and his presence on the battlefield, enabled him to
establish an extraordinary degree of personal contact, particularly with the Guard. One letter will illustrate his attention to details of morale. In May 1807 he wrote from Poland
to the Chancellor of the Legion of Honour thus: 'Write to
Corporal Bernaudet of the 13th of the Line and tell him not
to drink so much and to behave better. He has been given
the Cross because he is a brave man. One must not take it
away from him because he is a bit fond of wine. Make him
understand, however, that he is wrong to get into a state
which brings shame on the decoration he wears.' Marmont
writes that 'it was by familiarities of this kind that the
Emperor made the soldiers adore him, but it was a means
only available to a commander whom frequent victories had
made illustrious; any other general would have injured his
reputation by it'.

Napoleon played on the emotions of glory, adventure and
comradeship with the skill of a sorcerer. The Comte de
Narbonne, who was a survivor of the *ancien régime* and
went through the Russian campaign at the age of sixty,
described the spirit in Napoleon's army as 'a democratic
chivalry'. Wellington reckoned that the moral effect of
Napoleon's presence with his army was worth forty thousand men. Even Private Wheeler, of Wellington's army, records in his diary his admiration for 'Boney'. Not even
slaughter, defeat and disaster could break the bond. At the
costly battle of Essling in 1809 the Guard refused to fight
unless the Emperor retired to a less exposed position. In the
appalling conditions of the retreat from Moscow, there were
no signs of mutiny, even of grumbling; less so than in Wellington's army which was at the same time retreating from
Burgos. The most extraordinary example of Napoleon's mortal
ascendancy was on the return from Elba in 1815. When
Napoleon faced alone the battalion which had been sent to
stop him and cried: 'Kill your Emperor if you wish', they
ignored the commands of their officers to fire, broke ranks,
and crowded round him.

Much has been said of Napoleon's callousness about
human life, and on the battlefield. This is less shocking to
the professional soldier; even the amateur soldiers and civilian
combatants of twentieth-century wars have experienced the
strange, unfortunate capacity of the human race to suspend
the normal revulsion to death, wounds, and mutilation in the
heat and smoke of battle. Both Napoleon and his soldiers

knew well that, in the conditions of the time, a decisive
battle was far less costly in human life and misery than the
attrition of a protracted campaign. Disease and privation
were more to be feared than the risks of death in battle. A
Napoleonic veteran would greet the day of a decisive battle,
under the eye of the Emperor, as a *jour de fête*. The supply,
movement, medical services and even the training of the
Napoleonic armies continued the tradition of the revolutionary armies in being, in the words of Professor G.
Lefebvre, 'a continual improvisation'. The army was expected to live off the country; and everything was sacrificed
to mobility and the quick knock-out blow. As the conscript
armies grew in size and rawness, and as the campaigns
moved out of the fertile areas of Italy and Germany into
Poland, Spain and Russia, the inadequacy of this system
became steadily more serious, and wastage, pillaging, indis-
cipline mounted.

It is easy to exaggerate the manpower losses of the Napoleonic wars. Taine, writing immediately after the disastrous fall of the Second Empire, estimated that 1,700,000
French soldiers were killed between 1804 and 1815. This
figure would imply a casualty rate approaching one hundred
per cent, as the total number of men actually enrolled in the
army from the eighty-six Departments of France proper in
this period was little more than two million. Between 1800 and
1812, 1,400,000 men were enrolled out of 4,350,000 of military age. In 1813, after the losses in Russia, 800,000 men
were called up, and in 1814, for the first time, an entire
class was summoned without exemptions, though, in fact,
barely 100,000 new conscripts actually served. It is known
that 15,000 officers were killed or wounded between 1800
and 1815; and the proportionate casualties in the ranks
would not exceed 400,000. In the four years of the 1914–18
war, 1,360,000 French soldiers were killed.

The widespread unpopularity of the conscription dates
from 1813; before that date it was not unduly burdensome,
though there was resentment against the inequity of the
system. Selection was by lot, and the propertied classes could
evade service by buying a substitute. There is no evidence
that the Napoleonic wars permanently retarded the growth of
population in France: on the contrary the rush to evade
conscription by early marriage in the last three years of the
Empire caused a marked rise in the birthrate. The saying
often attributed to Napoleon that 'one night in Paris would

replace the losses of a battle' is much older and, in fact, goes back to Condé in the seventeenth century.

The Marshals, Generals, and staff officers frequently behaved like spoilt prima donnas; and Napoleon liked to manage them by keeping them in a constant state of jealous rivalry for his favours, by alternate slaps and caresses. When enraged with Napoleon, Marshal Lannes used to exclaim that 'he should be pitied for having conceived an unfortunate passion for this harlot'. When Lannes was killed at the battle of Essling, Napoleon wrote to his widow, "I lose the most distinguished General, my companion in arms for sixteen years, the man whom I considered my best friend'. On the evening after Essling, Napoleon sat with tears running down into his soup. No less genuine was his sorrow at the death of Bessières at the battle of Lützen and of Duroc at the battle of Bautzen in 1813. Junot, the companion of his youth, and Gourgaud, his aide who accompanied him to St Helena, tried Napoleon's patience by their tantrums of jealous devotion. Napoleon complained that Junot was *'sentimental comme une jeune fille allemande'*: that Gourgaud was 'jealous, in love with me. Hell . . . I was not his wife, and I could not sleep with him.'

Napoleon was a shrewd judge of the qualities and limitations of his Generals. He thought that Desaix would have been the first soldier of France, if he had not been killed at Marengo; Lannes might have become so. Ney and Murat were incomparably brave leaders of men on the battlefield, but no more. Berthier was a superb chief of staff, but a muddler if left to himself. Only Masséna, Davout, and possibly Soult were capable of independent command of large armies. Napoleon told Eugène in 1809 that 'Masséna has military talents before which one must bow'; but he also told Joseph that 'Masséna is no good at civil government: he is a good soldier, but he is completely dominated by the love of money'.

Napoleon frequently criticized his Generals' mistakes, but he never made any systematic attempt to teach them his methods, or to form a Staff College. He relied entirely on himself. But why did he put Junot in command of the Army of Portugal, knowing his inadequacy for command? Why did he make Marmont a Marshal, and leave him to face Wellington? Why did he continue to employ Bernadotte, whose defects he summed up in 1809, 'Bernadotte is an intriguer whom I cannot trust. He nearly lost me the battle of

Jena, he was mediocre at Wagram, he never turned up at Eylau, when he could have, and he did not do what he might have done at Austerlitz? The answer seems to be that Junot and Marmont were the companions of his youth; that Bernadotte had married Desirée, his ex-fiancée, and was Joseph's brother-in-law. Napoleon was, in fact, influenced by old associations and family ties a great deal more than he would have liked to admit; it may be a persisting trait of his Corsican origin.

This comes out most clearly in his dealings with his family. If they lacked Napoleon's ability, they were liberally endowed with individuality, self-will, and ambition; and they were seldom over-awed by their illustrious brother. Their grumblings, their sulks, and their demands so exasperated Napoleon that he complained, 'From the way they talk, one would think that I had mismanaged our father's inheritance.' It is true that Joseph, made first King of Naples and then of Spain, Louis, King of Holland, and Jerome, King of Westphalia, were put in an impossible position when they found they were expected to obey orders like Napoleon's Prefects: but it cannot be said that they deserved their positions on their merits.

Joseph and Lucien intrigued with the political opposition during the Consulate; and Lucien quarrelled with Napoleon after 1802 and retired into private life in Rome because Napoleon disapproved of his second marriage, which he considered to be a *mésalliance*. In December 1807, Napoleon had a long talk with Lucien at Mantua, trying to persuade him to assume his responsibilities as a member of the imperial family, at the price of a divorce. 'If you are not with me, Europe is too small for both of us.' But Lucien refused the bargain, and Napoleon wrote to Joseph, 'I have exhausted all the means of my power to make Lucien see reason.' Even Madame Mère, who had stood up to Napoleon for years on Lucien's behalf, finally lost patience with him. Two years later Lucien tried to take his family to the United States, was captured by the English, and spent several years as a country gentleman in Worcestershire, composing an interminable poem about Charlemagne, in which he took the side of the Pope.

Louis, married to Hortense Beauharnais and made King of Holland, quarrelled with his wife, refused to exchange the throne of Holland for that of Spain, and was finally removed from the throne of Holland in 1810 because he was too sympathetic to the Dutch in their resistance to the Continental System. Jerome incurred the Emperor's displeasure by marrying an American girl, Elizabeth Patterson. This marriage was annulled, and Jerome was provided with a wife, the Princess Catherine of Würtemburg, and the brand-new kingdom of Westphalia. The second marriage was a success, and Jerome led a debonair and spendthrift existence, supervised by Napoleon's civil servants.

Elisa, married to a Corsican officer, Bacciochi, was dissatisfied with her relatively minor position as Grand Duchess of Tuscany. Caroline, married to Murat, was never satisfied with her position, first as Grand Duchess of Berg and then as Queen of Naples. Napoleon complained that 'with the Queen of Naples I always have to fight a pitched battle'. Pauline, married first to General Leclerc, who died of yellow fever in San Domingo, and then to Prince Borghese, led a frivolous and dissipated life.

Madame Mère took no part in politics, and preferred a retired and frugal existence. Her parsimony became notorious. As she said, 'I may one day have to find bread for all these kings I have borne.' Napoleon bought for her the great château of Pont near Brienne, and gave her an income of a million francs. It is estimated that after the fall of the Empire she gave away nearly ten million francs to her family; and still managed to leave a comfortable fortune at her death. In family matters she remained the matriarch. When Napoleon once tried to make her kiss his hand as her Sovereign, he got a sharp rap over the knuckles. She was frequently at loggerheads with Napoleon, because she disapproved of the Beauharnais marriage, and took Lucien's side in his quarrel with Napoleon. Her simple view was that 'my favourite child is whichever one is in trouble'. In her fragmentary memoirs, dictated when she was old and blind, she wrote: 'Everyone called me the happiest mother in the world, yet my life has been a succession of sorrows and torments. Each time letters came I feared to read the disastrous news of the Emperor's death on the battlefield.' Stendhal wrote of her: 'Few lives have been so free from hypocrisy and to my mind so noble as that of Madame Letizia Bonaparte.'

The one question which united the Bonaparte family was disapproval of the Beauharnais relations. Napoleon found much more comfort in his step-children Eugène and Hortense than in his own family. He said in 1815 that 'Eugène was the only one of my family who has never caused me any trouble', and his affection for Hortense, and her eldest child, was such that it led to vile and improbable gossip that their relations were incestuous. But, in the end, the Bonaparte family hung together; the brothers, including Lucien, rallied to Napoleon in 1815. Only Caroline followed Murat in his squalid and disastrous treachery in the *débâcle* of 1814.

It was on this strong, underlying sense of family loyalty that Napoleon relied when he organized between 1806 and 1810 his 'federative' empire of vassal kings. But with a family as strongly individualist and independent as the Bonapartes it was far from successful: only his stepson Eugène fulfilled Napoleon's hopes. At St Helena Napoleon reflected: 'My family have not helped me.' After the birth of his son the King of Rome by his second wife, Marie-Louise (March 1811), Napoleon would have liked to disentangle himself from this system. More and more territories were brought under direct rule—Dalmatia and the Papal States in 1809, Holland and Hanover in 1810, the Hanseatic towns and Oldenburg in 1811. Rome was destined to be the second city of the European empire, and in 1811 designs were drawn up for a vast imperial palace to be built on the Capitoline Hill.

The ten years of the Empire cannot compare with the Consulate in constructive internal reform, partly because Napoleon was preoccupied with foreign policy and war, partly because the heavy hand of Napoleon's autocracy had a sterile touch. In 1807 the Tribunate, impotent since 1802, was finally abolished. In 1808 the inscription *République Française* disappeared from the coinage. The Senate was nominally the guardian of individual liberties, with its two standing committees on 'individual liberty' and on 'liberty of the press'. The first committee reversed ministerial decisions in a handful of cases: the second was not allowed to review the working of the daily and periodical press, and discussed only eight cases in ten years. The Ministry of Police, which had been suppressed in 1802, was revived in 1804, first under Fouché, and after 1810 under the more heavy-handed and less subtle Savary. The *lettres de cachet* of the *ancien régime* were openly revived by a decree of 1810, which established political prisons, and allowed detention without trial on an order of the *Conseil Privé*. The four legal codes produced under the Empire—those of Civil Procedure, Criminal Procedure, the Penal Code, and the Commercial Code—

followed much more closely than in the case of the Civil
Code the rules of the *ancien régime*. Trial by jury, introduced in the revolutionary period, was severely curtailed,
particularly in criminal cases, and special courts, reminiscent
of the *cours prévôtales* of the *ancien régime*, were permanently authorized for cases of rebellion, counterfeiting,
smuggling, and armed robbery.

Napoleon was firmly convinced that he could not dispense
with censorship of the press, not least for reasons of military
security. By 1811, there were four papers in Paris, and one
for each Department, all Government controlled. Napoleon
himself did much of the editing of the official organ, the
Moniteur. Censorship of books by the Ministry of Police
proved to be excessively heavy-handed; and in 1811 Napoleon put it under a special Director-General. To this official
he wrote from Moscow in 1812, 'My intention is that everything should be printed, absolutely everything, except ob-
scene works and those which tend to disturb the public
peace.' Yet it must be admitted that the parliamentary regime
of the Restoration found itself no more able than the Empire
to dispense with censorship.

Perhaps the most important institutional development of
the Empire was the organization of education in the 'University of France', established in 1808 after long delibera-
tions in the Council of State. Napoleon paid much attention
to this question, because of his need for trained officers and
civil servants; moreover the formation of opinion was an
important 'source of power'. The Revolution had proclaimed
the principle of free and compulsory State education; but
before the Revolution education had been entirely in the
hands of the Church, and the persecution of the priests
had reduced education, especially at the primary level, to
a low ebb. The Convention, while suppressing the moribund
theological universities, had made some progress in higher
education, by the foundation of the *Institut*, the *École
Polytechnique*, and about one hundred *Écoles Centrales*.
Their curriculum was progressive and modern, with emphasis
on mathematics, science and history; but they were viewed
with distrust both by Napoleon and by the middle class
because they were non-residential, and provided no discipline
or religious instruction.

After the Concordat there was a danger that the Church
would reassert its hold over education. Napoleon was content to leave primary education to the priests. A new Cate-

chism was approved by a majority of the Bishops in 1806, which contained the following clause: '*Q*. What should one think of those who would fail in their duties to our Emperor?' '*A*. According to the Apostle St Paul, they would resist the order established by God Himself, and would make themselves deserving of eternal damnation.' Napoleon summarily dismissed the question of the education of women, 'I do not think we need trouble ourselves with any plan of instruction for young females. Public education is not suited for them, because they are never called upon to act in public. Manners are all in all to them; and marriage is all they look to.'

For the secondary and higher education of the middle class, which was to provide his officers and civil servants, Napoleon disliked both clerical education and education which was 'ideological' and 'irreligious'. In 1803, he had suppressed the Section of Moral and Political Sciences of the *Institut*, because it was too 'ideological'. He wanted an education which was disciplined, modern, and scientific. At the Castle of Finkenstein in Poland in 1807, he drew up a project, which never materialized, for the reform of the *Collège de France*, which shows his preference for modern studies. He poured scorn on rhetoric and *belles-lettres*, and argued for the study of geography and recent history. 'All our youth finds it easier to learn about the Punic Wars than the American War of 1783. The whole of the revolutionary wars is fertile in lessons and yet to find them requires long application and research.' 'I desire these institutions; they have been long in my thoughts, because I have studied much and I have personally felt these needs.'

In 1802 Roederer, soon succeeded by the scientist Fourcroy, was made Director-General of Education under the Minister of the Interior. The *Écoles Centrales* were to be superseded by new *Lycées*, modelled on the *Prytanée Francais*, successor to the former Collège Louis-le-Grand. The *Lycées* were to be residential, with a strong element of military discipline, and a balanced curriculum of science and the humanities. Despite a lavish provision of state scholarships to the *Lycées*, it soon became apparent that the middle class preferred private, clerical education.

Napoleon was driven to a greater measure of State control of education, which emerged in 1808 as the 'University of France'. This was, in effect, a Ministry of Education, with a Grand Master directly responsible to the Emperor, controlling education at all levels. All teachers, whether private or government-controlled, had to be licensed by the 'University': in the State institutions the teachers' status, pay, and promotion were regulated by the 'University'. Napoleon wanted the State teachers to be a sort of lay Jesuit order, disciplined, dedicated and, in the lower ranks, celibate. 'My principal aim in the establishment of an official body of teachers is to have the means of directing political and moral opinion. Such an institution will be a safeguard against the re-establishment of the monks.' 'As long as one is not taught from infancy whether to be republican or monarchical, Catholic or agnostic, the State will not form one Nation.' Private schools were to be heavily taxed to reduce their competition with the *Lycées.* In 1811 Napoleon ordered the number of *Lycées* to be raised to one hundred, and the private schools and seminaries were to be curtailed and closely supervised. In higher education, the University promoted degree granting faculties in provincial centres, in addition to the special institutions of higher education such as the *École Polytechnique* and the *École Normale:* but these faculties were seldom grouped together to form a real university. With an output of nearly two thousand graduates in 1813, France retained her lead in higher education, inherited from the Enlightenment and from the scientific emphasis of the Revolution. But if Napoleon encouraged higher education he also, as with art and literature, stifled it; the faculties became increasingly vocational and utilitarian. Napoleon wrote to Fontanes: 'You are President of the Second Section of the Institute; I order you to tell them that I do not wish that politics should be discussed at their meetings. If they disobey I will suppress it as a dangerous club.' The *École Polytechnique* and the other institutions of higher education deteriorated in the later years of the Empire owing to militarization, and the desperate need for trained officers.

Napoleon's grandiose scheme for an exclusive State secondary education was never realized: even in 1813 the number of pupils in private secondary schools was still nearly as many as in the State schools. Apart from the heavy expense, the Church was too strongly entrenched. 'It was easier for the Emperor Napoleon in his omnipotence to send 100,000 conscripts to the battlefields of Spain and Russia than to obtain from the confidence and obedience of families a thousand more pupils for his *Lycées.'* Napoleon also made the mistake of passing over Fourcroy, because he was too tainted with 'Jacobinism', and appointing Fontanes as Grand Master of the University. Fontanes was a poet and classicist; he was also a crypto-royalist, who boasted under the Restoration that he had used his influence to favour clerical education and the traditional study of classics, rhetoric and *belles-lettres*. At St Helena Napoleon admitted that Fontanes had entirely perverted his conception of the 'University of France'. Napoleon bequeathed the plan of a unified system of education, and since his time successive French governments have wrestled with the problem of the *deux jeunesses*.

The honeymoon period of the Concordat with the Pope did not last long since it was based on a mutual misunderstanding. Napoleon intended to control both the Pope and the Bishops as his 'moral Prefects'. Napoleon reported to the Council of State in 1806 that 'The Catholic priests behave well and are a great help. They have contributed to the fact that the call-up this year has been much better than in previous years; morality has improved under their influence; it is through them that calm and tranquillity have been restored; as a corporate body they are foremost in speaking well of the Government.' Portalis, in charge of Public Worship, introduced the Organic Articles as placing 'not of the State within the Church, but the Church within the State'. The Pope reluctantly accepted the Concordat, with all its disadvantages, because of 'the power it gave to Rome over the episcopate throughout the world' through the recognition of the Pope's right of institution of Bishops: and because, as Cardinal Caprara told Cardinal Consalvi, 'Napoleon was alone in defending Catholicism in France.'

Napoleon's ultimate aim went beyond the pretensions of Charlemagne, to a revival of the Caesaro-Papism of Constantine and Justinian. At St Helena he claimed that 'I should have controlled the religious as well as the political world, and summoned Church Councils like Constantine.' But he completely misread the character of Pius VII, who was not a political prelate or a petty sovereign who could be bullied into serfdom, but a simple priest who would face martyrdom for his religious principles, and, like his successor Pius IX, regarded the Temporal Power as essential to the spiritual independence of the Papacy. Napoleon admitted in 1815, 'I was blind. I always believed the Pope to be a man of very weak character. When he began to resist me, I charged it to his weakness, which made him give in to the bad advice of his entourage.'

Pius had serious misgivings when the *Code Civil*, including divorce, was introduced into the Napoleonic Kingdom of Italy in 1805. In October 1805 French troops occupied the Papal port of Ancona, and Pius wrote a violent letter to Napoleon, threatening to break off diplomatic relations. This reached Napoleon at the most dangerous moment of the campaign of the Third Coalition, just before the battle of Austerlitz, and the timing of it made him suspect that the Pope was banking on an allied victory. The case for safeguarding Ancona was overwhelming on military grounds: at any moment it might be seized by the Anglo–Russian expedition which was threatening the flank of the *Grande Armée*.

The correspondence which ensued might have been written in the eleventh century; it posed in the starkest form the relations between Pope and Emperor. Napoleon wrote to Pius in February 1806: 'Your Holiness is sovereign of Rome, but I am its Emperor. All my enemies must be yours also. It is not fitting therefore that any agent of the King of Sardinia, any English, Russian or Swedish agent should reside in Rome or your States, or that any ship belonging to those Powers should enter your ports.' The Pope replied in March 1806 that 'there exists no Emperor of Rome.' But the final rupture was delayed for three years by Napoleon's difficulties in Poland, Spain, and Austria.

In February 1808 Napoleon, tightening the Continental System and his grip on Italy, ordered French troops to occupy Rome: the Pope shut himself up in the Quirinal. On May 17, 1809, from Vienna, Napoleon decreed the annexation of the Papal States to the Empire, with revenue and properties guaranteed to the Pope. Pius replied by a Bull of Excommunication of aggressors against the Holy See, but it stopped short of naming Napoleon specifically. Napoleon received the text of the Bull shortly before the battle of Wagram, and on June 20 wrote: 'He is a madman who should be shut up. Arrest Pacca and other followers of the Pope.' General Radet thereupon took the initiative of arresting the Pope and removing him to Grenoble. It does not appear that Napoleon had authorized or intended such drastic action, as he wrote to Cambacérès, 'It is without my orders and against my will', and to Fouché, 'I am annoyed that the Pope has been arrested; it is utter folly.

It was necessary to arrest Pacca and leave the Pope in peace at Rome. Now there is no remedy: what is done is done.' He ordered the Pope to be interned at Savona, on the Riviera coast near Genoa, where he was to remain until January 1812.

The effect of the Excommunication has often been exaggerated. It did not prevent the French Bishops from offering a *Te Deum* for the Peace of Schönbrunn nor His Apostolic Majesty of Hungary and Bohemia from giving his daughter in marriage to Napoleon. By January 1810, twenty-nine of the cardinals—a majority of the Sacred College—were installed in Paris, and most of them accepted the salaries provided by Napoleon. But thirteen cardinals, to be known as 'the black cardinals', refused to attend the wedding of Napoleon and Marie-Louise.

The line taken by Napoleon in the dispute was pursued with considerable success. He told the new deputies from the Roman Departments: 'I do not intend that there should be any change in the religion of our fathers; as the eldest son of the Church, I do not wish to leave its bosom. Jesus Christ did not consider it necessary to establish a temporal sovereignty for St Peter . . . Your Bishop is the spiritual head of the Church as I am its Emperor.' Pasquier, Prefect of Police under the Empire, remarked in his memoirs on the 'ease with which, despite the hostility of the Pope, Napoleon was able to maintain not only the loyalty of the Catholics who composed the vast majority of his subjects, but also the clergy. . . .' The *émigré* Damas thought that the 'Bull would rouse some fanatics in Spain. I very much doubt whether they still exist elsewhere.' The fanatical resistance of Spain and Calabria preceded the Bull, and would have arisen in any case over the application of the Codes. But it is noticeable that the loyalty to Napoleon of La Vendée and of Catholic Poland remained unimpaired.

It seemed therefore to Napoleon that sustained isolation and pressure on the Pope would bring him to accept the Caesaro-Papist principle. The Pope's most effective weapon was his refusal to grant investiture of bishops for vacant sees, and Napoleon called an Imperial Council of Bishops in 1811 to tackle this problem. A deputation, armed with an appeal from ten cardinals, waited upon Pius at Savona to obtain his agreement in principle before the Council met. Pius agreed that the Metropolitan should, as his deputy, institute, if there was a delay of more than six months; but

The earliest known drawing of Napoleon from life: as a Cadet at the École Militaire in 1785.

A medallion of 1832 by David d'Angers of Napoleon during the Italian campaigns of 1796-7, which reflects the influence of the Napoleonic legend.

A drawing by Appiani in 1796, after the battle of Lodi.

The centre-piece of the celebrated but idealized picture by J. L. David of Napoleon crossing the Alps in the Marengo campaign, 1800; in point of fact he crossed on a mule.

Portrait by Greuze of Napoleon in his official Consular uniform.

Portrait by Gérard, 1803.

Gros depicts the First Consul at a military review.

The centre-piece of J. L. David's huge picture of the Coronation, 1804.

Napoleon I in his Coronation robes, by Ingres.

A contemporary print of 1805.

Napoleon as Emperor of the French and Protector of the Confederation of the Rhine, 1806.

On leaving Tilsit, 1807, Napoleon decorated with the Legion of Honour the bravest soldier of the Russian Imperial Guard: picture by Debret.

Napoleon greeting Queen Louise of Prussia at Königsberg, 1807;
centre-piece of picture by Debret.

Napoleon in 1808; an unfinished portrait by J. L. David.

Napoleon in 1809, by R. Lefèvre.

Napoleon I, by Girodet.

Bust, from life, by Houdon.

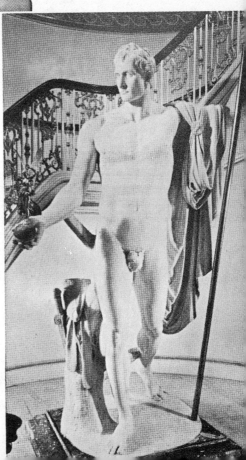

Statue by Canova, now in the possession of the Duke of Wellington, at Apsley House, London.

The plague of rats at Longwood was a favourite theme of caricaturists in the St Helena period.

A Gillray cartoon of 1808.

A Gillray cartoon of 1804.

A Gillray cartoon of 1805.

A German cartoon of 1813.

Napoleon in the campaign of France, 1814; picture by Meissonier, 1864.

Napoleon's farewell to the Old Guard at Fontainebleau, April 1814; contemporary print.

Napoleon as Père la Violette; Bonapartist propaganda during the First Bourbon Restoration, April 1814-March 1815.

L'Unique Pensée
de la France.

A Paris chez Delaunay rue Napoleon N.9.

Napoleon lands at Antibes, March 1815.

Napoleon wins over the 7th Infantry Regiment near Grenoble, March 1815.

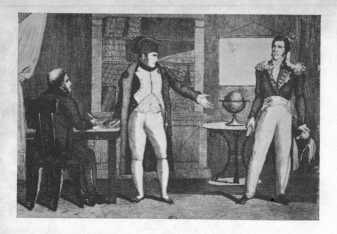

Napoleon's quarrel with the Governor of St Helena, Sir Hudson Lowe.

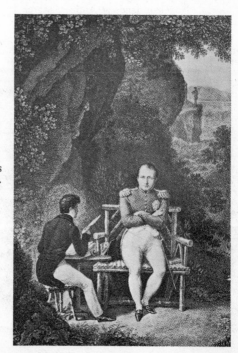

Napoleon dictates to Las Cases' son.

Napoleon meets Jane and Betsy Balcombe.

Napoleon gardening at Longwood: by an unknown artist.

The funeral cortège of Napoleon at St Helena, 1821.

The 'Sankey' death mask of Napoleon; see Appendix II.

Napoleon lying in state on his death-bed; drawing by an English officer.

Napoleon in captivity recalls his triumphs; the figure on the left with a harp is that of Ossian.

The Duke of Reichstadt, dying in 1832, joins his father.

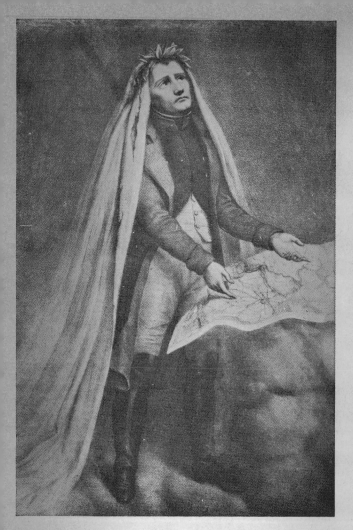

Napoleon as the champion of the Catholic faith; an exotic expression of the legend and the martyrdom of St Helena; the quotation from St Peter II, i, reads: 'Moreover I will endeavour that ye may be able after my decease to have these things always in remembrance.'

he withdrew his agreement as soon as the deputation left. When the Council met in June 1811, Napoleon's undisguised pressure on the proceedings hardened resistance; and a two-thirds majority declared that the Council was not competent to act without the Pope. Napoleon thereupon dissolved the Council, but succeeded in extracting individual agreement from a bare majority of the Bishops. He then blatantly overplayed his hand by extending the formula of institution, not only to the French sees, but throughout the Empire. From August 1811 to February 1812, a deputation waited in vain at Savona for Pius' agreement. In June 1812 the Pope was brought to Fontainebleau, on the ground that the English were preparing a descent on the coast to kidnap him.

After Moscow Napoleon tried to come to terms with the Pope by direct conversations, *tête-à-tête*, at Fontainebleau. The Pope signed 'preliminary bases' of a Concordat which recognized Papal sovereignty, delegation of institution of bishops to the Metropolitan after six months, an amnesty for the 'black' cardinals. Napoleon wrote to his sister Elisa on January 25, 1813: 'I am about to conclude a Concordat with the Pope. He may settle at Avignon.' Without waiting for ratification, he published the news of the Concordat; but in March Pius refused to sign. In December 1813 after Leipzig Napoleon offered to restore the Papal States without conditions. With the fall of the Empire in sight, Pius refused to negotiate except from Rome. On January 21, 1814, Napoleon gave orders for Pius to be escorted to Italy; he re-entered Rome on May 24, 1814, after Napoleon's abdication. It had been a long road from Napoleon's statesmanship and realism in 1801 when he told his agents to 'treat the Pope as if he had 200,000 men' to the insane pretensions of 1812.

It was noticeable after Tilsit that Napoleon's imperiousness had increased. Metternich, at that time Austrian Ambassador in Paris, had observed in October 1807 that 'there has recently been a total change in the methods of Napoleon: he seems to think that he has reached a point where moderation is a useless obstacle'. Even in 1806, Decrès, his Minister of Marine, had wrung his hands and exclaimed, 'The Emperor is mad and will destroy us all.' The United States Minister reported in a despatch, 'The aura which all about him manifestly feel is inconceivable to those who are not familiar with the excesses and extravagances of a man possessed of absolute power and actuated by violent and unmanageable passions.' A sense of disquiet had percolated

through the circles nearest to Napoleon. The shrewdest judge,
Talleyrand, insisted on resigning as Foreign Minister after
Tilsit; he was already beginning to dissociate himself from
the fortunes of the Emperor. In 1810 Fouché, the only
Minister apart from Talleyrand who could stand up to Napoleon, was dismissed. Chaptal, in his memoirs, said that
increasingly Napoleon wanted only valets, not counsellors.
Maret and Savary were blindly obedient, and poor substitutes
for Talleyrand and Fouché. Stendhal said of Napoleon's later
Ministers that 'Napoleon had no men of ability because he
wanted none'.

Chateaubriand wrote in his memoirs that 'Under the Empire we disappeared; there was no longer any mention of us
and everything belonged to Bonaparte.' 'I have ordered, I
have conquered, I have spoken: my eagles, my crown, my
blood, my family, my subjects.' In his proclamation to the
people of Madrid in 1808, Napoleon wrote that 'God has
given me the will and the force to overcome all obstacles.'
Such an attitude of mind sowed the seeds of the monstrous
miscalculations which were to follow.

10

The Continental System

IN NOVEMBER 1806, NAPOLEON issued the Berlin Decree which declared that 'the British Isles are in a state of blockade'; all commerce with them was prohibited, and all goods belonging to, or coming from, Great Britain and her colonies were to be seized. With the control of the North German ports, and with the adhesion of Russia and Austria after Tilsit, he was in a position to put teeth into the plan known as the Continental System.

Napoleon had inherited from the Revolution both the theory and practice of economic warfare. From 1793 the Convention had excluded British goods, and from 1803 onwards Napoleon had extended this exclusion into a 'coast system' extending as far as Hanover. After Trafalgar, direct naval action against England was indefinitely postponed, but the economic weapon might yet bring her to her knees. In August 1807 Napoleon wrote of 'her vessels laden with useless wealth wandering around the high seas, where they claim to rule as sole masters, seeking in vain from the Sound to the Hellespont for a port to open and receive them'. He told his brother King Louis of Holland, 'I mean to conquer the sea by the land.'

The Continental System was aimed at exports, not imports; it was in fact a boycott and not a blockade. The wild inflation caused by the paper money of the Revolution, the *assignats,* had been deeply impressed on Napoleon's mind; it was associated with the acute privations of his youth. England's National Debt in 1802 was enormous by the standards of the time—over £500 million; even a century later, in 1914, it had not reached £600 million. In 1797 Pitt had been forced to resort to paper money. If England's exports were stifled, her delicate balance of payments would be upset; she would be unable to subsidize Continental allies with her sovereigns, the *'Chevaliers de St George',* and then unemployment would either produce a revolutionary upheaval, or at least a public clamour which would force the English Government to make peace.

At first sight the statistics of English trade in the years 1806–14 appear to condemn the Continental System out of hand as a complete failure. The total volume of exports shows no considerable drop.[1] But the project cannot be properly assessed without a more detailed analysis of the fluctuations in the economic war. In the first place, the System was in full operation only for comparatively short periods. Great gaps were torn in it by the Peninsular War in 1808, by the Austrian War of 1809, and by the failure of the Russian campaign of 1812. Secondly, Napoleon himself wavered in his conception and application of the System.

English opinion at first greeted the Berlin Decree with derision; caricatures showed Boney blockading the moon. *The Times* wrote that 'His decree will have as little effect on British commerce as his navy has.' The coast system had proved quite ineffective in excluding English trade from the Continent, except for France, as it continued to flow through Holland and the North German ports. Even when the North German coastline was under French control after Jena, Bernadotte and Bourrienne, in charge of the administration, were pocketing large sums to connive at English trade. English agents took the view that the Continental System was simply a device to enrich French Generals. Moreover the markets of the New World were an expanding alternative to Europe. In the years 1803–5, Europe took only thirty-three per cent of English exports, the USA twenty-seven per cent, and the rest of the world, chiefly the English

[1] The English official figures (declared values) are:

1802	1803	1804	1805	1806	1807	1808	1809	1810	1811	1812
41·4m	31·4m	34·4m	36·5m	34·5m	34·5m	34·5m	50·3m	48·8m	32·4m	43·2m

colonies and South America, forty per cent. Contraband
trade with South America had been for some time considerable, and in 1806 great hopes were raised by the capture of Buenos Aires and Montevideo by English forces.

But after Tilsit the pressure began to be felt. In his Grand
Army Bulletin of July 1807, Napoleon warned that 'it is
probable that the Continental System will not be a vain
word'. Canning's decision to seize the Danish fleet meant
that English shipping had to be switched to Swedish ports.
In July 1807 there was also fear of war with the United
States, when the United States frigate *Chesapeake* was attacked and boarded by the Royal Navy, in search of deserters. A simultaneous closing of northern Europe and the
United States to English trade would be extremely serious,
as together they took sixty per cent of English exports. Moreover Napoleon's discrimination against English shipping
might divert the profitable trade in colonial produce to neutrals.

The English Government therefore replied to the Berlin
Decree with the Orders in Council of November and December 1807, requiring neutral ships to be furnished with a
license in an English port, if they wished to avoid capture
as lawful prize by the Royal Navy. Napoleon in turn in-
tensified the pressure on neutrals by the Fontainebleau and
Milan Decrees of October and December 1807 which declared that neutral ships complying with the Orders in Council would be treated as English ships. There were now to
be no neutrals: 'France by her decrees had resolved to abolish
all trade with England; England said, in return, that France
should have no trade but with England.' President Jefferson hoped by his Embargo Act of December 1807, which
prohibited United States ships from trading with Europe and
banned the import of specified English manufactured goods,
to force the belligerents to abandon their controls, but in
practice it caused more harm to United States' interests
than to the belligerents, and was repealed in March 1809.

Though the total figures of English exports for 1807 were
satisfactory, they conceal the fact that there was a serious
drop in the second half of the year, and this continued
through the first half of 1808. Exports to Europe sank to
£15 million as compared with £19½ million in the corresponding period in 1807. Grenville, who had been succeeded as Prime Minister by Portland in 1807, expressed
extreme disquiet. 'I am alarmed more than I can say. How

will our people live? How can we find in Government and Parliament the authority to control the wave of discontent that such misery will produce?'

This menacing situation was unexpectedly relieved by the opening of the Peninsular War. The flight of the Portuguese royal family to Brazil, and the refusal of the Spanish colonies to acknowledge Napoleon's brother, Joseph, as King of Spain, meant that English trade with South America was now open and official. The expeditionary force under Wellesley designed for the conquest of Mexico was cancelled. The Spanish rising in turn encouraged Austria to declare war on Napoleon, and during the Wagram campaign of 1809 Napoleon lost his grip on northern Europe.

English exports in 1809 reached a record height. As early as March 1809, Napoleon began to waver in his policy of strict prohibition. The success of the *'smogglers'* was such that he preferred to authorize limited trade with England in colonial produce, subject to high tariffs, in exchange for French wines and silks. This licence system was regularized by the Trianon Decree of 1810, but even at its height in 1812 it never yielded more than three per cent of English exports.

But after Wagram Napoleon was in a position to tighten his grip on Europe. Holland, the Hanseatic towns, and the Duchy of Oldenburg were annexed to the French Empire, and policed by the French Army. The ruthless Davout was put in charge of north Germany. The Fontainebleau Decrees of October 1810 ordered the seizure and burning of English manufactured goods, and the establishment of special tribunals for the trial of those engaged in the contraband trade. These measures hit the English economy when it was already running into a combination of difficulties. The Peninsular and Walcheren campaigns put a heavy strain on her gold reserves and balance of payments. The capacity of the South American market was wildly overestimated; some merchants even sent consignments of ice-skates to Buenos Aires. The colonial and New World markets might compensate for the loss of European markets, but in the long run these countries could only pay in colonial produce, of which Europe was almost the sole consumer. By 1810 a glut of colonial produce was piling up in English ports. The export figures for 1810 were only kept up by a large shipment to the USA in the spring, and the last quarter showed a big drop.

Napoleon had succeeded in embroiling England again with the USA. In May 1810, Congress had offered to the belligerents which respected neutral rights the reward of refusing trade with her enemy. Napoleon was the first to respond by declaring that the Milan decrees would be revoked on the understanding that the English Orders in Council would follow suit. In November 1810, President Madison gave the English Government three months to revoke the Orders, and in February 1811, failing to receive satisfaction, he reimposed the embargo. In October 1810 a large English convoy bound for Swedish ports was dispersed by storms, and sunk or seized in the Baltic ports. By September 1810 a wave of bank and commercial bankruptcies in England heralded a severe economic crisis.

Unemployment and distress were aggravated by the bad harvests of 1808 and 1809, and the Government were forced to import wheat in a hurry. Napoleon saw signs that the predicted crisis in England's credit was at hand, and encouraged the export of wheat from France and Holland for payment in gold. Would he have done better to withhold these shipments and so intensify the distress which manifested itself in the Luddite disturbances of 1811? Though local and un-coordinated, they were alarming enough, and required some twelve thousand troops to contain them. But it is unlikely that the Continental imports of wheat could have been decisive, as they amounted only to twenty-six per cent of the total wheat imports in 1810, and a reasonably good harvest in 1810 brought relief the following year.

The year 1811 was disastrous for English exports, and the outlook remained gloomy until Napoleon's retreat from Moscow. Throughout 1811 and 1812 northern Europe took only three per cent of English exports, though there was some compensation in southern Europe, where shipments through Malta showed a twentyfold increase. By the end of 1812 the Continental System had collapsed, and Napoleon was simply using the licence system as a means of raising revenue. 'It is necessary undoubtedly to injure our enemies, but above all it is necessary to live.' Meanwhile the persistence of the Tory Government in maintaining the Orders in Council had finally provoked the United States into declaring war on England in June 1812. In the same month, the Orders were revoked under pressure from the Whigs and the industrialists, but the news reached the United States too late.

This sway of fortune on the economic front reveals some

significant factors. When vigorously applied, the Continental System exerted considerable pressure on England. But it could only be decisive, if so applied over a fairly long period: and in fact it was effectively applied only from the middle of 1807 to the middle of 1808 and from mid-1810 to mid-1812. Secondly, the most dangerous threat to England was a conjunction of the Continental System with a rupture with the USA. Napoleon was not far wrong in thinking in 1812 that victory in Russia would also settle the fate of England.

In embarking on the Continental System he did, however, underestimate the toughness and resilience of the English economy and society. A clear realization that it was a question of 'export or die' united the governing class and the middle class. The working class, lacking in political consciousness and organization, would either follow their lead or be dragooned into doing so. A system of banking and credit, such as was unknown to France, had been built up since the days of Godolphin, Walpole, and the younger Pitt. Above all, Napoleon had not grasped the speed or the scope of the industrial revolution in England. In 1785, France and England were comparable in economic development. But between 1785 and 1800, while France was retarded by political strife, England was experiencing one of the major technological revolutions in human history. By 1800 Boulton and Watt had built and installed hundreds of their steam-engines, particularly in the all-important textile industry. When Watt died in 1819, Lord Liverpool rightly acknowledged that 'England could not have survived the Napoleonic Wars without the steam-engine'. Wellington's somewhat cryptic judgment that 'the battle of Waterloo was won on the playing-fields of Eton' presumably refers to one side of the picture: the toughness of the English leadership. It would be equally true to say that the battle was won in Boulton's engine-making works at Soho, Birmingham.

Napoleon had to pay a heavy price for his pursuit of the Continental System. He conceived it, not merely as a means of economic warfare, but as a decisive shifting of the axis of European trade from England to France. As in 1802, French industry at first welcomed the prospect of exploiting European markets free from English competition. But by the beginning of 1810 the French economy was running into serious difficulties. There were serious shortages of raw materials for industry, and the purchasing power of the Continent was reduced by the large war-indemnities and contributions from enemy and vassal-states which swelled Napoleon's war chest, the *Domaine Extraordinaire,* from 1805 onwards. By 1810 sums of the order of two thousand million francs had passed through the *Domaine.* In March 1811 Napoleon boasted in a speech to the Council of Commerce and Manufactures: 'The Bank is full of gold. There is nothing left in the English banks. I have brought back to France since 1806 more than a milliard of contributions. It is only I who have gold. Austria has gone bankrupt. Russia is about to do so, and England.' French overseas commerce which had been languishing from 1793 onwards was completely ruined as the System tightened: the great ports like Marseilles and Bordeaux seethed with discontent and latent royalism. The figures for French trade fell from 933 million francs in 1806 to 705 million francs in 1810.

In retrospect the general economic depression of 1810 to 1812 appears to the economic historian as the first of the cyclical depressions of the nineteenth century. But it was Napoleon's policy that took the blame for this new and dismaying phenomenon, despite his keen interest in industrial development, and his large subsidies to industrialists. By 1812 the depression was lifting, though the bad harvest of 1811 was a further complication. The confidence and support which Napoleon had won from the bourgeoisie during the Consulate were irretrievably dissipated by the crisis of 1810–11. French agriculture, which was always first in Napoleon's priorities, suffered less. It was helped by the export to England of surplus wheat and wines in 1810–11, and by the development of beet-sugar and indigo as substitutes for colonial products.

Until 1813 the finances of the Empire remained strong, thanks to the solid foundations of the tax system laid by Gaudin under the Consulate, and to the immense war indemnities flowing into the *Domaine Extraordinaire* between 1806 and 1810. From 1804 the indirect taxes of the *ancien régime,* a *gabelle* or salt tax and taxes on liquor and tobacco were revived in a rationalized and more efficient form. In 1811 tobacco became a state monopoly. These taxes yielded a large and increasing revenue till the end of the Empire. With his fanatical dislike of the financiers and war contractors associated with Barras and the régime of the Directory, Napoleon refused to resort to loans. Even in

1814 the national debt of France was no more than sixty-three million francs.

In 1805, when large armies were mobilized and the victory of Austerlitz had not yet been won, the Treasury was seriously short of cash, and in September 1805 the Bank of France had to limit payments in gold. In his embarrassment, Barbé-Marbois, the Minister in charge of the Treasury, had fallen into the hands of the financier-contractor Ouvrard, who advanced thirty millions. In return Ouvrard secured large contracts for the supply of the armies, to be paid in Treasury bills. After his visit to Spain in 1804, Ouvrard proposed to remedy the shortage of specie in France by tapping the vast bullion reserves in Mexico City. In this way Spain would be able to pay the subsidy of seventy millions a year which Godoy had promised to the French. But Ouvrard's grand design was frustrated by the English blockade.

With the Austrian war indemnity in his pocket, Napoleon was able to restore confidence on his return to Paris in January 1806. Barbé-Marbois was dismissed and replaced by Mollien; Ouvrard was made liable for 140 millions owed to the Government, and in 1807 was forced to declare himself bankrupt. Between 1809 and 1813 he was mostly in an open prison as a State debtor. However, Ouvrard had his revenge in the Hundred Days, when Napoleon had to turn to him for a loan to finance the Waterloo campaign. Ouvrard was actually present at the battlefield, and after the Bourbon Restoration played a considerable part in the negotiation by which the Baring banking firm was brought in to promote the payment of the French war indemnity by a large Government loan.

By his cat-and-mouse treatment of Ouvrard, Napoleon did not endear himself to the financial fraternity, and Ouvrard considered Napoleon's knowledge of economics both rudimentary and reactionary. 'Credit was to him an abstract idea, in which he saw merely the dreams of ideologists, and the empty notions of economists.'

The line which Napoleon took in his propaganda for the Continental System was that Europe must unite and undergo temporary hardship in order to achieve emancipation from 'the English tyranny of the seas' and commercial domination. He was helped by the bad impression created by the brutal English attack on the Danish fleet at Copenhagen in 1807. If he had genuinely aimed at fostering a free trade area in Europe, he might have won more support. But the Trianon tariffs of 1810 and the Fontainebleau decree of 1810 made it obvious that France was to enjoy exemptions from the hardships of the System, denied to the rest of Europe. Napoleon wrote to Eugène, his Viceroy in Italy, in 1810, 'My policy is France before all.' Metternich predicted that 'this mass of ordinances and decrees which will ruin the position of merchants throughout the Continent will help the English more than it harms them'. Moreover, with all Napoleon's efforts to develop roads and canals, it was hardly likely that land-transport in the pre-railway age could begin to compete with the relative cheapness of sea transport.

Not only in France but in Italy, Germany, and the Low Countries it was the bourgeois class that was most likely to respond to Napoleon's claim to stand for enlightenment and equality: and by the Continental System he forfeited their support. As will now be seen, his preoccupation with the System also contributed to the catastrophic mistakes of his regime—the Spanish entanglement, the breach with the Pope, the war with Russia.

II

The Spanish Ulcer

IT WAS NOT SOLELY the logic of the Continental System, which required control of the whole coast-line of Europe, that led Napoleon to intervene in Spain. He had an exaggerated notion of the latent Spanish resources, naval and economic, which a decadent Bourbon monarchy was failing to administer or exploit. The feeble and disreputable trio of King Charles IV, Queen Maria Luisa, and the favourite Godoy, are mercilessly revealed for all time in the portraits of Goya. Nor was the heir, Ferdinand, much better. When Napoleon met the royal family at Bayonne in 1808 he wrote that 'the Queen's love-life is written in her physiognomy; one need say no more'. And of Ferdinand he wrote, 'The King of Prussia is a hero beside the Prince of Asturias. He has not yet said a word; he is indifferent to everything, very materialistic, eats four times a day and has no ideas of anything.'

Godoy had kept Spain in uneasy alliance with France since 1804, in the hope of conquering Portugal and even of obtaining it for himself, if Ferdinand succeeded to the throne of Spain. During the Jena campaign Godoy had shown signs of disloyalty to the French alliance. The English capture of Buenos Aires in 1806 aroused fears in Spain of the loss of the whole of Spanish America. At the end of 1806, Napoleon retaliated by demanding that Spain should join the Continental System, and provide a Spanish corps for the occupation of Hanover. In July 1807 he began to concentrate troops at Bayonne for an invasion of Portugal. In October 1807, the secret Treaty of Fontainebleau provided for a partition of Portugal; the south as a principality for Godoy, Lisbon to be retained by Napoleon, the north as compensation for the Queen of Etruria, who was to be replaced in Tuscany by Napoleon's sister Elisa. Junot was put in command of the Army of Portugal, and in the course of his march to Lisbon was able to infiltrate troops into the northern fortresses of Spain.

Meanwhile Ferdinand, fearing that Godoy might usurp the throne of Spain at his father's death, was secretly seeking Napoleon's support against him. Godoy procured his arrest in October 1807, but he was reinstated on Napoleon's intervention. Two lines of policy thus presented themselves to Napoleon. He could exploit the dissensions in the royal family to bring about a deposition of the Bourbons, or he could back Ferdinand and arrange a marriage for him (as he was already a widower) with a Bonaparte princess. In December 1807 he met his brother Lucien at Mantua, but failed to persuade him to re-enter his 'system', or to allow his daughter Charlotte to remain in Paris. In February 1808 he wrote to Caulaincourt, 'As for Spain, I tell you nothing but you can understand that it is necessary for me to shake up this power, which is useless to the general interest.'

Events at Madrid now appeared to play into Napoleon's hands. As Murat, 'Lieutenant of the Emperor in Spain', was approaching Madrid in March 1808, riots at Aranjuez led to the fall of Godoy and the abdication of Charles IV. On receiving this news, Napoleon summoned the royal family to meet him at Bayonne, and wrote to his brother Louis to offer him the throne of Spain. The result of the meeting at Bayonne was that the King and Ferdinand, after mutual recriminations, both abdicated their rights to the throne, and Napoleon gave it to Joseph, after Louis had refused the offer. The royal family, still accompanied by Godoy, accepted luxurious exile; Ferdinand in Talleyrand's château of Valençay.

Napoleon had completely misread the temper of the Spanish people. They had so far kept quiet, because they thought that Napoleon was backing Ferdinand against the hated

Godoy. Murat had sent optimistic reports about his reception in Spain, because he was hoping to get the throne for himself, and was disappointed by the news that he was to replace Joseph at Naples. In April Napoleon had written to Murat that 'if there are movements in Spain, they will resemble those we have seen in Egypt'. On May 2, the population of Madrid, enraged by the departure of the entire royal family for Bayonne, rose against the French, and were sharply repressed by Murat's troops, with the loss of a hundred and fifty French and four hundred Spanish lives. Napoleon ignored this warning and wrote to Jerome, 'the battalions of fusiliers of my Guard and 400 cavalry have put everything right'. He wrote to Bessières, in command at Burgos, that 'the Spaniards are like other peoples and are not a class apart'. On May 18 he issued a Proclamation to the Spanish nation. 'I wish your descendants to say "He is the regenerator of my country." '

While an enlightened constitution for Spain on the French model was being elaborated under Napoleon's eye at Bayonne, the Spanish provinces were flaring into revolt, led by Juntas composed predominantly of nobles and clergy. Canning hastened to give English support to the insurrectionary Juntas, and an expeditionary force to Portugal defeated Junot at the battle of Vimiero (August 1808), and forced him to evacuate Portugal by the Convention of Cintra. At the end of May, Napoleon had ordered General Dupont, with one division, to press on through Andalusia and seize Cadiz, with support from Junot's Army of Portugal. In July Bessières easily defeated the main Spanish army at Medina del Rio Seco; but Dupont was caught at Baylen on July 19 by thirty thousand Spanish regular forces under Castaños, supported by guerrillas. Separated from his supporting division under Vedel, Dupont had only nine thousand men, mostly raw conscripts: nevertheless he was able to obtain a convention guaranteeing the evacuation and repatriation of the Army of Andalusia. Dupont was less lucky than Junot, for the Junta of Seville repudiated the convention, and barbarously imprisoned the twenty thousand men of his army. Napoleon ignored the fact that his orders to Dupont had exposed him to this disaster. He wrote, 'So then the Macks, Hohenlohes, etc. are justified. Nothing was ever so stupid, inept, cowardly.' He was particularly enraged by the false Spanish claims which spread all over Europe that veterans of the *Grande Armée* had been defeated by guerrillas.

In August 1808, Joseph wrote to Napoleon from Madrid, 'You cannot conceive how your name is hated here.' Already he was regretting Naples. But Napoleon could not face the loss of prestige in reversing his policy, once he had proclaimed Joseph as King of Spain. He was forced to recognize that he now had a full-scale war on his hands, and to transfer the bulk of the *Grande Armée* from Germany. At a conference with the Tsar at Erfurt in September 1808, Napoleon had at least assured himself of Russia's neutrality, though Alexander refused to commit himself to active intervention against Austria.

By the beginning of December Napoleon was in Madrid, having forced the Somosierra pass, between Burgos and Madrid, by a brilliant but costly charge of the Polish Lancers of the Guard. Moore, now in command of the English expeditionary force, moved north-eastwards to threaten the French communications with the Pyrenees. On December 20 Napoleon set out for Salamanca with Ney's corps, hoping to take Moore in the rear, while Soult held him at Burgos. But Moore's quick decision to retreat, and Napoleon's decision on January 3 to return to France and leave Soult in command, just saved the English army from annihilation at Corunna. The repercussions of Baylen had already produced a threat of war with Austria.

Despite Moore's costly retreat and evacuation, an English expeditionary force under Wellesley reappeared in Portugal in May 1809, and forced Soult to retreat. In retrospect this can be seen to be the crucial decision of the Peninsular War. The French armies in Spain, now exceeding two hundred thousand men, could easily defeat the Spanish forces in the field: and by 1810 guerrilla resistance was beginning to flag. Wellesley (raised to the peerage as Viscount Wellington in 1809) was quickly disillusioned about Spanish resistance. He wrote in August 1809, 'The Spanish troops will not fight; they are undisciplined, they have no officers, no provisions, no magazines, no means of any description.' And again in October 1809 he explained that, 'As to the enthusiasm, about which so much noise has been made even in our own country, I am convinced the world has entirely mistaken its effects. I fancy that upon reflection, it will be discovered that what was deemed enthusiasm among the French, which enabled them successfully to resist all Europe at the commencement of the Revolution, was force acting through the medium of popular societies and assuming the name of en-

thusiasm, and that force, in a different shape, has completed
the conquest of Europe and keeps the Continent in subjection.'

Until 1813, Wellington could never count on more than
thirty thousand English troops: and he could not hope to
face a concentrated French attack. But the regional Spanish
resistance, and the appalling attrition of guerrilla warfare,
never allowed the French to concentrate in sufficient force.
In the meantime Portugal provided the ideal foothold for
a small English army on the Continent. With command of
the sea, it could be easily supplied: and it could only be
reached by routes through the mountain-barrier which were
covered by the fortresses of Badajoz in the south, and
Ciudad Rodrigo and Almeida in the north. It was, therefore,
the combination of Spanish resistance with an English expeditionary force that was so effective.

The French effort was, moreover, fatally handicapped by
divided command. Napoleon, mistrusting Joseph's competence, never allowed him overall command in Spain until
1812, and even then he failed to provide him with an adequate chief of staff, in place of the incompetent Jourdan.
Joseph's view was that he must be given a free hand to
demonstrate to the Spanish that he was a genuinely independent and national monarch; but it is doubtful whether
he had the authority or ability to carry out such a policy.
Napoleon's orders to his Marshals were out of date by the
time they arrived, and out of touch with reality. In February
1810, he created four military governorships in the north
of Spain, independent of Joseph's Government at Madrid, as
a means of making the armies in these areas self-supporting.
The pay of the armies in Spain became irregular or non-
existent; corruption, pillaging, and atrocities led to a serious
deterioration of discipline in all ranks from the Marshals
downward. In September 1809, when Napoleon was in Vienna,
gossip reached him that Soult in northern Portugal was giving
himself the airs of a sovereign, and he sent him a sharp
letter warning him against the presumption of appearing to
usurp his authority. Miot de Melito notes that 'We may date
from this period the manifest moral change which took
place in the Frency Army.'

Napoleon told Caulaincourt in 1812 that the Marshals in
Spain 'hate each other to such an extent that they are desperate at the thought of carrying out a movement which
might add to the glory of another'. Only by taking command

personally in Spain could Napoleon have remedied this situation: but he never reappeared in Spain after the Corunna campaign. Wellington remarked after the battle of Fuentes d'Oñoro, 'If Boney had been here, we should have been beat.' In July 1809, Wellington won a tactical, defensive battle at Talavera, but was lucky to escape into Portugal, owing to the failure of Joseph to combine his movement from Madrid with that of Soult from Salamanca. In October–November 1809, two Spanish armies advancing from Galicia and Andalusia were heavily defeated, in the north at Alba de Tormes, and in the south at Ocaña.

After Wagram, Napoleon was able to reinforce the Peninsular armies substantially, and he sent Masséna, the Marshal whom he considered most capable of commanding large armies. But Masséna was already prematurely aged, and he did not create a good impression by bringing with him a mistress dressed in dragoon subaltern's uniform. It was not till August 1810 that Masséna's Army of Portugal reached its total of 130,000 men, and was ready to move on Lisbon. In the meantime Soult, following up the victory of Ocaña, occupied Andalusia and set siege to Cadiz. Wellington was thus given a breathing-space to prepare the defensive lines of Torres Vedras.

Masséna was quite unprepared for the fire-power of the English infantry line in skilfully chosen defensive positions, or for Wellington's ruthless 'scorched earth' policy. His massed columns were repulsed with heavy casualties at the ridge of Busaco (September 1810). For a month Masséna faced the lines of Torres Vedras, unable to force a battle or assault, with his army dwindling to fifty thousand men. For a further four months till March 1811 he remained at Santarem, hoping for reinforcements and for Soult's promised advance from the south. But Soult did not capture Badajoz till March 10, and five days earlier Masséna had been forced by sheer starvation to retreat.

The campaign of 1811 in Portugal centred on the struggle for the border fortresses. Masséna failed to break Wellington's siege of Almeida, after a costly two-day battle at Fuentes d'Oñoro (May 1811). He was then relieved in his command by Marmont. Soult, however, saved Badajoz by an inconclusive battle with Beresford at Albuera (May 1811) and was joined by Marmont. Their united force failed, however, to seize the chance of attacking Wellington. Marmont had to return to the north to counter Wellington's threat to Ciudad Rodrigo.

It was not till January 1812 that Wellington was able to storm the fortress in a winter campaign, and this was followed in March by the capture of Badajoz. By this time, the French armies in Spain were weakened by Napoleon's withdrawal of picked troops for the invasion of Russia. Wellington tempted Marmont to a battle by attacking Salamanca. Instead of waiting for ample reinforcements from the north and from Madrid, Marmont rashly attempted with barely equal numbers (forty thousand) to cut off Wellington's line of retreat by a flanking movement. In so doing, he over-extended his line, and the isolated left wing was crushingly routed by Wellington (July 1812). It was a resounding victory for Wellington, as the French losses in killed, wounded and prisoners amounted to fifteen thousand and Marmont himself was badly wounded. In August, Wellington entered Madrid. Soult was compelled to evacuate Andalusia and join King Joseph and Suchet's army at Valencia. While loosening the French grip on Spain, Wellington had compelled the French forces to concentrate. He could not hope to hold on to Madrid, and failed to take Burgos after a month's siege. In face of Soult and Souham's combined armies, which now amounted to a hundred thousand men, Wellington was forced into a costly winter retreat to Ciudad Rodrigo.

Despite this dispiriting check, Wellington was confident of a decisive campaign in 1813. Apart from the news of Napoleon's retreat from Moscow, his Anglo-Portuguese army was now reinforced to a total of seventy-five thousand men; and he had at last been appointed by the Cortes at Cadiz as Commander-in-Chief of all the Spanish armies. Soult and many more picked officers and men were withdrawn from Spain for Napoleon's spring campaign in Germany. By arranging for a naval supply base at Santander, Wellington was able to choose a line of operations from Braganza, much further north than the French deemed possible. When the campaign opened in May 1813, their right flank was repeatedly turned, and they were hustled back to Burgos.

At Vittoria (June 1813), Wellington had eighty thousand men concentrated against sixty-five thousand French, under King Joseph and Jourdan. Although the French lost far fewer men than at Salamanca, the defeat was decisive, as Wellington cut off their retreat by the main road to San Sebastian and Bayonne, and all their artillery and equipment, together wtih the treasure evacuated from Madrid, had to be abandoned. The news of Vittoria reached Napoleon at a critical moment of the armistice in Germany and the peace negotiations at Prague, and played no small part in Austria's decision to join the coalition against him.

Joseph retired in disgrace to Paris, and Soult was sent to defend the Pyrenees. His attempt to resume the offensive misfired, but he succeeded in delaying Wellington's invasion of France by four months. When Napoleon withdrew two divisions for the eastern frontier, Soult's army was reduced to fifty thousand men, and the collapse of the south-western front could not be long delayed. By the battle of Orthez (February 1814), Wellington opened the road to Bordeaux, which capitulated on March 12, and Soult's last battle at Toulouse (April 10) was actually fought after Napoleon's abdication at Fontainebleau.

It was only in the winter of 1813–14 that Napoleon attempted to negotiate with Ferdinand, and to restore him to the Spanish throne. By the Treaty of Valençay (December 1813) he recognized Ferdinand as King of Spain; but the Cortes at Cadiz refused to ratify it, and Ferdinand did not return to Madrid until March 1814. In November 1813 Napoleon exclaimed, 'I have sacrificed hundreds of thousands of men to make Joseph reign in Spain. It is one of my mistakes to think my brother necessary to assure my dynasty.' At St Helena, he admitted that 'the immorality of the proceedings at Bayonne had been too gross', and was an unforgivable shock to Spanish pride.

If he had turned to Ferdinand in 1812, he might well have used the veterans locked up in Spain to turn the scale in Germany in 1813. He had entertained the idea as early as 1810, and had sent a peace offer to Castlereagh early in 1812, on the basis of Ferdinand's restoration, but it had been left unanswered.

Both Soult and Marmont have recorded their opinion that a restoration of Ferdinand would have won over the Spanish people, as the English were hardly less disliked in Spain than the French. Their view is largely substantiated by the history of the French intervention in Spain in 1823. It was then generally expected that the Bourbon Government would be involved in the same sort of trouble that Napoleon had encountered in 1808. Nothing of the kind occurred, because on this occasion the Bourbons were intervening on behalf

of the monarchy and the Church against a minority of
liberal reformers.

Napoleon's initial and persistent error was in assuming
that there was a substantial middle class in Spain which
would welcome enlightened reform on the French model. It
is true that there was throughout the Peninsular War an ap-
preciable pro-French party, the *afrancesados,* among the
urban and official class, who disliked the anarchic violence
of the resistance and looked to the new monarchy of Joseph
for enlightened reform; but Spain was predominantly a
country of priest-ridden peasants. It is significant that the
first two provincial risings in 1808 were led by Canons of
the Church; and there is some truth in Napoleon's generaliza-
tion that it was a 'war of monks', like the wars of La
Vendée on a large scale. It is true that the insurrectionary Cortes at Cadiz contained delegates from all the
provinces, but the validity of the elections is dubious. The
Cortes produced an elaborate and radical Constitution culled
from the written constitutions of the French Revolution,
which outbid the Bayonne Constitution. Even so it is significant that the Inquisition was abolished only by ninety
to sixty votes.

It is difficult to believe that this Constitution represented
what most of the guerrillas were fighting for. The enlightened
reforms of the Bourbon King Charles III in the eighteenth
century had been greeted by the Spanish people with sullen
hostility. When Ferdinand returned to Madrid in 1814 he
summarily dismissed the Cortes and its Constitution and was
acclaimed with shouts of 'Long live the absolute King'. The
Spanish resistance to Napoleon had little in common with the
general movement of European nationalism in the nineteenth century, which sprang from the middle class.

12

Wagram and the Awakening of Europe

NOT ONLY IN SPAIN but elsewhere in the European vassal-states. Napoleon promoted the adoption of the *Code Napoléon*. At the Erfurt Congress in 1808, Napoleon urged the Kings of the Confederation of the Rhine to apply it in their States. The Code was the vessel in which the principles of the French Revolution were exported to Europe, even as far as Poland and Dalmatia.

Napoleon wrote to Jerome, King of Westphalia: 'In Germany, as in France, Italy and Spain, people long for equality and liberalism. The benefits of the *Code Napoléon*, legal procedure in open court, the jury, these are the points by which your monarchy must be distinguished. . . . Your people must enjoy a liberty, an equality unknown in the rest of Germany.' To Joseph, then King of Naples, he explained that 'You must establish the Civil Code in your States; it will fortify your power, since by it all entails are cancelled, and there will no longer be any great estates apart from those you create yourself. This is the motive which has led me to recommend a civil code and to establish it everywhere.' Northern Italy, western Germany and the Low Countries, un-

like Spain, had a substantial middle class which would welcome these reforms, until their benefits were effaced by the
hardships of the Continental System and conscription, and
by the slow awakening of a sentiment of national consciousness.

As the heir of the Enlightenment and a *déraciné* Corsican,
Napoleon's conception of Europe remained cosmopolitan. He
assumed that the basic ideological division in Europe was not
a vertical rift between nationalities but a horizontal one of
classes—the middle class and the peasants against decadent
dynasticism and feudalism. The destruction of the old regime
should therefore open the way to a common code of law, a
common administration and like-minded citizens throughout
Europe.

He did not foresee, until it was too late, that the sweeping away of the lumber of the old régime would only allow
the latent seeds of national sentiment to sprout. The middle
class to which he looked for support in his programme of
enlightenment would be the first to be affected by this sentiment. During the Hundred Days and at St Helena Napoleon
became aware of the trend of ideas, and carefully reinter-
preted his career as a struggle on behalf of the peoples and
nationalities against the dynasties. But the Napoleonic Empire,
while it lasted, was the negation of nationality, and never
more so than in its last phase after 1810.

Earlier in his career Napoleon seemed willing to encourage
national aspirations in Italy. The Cisalpine Republic acquired
in 1802 the name of the Italian Republic under the Vice-
Presidency of Melzi. But in 1806 the Kingdom of the Two
Sicilies was given to Joseph, and in 1808 to Murat. Various
principalities were carved out of Italian territories for the
benefit of the Bonaparte family and the imperial dignitaries.
In 1806 the Duchies of Parma and Piacenza were annexed
to the French Empire: in 1808 Tuscany also, and in 1809
the Papal States. The Illyrian provinces taken from Austria
in 1809 remained directly under the control of Napoleon
through a Governor-General. In 1811 the title of 'King of
Rome' for his son by Marie-Louise foreshadowed the merging
of Italy in a European empire.

The Napoleonic reforms in Italy, partial and inconsistent as
they were, are admitted by historians to be a landmark in
the development of the *Risorgimento*. Uniformity of law
and administration, and the institution of military conscription, helped to break down particularism. Italian troops,

mobilized in their own corps and divisions, fought well, particularly in Russia; and the Napoleonic officers and civil servants were to form the spearhead of the *Risorgimento* after 1815.

But it was only a handful of intellectuals like Alfieri and Foscolo who openly turned against Napoleon because he had betrayed their hopes of Italian unity. Active resistance to French rule was of a local, peasant and clerical character; and guerrilla warfare in Calabria between 1806 and 1808, which tied up considerable French forces, foreshadowed the Spanish reaction. When Murat tried to appeal to Italian nationalism against Austria in March 1815, he met with very little response.

In Germany Napoleon followed the traditional French policy of Richelieu and Louis XIV—that of keeping Germany divided, by fortifying the particularism of the client kingdoms, now grouped in the Confederation of the Rhine. Up to 1806, even Prussia had remained within Napoleon's system as a vassal-state: he was afterwards to regret that after Jena he had not taken the opportunity of eliminating the Prussian State altogether.

In 1807 the creation of the Grand Duchy of Warsaw appeared to be a step towards the restoration of the Polish State. But Napoleon was, in fact, only interested in Poland as a pawn in his strategy and diplomacy. At Tilsit he had first suggested that Prussia should take the whole of Poland, and that Silesia should be given to Jerome Bonaparte: the Grand Duchy was a compromise solution. In 1812 Napoleon continued to mislead the Poles by his evasive pronouncements about Polish independence.

Until 1806 the moral and ideological forces in Europe appeared to be on the side of Napoleon as the champion of enlightened reform. The day before the battle of Jena, Hegel wrote, 'Just as I did in former times, now everybody prays for the success of the French army.' After the shock of Jena the younger generation of intellectuals such as Fichte, Arndt and Schlegel began to formulate the concept of a united and independent Germany and to preach patriotic resistance to Napoleon. Whereas Arndt and Schlegel were anti-French from the start, Fichte only turned against Napoleon with reluctance. He wrote of him, 'With these elements of human greatness, tranquil lucidity, firmness of will with which he is endowed, he could have been the benefactor and liberator of humanity, if only the least trace of understanding of the moral destiny of the human race had illuminated his understanding.'

Yet German nationalism did not originate with Jena: it is discernible in the intellectual sphere long before it affected politics. The cultural renaissance of Germany at the end of the eighteenth century, headed by such great thinkers and writers as Kant, Goethe, and Schiller, was at first cosmopolitan in outlook. At the turn of the century, the romantic movement began to modify the rationalism and cosmopolitanism of the Enlightenment; by its interest in custom, history, and tradition, and in the language and literature of the *Volk,* pioneered by Herder, it gave a powerful stimulus to national consciousness.

The initial enthusiasm of German intellectuals for the French Revolution gave way to a conservative and religious reaction which condemned the anarchy and atheism of the Terror, and exalted the spiritual superiority of a distinct, unique German culture. But nationalism was still conceived in cultural, not political terms. Schiller wrote in 1802 that 'the greatness of Germany consists in its culture and the character of the nation, which are independent of its political fate'. Goethe remained uninterested in German political unity, and an admirer of Napoleon until the end of his life in 1832. After the battle of Leipzig in 1813 he wore his Cross of the Legion of Honour to receive an Austrian Field-Marshal. He translated Manzoni's *Ode on the death of Napoleon:*

> 'Was this true glory? Let succeeding time
> That arduous question ask.
> Ours be the simpler task
> Before the mighty maker's throne to bow
> Who in that towering genius deigned to show
> Of his Creator spirit an image, how sublime.'

The physical and moral collapse of the Prussian Government after Jena allowed the reformers to gain control. It is remarkable that few of them were Prussian by origin. Stein was a Rhinelander and a Freiherr (Imperial Knight); Hardenberg and Scharnhorst were Hanoverian; Gneisenau was a Saxon. Stein was a Prussian official in Westphalia until he became a Minister in Berlin in 1804. Influenced by Herder's ideas, he was anti-French and anti-cosmopolitan in outlook. 'The admirers of Napoleon hope that the Emperor will achieve his universal monarchy, and expect from this institution permanent peace and a splendid flowering of human forces. But the state of calm is prejudicial to the evolution of the human race.' Stein was dismissed by Frederick William III in February 1807 for demanding the reform of the King's Cabinet of incompetent favourites; and it was not till October 1807 that he was reappointed with wide powers. His appointment had the approval of Napoleon, who was apparently misled by General Clarke's advice that he was a sound man, and preferable to Hardenberg, Hanoverian and anglophil, who had been appointed Foreign Minister in April 1807.

In July 1807 the King of Prussia appointed a Commission for Military Reorganization which included Scharnhorst and Gneisenau. The reformers all realized the power which had been generated in France by the Revolution. Hardenberg wrote in a memorandum of September 1807, 'The French Revolution, of which the present wars are only a continuation, has given France, in the midst of stormy and bloody scenes, an unexpected power. The force of the new principles is such that the State which refuses to accept them will be condemned to submit or perish. . . . Democratic principles in a monarchical government—this seems to me the formula appropriate to the spirit of the times.' Gneisenau (who had seen the American militia in action in the War of Independence) wrote that 'the Revolution has set in motion the national energy of the entire French people, thereby putting the different classes on an equal social and political basis, thereby transforming the vital strength of the people and their resources into interest-bearing capital, thereby abolishing the former relationship of the states to one another and the balance of power. If the other states wish to re-establish this balance they must open and use these same resources.' All were agreed that reform must come from above, to avoid concessions to democratic principles and resistance from the Junker class.

It was these considerations that inspired the reforms initiated in Stein's ministry (1807–8)—emancipation of the serfs, municipal reform, foundation of the University of Berlin, ministerial reform, reform of the Army. The Emancipation Edict of October 1807 abolished personal serfdom, and allowed the free sale of all land.

But it did not succeed in establishing, as in France, a substantial class of peasant-proprietors. The Junker land-

owners were able to exploit the Edict by extending their
holdings, and reducing the peasants to paid labourers; they
retained control of manorial justice, and the peasants were
still burdened with the redemption of feudal dues. Stein's
reform of municipal administration was more far-reaching;
self-government was firmly established in the towns, and the
apathy of the middle class was transformed into a remarkable enthusiasm for the *Landwehr* militia of 1813. Stein intended this to be a stepping-stone to a form of national
representation on a corporative basis.

Stein created a unified Ministry of War (though Frederick
William refused to appoint a Minister of War) and prepared
a scheme for the reorganization of the central government
into five Ministries, forming a Council of Ministers. But
the King's Civil and Military Cabinets remained in being, as
indeed they were to do until 1918. Scharnhorst and Gneisenau were appointed to the Military Reorganization Commission, set up in July 1807. In the end only some two
hundred officers were weeded out for their incompetence in
the Jena campaign: but the Commission succeeded in re-
forming the cadet schools, and establishing a system of
selection and nomination of future officers. The foreign
mercenaries were eliminated, and degrading corporal punish-
ments abolished; new training manuals were devised, based
on a careful study of French tactics. The Commission recommended in 1808 that recruitment should be by conscription by ballot without exemptions, with provision for a reserve militia.

This plan was not realized until the mobilization of the
Landwehr in 1813. The King disliked a popular militia; and,
with the population of Prussia halved after Jena and the
finances ruined, the size of the Army had to be drastically
cut. By the Convention of September 1808, Napoleon imposed
a limit of forty-two thousand men for the Prussian Army,
and forbade a reserve militia. The *Krümper* system of
short-service training which was supposed by historians of
the nineteenth century to be deliberately designed to evade
the limit laid down in 1808 was, in fact, suggested by
Scharnhorst in 1807, and its effective application has been
greatly exaggerated. The regular army with its trained reserves did not exceed sixty-five thousand men at the beginning of 1813; but the application of conscription with
Prussia's entry into the war rapidly expanded it, and the

Landwehr added one hundred and twenty thousand second line troops.

The news of the Spanish rising and the battle of Baylen raised Stein's hopes of immediate action against Napoleon. Although he spoke contemptuously of the antics of the patriotic society, the *Tugendbund* or League of Virtue, as the 'rage of dreaming sheep', he planned to unleash against the French a popular militia or *Landsturm*, in concert with Austria. On August 25, 1808, Stein's correspondence was found on a Prussian official arrested by the French; in it he had written that 'the exasperation in Germany daily increases: we must keep it up and try to work on the people'.

Napoleon's reaction to this incriminating evidence was swift and violent. He forced the Prussian Government to accept the Convention of September 1808, and to dismiss Stein. In November 1808 Stein resigned and retired to exile in Prague; an imperial edict declared him to be an 'enemy of France and of the Confederation of the Rhine'. In his Bulletin announcing the capture of Burgos (November 1808) Napoleon gave a warning to Germany: 'It would be a good thing if men like M. de Stein, who, lacking regular troops which were unable to resist our eagles, entertain the sublime idea of arming the masses, could see the misfortunes which ensue, and the weakness of the obstacles which this resource can offer to regular troops.'

It is possible that Stein had been betrayed to the French by his Junker opponents, who were alarmed and exasperated by his far-reaching plans for reform. General von Yorck expressed the feeling of the Junkers when he wrote of Stein's dismissal: 'So one of these madmen has been eliminated; the rest of this brood of vipers will perish of their own poison.'

Yet despite the partial and half-hearted character of the Prussian reforms, the year 1807–8 can be seen as a landmark in the evolution of Prussia and of Germany. There was a moment after Jena when the artificial structure of the Hohenzollern state might have crumbled completely. Under the threat of extinction, Prussia was forcibly dragged into the nineteenth century by a handful of enlightened reformers, and set on the road which was to lead to the unification of Germany by Bismarck.

In Austria, too, reform was the work of a handful of

patriots, and was hampered by Emperor Francis' distrust
of 'Jacobinism'. In spite of the precarious Austrian finances,
the Archduke Charles, as Commander-in-Chief, had done
much to modernize the Army. Regiments of skirmishers and
sharpshooters on the French tactical model were raised; the
cavalry and artillery were grouped into larger units, and the
Army organized into army corps; mobility was increased
by lightening the supply services. In 1806, the volunteer
battalions of the *Landwehr* were instituted, and by 1809
they provided a reserve of 150,000 men. The Chancellor,
Stadion, allowed Hormayr, the State archivist, and Gentz to
unleash a propaganda campaign which exploited the Spanish example.

With the dismissal of Stein and the relapse of Prussia into
submission to Napoleon, the German patriots looked to Vienna. Stein was in Prague; Frederick and Auguste Schlegel,
and Madame de Staël, were in Vienna. But the propaganda
inspired by the Government recalled the historic mission
and the historic glories of the House of Habsburg; it was less
an appeal to German nationalism than to legitimism and
dynastic loyalty. Hormayr, a Tyrolean by origin, prepared an
insurrection in the Tyrol against Bavarian and anti-clerical
domination.

In September 1808 Gentz wrote that 'It is clear that luck is
leaving Bonaparte and that his frightful career has reached
its zenith. Europe can be saved through Spain, if Europe still
has the courage and determination to save itself.' He advised
Stadion at the beginning of 1809 that, with Napoleon's
Grand Army locked up in Spain, Austria must seize the opportunity and 'go it alone'. A successful Austrian offensive
might bring in Prussia, and even Russia; though Tsar Alexander had made it clear that he would not go beyond neutrality. England was prepared to promise subsidies and a
diversion in Northern Europe. Even the cautious Metternich
in Paris was persuaded that the time was ripe. The gathering
momentum of war fever and mobilization overbore the cau-
tion of the Emperor and the Archduke Charles. A French diplomat in Vienna reported in March 1809 that 'In 1805 the
Government alone wanted war, neither the army nor the people desired it: in 1809 Government, army and people want it.'

Napoleon had taken note of the Austrian war preparations
in good time. The Army of the Rhine still had ninety thousand
men at its disposal, augmented by a hundred thousand allied
and vassal contingents. The conscript class of 1809 had been

called to the colours in January 1808; in addition the class of 1810 was summoned for January 1809. The bulk of the Guard was withdrawn from Spain in the spring of 1809, bringing the forces available for Central Europe up to three hundred thousand. With a heavy dilution of raw conscripts, it was no longer the superb army of 1805; but the assumption that Napoleon was unable to fight on two fronts was quickly proved to be false.

When Austria declared war on April 9, 1809, the Guard had not yet arrived from Spain, and Napoleon's forces in Germany were scattered over a front of one hundred miles. The Archduke Charles had two hundred thousand men in Bohemia, despite detachments in the Tyrol, Croatia, and Galicia; but he missed the chance of a vigorous offensive before the French had concentrated. On April 17 Napoleon arrived at headquarters, and rapidly sorted out the mess caused by Berthier's faulty dispositions. He wrote to Masséna on April 18, 'Activity, activity, speed. I greet you.'

The series of battles in Bavaria between April 20-24 (Abensberg, Landshut, Eckmühl) were judged by Napoleon at St Helena to be among his most brilliant campaigns; and at Eckmühl he brought off one of his most cherished and rarely realized manoeuvres, that of taking the enemy in flank and rear by an unexpected arrival on the battlefield. It was not, however, as decisive as the manoeuvre of Ulm in 1805. The Archduke Charles was able to withdraw, after losing thirty thousand men. He wrote despondently to the Emperor Francis, 'If we have another engagement like this, I shall have no army left. I am awaiting negotiations.' The Austrians had lost the initiative, and were now limited to a defensive war. On May 12, Napoleon entered Vienna, while the Archduke Charles rallied his remaining army of a hundred thousand men on the left bank of the Danube.

As in 1805, Napoleon was anxious to maintain the momentum of his offensive in order to forestall a Prussian intervention. On May 20 he seized the island of Lobau, and on the following day crossed to the left bank of the Danube, occupying the villages of Aspern and Essling. Napoleon had underrated the Archduke's strength, and had only thirty-six thousand men on the left bank to oppose the hundred thousand Austrians. Moreover the Archduke had arranged for loaded barges to be sent down the river to smash the Lobau bridge. After a day of fierce defensive fighting, Napoleon repaired the bridge and brought across heavy reinforcements.

On the second day, Napoleon took the offensive and Lannes was developing a decisive attack on the enemy centre when Napoleon received news that the bridge had been smashed. The attack had to be halted through shortage of ammunition, and Lannes was mortally wounded in the costly withdrawal to Lobau. Napoleon was faced with a position similar to that of the Russians at Friedland, with his back against a dangerous bottleneck. Captain Coignet of the Guard wrote in his memoirs, 'This terrible battle cost us dear.' Both sides had casualties of twenty thousand killed and wounded. Napoleon could not unfairly claim that victory had been snatched from him by the collapse of the bridge: but the battle of Aspern-Essling created an even greater sensation in Europe than the battle of Eylau.

But, as so often before, Napoleon's military genius never shone more brightly than when he was in a tight corner, and his enemies remained unco-ordinated. By a stupendous feat of reorganization he turned the island of Lobau into a fortified base with the bridge protected by a flotilla of boats, and summoned his reinforcements. Eugène's corps, advancing from Italy, beat the Austrians at Raab (June 14)and joined up with Napoleon; so did Marmont's corps, advancing from Croatia. By the beginning of July, Napoleon had 180,000 men concentrated at Lobau.

The English expedition against Walcheren was not mounted until the end of July: the King of Prussia awaited the outcome of the next battle, and in the meantime the Prussian officers, Schill, Katte, Dörnberg and the Duke of Brunswick, who had tried to force his hand by leading isolated risings on their own initiative, had been rounded up.

Napoleon struck on July 5 before the Archduke John, rallying after his defeat by Eugène at Raab, could reach Vienna. The Archduke Charles, with no more than 135,000 men against Napoleon's 170,000, was unable to oppose the crossing of the Danube, and took up a defensive position, based on the village of Wagram. The first day's fighting consisted of probing the Austrian positions, and it was not till 7 pm that Napoleon had made up his mind that the Austrian front was over-extended, and that the decision was to be obtained by a rupture of the enemy centre, as at Castiglione in 1796. He kept his main forces massed in a space no more than one third of the Austrian lines and his wings relatively weak and extended, and lightly screened.

The weakness of the French left wing tempted the Archduke

Charles to take the offensive at dawn the following day, thereby giving Napoleon the chance of a fluid battle, which was all to his advantage. Masséna was able to check the Austrian threat on the left flank, when they captured Aspern and Essling, and the decision came when a massive column of thirty thousand men was thrown against the weakened Austrian centre.

But there was no rout and barely twelve thousand prisoners; the casualties exceeded twenty thousand on both sides, and the Archduke Charles was able to withdraw with an army of eighty thousand men still intact. But even before the battle he had written that 'it would be the throw of a gamester who risks his last win on one card'. On July 11 he asked for an armistice, and resigned his command, when the Emperor Francis and the war party refused to accept the necessity of an immediate peace. They were still hoping that English, Prussian or Russian intervention would save them.

By the autumn these hopes had faded, and Metternich was called in to replace Stadion, and sign the humiliating Peace of Schönbrunn (October 14, 1809). Austria lost three and a half million subjects—Salzburg to Bavaria, the Illyrian Provinces to Napoleon, and parts of Galicia to the Grand Duchy of Warsaw and to Russia. She had to pay an indemnity of eighty-five millions, limit her army to 150,000 men, and rejoin the Continental System.

Ostensibly the Wagram campaign had produced for Napoleon even more brilliant results than that of Austerlitz. But when, on his return to Paris, one of his Ministers spoke contemptuously of the Austrians, Napoleon replied sharply, 'It is evident that you were not at Wagram.' He had been impressed by the stoutness and enthusiasm of the Austrian resistance. The costliness of the Wagram battle, the greatest artillery battle yet known, which had caused some of his second line troops to panic, had shaken his confidence in battle as the trump card. In August 1809 he had written in an unaccustomed vein, 'Battle should only be offered when there is no other turn of fortune to be hoped for, as from its nature the fate of a battle is always dubious.'

It was not only in the military but also in the moral sphere that his confidence had been shaken. Shortly before he left Schönbrunn a young German student, Frederick Staps, had tried to assassinate him when presenting a petition at a military review. In the course of a long interview with this young man, Napoleon tried to persuade himself that the assassin was mentally deranged, but he refused to recant and went to his execution crying, 'Long live Germany. Death to the tyrant.' General Rapp wrote to the Burgomaster of Schönbrunn: 'You have no doubt heard of this man who wished to assassinate His Majesty last Thursday: it is I who was lucky enough to stop him. He has confessed everything to His Majesty. He is to be executed tomorrow. It is incredible that he is the son of a Lutheran minister from Saxony.' [1] Hitherto Napoleon had only had to face assassination from Bourbon agents: that an educated young man of the middle class should wish to murder Napoleon, the champion of enlightenment, he found puzzling and shocking. He was forced to recognize that there was a new spirit stirring in Europe.

[1] Curzon MSS b.27: Bodleian Library.

13

Catastrophe in Russia

IN MAKING PEACE WITH Napoleon at Schönbrunn, Metternich intended not only to liquidate the disastrous single-handed Austrian venture of 1809 but to supplant Russia as Napoleon's ally. The Emperor Francis was disgusted that he had been dragged into war by 'patriots' and 'Jacobins', and agreed with Metternich that, for the foreseeable future, the Napoleonic domination must be accepted and exploited to Austria's advantage.

According to Metternich's memoirs, Napoleon brutally demanded a marriage alliance from a reluctant and disdainful Habsburg court. The facts, as revealed by the Vienna Archives, were quite different. Countess Metternich was sent to Paris to work for an Austrian marriage, and when the contract was signed she wrote to her husband, 'Now the affair is successful, and is all that we could desire.' In a Privy Council of December 1809, Napoleon had finally taken the decision to divorce Josephine; and Metternich told the Prussian envoy that an Austrian marriage-offer was essential in order to forestall Russia. A *Senatus consultum* of December 16 announced the divorce, and the religious marriage of 1804 was annulled, in default of the Pope, by the Metropolitan Archbishop of Paris.

Since 1807 Napoleon had been trying to make up his mind about a divorce, painful though it would be to Josephine and to himself. 'I was not born of a tigress,' he once exclaimed, when the subject was broached. But the intrigues of Talleyrand in 1808 and of Fouché in 1809, during his prolonged absence from Paris, had convinced him that the security of the Empire demanded an heir. The death of Napoléon-Charles, the eldest son of Louis and Hortense in 1807, had deprived him of an adoptive heir: to adopt his stepson Eugène would be too great an affront to the Bonaparte family. By 1807 the doubts about his ability to beget children, arising from the sterility of his marriage with Josephine, had been removed. Eléonore Denuelle, a lady-in-waiting to Caroline Murat, and Maria Walewska had both borne him bastard sons, later to be known as the Comte Léon and the Comte Walewski.

At Erfurt the Tsar had been evasive when Napoleon suggested the possibility of his marrying the Tsar's sister, the Grand Duchess Catherine. In the meantime she had married the heir to the Duke of Oldenburg. Napoleon now made a formal offer for the hand of her younger sister Anna, who was barely fifteen. He had not much hope of success because of the fanatical hostility of the Dowager Empress, all-powerful in family matters, who regarded Alexander's Tilsit alliance as a 'pact with the devil'. She was also influenced by gossip, emanating ultimately from Josephine herself, in her desperate bid to avert a divorce, that Napoleon was incapable of begetting children.

At the beginning of February 1810, learning from his Ambassador Caulaincourt that the Tsar was making excuses for further delay, Napoleon made a formal offer to the Austrian Ambassador, which was immediately accepted, for the hand of the Archduchess Marie-Louise, eldest daughter of the Emperor.

The failure of the marriage negotiation with Russia was a symptom, rather than a cause, of the breakdown of the Tilsit alliance. When he returned from Tilsit, Alexander had to face fierce hostility among the Court and the nobility. Savary, replaced as Ambassador by Caulaincourt in December 1807, reported that 'the Emperor and Count Roumiantsov are the only friends of France in Russia'. Russia's adhesion to the Continental System meant ruin for many of the nobles, who relied on selling timber in large quantities to England. The efforts of Speranski, Alexander's new Minister, to reform

law and administration on French lines soon made him un-
popular. It was even rumoured that another palace revolution might be necessary, to remove Alexander in the same
way as his father, Paul. The feeling of guilt about the murder of his father haunted Alexander throughout his life, and
he dared not ignore public opinion for which the nobility
provided the only means of expression.

Roumiantsov, the new Foreign Minister, was eastern and
isolationist in outlook, and looked to Finland, Sweden and
Turkey for the advantages to be gained from Tilsit. Napoleon
was content to let Russia absorb Finland, but only one thing
could consolidate the alliance—Russian expansion to Constantinople and the Straits. In order to keep up the en-
thusiastic mood of Tilsit, Napoleon suggested in February
1808 a fantastic project for a joint Franco–Russian expedition to India. 'An army of fifty thousand men—Russians,
Frenchmen and perhaps even Austrians—marching by way
of Constantinople into Asia would have only to reach the
Euphrates in order to make England tremble and bring her
down on her knees before the Continent.'

But the Russian demand for Constantinople and the Straits
was soon revealed, and reduced the discussions to a deadlock. Alexander maintained that 'We must have something to
show to the nation that the alliance is not solely to your advantage.' In the first half of 1808 Napoleon thought that
Spain, including the Straits of Gibraltar, was about to fall
into his hands, and his Mediterranean ambitions had revived.
At the end of May 1808 he wrote to Caulaincourt, 'If Russia had an outlet on the Dardanelles, she would be at the
gates of Toulon, Naples, and Corfu. Thus you must make it
clear that Russia wants much too much, and that France cannot agree to such an arrangement, that this is a difficult problem to solve, which is the very reason why I tried to come
to an understanding at a conference. At bottom, the question
is always this: who shall have Constantinople?'

By the time Napoleon and Alexander met at Erfurt (October 1808) the 'spirit of Tilsit' had evaporated. To the re-
proaches of his mother, the Dowager Empress, Alexander replied by explaining that his policy was 'to gain a breathing-
space, and, during this precious interval, build up our resources. . . . Must we spoil all our work and raise suspicion
of our true intentions, just because Napoleon is temporarily
embarrassed?' At Erfurt, Alexander was secretly encouraged
by Talleyrand, Caulaincourt, and even Marshal Lannes, to

stand up to Napoleon and act as a mediator rather than an ally. The Erfurt Conference was therefore little more than an empty demonstration. Alexander refused to put pressure on Austria to stop her preparations for war; the questions of Turkey and a marriage alliance were shelved.

Once Napoleon had made the choice of the Austrian marriage, Franco–Russian relations deteriorated rapidly in the course of the year 1810. The Grand Duchy of Warsaw was always a source of irritation to the Tsar, and when it was enlarged by Galician provinces ceded by Austria in October 1809, he demanded a guarantee from Napoleon that an independent Poland would not be revived. An agreement to this effect signed by Caulaincourt in January 1810 was repudiated by Napoleon, and the modifications he proposed were unacceptable to Russia. In Sweden, the pro-French and anti-Russian party engineered the election of Bernadotte as heir to Charles XIII, on the death of the recognized heir, Augustenburg, in May 1810. Napoleon was suspicious of Bernadotte and would have preferred Eugène as a candidate: but the prospect of bringing Sweden into the war against England was too alluring, and he approved the nomination of Bernadotte by the Swedish Diet, at the cost of infuriating the Tsar. In pursuit of the Continental System, he annexed the Grand Duchy of Oldenburg, the heir to which was Alexander's brother-in-law.

Alexander's ukase of December 1810, which imposed high tariffs on French imports and opened his ports to neutral shipping, was a repudiation of the Continental System and convinced Napoleon that Russia was bent on war and a return to the English alliance.

At the beginning of 1811 Napoleon was warned by his Polish ally, Prince Poniatowski, that Alexander was planning a surprise attack on the relatively weak French forces left beyond the Elbe. Alexander had, in fact, sounded his friend, Prince Adam Czartoryski, about the possibility of rallying the Poles to his side: but Czartoryski warned him that only a Russian pledge of a united, autonomous Poland would wean the Poles from France. Alexander's approaches to Austria, Prussia, and Sweden were equally discouraging, and he drew back.

By August 1811 Napoleon had made up his mind that a showdown with Russia was inevitable. One more 'good battle' would settle all his problems. It would convince Europe of the impossibility of further resistance, seal up the gaps in the Continental System, and so bring England to her knees. It would mean nothing less than the mastery of the world. To the Comte de Narbonne, a *grand seigneur* and reputed illegitimate son of Louis XV, who had rallied to the Empire after being King Louis XVI's Minister of War in 1792, Napoleon hinted early in 1812 at his ultimate ambition: 'Alexander was as far as from Moscow when he marched to the Ganges. I have said this to myself ever since St Jean d'Acre.' Narbonne's private comment on this conversation was, 'What a man! What ideas! What dreams! Where is the keeper of this genius? It was half-way between Bedlam and the Pantheon.'

Caulaincourt, recalled from Russia in June 1811, warned Napoleon of the difficulties of the climate, the obstinacy of the Russians and their plan of luring him into the interior by a defensive strategy. Napoleon replied: 'Bah! a battle will dispose of the fine resolutions of your friend Alexander and his fortifications of sand. He is false and feeble.' Caulaincourt had guessed Alexander's new strategy correctly. Writing to the King of Prussia at the end of May 1811 Alexander said, 'The system which has made Wellington victorious in Spain, and exhausted the French armies, is what I intend to follow —avoid pitched battles and organize long lines of communication for retreat, leading to entrenched camps.' In April 1812 he told Czartoryski, 'A rupture with France seems inevitable. The object of Napoleon is to destroy or at least to humiliate the last Power in Europe which remains independent of him. He wishes all our trade with neutrals to be stopped but this is the only trade left to us.'

Nevertheless Napoleon had not forgotten the campaign of Eylau in 1807, nor did he ignore the difficulties of an invasion of Russia. Immense preparations were under way in the second half of 1811, and he fixed the month of June 1812 for the start of the campaign. He told one of his Councillors that he was embarking on 'the greatest and most difficult enterprise that I have so far attempted'. He wrote to Eugène in December 1811 that 'A Polish war is quite unlike the Austrian war; without supply-trains, everything will be useless.' Despite his commitments in Spain, Napoleon could mobilize six hundred thousand men in Poland, including the vassal and allied states. Of these a quarter of a million would be French, and the Imperial Guard, which Napoleon now regarded as the decisive and invincible weapon, would amount to not less than fifty thousand men.

In August 1810, Napoleon had issued to Bessières detailed instructions on the organization of the Guard, providing
for a reserve of a hundred battalions, which would bring its
strength up to eighty thousand men. Unlike the Guard formations of other armies, it was to be a self-contained force of
all arms, and its superb artillery was commanded by Drouot,
'le sage de la Grande Armée'. The expansion of the Imperial
Guard has often been explained by historians as a desperate
measure to offset the deterioration in quality of the line-
regiments. This may be true in relation to the campaign of
1813; but at the time when this important memorandum was
drawn up Napoleon was not faced with a shortage of manpower. Napoleon's plans for the Guard were cut short by the
Russian campaign; it was destroyed in the snows of Russia,
and had to be rebuilt in 1813 from the barest cadres. If this
superb fighting force had remained in being, Napoleon might
well have remained unbeatable in the field.

In the diplomatic campaign preceding the invasion Napoleon was out-manoeuvred. In March 1812 he constrained
both Prussia and Austria to sign agreements providing auxil-
iary corps for the Grand Army. But his peace offer to England in April 1812, on the basis of Portugal for the
Braganzas, Spain for Joseph, and Sicily for Ferdinand, ex-
King of Naples, was rebuffed. Swedish opinion was reduced
to desperation by the hardships of the Continental System
and the French occupation of Swedish Pomerania in January
1812. Bernadotte brought Sweden over to the Russian side in
April 1812, in return for Russian aid in the conquest of Norway. At the end of May 1812 the Turks finally signed the
Peace of Bucharest with Russia. Alexander was thus relieved
of anxiety about his northern and southern flanks, and could
concentrate his forces. Even so, his two main armies under
Barclay de Tolly and Bagration numbered no more than 160,-
000 men against the 450,000 which Napoleon brought across
the Niemen on June 25, 1812.

On June 6 Napoleon sent orders to his Ambassador in St
Petersburg to ask for his passports; and for Kurakin, the Russian Ambassador, to leave Paris. On June 22 he issued a
proclamation to the Army: 'This second Polish War will be
as glorious for French arms as the first has been: but the
peace we shall conclude will carry with it its own guarantee,
and will terminate the fatal influence which Russia for fifty
years has exercised in Europe.' Alexander's proclamation emphasized that it was a defensive war against an aggressor.

His last attempt at negotiation was the mission of General Balachov, who was received by Napoleon at Vilna on July 1 with boasts about the overwhelming size of his army. After the interview he told Caulaincourt: 'I have come to finish once and for all with the colossus of the barbarian North.' Yet a month later he told him: 'I am only waging a political war against Alexander; we can soon agree if he will negotiate.'

It is significant that the campaign of 1812 was the first in which Napoleon had a marked superiority of numbers. In accumulating such a mass of uneven quality, Napoleon defeated his object, which was to bring about another Austerlitz or another Friedland. Mobility was lost in the vast, empty spaces. Despite his careful organization of supply, commissariat broke down within a few days of crossing the Niemen. Only the Guard were amenable to march discipline, and pillaging, sickness, and desertion were soon rife on an unprecedented scale. By the time the army reached Vilna, twenty thousand horses had died, and wastage was equivalent to the losses of two big battles.

Napoleon would have done better with an army of half the size and higher quality. The disparity of numbers left the Russians no option but to avoid battle and repeatedly disengage; though their rearguard actions were fought with a courage and obstinacy which astonished even the French veterans. The Russian retreat was, in fact, dictated by necessity rather than by a coherent strategy. At the opening of the campaign Alexander was at headquarters, and under the influence of Phull, an *émigré* Prussian with a bogus reputation as a strategist, pinned his faith to the entrenched camp at Drissa. This was soon seen to be an illusion and a death-trap, and by July 18 Alexander was persuaded to leave the army to its Generals. But no commander-in-chief was appointed, and there was acute enmity and distrust between Barclay and Bagration, who complained that 'Minister Barclay himself is running away, yet he orders me to defend all Russia.'

While Napoleon failed to catch Barclay at Vilna, King Jerome and Davout, on the right wing, also failed to trap Bagration. Napoleon blamed his brother Jerome for his dilatory movements, and wrote to him on July 4, 'You compromise the success of the campaign on the right wing. It is impossible to make war in this way.' He was told in future to accept orders from Davout: but rather than submit to this

humiliation, Jerome preferred to retire in disgust to his
Kingdom of Westphalia.

Napoleon was delayed in Vilna by the political problem of
Lithuania. A deputation from the Warsaw Diet hoped that
Napoleon would proclaim the restoration of the Kingdom of
Poland. But Napoleon, bound by his engagements to Austria,
refused to speak the only word which could efface the de-
plorable impression made by the pillaging of the army. Prussian Poland showed no enthusiasm for its 'liberation'. The
troops, supplies and guerrilla fighters which Napoleon had
visualized never appeared.

Although the camp at Drissa was found abandoned, Napoleon was confident that the Russians would stand at Vitebsk;
Murat in the centre and Davout on the right wing had
fought stiff actions at Ostrovno and Moghileff. Napoleon was
correct in thinking that Barclay and Bagration were hoping
to unite and stand at Vitebsk and on July 27 he was in contact with Barclay's whole army. But Barclay now heard that
Bagration was deferring the junction till Smolensk: while
Napoleon prepared his attack for the 28th, Barclay slipped
away in the night.

At Vitebsk Napoleon conferred with Berthier, Murat and
Eugène, who implored him to halt the campaign, in view of
the enormous wastage and lack of supplies. He announced
that the campaign of 1812 was over, but two days later he
changed his mind and continued to advance. The Marshals'
reluctance was swept aside with the remark that 'I have made
my Generals too rich; they think only of pleasures, of hunting, of rolling through Paris in their magnificent carriages.
They have grown sick of war.' It was inconceivable to Napoleon that the Russians would surrender Smolensk or Moscow
without a fight. 'The very danger pushes us on to Moscow.
The die is cast. Victory will justify and save us.'

On August 17 at Smolensk, Napoleon thought he had at last
brought the Russians to bay. He was in no hurry to capture
the city, because he wanted a decisive battle: Junot was sent
ahead across the Dnieper to cut the Moscow road. But the
enveloping movement failed, through Junot's hesitancy; after
a two-day bombardment, Barclay abandoned the burnt-out
shell of Smolensk. Ney and Murat caught up with the Russian rearguard at Valutino on August 19, but, even at the
cost of six thousand casualties, did not succeed in halting
the Russian withdrawal.

Napoleon's striking force was now reduced to 160,000 men,

and the odds against a decisive victory were lengthening. A German captain, Roeder, recorded in his diary: 'Even if the Emperor manages to reach Moscow, unless he can first strike such a blow as to put Russia out of action, it will be impossible for us to hold the capital during the coming winter.' But he added later, 'Who, if he had been given the choice, would not have dared to gamble?' At Smolensk, Napoleon had reached the point of no return. Moscow was now only two hundred miles away: to halt the campaign at this stage would mean a humiliating retreat. On August 25 he resumed the advance.

On August 20 Alexander yielded to the pressure of public opinion and appointed Kutusov as Commander-in-Chief. Though sixty-seven and older than his years, no opponent could have been more dangerous to Napoleon. After his experience in the Austerlitz campaign, Kutusov never made the mistake of underrating Napoleon. When one of his aides spoke contemptuously of Napoleon, Kutusov replied: 'Young man, who gave you the right to jeer at one of the greatest of men? Stop all this unseemly abuse.' He knew that public opinion would force him to fight a battle for Moscow, but he would run no risks, and rely on the Russian spaces and the Russian climate as the decisive weapon. Clausewitz, in his account of the 1812 campaign, wrote, 'Kutusov, it is certain, would not have fought at Borodino where he obviously did not expect to win. But the voice of the Court, of the Army, of all Russia forced his hand.'

On September 5 Napoleon found the Russians entrenched on the banks of the river Moskova, their centre resting on the village of Borodino. He rejected Davout's advice to turn the Russian left wing: his one anxiety was to avoid another Russian withdrawal, by pinning them down with a frontal assault. He had 130,000 men available, with six hundred guns. Kutusov had slightly more and heavier guns, in prepared redoubts, but his 120,000 men included 10,000 crudely armed and trained militia from Moscow.

The main French attack started at dawn on September 7, and by the end of the day the Russian positions had been captured, but the Russian Army had not been broken; only seven hundred prisoners were taken. Many of his Generals criticized Napoleon for refusing to throw in the Guard at the climax of the battle. But the French casualties had been enormous—thirty thousand men and more than forty generals. Napoleon complained that 'these Russians get killed like machines: they are not taken prisoner. They are fortresses which have to be demolished by cannon.' Plagued by a heavy feverish cold, and the news of Marmont's defeat at Salamanca, he did not control the battle as closely as usual, and was not in a position to judge the extent of the much greater Russian casualties—over fifty thousand. 'If I throw in the Guard, with what shall I fight tomorrow?' Caulaincourt affirms that Berthier and Murat strongly advised him to withhold the Guard. At St Helena Napoleon said: 'The most terrible of all my battles was the one before Moscow. The French showed themselves worthy of victory, and the Russians worthy of being invincible.'

Kutusov made the difficult decision to abandon Moscow. 'As long as the army exists and is in a condition to oppose the enemy, we preserve the hope of winning the war: but if the army is destroyed, Moscow and Russia will perish.' On September 14 Napoleon saw the cupolas of Moscow sparkling in the sun. Marshal Ney, writing later to his wife, said: 'His joy was overflowing. The Russians, he thinks, will sue for peace, and I shall change the face of the world. Alas! how short was this moment of happiness!'

Napoleon expected to be met by a deputation of *boyars*. Instead he entered a silent, deserted city. That night fires began, and raged for five days, fanned by a strong wind. At first Napoleon attributed it to looting by drunken troops, but the fire-pumps had been removed, and it became clear that it was planned. The Moscow Police Superintendent's report leaves no doubt that the Governor, Rostopchine, gave the orders. Napoleon was unable to return to the Kremlin until September 18, where he awaited emissaries from Alexander. Kutusov encouraged fraternization between his Cossacks and Murat's cavalry outposts, in order to lull Napoleon into a false sense of security. Caulaincourt refused to undertake a mission to St Petersburg, and assured Napoleon that it was useless: finally Napoleon despatched General Lauriston on October 4.

In 1811, Alexander had told Caulaincourt, 'Convey to Napoleon this honest and final notice that once the war has begun—one of us, either Napoleon or I, Alexander, must lose his crown.' Napoleon was unable to grasp the fact that Alexander would not, and could not negotiate. The Tsar knew well that he would be deposed and assassinated if he tried to do so. On September 19, Alexander's sister wrote to him frankly: The capture of Moscow has caused intense irritation. Dissatisfaction has reached the highest point, and your person is far from being spared.' He was received in public with coldness and suspicion. In these trials Alexander fortified his spirit by reading the Bible, and his religious mysticism was confirmed by the apocalyptic experiences of 1812. Regardless of class, the Russian people were united in hatred of the invader. Napoleon had actually drafted an Edict of Emancipation of the serfs, but it had scant chance of rallying support after the events of the last few months.

Napoleon ignored Caulaincourt's warnings about the onset of the Russian winter. 'Caulaincourt imagines himself frozen already.' He declared that the Russian autumn was as fine as at Fontainebleau; he talked of marching on St Petersburg, of wintering in the Kremlin, of returning to Smolensk by the undevastated southerly road through Kaluga. He appears to have made no effort to discover the facts about winter in Russia, or to prepare his troops for it. Only Caulaincourt, on his own initiative, had the horses of Napoleon's household shod for ice. In fact, the records show that in 1812 October was unusually mild, that November was slightly colder than the normal, and that only in December and January did exceptional frosts set in.

On October 18 Kutusov surprised and defeated Murat at Winkovo, and Napoleon was forced to realize that the hope of peace negotiations was an illusion. On the 19th he left Moscow by the Kaluga road, with an army still a hundred thousand strong, but encumbered with its loot, its sick and wounded and its six hundred guns. Mortier was left with orders to blow up the Kremlin, a wanton and uncharacteristic act, which reflected Napoleon's desperate state of mind. His intention was to force Kutusov away from the Kaluga route, and to avenge the defeat at Winkovo. 'It must not be said in France that a check has forced us to retreat.'

On October 24 he found the way barred by the Russians at Malojaroslavetz, and in a desperate day's fighting, in which Eugène's Italian corps distinguished themselves, he lost five thousand casualties. To persist would mean a big battle on the following day, with casualties he could no longer afford. During the night he narrowly escaped capture by a surprise attack by Cossacks. Ironically, Kutusov was equally shaken, and refused to renew the battle. Having lost another week, Napoleon resigned himself to regaining Smolensk by the way he had come, hurrying past the dreadful battlefield of Borodino.

The first snow did not fall till November 5, but already the army was disintegrating through sheer hunger. Foraging was made impossible by the harassing of Cossacks and partisans. On November 7 Napoleon wrote that 'the cavalry is on foot, because the cold has killed all the horses.' But Caulaincourt explains that neither the cavalry nor the artillery had a single horse specially shod. 'Most of our losses must be attributed to this want of shoeing, that is, to our lack of foresight.' Napoleon, with the vanguard, reached Smolensk on November 8, but it proved to be a bitter disappointment. Most of the stores had been consumed by the reserves and communication troops, and discipline had collapsed to such an extent that rations could not be fairly distributed.

It seemed now that nothing could save the army from encirclement and destruction. Kutusov's main army, still fifty thousand strong, despite wastage, had attacked the French rearguard at Viazma on November 3, and Eugène had to send back two divisions to help Davout. On leaving Smolensk on November 14 with the Guard, Napoleon found Kutusov waiting for him at Krasnoi. To the astonishment of the Russians, Napoleon took the offensive in order to gain time for his remaining corps to join up. The Guard, which had been withheld at Borodino, were now thrown in, and such was their confidence that Kutusov was intimidated. If it is arguable that the Guard might have turned the scale at Borodino, it is certain that without them Napoleon could never have returned from Russia. Davydov, the Russian partisan leader, describes how 'the Guard with Napoleon passed through our Cossacks like a hundred-gun ship through a fishing-fleet'.

Napoleon dared not wait for Ney, commanding the rearguard, and gave him up for lost. From Orcha on the 20th he wrote: 'I have no news of Ney: I have given him up.' But the retreat was to be Ney's finest hour. He refused to surrender, spurred his men to a series of fantastic feats, crossed the Dnieper northwards over the ice, and rejoined Eugène's corps near Orcha, with eight hundred men left out of eight thousand.

On November 22 Napoleon received news that Minsk, his next supply depot, had been captured, and, two days later, that his bridgehead over the Beresina at Borissov had been destroyed. He was now looking into the abyss of disaster, and told Caulaincourt to burn his papers and prepare his personal arms. Wittgenstein, the commander of the northern Russian army, had beaten Victor and St Cyr, commanding the corps in reserve, at the end of October. Admiral Tchitchagov from the south had contained Schwarzenberg's flank-corps and advanced to Borissov. If Wittgenstein and Tchitchagov joined hands, there was no hope left. Meanwhile Napoleon had abandoned and burnt his pontoon train at Orcha.

Napoleon ordered Victor to hold Wittgenstein in check, and Oudinot to recapture Borissov, and make a feint of establishing a crossing to the south of the town. Meanwhile the brilliant sapper General Eblé (who died of exhaustion in January 1813) had improvised two bridges at Studianka to the north. The ruse deceived Tchitchagov into keeping his forces to the south of Borissov. On the 26th the cavalry swam across the Beresina and Oudinot's corps followed. On the 27th Napoleon and the Guard and all but Victor's corps crossed without opposition. By the evening of the 27th the Russian commanders had caught up, and Partouneaux' division of Victor's rearguard was surrounded and forced to surrender. It was the only unit of the *Grande Armée* to do so.

On November 28 there was violent fighting on both banks of the river, but Victor brought across his rearguard in the course of the night. The following morning Eblé set fire to the bridges, two hours after the time-limit. Including the reserve corps of Victor and Oudinot, fifty thousand effectives had got through, but thousands of stragglers fell to the Russian guns on the left bank of the Beresina. In a hurried letter to his wife, dictated to a staff-officer on the banks of the Beresina, Ney described the retreat. 'The Army marches covered in great snowflakes. The stragglers fall to the lances of the Cossacks. As for me, I cover the retreat. Behind, files the Army with broken ranks. It is a mob without purpose, famished, feverish. The Grand Army is surrounded by the Russians on the banks of the Beresina. It is necessary to construct a bridge. At the order of General Eblé, three hundred sappers hurl themselves into the icy water with a sublime devotion. The crossing begins and the Russian shells fall into the middle of this crowded mass, jostling and pushing—a dreadful sight. General Famine and General Winter, rather than the Russian bullets, have conquered the Grand Army.'

On November 29 Napoleon wrote to his Foreign Minister,

Maret, at Vilna, 'Food, food, food—without it there are no
horrors that this undisciplined mass will not commit at
Vilna. Perhaps the army will not rally before the Niemen.
There must be no foreign agents in Vilna; the army is not a
good sight today.' But there was worse to come. In the
first half of December the real cold set in, with frosts of
thirty degrees.

On December 6, at Smorgoni, Napoleon told his Marshals
that he was leaving for Paris, accompanied only by Caulaincourt. Murat was left in command, with Berthier as his
chief of staff. He read out a draft of his twenty-ninth Bulletin, describing the retreat. 'I will tell all.' Published on December 16, it was frank about the horrors of the retreat,
but everything was attributed to the unexpected severity of
the winter.

The Bulletin ended with the astonishing statement: "His
Majesty's health has never been better'; but it was not put
in without reason. On November 5, Napoleon had received
the news of General Malet's conspiracy which exploited rumours of his death. It was essential for him to be in Paris to
forestall the effect of the Bulletin, and to organize a new
army. It was not his troops who accused him of deserting
the army. Caulaincourt remarks that 'Not one murmur
against the Emperor was heard in the whole course of this
disastrous retreat.' It was his coolness and his presence in
the face of utter disaster that had kept them going. Caulaincourt was proud of the fact that the Emperor's household
was so well organized. 'Only the Emperor had been well
served throughout this retreat: he always had white bread,
linen, his Chambertin, good oil, beef and mutton, rice and
beans or lentils, his favourite vegetables.' Unannounced and
travelling with the barest escort, Napoleon arrived at the
Tuileries on the night of December 18–19.

Napoleon made a mistake in leaving Murat, rather than
Eugène, in command. Murat and Berthier had lost their
nerve, and gave no orders. Murat wrote to Napoleon on December 11 despairingly: 'Every human effort is hopeless to
remedy the disorder. One can only resign oneself.' By the
middle of January Murat handed over the army to Eugène,
and retired to Naples, on the plea of shattered health. On
December 12, Berthier reported to Napoleon: 'The whole
army is completely disbanded, even the Guard which has
only 400–500 men. Twenty-five degrees of cold and heavy
snow on the ground are the cause of the disastrous state of

the army, which no longer exists.' Murat had refused to
stand at Vilna, and on December 10 on the icy hill of
Ponarskaia, the last guns of the Guard, the baggage, and
the army-treasure were abandoned to the Cossacks.

When Ney, still in fighting trim, led the rearguard over
the Niemen on December 14, he had barely a thousand
men fit for action. When the stragglers regrouped behind
the Niemen, less than forty thousand men of the Grand
Army, excluding the flank-corps of MacDonald and Schwarzenberg, had survived.

14

Leipzig and Abdication

IN HIS ADDRESS TO the Senate on December 20, 1812, Napoleon wrote, 'My army has had some losses, but it was due to the premature rigour of the season.' On January 4, 1813, he ordered officers and cadres to be withdrawn from Spain, and wrote to Berthier on January 9: 'Everything here is in movement. Nothing lacks, neither men nor money nor goodwill, but we need cadres.'

Even when the full extent of the disaster to the *Grande Armée* was known in Europe, few could have predicted that the year 1813 would see the collapse of the Napoleonic Empire. The Russian army had suffered nearly as much as the French, and arrived at the Niemen with barely forty thousand effectives. Kutusov would have been content to halt at the frontier, and considered that it was no business of Russia's to liberate Europe. His death in April 1813 was a relief to Alexander, who now, under the influence of Stein, was determined to finish with Napoleon once and for all. He received unexpected encouragement when General Yorck, commander of the Prussian contingent, signed, on his own initiative, a Convention of neutrality at Taurroggen on December 30, and Schwarzenberg withdrew his Austrian contingent. Yielding to the patriots, King William signed a treaty of alliance with Russia at Kalisch on February 28, 1813, and authorized the calling out of the *Landwehr*. By the beginning of March, Eugène's weak covering forces had to retire behind the Elbe.

The way was still open to Napoleon to deal with the threat of a new coalition by skilful diplomacy and timely concessions, exploiting the war-weariness of Europe, the sovereigns' fear of popular movements, and their territorial jealousies. Talleyrand showed at the Congress of Vienna how this could be done when he wrote to Louis XVIII in January 1815: 'Now the coalition is dissolved.'

But such a policy would mean renouncing the 'Grand Empire' and the Confederation of the Rhine. If Napoleon had offered peace on the basis of the natural frontiers at the beginning of 1813, all France would have rallied to their defence, and the Powers would hardly have sustained a struggle to wrest them from France. In April 1813 the Emperor Francis wrote to Napoleon: 'Every prolongation of war, which does not allow the sovereigns to devote themselves seriously to stamping out the Jacobin ferment, which daily spreads, will soon threaten the existence of thrones.' Stein, the hero of the patriots, and administrator of the liberated German territories, was already being nicknamed 'the Emperor of Germany'. Under his influence the Tsar and the King of Prussia issued a proclamation from Kalisch which ended with the startling words: 'Germany, rejuvenated, vigorous, united, will once again take its place with advantage among the nations of Europe.' In March 1813 Metternich repudiated and suppressed the plans of the Archduke John and Hormayr for reviving the insurrection in the Tyrol. In his report to the Emperor Francis on his interview with Napoleon at Dresden in June 1813, Metternich regrets that Napoleon did not respond to his pleas that 'If your Majesty loses this opportunity what limit can there be to revolutions?'

In his Memoirs, Metternich presents himself as the arbiter of Europe who lured Napoleon to destruction by a subtle and far-sighted diplomacy. According to this version his peace negotiations were never genuine, but only intended to brand Napoleon as the warmonger, and to gain time to complete the Austrian mobilization and bring her over to the side of the Allies. The great French diplomatic historian, Sorel, accepted and developed this theme, which justified Napoleon's intransigence.

But the views of the Emperor Francis and of Metternich, as expressed in 1813 and as late as February 1814, point to the different interpretation that they would have preferred a negotiated peace which would perpetuate a Bonaparte-Habsburg dynasty in France. In June 1813 the Emperor Francis had no confidence in the ability of Russia and Prussia to withstand Napoleon, and feared that 'armed mediation' would expose him to Napoleon's vengeance. A Russian victory would be equally unwelcome. The English agent in Vienna reported in December 1812 that 'a General Peace is the everlasting theme of the Austrian Minister; all thoughts of resisting or of being able to resist the power of France are far removed from his mind'. Even after the news of the retreat from Moscow he reported that 'The Court is extremely jealous of Russia and would unwillingly see and still less contribute to her becoming the preponderant Power on the Continent. Austria, in a word, wishes for the humiliation in a certain degree, but not the total destruction of Bonaparte.'

At the Congress of Vienna, Princess Bagration remarked to Metternich, 'You find it more difficult to divide the booty than you did to conquer Napoleon.' He replied: 'That is why, Madame, I wished to keep him. That is the whole clue to my politics.' Metternich's diplomacy was so supple and evasive that it was adapted to any eventuality. He recognized, from the end of 1812, that a reasonable, negotiated peace, however desirable, was likely to be psychologically impossible for Napoleon. If so, the issue must be settled by force, and Austria must be prepared, by way of 'armed mediation', to throw in her lot with the allies.

Napoleon was not ready to face the loss of prestige involved in the sacrifice of the 'Grand Empire'. The critical attitude of the Legislature at the beginning of 1813 convinced him that it would also mean the end of his autocracy in France. As he explained to Metternich at Dresden in June 1813, 'Your Sovereigns born on the throne can let themselves be beaten twenty times and return to their capitals. I cannot do this because I am an upstart soldier. My domination will not survive the day when I cease to be strong and therefore feared.' He told Caulaincourt as they travelled from Smorgoni to Paris in December 1812, 'In this world there are only two alternatives—to command or to obey.' Thus the suspicion spread in French public opinion, and even among the Marshals, that Napoleon was no longer fighting for France, but to satisfy his own personal pride. Schwarzenberg, returning to Paris as Ambassador in April 1813, reported that 'Napoleon seemed like a man afraid of being deprived in other people's opinion of the prestige surrounding him'. 'Everybody, without exception, is tired of the war. Everything depends on a single man—the Emperor.'

In January 1813 Napoleon made a derisory offer to Austria to maintain the alliance—merely the return of her Illyrian provinces. He refused to believe that the Emperor Francis would ever fight against his son-in-law, and in order to emphasize the dynastic tie, he conferred on the Empress Marie-Louise the position of Regent during his absence from France. Yet Metternich had already proposed 'mediation' and expressed the view that only a general peace settlement would satisfy Austria.

If Napoleon rejected a peace settlement based on a 'European balance'—an issue on which he had already parted company with Talleyrand in 1807—the alternative must be rapid and ruthless military action. He had good grounds for thinking that by the spring of 1813 he would have an ample superiority of numbers in Germany against the Russians and Prussians, who together would have no more than a hundred thousand men. The conscripts of the 1813 age-group had already been summoned to the colours in September 1812; he now summoned the 1814 age-group, and combed out those of 1809–12. In addition a hundred thousand of the National Guard were made available for foreign service. On paper six hundred thousand men would be available for the campaign of 1813, and one hundred and fifty thousand could be mobilized in Germany by April. The material lost in Russia could be replaced in quantity if not in quality. The greatest difficulty was the shortage of cavalry: the loss of eighty thousand horses in Russia was irreparable. On April 24 Napoleon wrote, 'I would be in a position to settle the affair quickly if I had fifteen thousand more cavalry, but I am rather weak in this arm.' The trained cavalry still locked up in Spain might well have turned the scale in the campaign of Germany. He admitted at St Helena, 'After Russia I should have made a bargain with Spain, at Valençay, as I had with the Pope. With this army I should have been master of Germany.'

When Napoleon joined Eugène on April 28, 1813, he planned to capture Leipzig and draw the allied army away from its bases. Blücher attacked Ney's corps at Lützen,

south-east of Leipzig, on May 2; a general engagement ended
in an allied retreat, but Napoleon's manoeuvre to attack the
allied flank and rear miscarried. It was only a partial victory, but it was enough to bring the King of Saxony and his
army back to the French alliance.

On May 20 the allies again accepted the battle at Bautzen;
the following day Napoleon hoped that Ney would arrive in
time from the north to crush the allied right flank and rear.
Again the manoeuvre failed to be decisive, though the allies
were shaken and despondent.

On June 4, Napoleon agreed to an armistice, and a Peace
Congress at Prague. He wrote to his Minister of War, 'I
decided on an armistice for two reasons, my lack of cavalry,
which prevents me from making decisive blows, and the hostile attitude of Austria.' His young conscripts had fought
magnificently, but they were not trained for forced marches,
and wastage through sickness was excessive. The Generals
were war-weary and depressed by the loss of Bessières at
Lützen and of Duroc at Bautzen. 'The turn of the wheel of
fortune had ravaged these souls of iron,' wrote Baron Fain,
Napoleon's secretary.

Narbonne, Napoleon's ambassador in Vienna (whom Napoleon judged, at St Helena, to be the best of his diplomats
after Talleyrand), had already warned him in April that Austrian terms for mediation would include not only the return
of Illyria, but the suppression of the Duchy of Warsaw and
of the Confederation of the Rhine. Metternich announced
that 'Austria cannot fight to maintain the Confederation of
the Rhine for France'. After Lützen, Metternich appeared
to lower his terms—only the French annexations in Germany of 1810 were to be given up, in addition to Illyria and
the Grand Duchy of Warsaw. Napoleon was well aware that
these terms were only preliminary bases for negotiation,
which would be raised in the course of a Peace Congress.
If he was unwilling to accept the Rhine frontier, was there
any point in negotiating?

But he was now caught in a diplomatic trap; if he refused
to accept Austria's mediation, Metternich would be able to
brand him in the eyes of France and Europe as the eternal
warmonger, who had refused ostensibly favourable peace-
terms. Meanwhile he tried a separate peace-negotiation with
the Tsar through Caulaincourt, who was rebuffed. The Tsar
and the King of Prussia had already signed treaties on June
14 with Castlereagh's representatives, which pledged them,

in return for subsidies, to make no separate peace. Napoleon succeeded only in alarming Metternich, who drew closer to the allies. On June 24 at Reichenbach, Metternich agreed that Austria would declare war on France and join Russia and Prussia if France had not accepted by July 20 four conditions for a preliminary peace—dissolution of the Duchy of Warsaw, enlargement of Prussia, restoration of Illyria to Austria, cession of the Hanseatic towns and North German territories annexed in 1810.

On June 26, Metternich had a long interview with Napoleon at Dresden. It was the last time they were to meet. Although Metternich's account has obviously been touched up in retrospect, it agrees substantially with the record left by Fain, Napoleon's secretary. Their conversation lasted nine hours, and was sufficiently dramatic. It was the moment of truth, not only for two completely contrasting personalities, but for a whole historical epoch: the confrontation of the old order and the new.

Napoleon told Metternich, 'I have offered you Illyria as the price of neutrality. Do you agree? If I accept your policy I am required to evacuate Europe, half of which I still hold, lead back my legions across the Rhine, the Alps and the Pyrenees and, signing a treaty which amounts to a vast capitulation, deliver myself like an idiot to my enemies, and rely for a doubtful future on the generosity of those whom today I am conquering. It is my father-in-law who entertains such a project! In what position does he want to put me in face of the French people? He deceives himself if he thinks that in France a mutilated throne can shelter his daughter and grandson. Everything confirms that I have made an irreparable mistake in marrying an Archduchess of Austria. I wished to unite the past and the present—gothic prejudices and the institutions of our century. I was mistaken and I see now the full extent of my error.' Metternich held to his position. 'Between Europe and the aims you have hitherto pursued there is an absolute contradiction. Your treaties have never been more than a truce. Today you can still conclude peace; tomorrow it may be too late.'

Metternich came away convinced that a genuine negotiation with Napoleon was impossible. The news of Joseph's defeat at Vittoria reached Napoleon the same night, and when it was known in Germany it removed the last chance of Austrian neutrality. Nevertheless the following day Napoleon agreed to an extension of the armistice till August 10 and to a

Peace Congress at Prague. Napoleon welcomed the chance
of building up his army: so also did Schwarzenberg, the
Austrian commander. Both sides regarded the Congress as a
sham, and the allies refused to meet Caulaincourt in plenary
session until the preliminary conditions had been accepted.
Napoleon refused Caulaincourt the authority to do so, and
wrote on August 4: 'There is nothing doing at the Congress of Prague. There can be no result, and the Allies intend to denounce the armistice on the 10th.'

By that date Napoleon had brought his forces in Germany
up to nearly 470,000 men. He now had forty thousand cavalry, and the Guard numbered over fifty thousand. In June
he had written to his Minister of War: 'In most battles the
Guard artillery is the deciding factor, since, having it always
at hand, I can take it wherever it is needed.' On the other
hand, the Russians and Prussians had greatly increased their
forces; with the adhesion of Austria and Bernadotte's Swedes,
the allies entered the autumn campaign with over half a
million men, and ample reserves. They were grouped in
three armies—the north under Bernadotte, the centre (Silesia)
under Blücher, the southern (Bohemia) under Schwarzenberg. Moreau had joined allied headquarters from the USA,
and Jomini, Napoleon's Swiss staff-officer, had deserted to the
allies. Of Jomini, Napoleon wrote, 'He is a soldier of no
great note, but he is a writer who has grasped some ideas
of war.' These men, like Bernadotte, were familiar with
Napoleonic strategy, and their advice was sound. Moreau
told the Tsar: 'Expect a defeat whenever the Emperor attacks
in person. Attack and fight his lieutenants whenever you can.
Once they are beaten, assemble all your forces against Napoleon and give him no respite.'

Napoleon's attitude in the autumn of 1813 was strangely
hesitant and defensive. His normal strategy would have led
him either to concentrate his forces behind the Elbe, and
await the opportunity to attack converging forces successively, as he had so brilliantly done in the campaign of 1796,
and was to do again in 1814; or to deal rapidly with the
Army of the North, and then, reinforced by the northern
garrison, turn on Blücher and Schwarzenberg. But doubts
about the mobility of his raw recruits and about the loyalty
of his Saxon ally persuaded him to base his operations on
Dresden.

He detached inadequate forces to the north, and advanced
against Blücher. The news that the Army of Bohemia was

attacking Dresden brought him back by forced marches. In a two-day battle in the suburbs of Dresden (August 26–7) Napoleon won a brilliant tactical victory; but he failed to turn the allied retreat into a rout. Napoleon, as well as his troops, was exhausted and ill after five days' incessant marching and fighting in heavy rain, and Vandamme, entrusted with the pursuit, ran into a trap and was forced to surrender at Kulm (August 30). Meanwhile Oudinot had been defeated by Bülow and Bernadotte at Gross Beeren (August 23); MacDonald was defeated by Blücher at the Katzbach (August 26). Napoleon was unable to follow up the disorganized Army of Bohemia: he again failed to catch Blücher, and Ney, sent to the north, lost fifteen thousand men at Dennewitz (September 6). After the narrow escape from disaster at Dresden (where Moreau was killed), the allies were following with increasing success Moreau's legacy of advice. Twice again Blücher evaded Napoleon's clutches, and these abortive marches wore down Napoleon's army. In the two months since the armistice the balance of numbers, through losses in battle, sickness and desertion, had irretrievably tilted against Napoleon.

Belatedly he decided to fall back and await the chance of striking separately at the converging armies. On October 13 he wrote to Ney that 'undoubtedly a great battle will take place at Leipzig'. Even so, he had left strong forces with St Cyr at Dresden and with Davout at Hamburg, and could concentrate only 160,000 men against an allied total of more than 300,000. On October 15, he could have overwhelmed Schwarzenberg before Blücher and Bernadotte came up, but he waited for Ney to join him. On October 16, his offensive against Schwarzenberg did not start till 2 pm and bogged down. On the following morning it was clear to Napoleon that the three allied armies had joined up, but he did not prepare for a retreat until the 18th.

The fighting on the 18th and 19th was a holding operation to allow an orderly retreat, which was precipitated by the desertion of the Saxons on the left wing on the 18th. In the confusion of the retreat through the city of Leipzig, the one bridge over the Elster was blown up too soon, and the rearguard was trapped. The French losses amounted to sixty thousand, including twenty thousand prisoners; the allied casualties were no less.

Meanwhile Bavaria had gone over to the allies on October 18, and Wrede's army barred Napoleon's retreat at Hanau

on October 30. The Guard and its artillery were still intact,
and summarily disposed of the Bavarians. But the 100,000
men who got away from Leipzig had melted to 60,000 by
the time Napoleon crossed the Rhine on November 2; more
than 100,000 remained locked up in the German fortresses.

Although the eastern frontier of France was now wide open
to the immense allied forces, they hesitated to invade. The
memories of the French *levée en masse* which had defeated the First Coalition in 1792–4 weighed on them. Metternich, increasingly suspicious of Alexander's patronage of
Stein in Germany and of Bernadotte as a possible successor to
Napoleon in France, was willing to attempt another peace negotiation. If Napoleon accepted the offer, which was still unlikely, Metternich could reassure his allies, as at Reichenbach,
that the preliminary terms could be modified. If Napoleon
refused to negotiate, he would lose the support of French
public opinion and the French war effort would be undermined.

Baron St Aignan, French Minister at Weimar and brother-
in-law of Caulaincourt, had been captured and could be
used as an intermediary. He met Napoleon in Paris on November 15, and let it be known freely in the Paris salons
that the Allies were offering peace on the basis of the 'natural
frontiers'—the Rhine, Alps and Pyrenees. The best counter
to Metternich's peace propaganda would have been an immediate public declaration from Napoleon that he would
accept peace on these terms. But he still hesitated, dreaming
of a military miracle; it was not till the end of November
that he replaced Maret by Caulaincourt as Foreign Minister,
and authorized him to accept the St Aignan proposals.

In the meantime the allies had published the Declaration
of Frankfort of December 4 in evasive terms: 'The Powers
guarantee to the French Empire an extent of territory unknown to France under her kings.' Twenty thousand copies
were printed for distribution in France. In the sessions of
the Senate and Legislature which opened on December 9, Napoleon refused Caulaincourt's advice to publish the St Aignan terms and his acceptance. Consequently Fontanes in the
Senate, and Lainé in the Legislature, were able to refer to the
Frankfort Declaration, and, by calling on Napoleon to accept
it, gave public opinion the impression that Napoleon was still
refusing peace terms.

Lainé went further and persuaded the Legislature to pass

an address demanding civil and political liberties. Napoleon thereupon prorogued the Legislature: 'You are not the representatives of the nation. The true representative of the nation is myself. France has more need of me than I have need of France.' On the Frankfort terms, he would only say, 'The foreigner will either retire or sign the conditions which he has himself proposed. There is no longer any question of recovering the conquests we have made.'

On January 4, Napoleon wrote to Caulaincourt, 'I think it doubtful whether the allies are acting in good faith, and that England wants peace. I have accepted the Frankfort basis, but probably the allies have other ideas; their propositions have only been a mask.' The English Government had, in fact, been alarmed by the Frankfort proposals, and it was decided that Castlereagh, the Foreign Secretary, must himself go to Allied Headquarters. In his Instructions of December 26, the independence of Holland and Antwerp, of Spain and Portugal, were to be the *sine qua non* of English participation in a general peace: if the war went well, he was to favour the restoration of the Austrian Netherlands and of Piedmont. Subject to these conditions, subsidies of five million sterling were to be offered to the Allies. Castlereagh's own opinion was that 'peace with Bonaparte, whatever the terms, will never be popular, because no one will believe that he can submit to his destiny'.

As soon as Castlereagh arrived at Basle, Metternich realized that the Frankfort terms were out of date, because he needed Castlereagh's support against the Tsar's intrigue with Bernadotte. Castlereagh reported to the Cabinet that 'We may now be considered as practically delivered from the embarrassment of the Frankfort proposals.' When the peace conference with Caulaincourt opened on February 7 at Châtillon-sur-Seine, he was told that the terms were no longer those of Frankfort but the frontiers of 1792.

The patent war-weariness of France had now made the Allies over-confident. Napoleon made half-hearted efforts to revive the spirit of 1793 by ordering barrel-organs to play the *Marseillaise*, and appointing *Commissaires* to the Departments: but in contrast to the *Représentants en Mission* of the Convention in 1793, they were elderly and exhausted imperial officials, with an average age of sixty. When Napoleon's advisers talked of the 'spirit of 1793', he was sceptical. 'Rouse the nation, when the Revolution has destroyed the nobles and priests and I myself have destroyed the Revo-

lution?' Only in the eastern departments were there local
stirrings of the peasants, roused by the pillaging and indis-
cipline of Prussians and Cossacks. Wellington reported from
the south of France in November 1813, 'All except the
officials are sick of Bonaparte, because there is no prospect
of peace with him.'

The nemesis of the Napoleonic autocracy was all too clearly seen; for nearly fifteen years he had asked for nothing
but passive obedience. The Minister Réal wrote to Savary,
the Minister of Police: 'Where today are the men one
could employ for carrying out a big and bold measure?
For ten years have they not scattered, persecuted, extinguished almost all the energetic men who rendered such great
services at the decisive epoch of the Revolution?' As an eye-
witness Stendhal wrote, 'In January 1814 the most vital people in Europe were, as a nation, nothing better than a
corpse. That was what despotism did to one of the greatest
geniuses who ever lived.'

In spite of flagging impetus, the imperial administrative
machine could still grind out a certain number of conscripts.
On November 12 Napoleon wrote to Eugène, 'I am trying to
raise 600,000 men.' In October, before Leipzig, he had summoned to the colours 120,000 men from the older age-groups,
and 160,000 men from the 1815 age-group. In November, a
comb-out of the older age-groups from 1803 was intended to
produce 300,000 men. In December and January, the National Guard were mobilized, some of them for active service in
the field. Of all this mass of manpower on paper, barely
120,000 saw active service in 1814, owing to wholesale evasion of the call-up and shortage of equipment. The announcement of heavy increases in taxation merely inflamed opinion without producing results. The *Domaine Extraordinaire*
had been exhausted by the 1812 and 1813 campaigns; there
remained only the last reserve, Napoleon's private *Trésor des
Tuileries*, which sank from 75 to 10 millions between January and April 1814. The army contractors had to be content
with promissory notes.

When Napoleon left Paris for the army at the end of January 1814 he said to Berthier, 'Come, we must repeat the campaign of Italy.' As a military *tour de force* the campaign of
1814 will stand comparison with that of 1796. Wellington
long afterwards said that 'the study of it has given me a
greater idea of his genius than any other. Had he continued
that system a little while longer it is my opinion that he

would have saved Paris. But he wanted patience. He did
not see the necessity of adhering to a defensive warfare.'
This comment does not take account of the political factor
which was decisive. Napoleon's 'system' of attacking the flank
and rear of the allied march on Paris presupposed that Paris
would hold out, at least for a certain number of days, as a
fortified base. On January 12 he had given orders that Paris
was to be prepared as a fortress. Once the allies had reliable
information that Paris would not resist, Napoleon's bluff was
called. It was here that Napoleon made an error, possibly
fatal (which he was later to regret bitterly)—the appointment of Joseph, in compensation for the loss of his Spanish
crown, as Lieutenant-General to the Empress' Council of
Regency.

The disparity of numbers in 1814 was far greater than in
1796. In January 1814, Napoleon told one of his Ministers
confidentially that he would be lucky to collect forty thousand men. He would be starting the campaign with an inferiority of at least one to four. He hoped that, given time,
his agreement to restore Ferdinand to Spain would release
some of the divisions from Suchet's Army of Catalonia.
Meanwhile his one asset was the incomparable Guard. He
also ordered Eugène's Army of North Italy to fall back
through the Alps to Lyons. Murat had at last decided to become 'the Bernadotte of the South'. As early as April 1813
he had opened secret negotiations with Metternich but drew
back and joined Napoleon at Dresden and Leipzig. In January 1814 he signed an alliance with Metternich, and marched
north with thirty thousand men to support the Austrians in
Italy. On January 30 he issued a proclamation from Ancona
denouncing the 'mad ambition of Napoleon'. Murat's intrigues were known to Napoleon, and he wrote on February
13: 'The conduct of the King of Naples is infamous, and
the Queen's unspeakable. I hope to live long enough to
avenge for myself and for France such an outrage and such
horrible ingratitude.'

By a nice twist of fate Napoleon's first encounter with
Blücher on January 29, which was successful, was at Brienne,
where he had been a schoolboy. But on February 1 he found
Blücher and Schwarzenberg combined, at La Rothière, suffered heavy casualties, and had to fall back on Nogent. The
Allies assumed that Napoleon was finished, and the Austrians
and Prussians began their march on Paris.

On February 8 he received Caulaincourt's report on the

new allied peace terms at Châtillon. In an agony of despair he gave Caulaincourt *carte blanche* to sign, and wrote to his brother Joseph: 'I tell you again, in a word, that Paris will never be occupied while I live. If Talleyrand is involved in this idea of leaving the Empress in Paris if the enemy arrives, it is treason. I repeat—beware of this man. I have done so for sixteen years, though I have even favoured him, but he is certainly the greatest enemy of our House, ever since fortune has abandoned him. If I lose a battle and there is news of my death, you will hear of it before my family. Get the Empress and the King of Rome to leave for Rambouillet: order the Senate, the Council of State, all the troops to gather on the Loire. Never let the Empress and the King of Rome fall into the hands of the enemy. . . . I would prefer my son to be killed rather than see him brought up in Vienna as an Austrian prince. Still, it is possible that if the enemy marches on Paris, I should defeat them.'

Early the following morning Napoleon received news from Marmont that the allied armies had separated; Schwarzenberg was marching on Paris by the Seine valley, Blücher by the Marne. He exclaimed, 'Now it is another matter. I am going to beat Blücher, who is marching up Montmirail.'

At Champaubert (February 10, 1814) and Montmirail (February 11) he caught Blücher's Russian corps in flank and rear, and inflicted heavy casualties. On the evening after Champaubert Napoleon boasted, 'If we beat Sacken tomorrow, the enemy will retreat across the Rhine quicker than he crossed it, and I shall again be on the Vistula.' After Montmirail he wrote to Joseph that 'The Old Guard has exceeded all that I could expect from an *élite* corps. It was absolutely like the head of Medusa!'

On February 14 Napoleon caught Blücher himself at Vauchamps and routed him; Blücher lost ten thousand men. He now turned on Schwarzenberg and won an inconclusive victory at Montereau (February 18); it was to be his last. Schwarzenberg retreated hurriedly and offered an armistice. Napoleon now told Caulaincourt that he would only treat on the Frankfort terms: he even sent a message to Eugène to stand fast, as 'there was a hope of keeping Italy'. He urged Augereau, unaccountably inactive at Lyons, 'to forget his 56 years and remember the great days of Castiglione'.

But from this point everything started to go wrong for Napoleon. Castlereagh rallied the allies from the shock of the recent reverses, and persuaded them at the beginning of

March to sign the Treaty of Chaumont, which pledged them against any separate peace, and bound them to continue the war, if necessary, for twenty years. Soult had been beaten at Orthez at the end of February, and on March 12 the standard of Louis XVIII had been raised at Bordeaux.

At the beginning of March Napoleon was still hoping to crush Blücher before Schwarzenberg resumed his advance. While Marmont was pushed westwards by Blücher, Napoleon moved north from Troyes to take him in the rear. The manoeuvre was ruined by the sudden capitulation of the French commander at Soissons. On March 7 in a stiff battle at Craonne, Napoleon lost six thousand men which he could not afford: in the following two days, he was fighting in inferior force at Laon. On March 11 he wrote despondently: 'The Young Guard melts away like snow.'

But when Joseph wrote to him after Craonne that 'after this new victory, you can sign with glory peace with the ancient limits', Napoleon defiantly replied: 'Today as at Austerlitz I am the master.' He was furious on hearing from Marie-Louise that Joseph was trying to organize an address to the Emperor from the Council of State and the National Guard in favour of peace. He replied: 'Everyone has betrayed me. Will it be my fate to be betrayed also by the King? . . . Mistrust the King: he has an evil reputation with women, and an ambition which grew upon him whilst he was in Spain.' He wrote to Savary on March 14: 'Let them know that I am still the same man as I was at Austerlitz and Wagram. I want no tribunes of the people: let them not forget that I am the great tribune.'

Napoleon now decided to move back to the Seine and threaten Schwarzenberg. Meanwhile he had recaptured Rheims, and cut up General St Priest's Russian division. On the 19th he had crossed the Seine and Aube, and cut the main road from Paris to Troyes. But Schwarzenberg's forces were not as dispersed as he had hoped; on the 20th he repulsed General Wrede's Bavarian corps at Arcis-sur-Aube, but the following day he found Schwarzenberg's whole army concentrated. Outnumbered by three to one he only extricated himself from disaster with considerable loss.

With dwindling numbers, his intention now was to retire eastwards, collect reinforcements from his garrisons in Lorraine, and, in conjunction with the local partisan resistance, operate against the allied line of communications. If Paris held out this plan offered a considerable chance of turning the allied march on Paris into a precipitate retreat.

But it was ruined by two fatal leakages of information. On March 10, Vitrolles had arrived at Châtillon with a message from Talleyrand revealing the weakness of Napoleon's political hold on Paris. On March 23, allied patrols captured a courier carrying a letter from Napoleon to Marie-Louise, in which he rashly revealed his plans. 'I decided to make for the Marne and his [the enemy's] line of communications, in order to push him back further from Paris and draw nearer to my fortresses. I shall be at St Dizier this evening.' The first reaction of the allied Generals to this news was to pursue Napoleon, but Alexander persuaded them to ignore him, and to march on Paris with their united armies.

Marmont and Mortier had barely twenty thousand men to cover the capital, and they were roughly handled at La Fère-Champenoise on March 25. On March 30 the last battle was fought at Montmartre; on that night Marmont signed the capitulation of Paris. Unaware of the capture of vital information, Napoleon could not believe that the Allies would hurry on to Paris, while he threatened their communications. It was not till March 27 that news reached him of the situation in Paris, and he arrived at Fontainebleau on March 31, only to learn of Marmont's capitulation a few hours before.

Could he have expected the capital to hold out longer? On a purely military calculation it was reasonable to do so. He refused to listen to Joseph's complaints that there were no muskets available, and wrote that, 'it is the first time I have heard that a population of 300,000 men cannot survive for three months.' Partly out of fear of arming the populace, Joseph had raised no more than twenty thousand National Guards. There were masses of cannon at Vincennes, but hardly any gunners to serve them. Alexander himself had said that it was essential for Paris to capitulate within twenty-four hours; otherwise difficulties of supply and anxiety about their lines of communication would force the allied army to retreat.

But the crucial failure was political—the weakness (if not worse) of King Joseph and the treachery of Talleyrand. Joseph used Napoleon's letter of February 8 to convince the Empress and the Council of Regency that the Court must leave for Rambouillet on March 29. But he ignored Napoleon's instructions that not only the Court but the whole of the Government should also leave. Talleyrand arranged

to stay in Paris by the simple process of presenting himself
at the City barrier without passports, and being turned
back. Joseph's action therefore ensured that the dynasty
would be doubly handicapped: the chances of a Regency
were greatly diminished by the departure of the Empress,
and a Government was left in Paris to negotiate with the
enemy.

The Empress complained of this decision in a letter of
March 29 to Napoleon, but she had not the strength of will
to contest it. 'They insist on my going, only M. Boulay and
the Duc de Cadore, with myself a third, are opposed to the
idea. I should have been quite brave enough to stay, and I
am very angry that they would not let me, especially when
the Parisians are showing such eager determination to defend
themselves. . . . But the whole lot of them have lost their
heads except me, and I hope in a day or two you will be
telling them I was right in not wanting to evacuate the capital for a mere 15,000 cavalrymen who would never have got
through the streets. I am really angry at having to go, it
will have terrible disadvantages for you, but they pointed
out to me that my son would be running into danger, and
that was why I daren't contradict them once I had seen the
letter you wrote to the King.'

For Talleyrand treason was 'a matter of dates', and he had
prepared for any eventuality, including an assurance from
Louis XVIII that he had been forgiven. He afterwards maintained that he voted at the Council of Regency that the
Empress should remain in Paris only because his opinion
would sway the decision the other way. But on March 17
he wrote: 'If the Emperor were killed we should have the
King of Rome and the Regency of his mother,' and he told
Caulaincourt a few days later that everything was lost by
the departure of the Empress.

There was no manifestation of support for the Bourbons in
Paris, until the allied forces marched into the city wearing
white arm-bands. This was purely a military precaution
to identify the allied troops, but it was misunderstood to
mean that the allies had declared for the white flag of the
Bourbons. Alexander himself was hostile to the Bourbons
until he met Talleyrand. On April 1, Talleyrand formed a
provisional government, and two days later persuaded the
rump of the Senate to proclaim the deposition of Napoleon.

There was still one card left in Napoleon's hand, at least
to save the throne for his son—the loyalty of the army. On

April 2 Caulaincourt met Alexander, and reported to Napoleon that, while the allies were firm in their refusal to negotiate with him, the possibility of a Regency was not excluded and Alexander pledged himself to secure a suitable retirement for Napoleon, such as Elba.

When Napoleon still talked of marching on Paris the Marshals, led by Ney, Lefebvre and Moncey, rebelled. On April 4 Ney told Napoleon bluntly: 'The army will not march.' 'The army will obey me.' 'The army will obey its chiefs.' Napoleon thereupon wrote out a conditional abdication, provided that his son was first recognized as his successor. Caulaincourt, MacDonald, Ney, Marmont were appointed to take this offer to Paris. Meanwhile Marmont had been flattered by Talleyrand with the prospect of playing the part of General Monk. While Caulaincourt was pleading with Alexander the cause of the Regency and the Marshals had emphasized that the Army would fight rather than accept the Bourbons, a message was brought to the Tsar that Marmont had signed an armistice with Schwarzenberg, and that his troops were already moving into the Austrian lines. When Napoleon heard of Marmont's defection, he exclaimed: 'Unhappy man! His fate will be worse than mine.' The Marshals now insisted on unconditional abdication, and Napoleon signed on April 6. 'You wish for repose. All right—you shall have it.' On the same day the Senate under the leadership of Talleyrand voted the recall of Louis XVIII.

15

The Hundred Days and
Waterloo

THE TREATY OF FONTAINEBLEAU of April 11, 1814, signed
by the allies and Napoleon, guaranteed him the title of Emperor, the sovereignty of Elba with a revenue of two million
francs from the French funds: and to the Empress Marie-
Louise the Duchy of Parma with reversion to her son, and
pensions for the Bonaparte family. Napoleon stayed at Fontainebleau till April 20, deserted by all his Ministers but Caulaincourt; even his valet Constant and his Mameluke, Roustam, left him at the end. We owe to Caulaincourt's memoirs
a detailed, sober, and moving account of these days of fallen
grandeur.

Napoleon took little interest in the arrangements about
Elba, and his letters to Marie-Louise, now at Blois, were
strangely evasive. He would not order her to Fontainebleau,
and she sent him alarming accounts of her health. On April 8
he wrote: 'I am sorry to have nothing left but to have you
share in my evil fortunes.' On the 10th he sent a message
to Méneval, the Empress' secretary: 'Try to penetrate the real
intentions of the Empress, and to find out whether she pre-
fers to follow the Emperor amid all the hazards of his ill-

217

fortune, or to retire, either to a State which would be given to her, or to the Court of her father, together with her son.' On the 11th he wrote to her: 'You are to have at least one mansion and a beautiful country when you tire of my island of Elba, and I begin to bore you, as I can but do when I am older and you still young. . . . My health is good, my courage unimpaired, especially if you will be content with my ill-fortune and if you think you can still be happy in sharing it.'

While Napoleon was too proud and too ashamed to force Marie-Louise to join him, she was too weak to act on her own initiative. On April 8 she wrote to Napoleon that she had resisted strong pressure from Joseph and Jerome Bonaparte to seek Austrian protection: 'So now I am waiting orders from you, and I do beseech you to let me come.' But on the 10th she wrote that 'if you agree to let me go and see my father, I feel sure, almost positive, that I can get Tuscany'.

The failure of his wife to join him with the King of Rome added to Napoleon's depression: he must have guessed that once they were in the hands of the Emperor Francis and Metternich he was unlikely to see them again. On April 12 Caulaincourt brought him the draft Treaty of Fontainebleau to sign, and Napoleon remarked, 'I shall not need anything; a soldier does not need much space to die in'. He dined alone with Caulaincourt and talked at length about his reign, as if, Caulaincourt recalls, 'he was talking of someone else'. He was still unable to see the basic contradictions in his policy. 'The oligarchy fear me because I am the king of the peoples.' The next moment he complained that 'I have behaved to the Kings as a sovereign, they have behaved to me like Jacobins. That is the reward of my generosity.' Finally he told Caulaincourt that 'life had become intolerable'.

His chamberlain, Turenne, had taken the precaution of removing the powder from his pistols; but in the small hours Caulaincourt was summoned to Napoleon's bedside, where Napoleon confessed that he had taken poison. 'I did my best to get killed at Arcis.' But the poison came from the phial which Napoleon had carried in the retreat from Moscow, and had lost its potency. After severe vomiting and convulsions Napoleon survived, and was able to appear the following day. He never contemplated suicide again, and the secret was so well kept that the attempt remained an unconfirmed rumour until Caulaincourt's detailed eyewitness account in his memoirs (which did not appear until 1933) corroborated the recollections of Constant and Méneval.

Napoleon's recovery was helped by the arrival of a scribbled note from Marie-Louise, now on her way to Rambouillet to see her father. 'I am sending you a few lines by a Polish officer who has just brought me your note to Angerville; you will know by now that they have made me leave Orléans and that orders have been given to prevent me from joining you, and even to resort to force, if necessary. Be on your guard, my darling, we are being duped, I am in deadly anxiety on your behalf, but I shall take a firm line with my father. I shall tell him that I absolutely insist on joining you, and that I shall not let myself be talked into doing anything else.' On April 15 Napoleon wrote, 'You must have met your father by this time. I wish you to come to Fontainebleau tomorrow, so that we may set out together for that land of sanctuary and rest, where I shall be happy— provided you can make up your mind to be so and to forget worldly greatness.'

On his way to Elba and through the summer he continued to suggest plans to Marie-Louise for joining him, but the letter he had received from the Emperor Francis before he left Fontainebleau had confirmed his worst fears of Metternich's intentions for his wife and son. 'I have decided to propose that she should pass some months in the bosom of her family. Her need of rest and quietness is urgent, and Your Majesty has given her too many proofs of real attachment for me to doubt that you will share my wishes on the subject and approve of my decision. Once she has regained her health, my daughter will proceed to assume the sovereignty of her country and this will naturally bring her near to Your Majesty's place of abode. It is superfluous, I take it, for me to assure Your Majesty that her son will be accepted as a member of my family, and that during his residence in my dominions he will enjoy his mother's constant care.'

If the discovery (in 1934) of Napoleon's letters to Marie-Louise had not been completed by the discovery (in 1955) of Marie-Louise's letters to Napoleon, it would be possible to believe that Napoleon's second marriage was never more than a *mariage de convenance*, and that Marie-Louise remained the 'Austrian heifer sacrificed to the Minotaur'. When Marie-Louise heard the news of Napoleon's death in 1821 she wrote to her friend Victoire de Poutet: 'Although

I never entertained any strong sentiment of any kind for him, I cannot forget that he is the father of my son, and far from treating me badly as most people believe, he always manifested the deepest regard for me—the only thing one can expect in a political marriage.'

But it is impossible to read her long, spontaneous, and affectionate letters to Napoleon, right up to May 1814, without coming to the conclusion that, at the time, she was genuinely in love with him. She had been brought up to believe that Napoleon was a monster: but she had inherited a strongly sensual nature from her father, and the discovery that Napoleon was not only a passionate, but a considerate lover, altered her ideas. On April 24, 1810, she had written from Compiègne during her honeymoon to Victoire, 'Heaven has granted your prayers—may you soon enjoy a happiness equal to mine.' At the same time she wrote to her father about Napoleon. 'I find that he gains considerably by closer acquaintance; there is something very captivating and forceful about him which it is impossible to resist. I cannot thank God enough for granting me such great happiness and you, dear Papa, for not listening to my entreaties. . . .' On March 20, 1814, she wrote to Napoleon: 'I have been thinking about you so much today, it is three years since you gave me so moving a proof of your love that the tears come whenever I think of it, so it's an exceedingly precious day to me.' This was the anniversary of the difficult birth of the King of Rome, when Napoleon insisted that the mother's life should be saved, even if it meant losing the child.

When Marie-Louise returned to Vienna her grandmother, the formidable Marie-Caroline of Naples, sister of Marie-Antoinette and implacable enemy of Napoleon, gave her strong advice. 'Your father, my son-in-law, was never my ideal, but now I consider him criminal. He is entirely pushed from side to side by Prince Metternich, and between them they are behaving like scoundrels. The unscrupulous manner in which they are depriving the Emperor Napoleon of his only consolation in his misery is atrocious. If they still oppose your reunion, you must defy them. If they are adamant you must tie the sheets of your bed to your window and escape disguised. That is what I would do.'

When Marie-Louise insisted on setting out for a cure at Aix-les-Bains, still hoping to escape to Napoleon, her son was kept in Vienna, and Metternich chose as her aide-de-camp

General Neipperg, a subtle and accomplished lady-killer. By September he had seduced Marie-Louise and became her lover. The memory of Napoleon faded and she had two children by Neipperg before Napoleon died. As Duchess of Parma, she married Neipperg after Napoleon's death, and when he died, married her Prime Minister, the Comte de Bombelles.

She had proved to be pitiably inadequate to a tragic destiny, and she was no match for Metternich's cynical manipulation, backed by the dominating influence of her father. Both before and after her marriage she had led too sheltered an existence to develop any initiative. All her life she remained dependent on personalities nearest to her. Prokesch von Osten, the King of Rome's one intimate friend when he grew to manhood, wrote of Marie-Louise: 'One cannot attribute her faults which led to the fall of her husband and his death in exile, and her subsequent vagaries, except to the pernicious result of the education of Viennese girls, incapable of decision and consequently a prey to the first seducer.' Her private diaries, left behind in the Tuileries in her hurried flight in March 1814, show that even as Empress she was hardly more than a schoolgirl. On February 2, 1814, she had written to Napoleon pathetically, 'I myself am growing very brave since your latest successes, and I hope I don't deserve to be called a child any longer— that's what you used to like to call me before you went away.' The fate of the King of Rome, in the hands of Metternich, was to be infinitely more tragic.

It was arranged that Napoleon should travel to Elba, escorted by detachments of his Guard, under General Drouot, his Grand Marshal Bertrand, and four Allied Commissioners. Sir Neil Campbell, the English Commissioner, records his first meeting with Napoleon. 'I saw before me a short, active-looking man, who was rapidly pacing the length of his apartment, like some wild animal in his cell. He was dressed in an old green uniform with gold epaulets, blue pantaloons, and red topboots, unshaven, uncombed, with the fallen particles of snuff scattered profusely upon his upper lip and breast.' On the morning of his departure, April 20, Napoleon again referred to the separation from his wife and child, 'and the tears actually ran down his cheeks'.

There followed Napoleon's farewell to his Old Guard in the courtyard of the Château of Fontainebleau, now known as the *Cour des Adieux*. After explaining the reasons for his

abdication, Napoleon concluded: 'I have sacrificed all my
rights, and am ready to sacrifice my life, for the aim of
my whole life has been the happiness and glory of France.
. . . The happiest occupation of my life will henceforward
be to tell for posterity your great deeds, and my only consolation will be to know all that France is doing for the
glory of her name.' With this scene, so congenial to the
poets and artists of the Romantic Movement, the Napoleonic
legend was already taking shape.

Napoleon unwisely chose the Rhône Valley route to the
south (now the *Route Nationale 7*), possibly because he still
hoped to meet Marie-Louise on the way. At first Napoleon
was received with cries of *'Vive l'Empereur'*, but as he approached Provence, hostile demonstrations increased. Provence, with its fanatically royalist factions, was to be the
scene of the savage White Terror after Waterloo, in which
Marshal Brune was assassinated. At Avignon his carriage was
stopped by an ugly crowd, and for a few minutes there was
a risk of his being lynched. A few miles further on, at Orgon,
he was forced to see himself hanged in effigy. Napoleon
feared, not without reason, that Bourbon agents were being
sent to organize his murder. As for the Provençaux, 'They
can shout, but they are good for nothing else.'

His nerve, never good in the face of mob hysteria, temporarily broke. He disguised himself in an Austrian uniform,
and refused to touch the food in the local inns. On the last
lap of his journey he stayed with his sister, Pauline, at her
villa at Le Luc. Campbell noted that 'it was evident during
his stay at Fontainebleau and the following journey that
he entertained great apprehension of attacks upon his life,
and he certainly exhibited more timidity than one would
have expected from a man of his calibre'. Napoleon admitted to the Austrian Commissioner, General Koller, 'As
you know, my dear General, I showed myself at my very
worst.'

He felt much safer in the English frigate *Undaunted,* which
carried him to Elba, and enjoyed his conversations with
Captain Ussher about naval warfare. Ussher recalled Napoleon's 'unfailing cordiality and condescension', and Napoleon always spoke of him with regard and affection. A year
later, this impression was to have important effects.

On May 4, Napoleon took possession of Elba, and hoisted a
new flag, with the emblems of the imperial bees. The etiquette
of his miniature court was strictly maintained, and his

dominion of 112,000 souls was organized with the energy which had been applied to the whole of Europe. Inevitably, the English press indulged in bad puns about 'lack of Elba-room'. Campbell complained, 'I have never seen a man in any situation of life with so much activity and restless perseverance. . . . His thoughts seem to dwell perpetually on the operations of war.' Seven hundred volunteers from the Old Guard (nearly double the number stipulated by the Treaty of Fontainebleau) arrived after a march through Italy.

Madame Mère and Pauline arrived in July to keep him company. Pauline had written to her mother, 'We must not leave the Emperor alone. It is now that he is un-happy that we must show our attachment to him.' Madame Walewska brought her son for a secret visit of a few days. Napoleon amused himself by cheating at cards with his mother and sister, and playing practical jokes on Bertrand, such as slipping a fish into Bertrand's pocket, and then ask-ing him for a loan of his handkerchief. English visitors found Napoleon corpulent and affable, lavish with assurances that he was now a 'dead man'. A Cambridge undergraduate thought that 'his figure is decidedly the reverse of heroic'. But, as Castlereagh had feared, Elba was close enough to the mainland to allow plenty of information to reach Na-poleon: and he was keeping a close watch on developments in France and at the Congress of Vienna, which opened in October 1814.

Even before he left Paris, Tsar Alexander had said of the Bourbons, 'These people will never establish themselves.' Louis XVIII accepted the bases of the Constitution put for-ward by the Napoleonic Senate to guarantee the revolutionary settlement, but insisted on promulgating it as a 'Charter' freely granted by divine right. Joseph de Maistre, the cham-pion of legitimism, admitted that 'the Bourbons were as un-known in France as the Ptolemies' and that 'Louis XVIII had not returned to the throne of his ancestors; he had sim-ply ascended the throne of Bonaparte'.

Yet the 'cascade of disdain' which had undermined the *ancien regime* started up again. Ney's wife was received at Court as she was of the *noblesse* by birth, but she and her husband were treated with such contempt that they soon refused to attend. No attempt was made to remove the un-popular taxes and conscription which the Comte d'Artois, as Lieutenant-General until Louis XVIII's arrival from England, had promised to abolish. The proposal to return the unsold national lands to their former owners, the Church and the *emigrés*, reopened the whole question of the revolutionary land settlement, and alarmed the middle class and the peasants.

The Government were faced with a difficult problem in demobilizing the Army, still more loyal than the Marshals to Napoleon. A famous, if over-dramatized passage in Chateaubriand's memoirs describes the reception given to Louis XVIII by the Imperial Guard when he entered Paris: 'I suppose that such menacing and terrible impressions have never been seen on the human face. Some, wrinkling their foreheads, made their bearskins fall over their eyes to shut out the sight; some drew down the corners of their mouths in contempt and rage; others showed their teeth, through their moustaches, like tigers. When they presented arms it was with a movement of fury, and the noise of their weapons made one tremble.'

At the start it was hardly tactful to appoint as Minister of War Dupont, the General who had been disgraced by Napoleon for surrendering at Baylen. It would have been a wise precaution either to win over the Guard by making it the Royal Guard, or disbanding it. Instead the *Maison du Roi* was revived, with lavish posts for *emigré* nobles who had never seen a battlefield, and the Imperial Guard was retained, but degraded in status to *'Grenadiers de France'*. In all, thirty thousand officers of the Imperial Army were put on half-pay. The Duc de Berri made himself ridiculous by trying to ape Napoleon's familiarities with his *'grognards'*, who cherished Napoleon's memory under the nicknames of *Jean de l'Epée* or *le Père Violette*. By March 1815, the Generals Lallemand and Drouet were preparing to lead their troops on Paris.

It was evident by December 1814 that the Congress of Vienna had reached a deadlock over the settlement of Germany. Alexander was demanding the whole of Poland, with Saxony as compensation for Prussia. Metternich refused to allow Russia into Central Europe and Prussia on the borders of Austria: Castlereagh wanted Prussia on the Rhine as a buffer state against France. Talleyrand preached the principle of the 'legitimate rights' of the King of Saxony in order to foment the split and to oust Murat from Naples in favour of the Bourbon, Ferdinand. Although the secret treaty of January 1815 between England, Austria and France to resist the demands of Russia and Prussia was not known, it was rumoured that war between the allies might break out at any moment. Murat now felt so uncertain on his throne that he was prepared to raise Italy against Austria, and was secretly in touch with Napoleon.

Apart from these tempting political developments Napoleon could not feel secure in Elba. The Bourbon Government refused to pay the pensions guaranteed by the Treaty of Fontainebleau. Napoleon had left Fontainebleau with some four million francs, partly from the army pay-chest and partly from the treasure removed to Blois: when this ran out, he would be unable to pay his Guard, or live off the Elban revenues. As an additional insult Bourbon agents had, moreover, forged and published a letter purporting to be from Pauline recounting her incestuous relations with Napoleon. There was talk at Vienna of removing him to the Azores, the West Indies or St Helena; and it looked as if the allies were seeking an excuse by provoking him into leaving Elba. Campbell warned Castlereagh that 'If pecuniary difficulties press on Napoleon much longer, I think he is capable of crossing over to Piombino with his troops, or of any other eccentricity.' He was reassured by a meeting with an Under-Secretary of the Foreign Office, who, with singular complacency and lack of prescience, told him, 'When you return to Elba, you may tell Bonaparte that he is quite forgotten in Europe; no one thinks of him now.'

Meanwhile Fleury de Chaboulon, one of Napoleon's *auditeurs*, had arrived at Elba with authoritative information from Maret, his former Minister, about the situation in France. Although the wise Drouot disapproved, the influence of Madame Mère was on the side of adventure. His mother told him 'Go, my son, fulfil your destiny. You were not made to die on this island.' At St Helena Napoleon admitted the decisive motive. 'The fact is that what instigated me to return was the accusation of cowardice; at last I could stand it no longer.' 'It was the talk about his fear of death and his cowardice and, generally speaking, a feeling of despair that had made him go back to France.' Chateaubriand's comment on the Hundred Days was that 'in this fantastic undertaking there lay a ferocious egoism and a terrible lack of gratitude and generosity towards France'.

On February 16, Campbell left for a visit to Italy, and the next day Napoleon ordered his one warship, the brig

Inconstant, to be repaired and stocked for a voyage. When Campbell returned on February 28, he found that Napoleon and his Guard had sailed two days before. The English warship within call was too late to catch up with the *Inconstant*. One of three French ships cruising on the route actually hailed the *Inconstant*, but her captain, whether by error or connivance, was satisfied with the reply that Napoleon was still at Elba. On March 1, 1815, Napoleon was able to land unmolested near Antibes.

Napoleon told his 'handful of braves'—less than a thousand armed men, including a few mounted Polish lancers—that he 'would be in Paris without firing a shot'. He staked everything on his ascendancy over the minds of the French soldier and peasant. The bitter memories of the year before warned him to avoid Provence, and he chose the mountain road through Grasse, Digne, Grenoble, now known as the 'Route Napoléon'.

He was greeted enthusiastically by the peasants of Dauphiné, but the most critical test came before Grenoble, where there was a strong garrison under a royalist commander. Napoleon knew, however, before he left Elba that Colonel La Bedoyère, one of his former aides-de-camp, was in command of one of the regiments. The troops were already restive at the news of Napoleon's approach and when they were paraded for an address from the General, pointing out that Napoleon had only a thousand men, there were shouts from the ranks. 'What about us? Don't we count?'

Informed of these reactions Napoleon took a bold decision when his small force found an infantry regiment barring the road. He ordered his men to trail their muskets, and advancing alone in his familiar grey overcoat, he shouted 'Kill your Emperor, if you wish.' A single shot would have finished the adventure; but the regiment, ignoring all commands to fire, broke ranks and surrounded Napoleon with acclamations of 'Vive l'Empereur'. When Napoleon appeared at the gates of Grenoble the gunners refused to fire and the whole garrison went over to him. 'Before Grenoble I was an adventurer; at Grenoble I was a reigning prince.' The crucial first round had been won.

When the news of Napoleon's landing at Antibes reached Paris on March 5, it was not taken seriously and Ney promised the King that he would bring Napoleon to Paris 'in an iron cage'. The Comte d'Artois and MacDonald were received with hostility by the troops and populace at Lyons, and had to abandon the city. From Lyons Napoleon wrote to Ney a calm and polite order to join him. 'I will receive you as I did on the morrow of the battle of the Moskowa.' Ney was already shaken by the popular rage against the Bourbons, and this appeal to old memories, so subtly calculated, brought him over. He announced to his troops that 'the cause of the Bourbons is lost for ever'.

Napoleon had already sent a secret message to his Guard officers at Metz to ignore their commanders and march on Paris. When Ney's defection was known, Louis XVIII left Paris hurriedly for the north on March 19, and on the evening of March 20 Napoleon was carried up the steps of the Tuileries by a crowd which almost suffocated him in their excitement. As Balzac later wrote: 'Before him did ever a man gain an empire simply by showing his hat?'

The exhilaration of the march from Cannes to Paris which Napoleon recalled as 'the happiest period in my life' did not last long. He remarked to Molé, one of his former Councillors: 'Nothing astonished me more, in returning to France, than this hatred of priests and nobles, which I found to be as widespread and violent as at the beginning of the Revolution. They have reopened everything which had been settled.' Enlightened by La Bedoyère, who told him frankly, 'You can no longer reign in France except on liberal principles,' he had issued from Lyons a proclamation summoning the Electoral Colleges; and pledging himself to a reform of the Constitution. He recalled Fouché as Minister of Police to reassure the Jacobins and combat the royalists. Carnot, a staunch opponent of the autocratic Empire, became Minister of the Interior; even Lucien Bonaparte was reconciled.

Benjamin Constant, protégé of Madame de Staël and leader of the liberal opposition in the Tribunate in 1802, was invited to draft an 'Additional Act to the Constitution of the Empire'. The Council of State and the plebiscite based on universal suffrage were retained; otherwise it followed closely Louis XVIII's Charter, with guarantees of civil liberty, responsibility of Ministers, a hereditary upper house, and a lower house elected on a complicated and restricted franchise. Napoleon professed to be 'inaugurating a constitutional monarchy'. Napoleon told General Rapp, 'My system has changed—no more war, no conquests. Can one be as fat as I am, and have ambition?' He assured the Council of State, 'I have renounced the ideas of the Grand Empire which during the last fifteen years I had only begun to found. Henceforth the happiness and consolidation of the French Empire will be the objects of my thoughts.' The ceremony of the *Champ de Mai* (June 1), the formal promulgation of the *Acte*, was a bizarre and contradictory affair, at which Napoleon appeared for the last time in his velvet pseudo-Renaissance Coronation robes.

On June 7, the Chambers met, and the lower house proceeded to elect as their President not the Government nominee, Lucien Bonaparte, but Lanjuinais, an ex-Girondin revolutionary, and an ideologue of the type most objectionable to Napoleon. Napoleon afterwards admitted that he would have taken the first opportunity to get rid of the Additional Act. He warned the Chambers, 'Let us not imitate the example of the later Roman Empire, which, invaded on all sides by the barbarians, made itself the laughing-stock of posterity by discussing abstract questions when the battering-rams were breaking down the city gates.'

The same pacific assurances were given to Europe, but the diplomatic outlook was now far less favourable than in February. The Congress of Vienna was still sitting, and the allies had resolved their differences over Poland. On March 13, at the instance of Talleyrand, they committed themselves to a proclamation of outlawry against 'Buonaparte'. His breach of the Treaty of Fontainebleau placed him 'beyond the pale of civil and social relations' and he was 'delivered to public vengeance'. From such a novel and drastic application of international law the allies could not recede. Napoleon found in the Tuileries the secret treaty of January 1815 between England, Austria and France and sent it to Alexander, hoping to embroil the allies: it cost Metternich a bad quarter of an hour with Alexander, but made no difference to their plans for mobilization.

Napoleon's only ally was the unreliable Murat, to whom Napoleon wrote at the end of March: 'I will support you with all my forces. I count on you.' Having ruined Napoleon's chances in the campaign of 1814, Murat now rashly moved northwards in April with a Neapolitan army of dubious quality. He was checked at Ferrara by the Austrians, and routed at Tolentino (May 3). When he arrived in the south of France as a refugee, Napoleon refused to employ him or see him.

With a divided and apprehensive nation Napoleon dare not risk a defensive campaign. His only chance was a quick and resounding victory which might rally France behind him and shatter the allied unity. In contrast with 1814 Napoleon now had plenty of veterans, including the returned prisoners of war. The National Guard battalions could be used for fortress duty, to release every available man for the field-army. Napoleon hesitated until June before applying the hated conscription. In March the army had barely two hundred thousand men in service; in June its strength still did not reach three hundred thousand. Of these Napoleon had to leave nearly a hundred thousand, supported by National Guards, to hold the Alps, Pyrenees, Alsace, and even La Vendée, where a royalist resistance movement broke out in May. His available striking force at the beginning of June was no more than 130,000 men.

The choice of available Generals was dangerously limited. Apart from Murat, four of the Marshals, including Berthier, were struck off the list for leaving Paris with Louis XVIII. Napoleon still hoped that Berthier would return. 'That ass Berthier. I will pardon him, but on the condition that he appears before me in his Royal Bodyguard uniform.' But Berthier, exhausted and disillusioned, retired to Bamberg. and fell to his death from a window on June 1. Suchet was left in command of the Alps, and Davout remained in Paris as Minister of War. Soult, without any experience as a chief of staff, filled the place of Berthier; of the available Marshals, Ney was an inspiration to the troops, but his record as an independent commander was dubious, and his mind was desperately troubled by his rapid change of allegiance; Grouchy was a good cavalry-leader, but completely untried in independent command. The faithful Junot had never recovered from the Russian campaign. His mind gave way and Napoleon had to remove him from the Governorship of Venice when he took to parading in the streets of the city clad only in his epaulettes and sabre; he died in 1813.

The allied forces within reach were strung along the Belgian frontier—30,000 English and 70,000 Belgian, Dutch and Hanoverian under Wellington, and 120,000 Prussians under Blücher. The Russian and Austrian armies could not reach the eastern frontiers before July. Napoleon's problem, with markedly inferior numbers, was to prevent a junction of the two allied armies in the north, and to beat them separately. He hoped to surprise them while they were still dispersed; and the concentration of his Army was as brilliantly conceived as ever.

By June 14 he had 120,000 men massed on the frontier

at Charleroi, before Blücher and Wellington were even
aware that he was taking the offensive. The Guard did not
leave Paris till June 5, and Napoleon delayed his departure
till the last minute, June 12. He then told the Marshals that
he intended to operate with two wings and a reserve. This
formation was perfectly adapted to his purpose, as the weight
of the reserve could be thrown on either wing; but it would
require accurate staff work and timing, and a clear grasp of
Napoleon's intentions by the wing commanders. On June 15
the bulk of the French Army was across the Sambre, and in
touch with one Prussian corps.

On that evening, the strategic situation was highly favourable as Napoleon had succeeded in massing his Army within
a ten-mile square between the converging allied forces. Wellington had been slower than Blücher to react, and if
Blücher chose to stand and fight on the following day, he
could be crushed before Wellington's forces appeared in
sufficient strength.

But it was not till midday on June 16 that it became
clear to Napoleon that Blücher was concentrating in force
round Ligny, and at 2 pm Soult sent a message to Ney,
commanding the left wing, that 'the intention of His Majesty
is that you attack whatever is before you and after vigorously
throwing them back, join us to envelop this corps'. Napoleon intended to tie down the Prussians by a frontal assault,
and then smash their right wing, forcing them on a line
of retreat eastwards away from Wellington. 'In three hours
the fate of the campaign will be decided. If Ney carries
out his orders thoroughly, not a man or gun of this army
in front of us will get away.'

Unfortunately Ney's written instructions at no point made
it clear that his action at Quatre-Bras was to be a holding
one, and he was meeting stiffer opposition as the English
reserves came up. At 4 pm General La Bedoyère, using
his authority as the Emperor's aide-de-camp and an unsigned
pencil note, which he may have written himself, diverted
D'Erlon's reserve corps towards the right wing. As soon
as he heard of this Ney, knowing that this corps had been
allotted to his left wing, countermanded the order.

He did not stop to think that this countermanding would
ensure that D'Erlon's corps could not arrive at either battlefield in time. Ney reported to Soult at 10 pm: 'I have attacked
the English position at Quatre-Bras with the greatest vigour:
but an error of Count d'Erlon's deprived me of a final vic-

tory, for at the very moment when the 5th and 9th Divisions of General Reille's corps had overthrown everything in front of them, the 1st corps marched off to St Amand to support His Majesty's left; but the fatal thing was that this corps, having then countermarched to rejoin my wing, gave no useful assistance on either field.'

By 8 pm Napoleon had put in the Guard at Ligny, and had broken and partially routed the Prussians. About eighty thousand men had been engaged on each side: the Prussians had lost sixteen thousand men and the French over eleven thousand. Nightfall prevented Napoleon from completing the rout by launching the cavalry. Blücher gave the order to retire on Tilly and Wavre.

But for the confusion in D'Erlon's orders, Ligny might have been a decisive victory; but the possibilities for the following day were still immense. Napoleon could either complete the rout of the Prussians, or move to the left wing and smash Wellington while the Prussians were still out of action. Yet within a few hours Napoleon had lost the initiative. As the English military historian Captain Becke points out: 'It was in these 12 hours from 9 pm on the 16th to 9 am on the 17th that the campaign was lost.'

It was not till 11 am on June 17 that Napoleon ordered Grouchy to pursue the Prussians with thirty-three thousand men, and the Guard to move to Quatre-Bras. In the meantime Ney had been left without instructions to pin down the English by renewed attacks. When Napoleon joined Ney at 2 pm, Wellington, informed of Blücher's defeat, had disengaged to retire on Mont St Jean. Napoleon's belated and desperate attempts to pin down Wellington in the afternoon of the 17th were delayed by thunderstorms.

On the morning of June 18 Napoleon with seventy-four thousand men faced Wellington with sixty-seven thousand men. Confident that the Prussians were out of action or contained by Grouchy, Napoleon's only fear was that Wellington would retreat. Although he had left seventeen thousand men out of reach at Halle to secure his bases in case of a defeat, Wellington had decided to fight it out, on Blücher's assurance that at least one Prussian corps would reach him by midday. He had chosen his favourite defensive position on a rise, where the reverse slopes would shelter his infantry from plunging artillery fire, and he carefully distributed his English divisions to stiffen the Belgian-Dutch. 'Had I employed them in separate corps I should have lost the battle.'

Napoleon ignored the warnings of his Peninsular War Generals about the fire-power of the English infantry, and decided on a frontal attack on the centre. 'I tell you that
Wellington is a bad General, that the English are bad troops,
and it will be a picnic.' He was in no hurry to start the
battle, and Drouot advised him to let the ground dry out
till midday, so that the twelve-pounder batteries could get
into position.

At 12.30 pm a column approaching on his right flank
was identified as Prussian. Napoleon could have called off
the battle at this point, but the campaign would have been
lost, and he preferred the chance of smashing Wellington
before the Prussians could intervene. If all went well, the
Prussians would be involved in the English rout.

What had happened to Grouchy since he parted from Napoleon on the morning of June 17? In his written orders
to Grouchy, dictated to Bertrand, Napoleon told him: 'Proceed to Gembloux. . . . You will reconnoitre towards Namur
and Maastricht, and you will pursue the enemy. . . . It is
important to discover what the enemy intend doing, whether
Blücher is separating himself from Wellington, or whether
they meditate uniting to cover Brussels and Liège by risking
the fate of another battle. . . . Place cavalry detachments
between us, so as to keep up communication with Headquarters.'

At 2 am on June 18 Napoleon received a message from
Grouchy, still at Gembloux, that one Prussian corps had withdrawn on Wavre. Not till 10 am did Soult dictate a message
to Grouchy to 'direct his movements on Wavre, to draw
near us, and establish communication with us.'

By the time he heard the opening guns of Waterloo
from Walhain, between Gembloux and Wavre, Grouchy correctly judged that it was too late to cross the River Dyle,
and rejected General Gérard's plea that they should march
to the sound of the guns. Soult's subsequent message of
1 pm 'not to lose a moment in drawing near to us, and
affecting a junction with us, in order to crush Bülow whom
you will catch in the very act of concentrating' did not
reach him till 4 pm. By this time Grouchy was engaging
in a frontal assault on the Prussians in Wavre.

If he had displayed more energy and appeared in force
at Wavre on the morning of the 18th he might well have
deterred or decisively delayed the Prussian flank march from
Wavre to Mont St Jean. Gneisenau, Blücher's chief-of-staff,

was, in fact hesitant in committing his army to an advance, even though he estimated Grouchy's force at no more than fifteen thousand men.

In his Memoirs Napoleon was contemptuous of Grouchy: 'Marshal Grouchy with 34,000 men and 108 guns had discovered the secret, which seemed impossible, of being neither on the day of 17th nor the night of the 17th and the morning of the 18th on the battlefield of Mont St Jean or at Wavre.' But his failure was due to a combination of his own inadequacy and Napoleon's errors. Grouchy's defence after the catastrophe revealed his character. 'Inspiration in war is appropriate only to the commander-in-chief, and his lieutenants must confine themselves to executing orders.' This was a doctrine which Napoleon had impressed on his Generals and Ministers only too well in the later years of the Empire. Lacking initiative, authority and energy, Grouchy took refuge in a literal obedience to orders. But the orders he received from Napoleon were lacking in precision and too late.

It is clear from the written instructions to Grouchy of the morning of the 17th and the morning of the 18th that Napoleon did not take seriously the possibility that Blücher would recover from Ligny in time to join Wellington. If he had done so, he would have given precise orders to Grouchy on the morning of the 17th to make for Wavre with all speed and to seize the crossings over the Dyle. It was, moreover, contrary to the principles of his own strategy and particularly of the strategic formation adopted at the start of the campaign, to allow a detached wing to be out of reach for the decisive battle. Napoleon had nearly lost the battle of Marengo by taking this risk, when Desaix was able to rejoin Napoleon in time only because he had been delayed by bad roads.

By his underestimate of Blücher, the more surprising because he had experienced his pertinacity in 1813 and 1814, Napoleon had allowed himself to be strategically outmanoeuvred. But everything could still be retrieved by a tactical triumph on the field of Waterloo. The conduct of the battle was an unimpressive performance by Napoleonic standards, and this was primarily due to the decision to leave the tactical handling of the battle to Ney, whose heart was a great deal better than his head on this occasion. It was also a serious misfortune for Napoleon that Drouot, the great artillery expert, had to replace Marshal Mortier,

commander of the Guard, who was ill; and he was therefore unable to take personal direction of the Guard artillery,
whose commander was killed early in the battle.

At 1.30 pm Ney launched the first main attack, when four
densely massed infantry columns were repulsed with heavy
loss. They were unable even to deploy before they were
decimated by the English volleys, and thrown into confusion
by a well-timed charge of Lord Uxbridge's cavalry. At 3.30
pm Ney misinterpreted movements in the English line as
signs of a general retreat, and sent in the cavalry alone.
For two hours the superb French heavy cavalry were worn
down against the unbroken English squares, and were unable
even to spike the guns which the enemy had temporarily
to abandon. Napoleon exclaimed: 'There is Ney hazarding
the battle which was almost won; but we must support him
now, it is our only chance.'

By 6 pm Napoleon had been forced to use fourteen thousand men of his general reserve to hold up Bülow's Prussians, and when Ney captured La Haye Sainte at 6.30 pm,
and demanded the Guard infantry for a final decisive assault on the English centre, he refused: 'Troops? Where do
you suppose I shall find them? Do you expect me to make
them?'

It was not till 7.30 pm that he released five battalions of
the Guard for Ney's final assault. When this failed, shouts of
despair were heard. 'The Guard is retreating.' As Wellington put in his cavalry, the French Army broke in panic
and rout. Barely eight thousand men escaped in fighting
formation.

Ney's fundamental error was in first sending in the infantry column unsupported by cavalry, and then the cavalry
unsupported by infantry. After the tremendous artillery prepa-
ration, a combined assault of all arms would have forced
the enemy to form into squares, which could then have
been ripped to pieces with caseshot from the horse and divisional artillery. Even as it was, Wellington wrote on the
day after the battle: 'It was the most desperate business
I ever was in: I never took so much trouble about any
battle, and never was so near being beat. Our loss is immense, particularly in the best of all instruments, the British
infantry. I never saw the infantry behave so well.'

Napoleon was so tired at the end of the battle that he
had to be held on his horse as he escaped to Charleroi. It
is evident that, from the start of the campaign, he no longer

had the capacity, on which he had always relied, to ignore fatigue, to make and communicate precise decisions and keep things moving. But on June 19 he was writing to Joseph: 'All is not lost. I suppose that I shall still have 150,000 men, if I collect my forces.'

It was impossible, however, to conceal the magnitude, moral and material, of the disaster; and, remembering his mistakes of March 1814, Napoleon hurried back to Paris. Lucien and Davout advised him to dissolve the Legislature, and proclaim a dictatorship. But Napoleon could not face the prospect of 'reigning by the axe'. 'I should have had to make myself the Marius of the Revolution, and shed blood.'

Within a few hours the decision was out of his hands as the Chambers met the same day that Napoleon reached Paris, June 21, and resolved that a decree of dissolution would be treason. The National Guard were summoned for their protection. On the following day Napoleon signed his second abdication. 'My political life is over and I proclaim my son Napoleon II, Emperor of the French.'

But only a handful of Peers supported Lucien's motion to proclaim Napoleon II, and the Chamber voted for a provisional government headed by Fouché. Throughout the Hundred Days Fouché had prepared the way for the moment when he would take over the part played by Talleyrand in 1814. He would have preferred Louis-Philippe, Duc d'Orléans, to a restoration of Louis XVIII, but the rapid advance of Wellington and Blücher gave him no time to bargain. Davout signed a capitulation of Paris on July 3, and withdrew the Army to the Loire. On July 8 Louis XVIII re-entered Paris 'in the baggage-train of the allies'.

16

St. Helena

ON JUNE 23, 1815 Napoleon asked Decrès, the Minister
of Marine, to prepare two fast frigates at the Atlantic port,
Rochefort. Fouché at first refused to release the frigates
unless they were provided with safe-conduct passes from the
allies. But he had to drop this condition as Napoleon's popularity with the army and the populace was unbroken, and if
the possibility of escape were blocked, he might be driven
to put himself at the head of the army, which was regrouping on the Loire.

Fouché had persuaded Napoleon to leave the Elysée on
June 25 for Malmaison. In a last spurt of energy Napoleon
sent an offer on June 29 to the Provisional Government
to throw back the allies before retiring to the USA. Fouché
refused the offer, but withdrew the stipulation about safe-
conduct, and asked Napoleon to leave for Rochefort 'without
delay, as the Prussians are marching on Versailles'. Their
guns could already be heard from Malmaison, and Blücher,
relying on the allied declaration that Napoleon was an
'outlaw', had sworn to shoot Napoleon if he captured him.
On the evening of June 29 Napoleon left for Rambouillet
incognito, and without escort.

At Malmaison Napoleon had been the guest of his step-

daughter, Hortense, who inherited it on Josephine's death
in May 1814, and he had time to arrange his affairs and
receive visitors. Six million francs from the Tuileries treasure
were handed over to Laffitte, the banker, for safe-keeping.
Hortense insisted on sewing her diamonds into his belt. His
two bastard sons, the Comte Léon and Alexandre Walewski,
were brought to see him. Hortense remarked that Léon was
the 'image of the King of Rome'. Besides Maria Walewska,
two of Napoleon's former mistresses, Madame Duchâtel and
Madame Pellapra, also came. Napoleon's last farewell was
to his mother. The suite which was to follow him to Rochefort was a haphazard collection of courtiers, officers and
servants, some of them with their wives and children.

The last part of the route to Rochefort—Chartres, Tours,
Poitiers, Niort—was on the border of La Vendée, which
might well expose Napoleon to royalist attacks. To his surprise, he was received with popular acclaim at Niort, where
he was recognized by a detachment of a hussar regiment.
Rochefort, which he reached on July 2, was also Bonapartist.
Napoleon rejected the last, lingering temptation to plunge
France into civil war by joining the Army of the Loire,
and considered the various plans of escape offered to him.

Besides the frigates, two sea-captains with smaller vessels
were prepared to run the English blockade. Napoleon's
brother Joseph offered to stay and impersonate him. A quick
decision to run for the USA might well have succeeded,
as Admiral Hotham, commanding the Channel squadron, was
not told till July 5 that Napoleon was making for Rochefort,
and Captain Maitland of the *Bellerophon* received orders to
intercept the frigates only on July 7. But Napoleon hesitated
at the prospect of a furtive, risky and undignified escape; subconsciously the grandiose gesture of an appeal to English
hospitality was forming in his mind.

When, on July 10, Napoleon sent Savary and Las Cases
to negotiate with the commander of the *Bellerophon,* there
was really no alternative left; a Bourbon Prefect was on
the way from Paris to take charge at Rochefort. Captain
Maitland explained that he had orders to intercept the frigates if they put to sea, and he took the initiative in suggesting
that Napoleon should seek asylum with the English. He was
anxious to carry out his orders, and to gain the kudos of
so great a prize; but he was careful to make it clear that
he could offer no guarantees on behalf of the English Government. It must be surrender at discretion.

Three days later Napoleon took the final decision to embark voluntarily in the *Bellerophon*. He knew perfectly well
what was involved, as he told Bertrand: 'There is always a
danger in entrusting oneself to one's enemies, but it is better
to risk relying on their sense of honour than to be in their
hands as a prisoner of war.' He then signed the famous letter to the Prince Regent which now reposes in the Royal
Library at Windsor. 'Pursued by the factions which divide
my country and by the hostility of the Powers of Europe,
I have finished my political career, and I come, like
Themistocles, to sit at the hearth of the British people. I put
myself under the protection of the laws which I claim from
your Royal Highness as the most powerful, constant and
generous of my enemies.' Napoleon's subsequent charges of
perfidy against the English Government were no more than
a bluff. He was banking on the prestige of his name and
the fascination of his personality. Had not his first patron,
Paoli, and his brother Lucien spent many happy years of
exile in England? Had not Captain Ussher and Sir Neil
Campbell proved to be congenial company at Elba?

On board the *Bellerophon*, and in the *Superb*, where Napoleon lunched with Admiral Hotham, Napoleon was treated
as a royal personage. In fact the Admiral went further than
Captain Maitland and made a point of uncovering in Napoleon's presence. On July 23 Napoleon caught a last glimpse
of the coast of Europe off Ushant, and was on the poop
with his spy-glass from dawn till midday. In the ten days
of the voyage Napoleon won the respect and affection of
the officers and the crew. Maitland records that 'from the
time of his coming on board ship, his conduct was in-
variably that of a gentleman'. Lieutenant Bowerbank thought
that, upon the whole, he was a good-looking man, and when
young must have been handsome. 'His manners struck me
as very engaging.' Midshipman Home thought that 'his mouth
had a charm about it that I have never seen in any other
human countenance'. The crew put on a play for Napoleon's benefit, and he remarked that the midshipmen did
well in the female roles.

When Maitland asked his servant what the ship's company
thought of Napoleon, he replied, 'I heard several of them
conversing this morning and one observed, "Well, they may
abuse that man as much as they like, but if the people of
England knew him as well as we do, they would not hurt a
hair of his head." They all agreed.' At Torbay and Plymouth,

boatloads of sightseers besieged the *Bellerophon*. Bowerbank
was 'surprised at not hearing a disrespectful or abusive
word escape from any one. On the contrary the spectators
generally took off their hats when he bowed.' Many years
later Palmerston reminded Queen Victoria that 'The people
of this country are remarkable for their hospitable reception
of foreigners, and for their forgetfulness of past animosities.
Napoleon Buonaparte, the greatest enemy that England ever
had, was treated with respect while at Plymouth and with
consideration while at St Helena.'

By this time Napoleon was discussing hunting and shoot-
ing with Maitland, and was looking forward to the life of
an English country squire. All the more bitter, therefore,
was the moment when Admiral Lord Keith announced to
him the decision of the English Government that his destination was to be St Helena. He was to be treated no longer
as ex-Emperor, but as a General on retired pay. It was particularly embarrassing for Keith as he had to thank Napoleon for the life of his nephew, wounded at Waterloo and
carried to safety by the personal order of Napoleon. He
later wrote to Napoleon of his 'sincere regret' at the 'painful
duty of conveying disagreeable news'. Napoleon asked him
to forward to the Government a formal protest. 'I am not
the prisoner, but the guest of England. If the Government,
in ordering the captain of the *Bellerophon* to receive me,
as well as my suite, desired only to set a trap, it has forfeited its honour and sullied its flag.'

By a Convention signed at Paris on August 2, 1815, the
four allies declared that Napoleon was their prisoner. England was to be responsible for choosing and guarding his
place of confinement; the other three Powers could send
Commissioners as observers. It was only by a narrow margin
that, as Lord Rosebery wrote in his study of Napoleon at
St Helena, *The Last Phase*, 'though no thanks to our Ministers,
we are spared the memory of their having handed over Napoleon to the French Government to be shot like Ney'.
Lord Liverpool, the Prime Minister, had written to Castlereagh, 'We wish that the King of France would hang or shoot
Buonaparte, as the best termination of the business.'

Even if the English Government had been disposed to be
magnanimous, as Lord Holland and HRH the Duke of Sussex
publicly urged, it was politically impossible to keep Napoleon in England. Lord Liverpool reminded Castlereagh: 'You
know enough of the feelings of people in this country not

to doubt he would become an object of curiosity immediately, and possibly of compassion, in the course of a few months.' The behaviour of the Fleet and the demonstrations at Plymouth confirmed this fear. On August 4 Maitland was ordered to leave harbour and cruise off Start Point pending the arrival of the *Northumberland* which, under the command of Admiral Cockburn, was to take Napoleon to St Helena.

Apart from his personal fascination, Napoleon was still the symbol of the Revolution, whom the Whig and Radical opposition would have welcomed and exploited against a shaky Tory Government. Moreover it was a Government committed to support of the Bourbons in France, for whom Napoleon as an exile in England would have been a source of endless alarm and suspicion.

The decision to recognize 'General Buonaparte' but not the 'ex-Emperor' seems both arbitrary and maladroit. As Napoleon remarked, General Bonaparte had not been heard of since Egypt. The question could probably have been settled at the start by a tactful suggestion that Napoleon should adopt an incognito, which he already had in mind in the form of 'Colonel Duroc' or 'Colonel Muiron', the names of his former aides-de-camp who had been killed in battle.

But for this inescapable situation, posterity might have been enriched by a record of many fascinating conversations. What would the historian not give for a conversation between Napoleon and Wellington or Canning, Palmerston or Disraeli! Some idea of the possibilities is given by a long conversation between Napoleon and Mr Lyttelton, a Whig member of Parliament and friend of Admiral Cockburn, shortly before the *Northumberland* sailed for St Helena. It ranged frankly and easily over the most contentious topics, and Lyttelton found it 'impossible not to admire his quickness, adroitness and originality'. Even so, Napoleon's conversations at St Helena add immensely to our knowledge of his character and career.

Napoleon's valet, Marchand, was momentarily afraid that he would commit suicide rather than go to St Helena. But Napoleon showed more stoicism than his followers, who were unrestrained in their rage and despair. Bertrand's wife, Fanny, had hysterics and tried to throw herself out of a cabin window. Napoleon had to select his companions as the instructions of the English Government allowed him three officers and twelve servants. General Savary and General Lallemand were expressly excluded as they were wanted for trial

by the French Government. It was only on the intervention
of Captain Maitland that they were promised internment
at Malta. Napoleon chose Bertrand, his Grand Marshal, two
court chamberlains, Montholon and Las Cases, and Colonel
Planat, his aide-de-camp. At the last minute General
Gourgaud was substituted for Planat, to appease Gourgaud's
hysterical jealousy. Las Cases and his young son were admitted as civilians. Bertrand and Montholon brought their
wives and children. Napoleon's doctor refused to go, and
his place was taken by Dr Barry O'Meara, a surgeon of
the Royal Navy, who was, in fact, a spy for the English
Government.

During the three months' voyage, Napoleon adapted himself with good humour to crowded quarters and a reduced
status. He spent his evenings playing vingt-et-un and whist
with Admiral Cockburn and his officers, and started to learn
English from Las Cases. The only known example of Napoleon's attempt at English composition is not impressive. 'Count
Lascases. Since sixt wek, y leave the english and y do not
any progress. Sixt week do fourty and two day. If might have
learn fivty word, for day, I could know it two thousands
and hundred. . . .' Cockburn wrote that 'he has descended
from the Emperor to the General with a flexibility of mind
more easily to be imagined than described'. Yet he was
disconcerted by Napoleon's habit of leaving the Admiral's
dinner table as soon as he had eaten, as he was accustomed
to do at the Tuileries. Cockburn wrote: 'It is clear he is
still inclined to act the Sovereign occasionally, but I cannot
allow it, and the sooner therefore he becomes convinced
it is not to be admitted the better.'

Napoleon was depressed by his first sight of St Helena—
a mass of bare volcanic granite rising steeply out of the
sea, barely twenty-eight miles in circumference. What a prospect! He was forty-five years old, and his health had improved on the voyage. 'I should have done better to have
stayed in Egypt.' He spent the first night on shore at a
boarding-house in the port of Jamestown, while Admiral Cockburn looked over the available houses on the island. There
were few of any size, and the best, Plantation House, had
been reserved by the East India Company when they agreed
to hand over the island to the Government. Cockburn chose
Longwood, the summer seat of the Lieutenant-Governor, on
a high plateau, 1,700 feet above the sea. It was ideally
situated for security as it was five miles from the port, and

was overlooked by the army encampment at Deadwood.
He could fairly tell Napoleon that it had a cooler climate
than Jamestown, and although it was no more than a bunga-
low, it could be rapidly extended to provide forty-four rooms
of a sort.

After looking at Longwood with the Admiral, Napoleon observed with pleasure the fine garden of a house called 'The
Briars,' the residence of William Balcombe, the East India
Company agent. Napoleon was determined not to spend another night in Jamestown, and arranged on the spot with the
Admiral and the Balcombes to settle into the pavilion in
'The Briars' garden. It was often used as a rest-house for
travellers, and Wellington had in fact occupied it on his way
back from India. In 1816 Wellington wrote (not in the best of
taste) to Admiral Malcolm, Cockburn's successor, 'Tell Boney
that I find his apartments at the Elysée-Bourbon very comfortable and I hope he has enjoyed mine at the Balcombes.'

No writer would dare to invent a situation in which the
first stage of Napoleon's captivity at St Helena was to expose
him to the ragging of two English teenage girls. Yet such was
his fate. It is one of the most bizarre encounters in history.
The two Balcombe daughters, Jane, aged sixteen, and Betsy,
aged fourteen, were suddenly faced with the 'Corsican ogre',
dressed, as they had often seen in pictures, in his cocked hat
and the green uniform of the Guard. Betsy was learning
French and was promptly given a *viva voce* examination by
Napoleon.

'What is the capital of France?'

'Paris.'

'Of Italy?'

'Rome.'

'Of Russia?'

'Petersburg now, and Moscow formerly.'

'Who burnt it?'

'I do not know, Sir.'

'Yes, yes. It was I who burnt it.'

'I believe, Sir, the Russians burnt it to get rid of the
French.'

Napoleon shook with laughter, and the ice was broken. Betsy, whom Glover, Cockburn's secretary, describes as 'a pretty
girl and a complete romp when out of sight of her father',
proceeded to adopt Napoleon as a favourite uncle, and as her
capacity for crude practical jokes was a match for Napoleon's,
the fun became fast and furious. Having been brought up in

a large, noisy and hard-hitting family, Napoleon was completely natural and at ease with children.

The two months which Napoleon spent at 'The Briars' were one of Napoleon's rare holidays, and as there was only room at the pavilion for his valet and the two Las Cases, Napoleon was free of his tiresome 'Court'. Las Cases was outraged by the liberties taken by the Balcombe children, but Napoleon was enjoying himself. 'We are at a masked ball.'

It was a rare experience for Napoleon to have a completely disinterested friend. He helped Betsy with her French lessons, showed her pictures of the King of Rome, and the magnificent Sèvres porcelain dinner-service depicting his victories. When he teased her about English roast beef, she retaliated by producing a caricature of a Frenchman with a frog jumping down his throat. He incautiously allowed her to handle one of his ceremonial swords, and she pinned him in a corner with it, while Las Cases gibbered in the background. But she went too far when she produced a new toy which made Boney climb up a ladder and then fall down to St Helena. Napoleon played with it, and sighed 'Ah well!' Her mother was extremely angry, and shut her in a cellar; Napoleon fed her with sweets through the bars. Betsy talked about her friend who was terrified of meeting the 'ogre'; when she called at 'The Briars' Napoleon made a horrible face and growled at her. When Betsy accused him of cheating at whist, he went off with her new ball-dress, and refused to return it until the carriage was at the door. 'Enjoy yourself and don't forget to dance with Gourgaud.' This was a sore point as Gourgaud was paying court to the Governor's daughter and ignored the Balcombe girls as mere children.

When Napoleon moved to Longwood in December 1815, the Balcombe family were frequently visitors, until they left the island in 1818. By this time Betsy had grown from a wild tomboy into a beautiful young debutante, made self-conscious by the ridiculous gossip which circulated on the island and even in England about her relationship with Napoleon. This gossip emanated from the French Commissioner, Marquis de Montchenu, an absurd relic of the *ancien régime*, who rapidly acquired the nickname of 'Monsieur Montez-chez-nous' as he became notorious as a social bore. Napoleon suggested to Betsy that she should teach him a lesson by cutting off his pigtail. But she never lost her affection for Napoleon, and he gave her a lock of his hair as a memento. At their last meeting she thought he had the look of a dying man. Long after, she wrote her memoirs, and met Napoleon III, who gave her an estate in Algeria. He was disappointed to be told by Betsy that he did not resemble his uncle. Her younger brother's descendant, Lady Brookes, has recalled 'The Briars' episode in her *St Helena Story*, and bequeathed 'The Briars' pavilion to the French nation. Her grandfather remembered well how as a small boy he sat on Napoleon's lap.

Though Napoleon refused to accept official invitations because they were addressed to 'General Buonaparte', he rode and walked and met the islanders freely while he was at 'The Briars'. Admiral Cockburn imposed no military guard at 'The Briars' apart from the orderly officer, Captain Poppleton. At Longwood he could ride for twelve miles without supervision, and Bertrand was authorized to issue passes for visitors. In the first two years Napoleon received over a hundred. Dr Warden, the intelligent and cultured surgeon of the *Northumberland*, who was a frequent visitor at 'The Briars' and Longwood, described a drive round the Longwood plateau, when Napoleon was the 'life and soul' of the party. He practised his English, deliberately getting the words wrong, and flirted outrageously with Fanny Bertrand.

But the arrival of Sir Hudson Lowe as Governor, in April 1816, armed with new instructions from Lord Bathurst, the Colonial Secretary, produced a violent clash of wills, and a state of cold war between Plantation House and Longwood. Even today, with the immense documentation on St Helena, it is difficult to determine whether it was due to the personality of Lowe or to a deliberate plan of campaign adopted by Napoleon. Napoleon always insisted that if he had had to deal with a 'man of honour' like Cornwallis (who had signed the Treaty of Amiens) there would have been no unnecessary friction. But from the start, Napoleon told his followers that it 'was their duty to complain'. Oblivion was the one thing he dreaded; persecution and 'martyrdom' were preferable. He would not receive the allied Commissioners sent to St Helena as 'observers', because he refused to recognize the allied Convention prescribing his detention. 'What folly it is to send these Commissioners out here without charge or responsibility. They will have nothing to do but to walk about the streets, and creep up the rocks.'

Until the Congress of Aix-la-Chapelle in 1818 reaffirmed the conditions of his detention, he did not give up hope that political developments in Europe would extricate him from

St Helena. Even in 1821, in the last six months of his life, he
still hoped that a change of Government in England would
release him. The arrival of every ship brought wild rumours.
In moments of disillusionment Napoleon said: 'We are behaving like grown-up children, and I, who should be giving
an example of good sense, am as bad as any of you. We
build castles in Spain.'

Meanwhile the more fuss, protest and propaganda the better. If he could not wear an imperial crown, he would wear
'a crown of thorns'. Prince Eugène interceded privately and
perfunctorily with the Tsar, while Madame Mère and Jerome
wrote to the Prince Regent. It was the saintly Pope Pius VII
who made the strongest appeal to the Prince Regent for
generosity. 'The pious and courageous initiative of 1801
moves us to forget and pardon the subsequent wrongs.
Savona and Fontainebleau were errors of judgment or the
excesses of human ambition: the Concordat was a Christian
and heroic act of healing. It would bring the greatest joy to
our heart if we could help to diminish Napoleon's torture.
He cannot be a danger to anyone; we desire that he should
not be a cause for remorse.' None of these letters was answered.

There is no evidence that Napoleon seriously thought of
escape, though it was discussed in a desultory sort of way at
Longwood, and Napoleon had little difficulty in getting secret
messages out of the island. If he had had such plans, he
would have lulled English suspicions, instead of provoking
them. St Helena was a different proposition from Elba. It was
over a thousand miles from any mainland, and the nearest
island, Ascension, six hundred miles away, was occupied by
the Royal Navy. Besides a squadron of frigates on constant
patrol, there was a military garrison at St Helena of nearly
three thousand men. There were few beaches to guard, and
Admiral Malcolm, Cockburn's successor, thought that no
further measure of security was necessary. Long afterwards
Wellington agreed with this view. 'If I had been Lord Bathurst
I would have adopted a different plan for his confinement.
There are only some five landing places along the coast of St
Helena. As for the means of keeping him there, there was
never anything so damned absurd. I know the island of St
Helena well.'

Sir Hudson Lowe appears to have been chosen as Governor
mainly for his knowledge of French and Italian, and his ef-

ficient staff work. Son of an army surgeon, he was not an
aristocrat with the assurance, tact and knowledge of the
world possessed by the naval officers whom Napoleon had
hitherto encountered. After Waterloo there were plenty of
distinguished Admirals available who would not have refused
a post carrying a salary of £12,000 a year. But perhaps the
Admirals had already shown themselves too liable to suc-
cumb to Napoleon's charm.

Lowe's military record was undistinguished; he had commanded a regiment of Corsican Rangers in the Mediterranean.
As the Rangers were royalist *emigrés* and deserters, it was a
record hardly likely to commend itself to Napoleon, and was
bound to be construed as a deliberate insult. There can be
little doubt that this exceedingly tactless appointment was
the initial and basic bone of contention between Lowe and
Napoleon. In 1819 Napoleon told Ricketts, a diplomat and
nephew of Lord Liverpool, who called on his way home
from the East, that 'Sir Hudson Lowe, as Colonel of the
Corsican battalion, was one of the few men that your uncle
should never have sent here'.

It was not only the French who found Lowe exasperating.
Admiral Malcolm tried to mediate between Lowe and Napoleon, and ended by quarrelling with Lowe. The Austrian and
Russian Commissioners, Balmain and Sturmer, were furious
at Lowe's rudeness and the odious system of espionage which
he organized throughout the island. Balmain reported that
'the English treat Bonaparte very shabbily'. Sturmer thought
that 'it would have been impossible to make a worse choice.
It would be difficult to find a man more awkward, extravagant
and despicable.' 'The English fear and avoid him, the French
make a mock of him, the Commissioners complain of him,
and everybody agrees that he is touched in the head.' Wellington, who had got rid of Lowe from his staff just before
Waterloo, thought that 'he was a damned fool'. Lowe was
fundamentally well-meaning in a fussy, unimaginative way,
but he was morbidly anxious and suspicious, and lacked the
assurance even to exercise the discretion given to him by his
instructions from Whitehall.

The responsible Minister, Lord Bathurst, the Colonial Secretary, was a man of similar mentality. It is impossible for an
Englishman to read the Lowe-Bathurst correspondence without
blushing for his country. They were small-minded, frightened
men, fumbling with a genie in a bottle. Bathurst wrote to
Lowe in 1817, 'No doubt, however, can be entertained that

attempts are making at clandestine communications, which will be much encouraged if it be once understood that your vigilance abates. The turbulent and seditious in this as well as in every other country, look to the escape of General Bonaparte as that which would at once give life and activity to the revolutionary spirit which has been so long formidable to the best interests of Europe, and which they have all a common object in endeavouring to revive.'

Bathurst's stature may be measured by the following letter: 'In case of any present being hereafter forwarded to General Buonaparte to which emblems or titles of sovereignty are annexed, you are to consider that circumstance as altogether precluding its delivery, if they cannot be removed without prejudice to the present itself.' In October 1816 Napoleon suggested to Lowe that the disputes about his 'title' should be solved by adopting the incognito of 'Colonel Muiron' or 'Baron Duroc'. Bathurst ruled that this should be ignored as 'there may arise much embarrassment in formally acquiescing in it'.

Lowe's first interview with Napoleon passed off correctly, but he lost no time in informing Bertrand of the new instructions laid down by Bathurst. Napoleon's household was to be reduced at once by four, and the annual expenditure was to be limited to £8,000. Those who wished to remain must sign a declaration committing themselves to staying indefinitely. No correspondence was to take place except through the Governor, and only he could issue passes to visit Longwood. The riding limits without supervision were to be restricted. Napoleon's presence was to be checked twice daily by the orderly officer. Lowe personally interrogated the servants about the declaration, and hoped to find a pretext for deporting most of Napoleon's suite. He wrote to Bathurst, 'With the present feelings of the persons attached to General Buonaparte, I conceive the whole of them, with the exception, perhaps of Las Cases, had better be removed.' Lowe was horrified by the free and friendly relations which the French had established with the English residents: they were making Longwood the centre of island society.

Not surprisingly, Lowe's programme produced an explosion of wrath at Longwood. The Marquis de Montchenu, reporting on Lowe, wrote: 'If I was in his place, I would not permit a single stranger to visit Longwood, for they all leave transported with devotion, and take this sentiment to Europe.' Bertrand thought it a deliberate attempt to isolate Napoleon.

At a second interview on April 30, Napoleon told Lowe: 'If the Government has approved the limits, and if you cannot give us the freedom of the island, you can do nothing for us. No doubt the Admiral had instructions from the Government to kill us by degrees. I see that you have the same orders. I would prefer that you should do as the Calabrians did with Murat and put two shots through my head.' Napoleon told Bertrand that 'I believe this man has sinister intentions, even more than we suspect.' These charges Napoleon repeated in more insulting terms at their next meeting, and Lowe told Bertrand that 'Napoleon had created an imaginary Spain, an imaginary England, and now an imaginary St Helena'.

In the meantime Lowe had made a clumsy attempt at conciliation by inviting 'General Bonaparte' to dine at Plantation House to meet the Countess of Loudon: he was surprised and annoyed when he received no reply. Napoleon told Admiral Malcolm that Lowe was 'a disagreeable man in everything, even when he wished to oblige. Everything is offered with such a bad grace that if he came to announce an order to take me back to Toulon to return to the throne, he would manage to make that disagreeable.' Malcolm explained frankly to Napoleon why it was politically impossible for him to reside in England, and advised him to make the best of St Helena.

On August 18, 1816, Napoleon and Lowe met for the last time, in the presence of Admiral Malcolm and Lowe's staff. Napoleon completely lost his temper and repeated his insults against Lowe as a 'staff-clerk' and an 'executioner'. 'Five hundred years hence the name of Napoleon will resound in Europe and the name of Castlereagh and yours will only be known for the shame and injustice of their conduct to me.' Afterwards he admitted: 'It is the second time in my life that I have messed up my affairs with the English. I do not wish to see the Governor again, he makes me too angry and I lose my dignity.'

Lowe's gaucheries multiplied. He sent an invitation to the 'General' for a party at Plantation House to celebrate the birthday of the Prince Regent. He confiscated the present of a book because it was inscribed *'Imperatori Napoleoni'*. He wondered whether a marble bust of the King of Rome should be delivered to Napoleon because it might contain a secret message.

Meanwhile Napoleon's campaign of propaganda against Lowe was having repercussions in Europe. 'The more I am

persecuted the more noise it will make in Europe.' Napoleon
drafted a *Remonstrance* which, copied microscopically on
silk, was smuggled into Europe by Santini, one of the servants selected for deportation under Bathurst's orders. With
the help of Lord Holland Santini published an *Appeal to the
English Nation*. Dr Warden had already published *Letters
from the 'Northumberland' and St Helena*, which gave a
vivid and not inaccurate picture of Napoleon. As it was em-
barrassingly favourable to Napoleon, Warden was cashiered
and dismissed from the Service. Napoleon replied anony-
mously to Warden's work in *Letters from the Cape*. The
Manuscrit Venu de Ste-Hélène was widely read, and was
thought to be by Napoleon: in fact it was a forgery by Lullin
de Chateauvieux.

Lowe's attempt to reduce the expenses of Longwood turned
to Napoleon's advantage. The English colony at St Helena
knew only too well that the cost of living was very high.
Napoleon was willing to draw on his funds in Paris and London but refused to reveal their source by submitting to
Lowe's censorship of correspondence. To add to the embarrassment of the English Government he had a large quantity
of his silver plate broken up and publicly sold in Jamestown.
In March 1817 Lord Holland opened a debate in the House
of Lords on the conditions of Napoleon's detention, to which
Lord Bathurst replied.

Although the motion was heavily defeated, the publicity
forced Bathurst and Lowe to change their tune. Napoleon
sent his *Observations on the Speech of Lord Bathurst*. The
allowance for Longwood was restored to £12,000. Lowe
dared not enforce the regulation that Napoleon should show
himself twice a day to the orderly officer, as Napoleon threatened to shoot anyone who forced his private apartments. In
February 1817 Bathurst suggested to Lowe that the original
twelve-mile limit should be restored 'if it would reconcile
him to more frequent exercise in fresh air'. Later he even suggested that Napoleon should be given the freedom of the
island if he would agree to show himself to the orderly officer twice a day. So much for the security precautions which
Bathurst had originally laid down as 'essential'. But these
second thoughts came too late, as Napoleon's health had begun to deteriorate as soon as he gave up riding as a protest
against Lowe's restrictions.

The increasing isolation of Longwood preyed on the
nerves of Napoleon's suite. Bertrand was affronted because

Montholon was put in charge of the household: Napoleon
thought that Bertrand spent too much time with his wife and
family. Gourgaud, the youngest, was too temperamental to
endure exile, and was jealous of Las Cases and Montholon.
Napoleon's preference for Las Cases' company turned all the
rest against him.

In November 1816 Las Cases was arrested and deported,
when his smuggling of secret correspondence was detected. It
may be suspected that Las Cases had provoked this incident
as a means of escape from St Helena, as he refused to return
to Longwood on the conditions offered by Lowe. Napoleon
was depressed by his departure, but thought that he might be
more useful as a propagandist in Europe.

By the end of 1817 Gourgaud's behaviour had become so
impossible that Napoleon granted his request to leave. He had
even threatened to challenge Montholon to a duel. Gourgaud
records in his *Journal* a painful scene when Napoleon accused him of constantly sulking. 'Don't you consider that
when I wake in the night I don't have bad moments, when I
recall what I was and what I am now?' In his exasperation
with the quarrels of his followers, Napoleon once told Gourgaud: 'If I had known what it would be like, I would have
brought nothing but servants.' 'After all, if one had nothing
else, one would have to find one's company in a green par-
rot.' Gourgaud's behaviour on his return to Europe was dis-
tinctly odd, and hardly helpful to Napoleon. He told Bathurst
that Napoleon's ill health was 'diplomatic', that he could escape from St Helena any time he wished, and that he had no
difficulty in conducting secret correspondence with Europe.
Bathurst naturally used these extraordinary admissions to
stiffen the determination of the Powers at the Congress of
Aix-la-Chapelle to confirm the strictness of Napoleon's detention. At the same time Gourgaud addressed sentimental
appeals to the Tsar and to Marie-Louise to release Napoleon,
as St Helena would kill him. It is significant that Gourgaud
was not mentioned in Napoleon's will.

In July 1819 the amiable Madame Montholon, who was, im-
probably, suspected of being Napoleon's mistress, had to
leave for reasons of health. From his servants, notably the intelligent and reliable valet, Marchand, Napoleon received
smooth and devoted service; though, being used to the lavish-
ness of palace life, they were extravagant and wasteful. The
sudden death of Cipriani the butler, in February 1818, was
a loss to Napoleon. He had formerly been an experienced

espionage agent, and entertained Napoleon with all the gossip
of the island.

In September 1819 reinforcements for the household arrived from Europe, sent by Madame Mère. Apart from the
servants, Coursot, one of Madame Mère's valets and formerly
a servant of Duroc, and Chandellier, one of Pauline's cooks,
trained in the Tuileries, they were not an impressive collection—two ignorant Corsican priests, Buonavita and Vignali,
and a bogus and bumptious young Corsican surgeon, Antommarchi. According to a letter Pauline wrote to Colonel
Planat in 1821, Madame Mère, under the influence of a German clairvoyante, had been convinced for some time that all
news from St Helena was false, and that Napoleon was no
longer there. She had therefore taken little trouble in her selection.

As early as 1816 Bertrand's diary notes that Napoleon's
health was frequently upset. Were these symptoms exaggerated in order to support Napoleon's contention that Longwood was unhealthy? Apart from the excessive humidity,
which was trying to a man of Mediterranean origin and up-
bringing, nothing serious can be alleged against the climate
of St Helena, which is temperate rather than tropical. But in
Napoleon's time, visitors to the island were plagued with
dysentery and disease of the liver, probably due to the bad
water supply which harboured virus infections. Glover, Cockburn's secretary, noted that 'the climate is by no means so
healthy as it is generally described to be, the children being
sickly and the adults suffering from the liver, of which complaint many of our men died'.

In the second half of 1817 Napoleon suffered increasingly
from swelling of the legs, and in October 1817 O'Meara
diagnosed hepatitis, and treated him with mercury. Lowe
distrusted O'Meara, who, on Napoleon's instructions, refused
to give the Governor detailed reports on Napoleon's health.
He resented the fact that O'Meara was corresponding directly with the Admiralty, and was determined to get rid of
him. In May 1818 he obtained Bathurst's permission to dismiss O'Meara. In an official report O'Meara wrote: 'I think
it my duty to state, as his late medical attendant, that,
considering the disease of the liver with which he is afflicted,
the progress it has made in him, and reflecting upon the great
mortality produced by that complaint in the island of St
Helena, so strongly exemplified in the number of deaths in
the 66th St Helena regiment, the squadron and Europeans

in general, and particularly in HMS *Conqueror,* it is my opinion that the life of Napoleon Bonaparte will be endangered by a longer residence in such a climate as that of St Helena.' On his return to England O'Meara complained of Lowe's tyranny and even hinted that Lowe had orders to hasten Napoleon's death. As a consequence O'Meara was court-martialled and dismissed from the Navy. He was a plausible, amusing, but untrustworthy Irishman, who had involved himself in the most tortuous position as a double agent. Napoleon was unaware that the man to whom he gave his confidence was secretly sending all the gossip of Longwood to the Admiralty for circulation to the Cabinet and the Prince Regent. Lowe was unaware that O'Meara had accepted a substantial gift of money from Napoleon.

Napoleon refused to see any doctor nominated by Lowe, pending the arrival of his own physician nominated by Madame Mère, and he was without medical attention for some months. In January 1819 he had a fainting-attack, and Dr Stokoe, a naval surgeon, was sent for. Stokoe confirmed O'Meara's diagnosis of chronic hepatitis. For this he incurred the wrath of Lowe, was court-martialled for collaboration with Longwood, and retired from the Service. One of the charges in Stokoe's court-martial was 'knowingly and wilfully designating General Bonaparte in the said bulletin in a manner different from that in which he is designated in the Act of Parliament for the better custody of his person'.

The last English visitor whom Napoleon received was a Foreign Office official, Ricketts, on his way home, who reported to Lord Liverpool that Napoleon's illness was 'diplomatic'. In August 1819, Napoleon had a return of his 'hepatic' symptoms, and dictated the first draft of his will. For nearly a year, however, he felt better, and busied himself with elaborate gardening projects. The whole household were made to rise at dawn, and labour under Napoleon's direction. In May 1820 he even resumed riding, but was forced to give it up because it fatigued him excessively. On October 4, 1820, he made his last excursion outside the grounds of Longwood, driving over to his neighbour Sir William Doveton, and picnicking on his lawn. Doveton thought him 'very pale', but 'fat and round as a China pig'.

On October 10, 1820, Napoleon again fainted after his bath, and his weakness, vomiting and lack of appetite became more marked and chronic. Napoleon told Montholon, 'There is no more oil in the lamp.' On March 17, 1821, Montholon wrote to his wife, 'One way or another, St Helena is nearing its end. It is impossible that He can live much longer.' Antommarchi diagnosed a gastric fever and prescribed a violent emetic. Meanwhile Lowe and Bathurst were still preoccupied with the danger of escape, and insisting that Napoleon should show himself to the orderly officer, or to an English doctor. Lowe threatened to force the door if his orders were not obeyed.

On April 1 Napoleon finally consented to see Dr Arnott, an army surgeon. He could find nothing serious and diagnosed hypochondria. On April 23, Arnott was still reporting that 'convalescence will be long and difficult, but he is not in danger'. It was not till the following day when Napoleon started to vomit matter which looked like 'coffee-grounds' that Arnott became alarmed.

Conquering his physical feebleness with an extraordinary effort, Napoleon dictated a lengthy will between April 12 and April 15, having ordered Marchand to burn the previous draft. On May 2 Napoleon received extreme unction from the priest Vignali, but in secret. A consultation between Arnott and Antommarchi, to which two more English doctors, Shortt and Mitchell, were added, decided that ten grains of calomel should be given. Marchand, much against his will, was forced by the doctors to give it to Napoleon in a drink. At 2 am on May 5, 1821, he uttered his last incoherent words, *'France, armée, tête d'armée, Joséphine.'* During the day the household of Longwood, including the children, gathered round his unconscious form and watched him die peacefully at sunset. At 5.51 pm Antommarchi pronounced him dead.

Lowe succeeded in being fatuous to the last. On hearing the news, he remarked to his aides: 'Well, gentlemen, he has been England's greatest enemy, and mine also, but I forgive him everything. At the death of a great man like him, we should feel only respect and regret.'

It was Napoleon's wish that there should be an autopsy to determine the cause of his illness. This was conducted by Antommarchi in the presence of the English surgeons. The stomach was found to be perforated by a hole 'large enough to admit a little finger', but adhering to the liver in such a way as to block the perforation. Dr Shortt strongly dissented from his colleagues who found no abnormality in the liver, and made a note that his opinion that the liver was enlarged was 'omitted by order of the Governor'. Antommarchi

refused to sign the report, and later said in his memoirs
that the liver was abnormally large. The official post mortem
report concluded that death was due to a 'cancerous ulcer'
of the stomach, which showed signs of lesions 'about to become cancerous'.

This report was highly convenient to Lowe and the English
Government, as it showed that Napoleon died of the same
disease as his father, but in view of the perfunctory nature
of the post-mortem and the rudimentary knowledge of path-
ology at the time it is not conclusive, and is still being
debated by medical experts.[1]

When Napoleon lay in state in his uniform, everyone remarked on the serene and youthful beauty of his face. It had
been fined down by his illness and resembled the face of the
First Consul at the age of thirty. Dr Shortt noted: 'In
death the face was the most splendid I have ever beheld; it
seemed moulded for conquest.' Dr Henry recorded: 'All
admitted they have never seen a face more noble, classical,
and peaceful.' These impressions are confirmed by the death-
mask which was taken with great difficulty at a late stage
when decomposition of the body was setting in. Dr Burton
just succeeded in time in finding a small deposit of suitable
plaster of paris on the island. The cast was taken in two
parts—the face and the skull. Even this operation, and the
interment, were bedevilled by political quarrels, as Antommarchi removed the cast of the face in Burton's absence,
and the cast of the skull was kept by Burton.[2] Napoleon
was buried in accordance with his wish, in Geranium Valley,
with full military honours organized by Lowe. Montholon
proposed that the inscription on the tomb should read:

Napoléon
Né à Ajaccio le 15 Août 1769
Mort à Ste-Hélène le 5 Mai 1821

Lowe insisted that it should read: 'Napoléon Bonaparte.'
In the end, the tomb was left nameless.

[1] See Appendix I.
[2] See Appendix II.

17

The Napoleonic Legend

IT MUST BE CONCEDED that Napoleon won his last battle at St Helena. Lowe was made the scapegoat of Bathurst's policy, and cold-shouldered on his return to England. When Alexandre Dumas' play *Napoléon Bonaparte* was performed in Paris in 1831, the character of Sir Hudson Lowe aroused such passions that the actor who took the part had to receive police protection. In 1840 Bertrand, Gourgaud, the young Las Cases, and Marchand (now married, in accordance with Napoleon's last wishes, to a daughter of one of Napoleon's Guards officers) sailed for St Helena to bring back the body of Napoleon and install it with pomp and ceremony in the Invalides in Paris. In 1855 Queen Victoria, a guest of the Emperor Napoleon III, visited the Invalides and bade her small son, the future King Edward VII, 'kneel down before the tomb of the great Napoleon'.

In contrast with his Memoirs, which are rather dull, impersonal accounts of his campaigns, Napoleon's will was a masterpiece of astute political propaganda. 'I die in the apostolic and roman religion in which I was born more than 50 years ago. . . . I desire that my ashes should repose on the banks of the Seine in the midst of the French people whom I have loved so much. . . . I have nothing but praise

for my dear wife Marie-Louise; I preserve in my last moments the most tender affection for her. . . . I recommend
my son never to forget that he is born a French prince, and
never to become an instrument of the triumvirate which
oppresses the peoples of Europe. He must never fight against
or injure France: he must adopt my motto: "Everything for
the French people" . . . I die prematurely assassinated by
the English oligarchy and their executioner: the English
people will soon avenge me.'

In 1822 O'Meara's *A Voice from St Helena* was published;
in 1823, Las Cases' *Mémorial de Ste-Hélène*. These were
the most widely read and influential evangelists of the captivity. Napoleon was well aware that they were recording
his conversations, and encouraged them to do so, telling them
that they would thereby make their fortunes. Through them
Napoleon told the world what he wanted it to hear, and re-
interpreted his career in accordance with the trend of opinion
and events since 1815. He claimed to be the champion of
equality, liberty and nationality against the Holy Alliance
which had defeated him. He was the *roi du peuple:* 'the
natural mediator in this struggle of the past against the
Revolution.' 'These truths will rule the world. They will be
the creed, the morality of all nations. And, no matter what
has been said, this memorable era will be linked to my
person, because, after all, I have carried its torch and con-
secrated its principles, and because persecution has now
made me its Messiah.' 'Every Frenchman could say in my
reign—I shall be minister, grand officer, duke, count, baron,
if I earn it—even king.' The function of the imperial nobility
was to 'remove the remnants of feudalism in Europe by at-
taching the idea of *noblesse* to services rendered to the State
and divorcing it from any feudal idea'.

His autocracy was now explained as a temporary necessity,
justified by the dangers of civil war and from the allied
Powers. If he had won in 1812, his 'constitutional reign
would have begun'. He had not aimed at 'universal monarchy': 'France has natural limits which I did not wish to
exceed.' The war of 1812 had been undertaken to convince
England of the necessity for peace, and to free Poland. He
was forced despite himself to conquer Europe. 'England had
determined to destroy France.' 'The vulgar have never ceased
blaming all my wars on my ambitions. But were they of my
choosing? Were they not always determined by the ineluctable
nature of things, by the struggle between the past and the

future, by the permanent coalition of our enemies, who put upon us the obligation of destroying them lest we ourselves be destroyed?'

Napoleon was now aware of the force of nationalism. 'The first ruler who embraces in good faith the cause of the peoples will find himself at the head of all Europe and will be able to accomplish everything he wishes.' If he had been given more time, he would have unified and freed the nationalities. 'There are in Europe more than 30 million French, 15 million Spanish, 15 million Italians, 30 million Germans. I would have wished to make each of these peoples a single united body.' He would have restored Polish independence, but Germany and Italy required time 'to simplify their complications'. His policy in Italy was intended 'to supervise, guarantee and promote the national education of the Italians'. His second son would have become King of Italy. He admitted his mistake in the handling of Spain: the removal of the Bourbon dynasty was done with the best intention of 'regenerating' Spain, but it would have been better to put Ferdinand on the throne, married to a Bonaparte princess. 'Europe thus divided into nationalities freely formed and free internally, peace between States would have become easier: the United States of Europe would become a possibility.' 'I wished to found a European system, a European Code of Laws, a European judiciary: there would be but one people in Europe.'

There was a sufficient core of truth in all this propaganda to make it plausible to the new generation which was frustrated by the policy of Metternich and had not seen the battlefields of the Empire. Even Wellington was constrained to admit that 'Napoleon was not a personality, but a principle'. But for Napoleon's real thoughts and the authentic style of his talk we must turn to the diaries of Gourgaud and Bertrand, which were not intended for publication. Gourgaud's *Journal* was not published till 1899, and Bertrand's *Cahiers de Ste-Hélène* were only deciphered and published in the period 1949–59. Gourgaud is astonishingly naïve, spontaneous and uninhibited: Bertrand puts down everything with calm objectivity, even the fact that Montholon and Antommarchi told him that Napoleon had quarrelled with Bertrand's wife, Fanny, because she refused to become his mistress. Bertrand thought that Napoleon's references in his will to the Catholic religion, and to Marie-Louise, were 'policy'. Napoleon was clearly aware that Neipperg had

seduced Marie-Louise, but he did not hold it against her, as
he understood the pressures to which she had been subjected.
He told Bertrand, 'I was really in love with Josephine, but
I did not respect her.' On the whole he preferred Marie-
Louise: 'never a lie, never a debt.'

Gourgaud, a good Catholic, depicts Napoleon as a cynical
agnostic, who believed only that 'a religion is necessary to
bind men together in society'. He argued with Gourgaud
that 'Jesus Christ had never existed', Mahomet had been a
ruler as well as a prophet, and Islam was a more effective
religion than Christianity. 'If I had gone to the Mosque at
Cairo with my Generals, who can tell what the effect would
have been? It would have given me 300,000 men and the
Empire of the East.' When told that in China the Emperor
was worshipped as a god, Napoleon exclaimed, 'That is as it
should be!' No doubt Napoleon was often tempted to pull
Gourgaud's leg, but in the last months of his life he also
told Bertrand, 'I am glad I have no religion. It is a great
consolation. I have no imaginary fears. I do not fear the
future.' But he told Bertrand on another occasion, 'It dis-
turbs me that I have no belief.' Bertrand explained that
'Napoleon died a theist but declares that he is a Catholic
because it is more conducive to public morality'. If Napoleon
remained an agnostic, he was neither a fanatical nor a willing
one.

His reflections on government take on a different aspect
when recorded by Gourgaud and Bertrand. Referring to the
Hundred Days, he told Gourgaud that 'these miserable liber-
als made me lose a lot of time in talking to me about a
Constitution'. It was a mistake, on his return from Elba,
to summon the Legislature and to have made Fouché a
Minister, instead of executing him. He remarked to Bertrand
that 'parliamentary government is no doubt better than the
rule of one man. But I doubt whether it can ever be possible
in France.' His study of the English Constitution prompted
the shrewd remark: 'I understand the English Government.
It is ridiculous to talk of balance of powers: it is Parliament
which governs by a section of its members.' Discussing with
Bertrand in 1818 his intention to refute current works on his
career, he said, 'he would explain when he conceived the
idea of becoming master of the world'. He regretted that he
had not died at the Kremlin. 'Then I should have had the
greatest glory, the greatest reputation that has ever existed.'

As he lost hope of a return from St Helena, Napoleon's thoughts for the future were concentrated on his son. He worried constantly about the lack of news from Vienna, and the education that his son might be receiving. The last direct news he had had was from Méneval, who had accompanied the Empress Marie-Louise to Vienna as private secretary after the first abdication. He was expelled from Vienna during the Hundred Days and reported to Napoleon in Paris. When he left, the small King of Rome had taken him aside and whispered, 'Monsieur Méva, you will tell my father that I still love him very much.' Since then Napoleon had received only a lock of his hair sent by his nurse, Marchand's mother. The Austrian Commissioner at St Helena, Sturmer, had nothing to report. Poor Gourgaud was snubbed by Napoleon when he tried to celebrate the birthday of the King of Rome. Exasperated, as usual, by Gourgaud's *Schwärmerei*, Napoleon declared, 'The King of Rome no more thinks about me than he does of you.'

He would have been gratified and touched to learn how far this was from the truth. Metternich's policy was to bring up Napoleon's son as a purely Austrian prince; he was not regarded as a 'prisoner' because, after all, he was the Emperor Francis' grandson, but he was in 'a special position'. In the case of a small boy of four, parted from his father at the age of three, and seen by his mother only on her rare visits from Parma to Vienna, this did not appear to be difficult.

In accordance with this programme of brain-washing, his French attendants were removed—his governess Madame de Montesquiou, Méneval, his nurse Madame Marchand. At the end of June 1815 Count Maurice Dietrichstein, a humourless, fussy pedant, was appointed his tutor. He wrote to Marie-Louise: 'It seems to me that the Prince whose education I have been given the honour of directing must be considered as of Austrian descent and brought up in the German fashion. Many of the tendencies of his precocious sensibility must be restrained, and many of the ideas which have been implanted must be gradually eradicated, without making him suffer and without hurting his pride more than is necessary.'

But how would the most expert psychologist deal with the case of a small boy, deprived of his parents, who since his birth had borne successively the titles of King of Rome, Prince Imperial, Prince of Parma, Napoleon II (if only for a

few days), and Duke of Reichstadt? Dietrichstein commented severely on his young pupil's habit of persistent bed-
wetting; a modern psychologist would recognize this at once
as a system of stress and anxiety. It was soon apparent that
he had inherited some, at least, of his father's character—
his power of memory, his soaring imagination, his self-
control and dissimulation, his ability to charm and persuade.
Napoleon had devoted a lot of time to his son in his infancy,
often allowing him to play in his study at the Tuileries
while he was working. When Marie-Louise broke the news of
Napoleon's death to her son she wrote: 'I am sure that your
grief was no less profound than mine, for you would be
an ungrateful wretch if you could forget the kindness he
showed you in your infancy. You must endeavour to imitate
his virtues, while avoiding the reefs on which he came to
grief.'

Such a powerful impression of his father was difficult to
eradicate. His assistant tutor, Foresti, commented that 'He
knows a great deal about the past, but in this connection
maintains a silence which is quite extraordinary in a child.'
The Archduke Rainer wrote that 'it is a curious psychological
phenomenon that a child of that age should know so
much about the past and about his father and that, far from
talking about it, he should keep that knowledge such a closely
guarded secret'. Dietrichstein wrote despairingly to Marie-
Louise: 'The Prince knows nearly everything about his father;
he hides it from us constantly.'

Dietrichstein began by removing all reminders of the name
'Napoleon' from the boy's surroundings, including the emblems on his clothes, and insisting that he should answer
only to the name of 'Francis'. He succeeded in making him
forget how to talk French, but he was forced into a change
of tactics and to answer the boy's queries about his father.
'A change had to be made. The embarrassment and silence of
the old system had become utterly unbearable.' Before his
French attendants were sent away the child must have gathered something about Waterloo because he remarked: 'It is
my dear papa; he is a bad man, are they going to kill him?'
He asked Foresti 'who had been Emperor in France?'; and
the tutor congratulated himself on his tactful reply: 'Prince,
it was your dear Papa, who lost his Crown and Empire on
account of his unfortunate propensity for war.' The boy
was quite aware that he had been called 'King of Rome',
and asked his grandfather the Emperor Francis what it

meant. The Emperor's reply was ingenious: it was a nominal title, like that of 'King of Jerusalem' held by the Emperors of Austria.

As he grew up, the position became more embarrassing. Gentz wrote: 'The young Napoleon, by the mere fact of so many wild hopes resting on his head among millions of Frenchmen (who cannot imagine that Austria has completely abandoned them), is an object of alarm and terror for most of the European cabinets.' The French Ambassador in Vienna wrote in 1824: 'I fear there will come a time when the position of this young man will become extremely embarrassing.' In accordance with his policy that the 'Prince Francis' was 'once and for all, excluded from all thrones', Metternich had refused to allow him the reversion to the Duchy of Parma, and in 1817 he was given the title of 'His Serene Highness the Duke of Reichstadt', with estates in the Bavarian Palatinate. By 1827 he had free access to the palace library and was able to read Las Cases' *Mémorial de Ste-Hélène*, which stimulated the hero-worship of his father. He wrote to Marie-Louise: 'I am indeed convinced of the need for study. . . . I am, therefore, trying as best I can to make up for lost time, in order to offer you, dear Mamma, on your return the sight of a morally superior and noble being and thus show you the foundations of a character which will remind you of my father's: for a soldier on the threshold of his career, can there be a finer and more admirable model of constancy, endurance, manly gravity, valiance and courage?'

In August 1828 the Emperor nominated him Captain in a Tyrolean regiment; 'the most agreeable event of my life'. In 1830 Reichstadt was emancipated from the tutelage of Dietrichstein and given the colonelcy of a battalion. In this year also he found his first real friend and confidant, the young Austrian officer Prokesch von Osten, who had written a eulogy of Napoleon's military genius. When Neipperg died in 1829, the fact that Marie-Louise's two children by him had been born before Napoleon's death could no longer be concealed from Reichstadt, and he confided to Prokesch: 'If Josephine had been my mother, my father would not have been buried at St Helena and I should not be at Vienna. My mother is kind but weak; she was not the wife my father deserved.'

The revolutionary movements in France, Belgium, Poland and Italy between 1830 and 1832 threw Reichstadt and

Prokesch into a frenzy of speculation. There was an outburst of Napoleonic plays in Paris and Napoleon's column in the Place de Vendôme was restored. But Metternich's policy of isolating Reichstadt in the Habsburg palace at Vienna had been effective. Reichstadt was regarded in France as a wholly Austrian prince. Méneval wrote to King Joseph that 'a profound obscurity surrounds this young prince, and greatly damages his cause'.

In July 1832 Prokesch called on Madame Mère in Rome and gave her news of her grandson. 'You will tell him,' she said, 'that above all else he must respect his father's wishes. His hour will come. He will ascend the throne of France.' Prokesch could not contain his tears, because he knew that already Reichstadt was mortally ill. From 1827 when he was aged sixteen his health had given cause for anxiety. He was too tall and thin, developed a persistent cough, and suffered from frequent chills. His physician persisted almost to the end in diagnosing a disorder of the liver, but to the layman it was painfully obvious that he was afflicted by the hereditary Habsburg tendency to tuberculosis. In January 1832 he caught pneumonia at a military parade, and went rapidly downhill, dying on July 22, 1832. On his coffin, he was described as 'Joseph Charles Francis, Duke of Reichstadt, son of Napoleon Emperor of the French, and of Marie-Louise, Archduchess of Austria'. It was not till 1940 that as one of Hitler's gestures towards Franco-German *rapprochement* his body was removed to Paris to lie beside that of his father in the Invalides.

At Vienna it was difficult to disguise a sense of relief at Reichstadt's death. Prokesch wrote, 'I cannot help thinking that an active and happy early life would have benefited his physical constitution and that his development was arrested by mental depression. I knew him well enough to realize that his health was profoundly affected by his melancholia.' Foresti wrote to Dietrichstein, 'I agree with you that it is better for the poor Prince to go to a more peaceful world. His position was so artificial, so full of constraints, his character so enigmatic and incomprehensible, the dangers so great for him, that he could not find in this world any true contentment or any prosperity.' The Emperor Francis, who was truly fond of his grandson, told Anatole de Montesquiou, Napoleon's former aide-de-camp and the son of Reichstadt's governess, 'His death was a good thing: his position in Europe was too difficult. His death was a misfortune for nobody except myself.' The Emperor had written to General Hartmann, appointed head of the Prince's military household in 1830, that 'It is possible that some of the passions and inclinations of the Prince's late father—most of which are extremely culpable—may have been handed down to his son.'

These suspicions were not allayed when, in the last year of his life, Reichstadt greeted Marshal Marmont, who was visiting Vienna, as his father's 'oldest comrade-in-arms' and insisted, in a long series of interviews, in hearing from him an eye-witness account of his father's campaigns. Marmont noted that 'his eyes, smaller than Napoleon's and deeper-set, had the same expression, the same fire, the same energy. . . . His forehead too, recalled that of his father, and there was an-other point of resemblance in the lower part of his face and chin. Finally his complexion was that of the young Napoleon; the same pallor and the same colour of the skin.' No-body meeting him could doubt that he was more the son of his father than of his mother; in the dull circle of Habsburg princes he stood out as sensationally different and exotically brilliant. But, as Metternich, who knew Napoleon intimately, remarked, 'Greatness rarely passes from father to son.'

Madame Mère was now past her eightieth year and the successive deaths of Napoleon, of Napoleon-Louis (the elder son of Louis Bonaparte, who joined the Carbonarist rising in the Romagna in 1831, and died of an epidemic of measles) and of Reichstadt in 1832, broke her spirit. She died in 1836 in her eighty-sixth year. Louis' younger son Louis-Napoleon, who had fought at his brother's side, was now the head of the younger generation of Bonapartes. His uncles Joseph, Lucien, Louis and Jerome had neither the enthusiasm nor the authority to lead a Bonapartist movement, and the mantle of Bonaparte pretender fell on his shoulders. After the fiasco of two abortive attempts at a military *putsch*, at Strasbourg in 1836 and at Boulogne in 1840, Bonapartism was given its second chance by the weakness of the Second Republic and the fear of the new socialist principles. Five million votes gave Louis-Napoleon the Presidency of the Republic in De-cember 1848.

The history of the Second Empire is beyond the scope of this book, but two curious parallels between the First and Second Empires may be noted. Louis-Napoleon had taken to heart Napoleon's lessons expounded from St Helena, and re-stated them in his book, written in 1839, *'Les Idées Napo-léoniennes'*. In accordance with the legend, the Bonaparte

dynasty must be based on the support of the principle of
nationality in Europe. But in a different way nationalism was
to cause the collapse of the Second Empire no less than that
of the first Empire. If his uncle ignored nationality until it
was too late, Napoleon III promoted it, but misconceived the
form it would take. He visualized an Italy independent but
organized as a confederation of states including the Papal
states. So also a North German confederation under Prussia
would be balanced by a confederation of South German
states under French patronage. A revision of the Vienna settlement would thus restore to France the natural frontiers and
secure her the moral hegemony of Europe. Napoleon III's
opponent Thiers admitted in 1865 that if he obtained the
Rhine frontier, the dynasty would be secure. But when it appeared that Napoleon III's disruption of the Vienna settlement was bound to produce strong unitary states in Italy and
Germany which would completely alter the balance of power
in Europe, the Second Empire was doomed. And after the
fiasco of Sedan a second Prince Imperial was to die young,
killed as an English officer by Zulu assegais in the war of
1879.

Napoleon pronounced his own epitaph at St Helena. 'If I had
succeeded, I should have been the greatest man known to
history.' But was the success he was aiming at ever within
the bounds of possibility? It is not inconceivable that he
could have won the game militarily in 1812, or even in 1813.
But it is hardly conceivable that the European or even the
world empire which appeared to be within his grasp could
have lasted more than a few years. The forces at work in
Europe would have shattered it into fragments—the rise of
the middle class, fostered by Napoleon as the basis of his
power, and soon to be immensely accelerated by the spread
of the industrial revolution. And it was this class which was
to be the spearhead in the demand for national self-determi-
nation and parliamentary government.

In France itself it was apparent even under the Empire
that the Napoleonic autocracy could only be ephemeral. Even
Napoleon was sometimes aware of this. 'All this may last my
lifetime but my son will have to govern very differently.' He
did not underrate the force of public opinion, though he
often misunderstood it. He remarked to Gourgaud at St
Helena, 'A man is only a man. His power is nothing if circumstances are not favourable. Opinion is all-important.' He

tried to harness to his ambition forces of 'opinion' which he only partially understood and could not in the end control. For that reason the title 'Emperor Napoleon the Great' did not survive his reign: though the reputation of Napoleon, the great man, cannot be effaced.

The legal, administrative and social institutions which he stamped on France, still malleable from the fiery furnace of the Revolution, remain the lasting monument to his genius. But for the mistakes of the last years of the Empire, a Napoleon II might have reigned in France. There was considerable force in Napoleon's claim at St Helena that only his dynasty could reconcile the Revolution with the past.

It would be futile to attempt a summing-up or a verdict on Napoleon as a man or as an historical phenomenon. It is better to try to let the facts, and the actors, speak for themselves; though no historian could, or would wish to, deny that the very process of historical thinking and writing necessarily involves a selection and an interpretation. As Professor Geyl, in his *Napoleon. For and Against*, concludes, 'The argument goes on.'

The most interesting retrospective judgments on Napoleon come from those who knew him well and stood up to him. Talleyrand, in conversation with Lord Holland after Napoleon's death, said, 'His career is the most extraordinary that has occurred for one thousand years. . . . He was certainly a great, an extraordinary man, nearly as extraordinary in his qualities as in his career: at least, so upon reflection I, who have seen him near and much, am disposed to consider him. He was clearly the most extraordinary man I ever saw, and I believe the most extraordinary that has lived in our age, or for many ages.' Metternich wrote a character-sketch of Napoleon in 1820. 'In order to judge of this extraordinary man, we must follow him upon the grand theatre for which he was born. Fortune had no doubt done much for Napoleon; but by the force of his character, the activity and lucidity of his mind, and by his genius for the great combinations of military science, he had risen to the level of the position which she had destined for him. Having but one passion, power, he never lost either his time or his means in those objects which might have diverted him from his aim. Master of himself, he soon became master of events. In whatever time he had appeared he would have played a prominent part.' In his Memoirs, Chateaubriand summed up Napoleon as 'the mightiest breath of life which ever animated human clay'.

In a sense Napoleon's life is both simple and symmetrical;
born in one small island, dying in another, and, in between,
such a fantastic career. In 1919 Archbishop Whately argued
amusingly and ingeniously in his *Historic Doubts Relative to
Napoleon Buonaparte* that Napoleon was a myth, and had
never existed. 'Now if a free-thinking philosopher—one of
those who advocate the cause of unbiased reason and despise
pretended revelations—were even to meet with such a tissue
of absurdities as this in an old Jewish record, would he not
reject it at once as too palpable an imposture to deserve even
any inquiry into its evidence?' 'Is it not just possible that,
during the rage for words of Greek derivation, the title of
Napoleon, which signifies "Lion of the Forest", may have
been conferred by the popular voice on more than one
favourite General, distinguished by irresistible valour? Is it
not also possible that "Buona Parte" may have been originally a sort of cant term applied to the "good", i.e. the
bravest or most patriotic part of the French army, collective-
ly, and have been afterwards mistaken for the proper name
of an individual?'

At St Helena Napoleon recalled that several times General
Paoli had said to him, 'You are a man of Plutarch, of
antiquity.' His career has, indeed the starkness of a Sopho-
clean tragedy; of hubris followed by nemesis. But it would
need a Shakespeare as well as a Sophocles to do justice to
the complexity of Napoleon's personality, which makes the
potentialities of his mind and character often more remarkable even than his achievements. We are confronted with the
enigma of a man of great intelligence, yet often startlingly
obtuse in his judgment of men and events; a man intensely
human, and even humane in his personal relationships, yet
possessed by a daemon of ambition which puts him beyond
the pale of humanity: in Aristotle's definition, 'either a
beast or a god'.

APPENDIX I

THE DIAGNOSIS OF NAPOLEON'S ILLNESS

IN VIEW OF THE PREVALENCE of liver-disease on the island in the early nineteenth century, the contention of the English Government that St Helena was healthy at this time cannot be sustained.[1] Dr Stokoe and Dr Antommarchi confirmed O'Meara's diagnosis that Napoleon was suffering from recurrent hepatitis, which he thought to be aggravated by his lack of exercise and addiction to prolonged hot baths.

It is less easy to determine whether these symptoms had any connection with his final, fatal disease. Surgeon-General R. Brice (*Le Secret de Napoleon*, 1936) thought that the perforated ulcer found at the post-mortem was caused by a rupture into the stomach of an amoebic liver abscess. Against this theory is the fact that no sign of an abscess of the liver was found at the post-mortem. Professor R. Leriche (*Souvenirs*, 1956) recalls that Lord Moynihan, President of the Royal College of Surgeons, showed him in 1927 a specimen preserved in the Hunterian Museum, supposed to be from the stomach of Napoleon. Professor Leriche thought that the perforation was probably dysenteric. The specimen was destroyed in the bombing of London in 1940, and in any case the attribution is doubtful. Bertrand and Marchand record that, on Lowe's instructions, great care was taken to see that the internal organs removed in the post-mortem were sealed up and placed in the coffin.

[1] See p. 251.

Dr J. Kemble (*Napoleon Immortal,* 1959) accepts the post-mortem finding that there was cancer of the stomach. The persistent vomiting in the last few months of his life are characteristic symptoms. But there remains the difficulty that this disease is usually accompanied by extreme emaciation; whereas Napoleon's abdomen was found to be encased in nearly two inches of fat. But Montholon noted that in the last few months Napoleon was suffering from extreme physical weakness, and that he was becoming 'as emaciated as in 1800'. Napoleon died before the cancer had run its full course. It is certain that, whatever the cause of the ulcer, the excessive dose of calomel administered on May 2, unwisely but in good faith by the assembled doctors, was rapidly fatal, by accelerating perforation and haemorrhage.

Dr Kemble writes that 'At forty, at the summit of his career, I think he undoubtedly became the subject of Fröhlich's disease' (*dystrophia adiposogenitalis*). One surgeon, but one only, Dr W. Henry, noted at the autopsy that there was atrophy of the genital organs; this, combined with the marked change from leanness to fatness in middle life, might suggest a deficiency of the pituitary gland. But endocrinologists today are far less confident about the diagnosis of Fröhlich's disease. Corvisart had warned Napoleon that too much desk work would make him fat, and in any case a number of English visitors who met Napoleon at St Helena thought that his corpulence had been exaggerated.

Recently hairs from Napoleon's head, preserved by the valets Marchand and Noverraz, have been tested for arsenic content, which was found to be abnormally high. It had already been noted in 1840 that Napoleon's body was perfectly preserved when the coffin was opened before it was removed to Paris. S. Forshufvud (*Who killed Napoleon?* 1962) has accordingly put forward the hypothesis that Napoleon's death was due to chronic arsenical poisoning, accidental or premeditated. It seems, however, impossible to base any conclusions on these findings, as arsenic was used so freely in the medicine of the time that an abnormal tolerance was built up.

In a sense, discussion of the physical cause of Napoleon's death is academic: the real cause was despair and frustration. A man of his temperament and past history, deprived of activity, interest and hope, was unlikely to survive for long.

APPENDIX II

THE DEATH-MASK OF NAPOLEON

STUDENTS OF NAPOLEON ARE greatly indebted to Monsieur E. de Veauce for his thorough investigation of the extant death-masks of Napoleon in '*L'Affaire du Masque de Napoléon*' (1957). Until the publication of this work, their origin and classification have been obscured by confusion and controversy. Since 1833 when Antommarchi raised a public subscription for the reproduction of the death-mask which he brought from St Helena, doubts have arisen about its authenticity. The low receding forehead, the weak chin, and the fine-drawn elegance of the face are in surprising contrast with the normal image of Napoleon. Yet Count Bertrand, and particularly Countess Bertrand, who was present at the taking of the cast, never repudiated the Antommarchi mask. Monsieur de Veauce shows by a comparison of the masks and by an analysis of the Marchand, Bertrand, Antommarchi, Burton and Lowe papers that the difficulties can be resolved.

Lowe wrote to Bathurst, 'Dr Burton, by a happy combination of dexterity and patience, succeeded—though with very imperfect materials—in obtaining an almost perfect cast. The Bertrands have kept the face; Dr Burton has kept the back part of the head, the craniological part.' For technical reasons the casts taken by Antommarchi and Burton together were probably in three rather than two pieces—the face from the temples to the mouth, the skull including the forehead, and the ears and lower jaw. No trace has been found of the part kept by Dr Burton, and as a result of the quarrel between

Dr Burton and Napoleon's household, which rumbled on
after their return to Europe, Antommarchi, in making his
copies, was left only with the cast of the face. To the authentic cast of the central part of the face, Antommarchi
therefore added an imaginative and unsatisfactory recon-
struction of the head and the periphery of the face. The cast
taken directly from the corpse would necessarily have been
destroyed in the process of reproduction.

Bertrand certifies in a letter of September 1, 1821, that
Antommarchi brought two copies from St. Helena. Bertrand
kept one, which was bequeathed by his descendants to Prince
Victor Napoleon. In order to avoid the French customs and
police, Antommarchi forwarded the other to Lord Burghersh,
British Consul at Leghorn, to be used by Canova as a model
for a marble bust. Bequeathed later to Lord Burghersh, the
mask was bought by Mme de Veauce at a sale of the Weigall
property, and is now in the Musée de l'Armée in Paris. Between Napoleon's death and the departure of the French from
St Helena, Antommarchi, now supplied with adequate plaster,
made more than two copies. The Reverend R. Boys, Vicar of
Jamestown, St Helena, until 1829, who was *persona grata* at
Longwood and had received a present of a snuff-box from
Napoleon for conducting the burial of his butler, Cipriani, obtained two. They remain the property of his descendants, Dr
L. Boys and Mrs Sankey, who has placed her copy on loan
with the Bodleian Library. A third was acquired by Colonel
Gilley, probably on a visit to St Helena in 1854, and is now
at Ffrankfort Castle, Tipperary.

The mask bequeathed to the Musée de Malmaison by the
Antommarchi family and the wax mask in the family of
Noverraz (Napoleon's footman at Longwood) were probably
made by Antommarchi after his return to Europe. ·

There are other masks purporting to represent Napoleon
which differ *in toto* from the Antommarchi masks. Dr
Arnott sold three masks in 1822. Unless Arnott succeeded in
taking a clandestine cast from Napoleon's corpse the day before Antommarchi and Burton, which is denied by the records of Bertrand and Marchand, these masks were probably
modelled from Arnott's drawing of Napoleon on his death-
bed.

The death-mask labelled 'Napoleon' in the Royal United
Services Museum differs so completely from the Antommarchi
masks and from the drawings of Napoleon on his death-bed
that it must be wrongly attributed.

SELECT BIBLIOGRAPHY

No attempt will be made here to reproduce the full bibliographies which already exist, or to list all the works consulted by the author. References to unpublished material quoted in the text have been made in the preface or footnotes. The reader may welcome, and may indeed expect, some guidance through the maze of Napoleonic literature, including recent works, even if it is the author's personal selection.

Books with useful bibliographies will be marked with an asterisk *.

English language editions will be quoted wherever they are available, and they are indicated by an English or American place of publication.

Full bibliographies will be found in:

Cambridge Modern History, Vol. IX (1906).

A. Fournier: *Napoleon I*, 2nd ed., London, 1914.

F. Kircheisen: *Bibliographie Napoléonienne*, Paris, 1912.

G. Pariset: *Le Consulat et L'Empire* (Hist. de France Contemporaine), Paris, 1921.

L. Villat: *La Révolution et l'Empire*, Vol. 2 (Clio Series), Paris, 1936.

G. Bruun: *Europe and the French Imperium* ('The Rise of Modern Europe' Series, ed. W. L. Langer), New York, 1938.

G. Lefebvre: *Napoléon* ('Peuples et Civilisations' Series), 4th ed., Paris, 1953. *Napoleon*, London, 1969.

Select List of Works on Europe, 1715–1815, by J. S. Bromley and A. Goodwin, Oxford, 1956. *Select Bibliography of Russian History, 1801–1917*, by D. Shapiro, Oxford, 1962.

The bibliography of the Napoleonic period is kept up to date, but only for books, by the valuable *Bulletins Historiques* (La période révolutionnaire et impériale) in the *Revue Historique*, Vols. 187

(1939), 196 (1946), 213 (1955), 221 (1959), 227–8 (1962), and by the periodical *French Historical Studies* (North Carolina).

Only occasional articles can be mentioned here out of the large number, contained especially in the *Revue des Études Napoléoniennes, Revue Historique, Annales Historiques de la Révolution Française, English Historical Review, American Historical Review, Journal of Modern History.*

For periodicals see: *Bibliographie der fremdsprachigen Zeitschriften literatur,* Leipzig, 1911–54.

Published Sources—The Bonapartes

Correspondance de Napoléon I, 32 vols., Paris, 1858–70.

(For additional collections of Napoleon's letters see Villat (Clio, *op. cit.*).

Lettres à Joséphine, ed. J. Bourgeat, Paris, 1941.

Napoleon's Letters to Marie-Louise, London, 1935.

Letters of Marie-Louise to Napoleon, ed. C. F. Palmstierna, London, 1958.

Lettres Personnelles des Souverains à Napoléon I, ed. Prince Napoléon et J. J. Hanoteau, Paris, 1939.

Napoleon's Memoirs, ed. S. de Chair, London, 1948.

Beauharnais, Eugène de: *Mémoires,* Paris, 1858–60.

Bonaparte, Joseph: *Mémoires,* Paris, 1853–4.

Bonaparte, Lucien: *Memoirs,* London, 1836.

Queen Hortense: *Memoirs,* New York, 1927.

Extracts

C. Herold: *The Mind of Napoleon,* New York, 1955.

J. E. Howard: *Letters and Documents of Napoleon,* Vol. I (1769–1802), London, 1961.

J. M. Thompson: *Napoleon's Letters,* Oxford, 1934.

The Principal Memoirs of Contemporaries

Abrantès (Laura Junot): *Memoirs,* London, 1929.

Beyle (Stendhal): *Life of Napoleon,* London, 1956.

Bertrand: *Cahiers de St. Hélène,* Paris, 1949–59; *Napoleon at St. Helena,* Vol. I, London, 1953.

Beugnot: *Life and Adventures,* London, 1871.

Bourrienne: *Memoirs of Napoleon Bonaparte,* London, 1923.

Caulaincourt: *Memoirs,* London, 1935.

Chaptal: *Mes Souvenirs,* Paris, 1893.

Chateaubriand: *Memoirs,* ed. R. Baldick, London, 1961.

Constant: *Memoirs,* London, 1896.

Fain: *Mémoires,* Paris, 1908.

Fouché: *Mémoires,* ed. L. Madelin, Paris, 1945.

Lavalette: *Memoirs,* London, 1831.

MacDonald: *Souvenirs,* Paris, 1892.

Marbot: *Memoirs,* London, 1892.

Marchand: *Mémoires,* Paris, 1952–5.

Marmont: *Mémoires,* 1857.

Masséna: *Mémoires,* 1848.

Méneval: *Memoirs,* London, 1894.

Miot de Melito: *Mémoires,* Paris, 1858.

Metternich: *Memoirs,* London, 1880.

Molé: *Life and Memoirs,* by H. de Noailles, London, 1923.

Pasquier: *Memoirs,* London, 1893.

Rapp: *Mémoires,* Paris, 1896.

Rémusat, Madame de: *Memoirs,* London, 1880.

Roederer: *Bonaparte me disait,* Paris, 1942; *Oeuvres,* Paris, 1853–9.

Savary: *Memoirs,* London, 1891.

Thiébault: *Memoirs,* London, 1896.

Memoirs such as Abrantès, Bourrienne, Constant, Marbot, Rémusat are lively but unreliable. A useful selection of the memoirs of contemporaries is in: J. Savant: *Napoleon in His Time,* London, 1958, but it relies heavily on biased accounts written soon after the fall of the Empire.

Bertrand and Caulaincourt are of outstanding importance for their intimacy and objectivity.

The Principal Biographies of Napoleon

A. Fournier: Leipzig, 1886–9; London, 1911.

J. Holland Rose: London, 1902.

F. Kircheisen, London, 1931.

E. Tarlé: London, 1937.

J. M. Thompson: Oxford, 1952.

Short Lives

H. A. L. Fisher, Oxford, 1912.

J. Colin, Paris, 1914.

J. Bainville, London, 1932.

H. Butterfield, London, 1939.

F.M.H. Markham, London, 1954.

A. J. Guérard, London, 1957.

Secondary Works—General

G. Bruun: *Europe and the French Imperium,* New York, 1938.*

Cambridge Modern History, Vol. IX, Cambridge, 1906.* (New Vol. IX, 1965.)

E. Dard: *Napoleon and Talleyrand,* London, 1937.

E. Driault: *Napoléon et l'Europe,* Paris, 1912–27.

A. Duff-Cooper: *Talleyrand,* London, 1932.

A. Fugier: *La Révolution Française et l'empire napoléonienne,* Paris, 1954.*

L. Garros: *Itineraire de Napoléon Bonaparte,* Paris, 1947.

P. Geyl: *Napoleon—For and Against,* London, 1949.

J. Godechot: *Les Institutions de la France sous la Révolution et l'Empire,* Paris, 1951.*

F. Kircheisen: *Napoleon I, sein leben und seine Zeit,* Munich, 1911–34.

G. Lacour-Gayet: *Talleyrand,* Paris, 1928–32.

G. Lefebvre: *Napoléon,* 4th ed., Paris, 1953.*

A. Lobanov-Rostovsky: *Russia and Europe,* 1789–1825, Duke, 1947.

L. Madelin: *Fouché,* Paris, 1900; *Histoire du Consulat et de l'empire,* Paris, 1937–54.

F. Masson: *Napoléon et sa famille,* Paris, 1897–1919.

G. Pariset: *Histoire de France Contemporaine,* Vol. 3, Paris, 1921.*

F. Rocquain: *Napoléon I et le Roi Louis,* Paris, 1875.

J. H. Rose: *Napoleonic Studies,* London, 1904; *The Personality of Napoleon,* London, 1906.

H. Srbik: *Metternich,* Munich, 1925.*

A. Sorel: *L'Europe et la Révolution Française,* Paris, 1885–1904.

L. Strakhovsky: *Alexander I of Russia,* New York, 1947.*

A. Vandal: *Napoléon I et Alexandre,* Paris, 1891–6; *L'Avènement de Bonaparte,* Paris, 1903–5.

J. S. Watson: *The Reign of George III (Oxford History of England*, Vol. 12), Oxford, 1960.*

Additional sources and works on particular periods and aspects are listed under the relevant chapters.

CHAPTER I

Published Sources
J. Boswell: *An Account of Corsica*, London, 1768.
F. Masson and G. Biagi: *Napoléon Inconnu, papiers inédits, 1769–1793*, Paris, 1895.
T. Nasica: *Mémoires sur l'enfance et la Jeunesse de Napoléon*, Paris, 1852.
Secondary Works

A. Chuquet: *La Jeunesse de Napoléon*, Paris, 1897–9.*
P. Bartel: *La Jeunesse Inédite de Napoléon*, Paris, 1954.
J. Colin: *L'Éducation Militaire de Napoléon*, Paris, 1900.*
A. Decaux: *Napoleon's Mother*, London, 1962.*
H. Larrey: *Madame Mère*, Paris, 1892.

CHAPTER II

Published Sources
Barras: *Mémoires*, ed. G. Duruy, Paris, 1895.
Pontécoulant: *Souvenirs*, 1861.
La Revellière-Lépeaux: *Mémoires*, Paris, 1895.
Maximilien Robespierre: *Correspondance*, ed. G. Michon, Paris, 1941.

Secondary Works
H. Cole: *Josephine*, London, 1962.
C. J. Fox: *Napoleon Bonaparte and the Siege of Toulon*, London, 1902.

J. Godechot: *La Contre-Révolution*, Paris, 1961.
G. Lefebvre: *Le Directoire*, Paris, 1946.*
A. Meynier: *Les Coups d'État du Directoire*, Paris, 1927–9.
M. Reinhard: *Carnot*, Paris, 1950–2.
M. J. Sydenham: *The Girondins*, London, 1961.
H. Wallon: *Les Représentants du Peuple en Mission*, Paris, 1899.
S. Wilkinson: *The Rise of General Bonaparte*, Oxford, 1930.

CHAPTER III

Published Sources
M. Reinhard: *Avec Bonaparte en Italie—Lettres de J. Sulkowski*, Paris, 1946. See also General Bibliography—Letters a Joséphine, Mémoires of Barras, Miot de Melito, Masséna.

Secondary Works—Political
S. Biro: *The German Policy of Revolutionary France, 1792–1797*, Harvard, 1954–7.*

G. Candeloro: *Storia dell' Italia Moderna*, Vol. I, Milan, 1956.*
G. Ferrero: *The Gamble*, London, 1939.
A. Fugier: *Napoléon et l'Italie*, Paris, 1947.*
P. Gaffarel: *Bonaparte et les Républiques Italiennes*, Paris, 1895.
J. Godechot: *Les Commissaires aux Armées sous le Directoire*, Paris, 1938*; *La*

Grande Nation, Paris, 1956.

R. Guyot: *Le Directoire et la Paix de l'Europe*, Paris, 1911.

E. Y. Hales: *Revolution and Papacy*, London, 1960.*

G. MacLellan: *Venice and Bonaparte*, Princeton, 1931.

B. Nabonne: *La Diplomatie du Directoire et Bonaparte*, Paris, 1952.

P. Rain: *La Diplomatie Française de Mirabeau à Bonaparte*, Paris, 1950.

E. P. Noether: *Seeds of Italian Nationalism, 1700–1815*, New York, 1951.

Napoleonic Warfare—General

P. Aubry: *Monge*, Paris, 1954.

P. de Bourcet: *Principes de la Guerre des Montagnes*, new ed., Paris, 1888.

H. Camon: *La Guerre Napoléonienne*, 4 vols., Paris, 1903–10; *Le Système de Guerre de Napoléon*, Paris, 1923.

D. Chandler: *Campaigns of Napoleon*, London, 1967.

C. Clausewitz: *On War*, London, 1908.

J. Colin: *L'Éducation Militaire de Napoléon (op. cit.)*; *The Transformations of War*, London, 1912.

E. M. Earle: *Makers of Modern Strategy*, Princeton, 1943.*

J. Guibert: *Essai general de Tactique*, Liège, 1775.

H. Jomini: *Life of Napoleon*, New York, 1864; *Art of War*, ed. J. D. Hittle, Harrisburg, 1947.

M. Lauerma: *L'Artillerie de Campagne Française pendant les guerres de la Révolution Française*, Helsinki, 1956.

B. H. Liddell-Hart: *The Ghost of Napoleon*, London, 1933.

J. Marshall-Cornwall: *Napoleon As Commander*, London, 1967.

J. U. Nef: *War and Human Progress*, Cambridge, Mass., 1950.*

C. Richard: *Le Comité de Salut Public et la fabrication des munitions de Guerre*, Paris, 1922.

T. Ropp: *War in the Modern World*, N.C., 1959.*

R. Quimby: *Background of Napoleonic Warfare*, New York, 1957.

S. Wilkinson: *French Army before Napoleon*, Oxford, 1915; *Rise of General Bonaparte*, Oxford, 1930 *(op. cit.)*.

S. T. McCloy: *French Inventions of the 18th century*, Lexington, 1952.

Campaign of 1796–7

J. Colin: *Campagne de 1796–1797*, Paris, 1898.

C. von Clausewitz: *La campagne de 1796 en Italie*, tr. J. Colin, 1899.

W. G. F. Jackson: *Attack in the West*, London, 1953.

For subsequent campaigns, see bibliography in G. Lefebvre, *Napoleon (op. cit.)*, which includes the campaign histories published by the French General Staff.

CHAPTER IV

Published Sources

R. N. Desgenettes: *Souvenirs d'un médecin de l'expédition d'Égypte*, Paris, 1893.

Desvernois: *Mémoires*, Paris, 1893.

Nelson, Horatio: *Letters and Dispatches*, ed. Nicholas, Vol. III, London, 1844.

Secondary Works

J. Barrow: *Life and Correspondence of Sir Sidney Smith*, London, 1848.

R. Cavaliero: *The Last of the Crusaders: the Knights of St.*

John and Malta in the 18th Century, London, 1960.

F. Charles-Roux: Bonaparte: Governor of Egypt, London, 1937; Les Origines de l'expédition d'Egypte, Paris, 1910.

P. G. Elgood: Bonaparte's Adventure in Egypt, London, 1931.

S. Ghorbal: The Beginnings of the Egyptian Question, London, 1928.

C. Herold: Bonaparte in Egypt, London, 1963.*

C. de la Jonquière: L'Expédition d'Égypte, Paris, 1899–1907.*

A. Moorehead: The Blue Nile, London, 1962.

O. Warner: Battle of the Nile, London, 1960.

CHAPTER V

Published Sources
Gaudin: Mémoires, new ed., Paris, 1926.

Gohier: Mémoires, 1824.

Pelet: Napoleon in Council, Edinburgh, 1837.

Thibaudeau: Bonaparte and the Consulate, London, 1908.

Secondary Works
H. Acton: The Bourbons of Naples, London, 1956.

A. Aulard: Political History of the French Revolution, London, 1910; Études et Leçons, Vol. VII, Paris, 1913.

P. Bastid: Sieyès, Paris, 1939.

J. Bourdon: La Constitution de l'An VIII, Paris, 1941.

C. Durand: Études sur le Conseil d'État napoléonien, Paris, 1949; Le fonctionnement du Conseil d'État napoléonien, 1954; Les Auditeurs au Conseil dÉtat, Aix-en-Provence, 1958.

A. Gobert: L'opposition des Assemblées sous le Consulat, 1925.

G. Lefebvre: Le Directoire, Paris, 1946.*

A. Ollivier: Le Dix-Huit Brumaire, Paris, 1959.

J. Régnier: Les Préfets du Consulat et de l'Empire, Paris, 1913.

A. Vandal: L'Avènement de Bonaparte, 1903.

Articles
A. Goodwin: The French Executive Directory—a Revaluation—History, 1937.

CHAPTER VI

Published Sources
Consalvi: Mémoires, Paris, 1864.

Secondary Works
A. Aulard: 'Le centenaire de la Légion d'honneur', Études et Leçons, Vol. IV, Paris, 1904.

F. Baldensperger: Le Mouvement des Idées dans l'émigration française, Paris, 1925.

A. Dansette: Religious History of Modern France, London, 1961.

B. Delacroix: Réorganisation de l'Église de France après la Révolution, Paris, 1962.

H. C. Deutsch: The Genesis of Napoleonic Imperialism, Harvard, 1938.

E. Y. Hales: Napoleon and the Pope, London, 1960.

A. Latreille: Napoléon et le Saint-Siège, 1935*; L'Église

Catholique et la Révolution française, Paris, 1946–50.
J. Leflon: *Pie VII*, Paris, 1958.
F. Ponteil: *Napoléon 1er et l'organisation autoritaire de la France*, Paris, 1956.*
P. Sagnac: *La législation civile de la Révolution Française*, Paris, 1898.

CHAPTER VII

Published Sources
Letters of Charles, Lord Barham, ed. J. K. Laughton, London, 1907–11.
O. Browning: *England and Napoleon in 1803—Dispatches of Lord Whitworth*, London, 1887.
Letters and Dispatches of Horatio, Viscount Nelson, ed. Nicholas, London, 1844, Vols. VI and VII.

Secondary Works
J. G. Alger: *Napoleon's British Visitors and Captives*, London, 1904.
A. Broadley: *Napoleon in Caricature*, London, 1911.
J. S. Corbett: *The Campaign of Trafalgar*, London, 1910. *The Naval Campaign of 1805*, Oxford, 1933.
E. Desbrières: *Projets et Tentatives de debarquement aux Îles britanniques, 1793–1805*, Paris, 1905–12.
D. George: *English Political Caricature*, Oxford, 1959.
G. S. Ford: *Hanover and Prussia, 1795–1803*, New York, 1903.
H. Gaubert: *Conspirateurs sous Napoléon 1e*, Paris, 1962.
B. de Jouvenel: *Napoléon et l'Économie Dirigée*, Paris, 1942.
M. Lewis: *The History of the British Navy*, London, 1959; *A Social History of the Navy*, London, 1960; *Napoleon and His British Captives*, London, 1962.
P. G. Mackesy: *The War in the Mediterranean, 1803–1810*, London, 1957.
A. T. Mahan: *The Influence of Seapower upon the French Revolution and Empire*, London, 1892; *Life of Nelson*, London, 1898.
B. Melchior-Bonnet: *Le Duc d'Enghien*, Paris, 1961.
F. J. McCunn: *The Contemporary English View of Napoleon*, London, 1914.
A. Pingaud: *Bonaparte Président de la République Italienne*, Paris, 1914.
D. Pope: *England Expects: Trafalgar*, London, 1959.
A. Thomazi: *Napoléon et Ses Marins*, Paris, 1950.*

Articles
Critical discussion of the Enghien affair remains embedded in articles:
G. Caudrillier: 'Le Complot de l'An XII', in *Revue Historique*, Vols. 74 (1901), 75 (1901), 78 (1902); *Revue des Études Napoléoniennes*, May 1922.
J. Doutenville: 'Le Catastrophe d'Enghien', in *Revue des Études Napoléoniennes*, Vol. 25, 1925.
See also Chapter XIX of J. Holland-Rose, *Life of Napoleon* (11th ed., 1934).

CHAPTER VIII

Published Sources
A. Czartoryski: *Memoirs and Correspondence,* ed. A. Gielgud, London, 1888.
Leveson Gower, Lord Granville: *Correspondence,* London, 1916.
Nesselrode: *Lettres et Papiers,* Paris, 1904–8.

Secondary Works
H. Butterfield: *The Peace Tactics of Napoleon, 1806–1808,* Cambridge, 1929.
G. Craig: *The Politics of the Prussian Army,* Oxford, 1955.
H. A. L. Fisher: *Napoleonic Statesmanship: Germany,* Oxford, 1903.
A. Handelsman: *Napoléon et la Pologne, 1806–1807,* Paris, 1909.
M. Kukiel: *Czartoryski and European Unity,* Princeton, 1955.
H. T. Parker: *Three Napoleonic Battles,* Durham, N.C., 1944.
K. Waliszewski: *Le Règne d'Alexandre 1ᵉʳ* (St. Petersburg, 1912).
J. Rambaud: *Naples sous Joseph Bonaparte, 1806–1808,* Paris, 1911. See also under Chapter XII.

CHAPTER IX

Published Sources
See General Bibliography.
Bausset: *Mémoires,* Paris, 1829.
Coignet: *Narrative of Captain Coignet,* ed. L. Larchey, New York, 1890.
Fouché: *La Police Secrète du premier empire: bulletins quotidiens,* ed. F. d'Hauterive, Paris, 1908.
Wheeler: *The Letters of Private Wheeler,* ed. B. H. Liddell-Hart, Boston, 1951.

Secondary Works
A. Aulard: *Napoléon et le Monopole Universitaire,* Paris, 1911.
H. Aureas: *Miollis,* Paris, 1960.
J. Bourdon: *L'Administration Militaire de Napoléon I,* Paris, 1917.
O. Connelly: *Napoleon's Satellite Kingdoms,* New York, 1965.
P. Ganière: *Corvisart,* Paris, 1951.
C. Herold: *Madame de Staël,* London, 1959.*
F. Healey: *Rousseau et Napoléon,* Geneva, 1957; *The Literary Culture of Napoleon,* Geneva, 1959.
R. B. Holtman: *Napoleonic Propaganda,* Baton Rouge, 1950.
J. Kemble: *Napoleon Immortal,* London, 1959.*
H. Lachouque: *The Anatomy of Glory, Napoleon and His Guard,* Providence, 1961.
F. Masson: *Napoleon at Home,* London, 1894.
A. Meynier: *Une Erreur Historique: Les Morts de la Grande Armée et les Armées ennemies,* Paris, 1934.
J. Morvan: *Le Soldat Impérial,* Paris, 1904.
C. Schmidt: *La Réforme de l'université impériale en 1811,* Paris, 1905.
H. Welschinger: *La Censure sous le Premier Empire,* Paris, 1882.
A. Wilson: *Fontanes,* Paris, 1928.
L. Hautecoeur: *David,* Paris, 1954.*

On Napoleon's Marshals and Generals, see:

G. Six: *Les Généraux de la Révolution et de l'Empire*, Paris, 1947.

And in lighter vein:

E. F. Delderfield: *The March of the Twenty-six*, London, 1962.

A. MacDonell: *Napoleon and His Marshals*, London, 1934.

Articles

F. Artz: 'L'Enseignement Technique en France (1789–1815)', in *Revue Historique*, Vol. 196 (1946).

G. Hanotaux: 'Du Consulat à l'Empire', in *Revue des Deux Mondes*, 7th Series, Vols. 26, 29 (1925); 'La Transformation Sociale', in *Revue des Deux Mondes*, 7th Series, Vols. 33, 34 (1926).

A Meynier: 'Levées et Pertes d'Hommes sous le Consulat et l'Empire', in *Revue des Études Napoléoniennes*, January 1930.

L. P. Williams: 'Science and the French Revolution', in *Isis*, Vol. 44; 'Science and Napoleon', in *Isis*, Vol. 47.

CHAPTER X

Published Sources

Mollien: *Mémoires*, Paris, 1898. See also Chaptal, Gaudin, *op. cit.*

Secondary Works

C. Ballot: *L'Introduction du Machinisme dans l'industrie française*, Paris, 1923.

R. Cameron: *France and the Economic Development of Europe, 1800–1914*, Princeton, 1961.*

S. B. Clough: *France, a History of National Economics*, New York, 1939.

F. Crouzet: *L'Économie britannique et le blocus continental, 1806–1813*, Paris, 1958.*

A. Cunningham: *British Credit in the Last Napoleonic War*, Cambridge, 1910.

M. Dunan: *Napoléon et l'Allemagne: Le Système Continental et les débuts du Royaume de Bavière, 1806–1810*, Paris, 1942.

W. F. Galpin: *The Grain Supply of England during the Napoleonic Period*, New York, 1925.

S. E. Harris: *The Assignats*, Harvard, 1930.

E. F. Hecksher: *The Continental System*, Oxford, 1922.

E. Hobsbawm: *The Age of Revolution*, London, 1962.

M. Marion: *Histoire Financière de la France*, Vol. IV, Paris, 1914–25.

F. Melvin: *Napoleon's Navigation System*, New York, 1914.

H. Sée: *Histoire Économique de la France*, Vol. 2, Paris, 1942.*

E. Tarlé: *Le blocus continental et le royaume d'Italie*, Paris, 1931.

O. Viennet: *Napoléon et l'industrie française*, Paris, 1947.*

O. Wolff: *Ouvrard*, London, 1962.

The best general survey of the Continental System is in:

G. Lefebvre: *Napoléon, op. cit.*, Bks. IV and V.

For the Anglo-French economic warfare the indispensable work is:

F. Crouzet: *op. cit.*, which

largely supersedes the earlier work of Hecksher, Galpin, Melvin, Cunningham and Holland-Rose. Crouzet's final chapter sums up his conclusions.

Hobsbawm and J. S. Watson (*Oxford History of England,* Vol. 12, Ch. 20) give the latest surveys of the progress of the industrial revolution.

CHAPTER XI

Published Sources

A. Brett-James: *Wellington at War: a selection of his wartime letters,* London, 1961.

M. Foy: *Histoire de la Guerre de la Péninsule,* Paris, 1827.

Jourdan: *Mémoires Militaires,* 1899.

La Forest: *Correspondance,* ed. G. de Grandmaison, Paris, 1905–7.

Soult: *Mémoires: Espagne et Portugal,* Paris, 1955.

Suchet: *Mémoires, Paris,* 1892.

Secondary Works

M. Artola: *Los Afrancesados,* Madrid, 1953.

J. Chastenet: *Godoy,* London, 1953.

P. Conrad: *La Constitution de Bayonne,* Paris, 1909.

G. Davies: *Wellington and His Army,* Oxford, 1954.

A. Fugier: *Napoléon et l'Espagne, 1799–1808,* Paris, 1930; *La Junte Supérieure des*

Asturies, Paris, 1930.

G. de Grandmaison: *L'Espagne et Napoléon,* Paris, 1908–31.

C. Grasset: *La Guerre d'Espagne,* Paris, 1914–32.

R. Herr: *The Eighteenth-century Revolution in Spain,* Princeton, 1958.

G. Lovett: *Napoleon and the Birth of Modern Spain,* New York, 1965.

J. Lucas-Dubreton: *Napoléon devant l'Espagne,* Paris, 1946.

C. W. Oman: *History of the Peninsular War,* Oxford, 1902–30.

S. P. G. Ward: *Wellington's Headquarters,* Oxford, 1957.

J. Weller: *Wellington in the Peninsula,* London, 1962.

The military side is well covered by Oman; but there is as yet no systematic treatment of the social and political background of the Peninsular War. Lucas-Dubreton provides a useful introduction.

CHAPTER XII

Published Sources

J. G. Fichte: *Addresses to the German Nation,* Chicago, 1922.

Hardenberg: *Denkwürdigkeiten,* Leipzig, 1877.

Karl Erzherzog von Oesterreich *Ausgewählte Schriften,* Vienna, 1893–5.

Stein: *Briefwechsel,* ed. Botzenhart, Berlin, 1931.

G. de Staël, *Germany,* London, 1813.

Secondary Works

E. N. Anderson: *Nationalism and the Cultural Crisis in Prussia, 1806–1815,* 1939.

R. Aris: *History of Political Thought in Germany,* London, 1936.

M. Boucher: *Le Sentiment National en Allemagne,* Paris, 1947.

G. Cavaignac: *La Formation de la Prusse Contemporaine,* Paris, 1891.

SELECT BIBLIOGRAPHY

281

J. Droz: *L'Allemagne et la Révolution Française*, Paris, 1949.

R. Ergang: *Herder and the Foundation of German Nationalism*, New York, 1913.

G. S. Ford: *Stein and the Era of Reform in Prussia, 1807–1815*, Princeton, 1922.

G. P. Gooch: *Germany and the French Revolution*, London, 1920.*

E. F. Henderson: *Blücher and the Uprising against Napoleon*, New York, 1911.

H. Kohn: *The Mind of Germany*, London, 1961; *The Idea of Nationalism*, New York, 1945.

C. Langsam: *The Napoleonic Wars and German Nationalism in Austria*, New York, 1930.*

F. Meinecke: *Weltbürgertum und Nationalstaat*, Berlin, 1908.

K. Pinson: *Modern Germany*, New York, 1954.*

S. Ritter: *Stein*, revised ed., Stuttgart, 1958.

A. Robert: *L'Idée nationale autrichienne et les guerres de Napoléon*, Paris, 1933.*

W. O. Shanahan: *Prussian Military Reforms, 1786–1813*, New York, 1945.

P. R. Sweet: *F. von Gentz*, Madison, 1941.

Articles

Napoleon's attitude to nationality is well analysed by:

A. Pingaud: 'La politique italienne de Napoléon I', in *Revue Historique*, January 1927, Vol. 154.

H. Kohn: 'Napoleon and the Age of Nationalism', in *Journal of Modern History*, March 1950.

CHAPTER XIII

Published Sources

Alexandre I—*Correspondance avec sa soeur la grande-duchesse Catherine*, ed. N. Mihailovitch, St. Petersburg, 1910.

Bourgogne: *Memoirs of Sergeant Bourgogne (1812–1813)*, London, 1899.

A. Chuquet: *La Guerre de Russie–Notes et documents*, Paris, 1912.

Fain: *Manuscrit de 1812*, Paris, 1827.

C. de Grunwald: 'Le Mariage de Napoléon et de Marie-Louise' (Letters of Comtesse Metternich, *Revue des Deux Mondes*, Vols. 38 and 41 (1937).

Roeder: *Diary of Captain Roeder*, London, 1960.

P. de Ségur: *Napoleon's Russian Campaign*, ed. J. D. Townsend, London, 1959.

Sir R. Wilson: *Narrative of Events during the Invasion of Russia*, London, 1860.

Secondary Works

C. von Clausewitz: *The Campaign of Russia in 1812*, London, 1843.

E. Dard: *Narbonne*, Paris, 1943.

A. Palmer: *Napoleon in Russia*, London, 1967.

V. Puryear: *Napoleon and the Dardanelles*, Berkeley, 1951.*

E. Tarlé: *Napoleon's Invasion of Russia, 1812*, London, 1942.*

F. D. Scott: *Bernadotte and the Fall of Napoleon*, Cambridge, Mass., 1935.

CHAPTER XIV

Published Sources
Fain: *Manuscrit de 1813,* Paris, 1824.
E. Odeleben: *Relation de la Campagne de 1813,* Paris, 1817.
Planat de la Faye: *Souvenirs,* 1895.
Vitrolles: *Mémoires,* Paris, 1883.

Secondary Works
C. S. Buckland: *Metternich and the British Government,* 1932.
E. V. Gulick: *Europe's Classical Balance of Power,* Ithaca, 1955.
H. Houssaye: *1814,* Paris, 1888.
R. M. Johnston: *The Napo-leonic Empire in Southern Italy,* London, 1904.
H. Kissinger: *A World Restored,* Boston, 1957.
H. Nicolson: *The Congress of Vienna,* London, 1946.
F. Ponteil: *La Chute de Napoléon,* Paris, 1943.*
R. Rath: *The Fall of the Napoleonic Kingdom of Italy,* New York, 1941.
J. Thiry: *La Chute de Napoléon,* Paris, 1938.*
C. K. Webster: *The Foreign Policy of Castlereagh, 1812–1815,* London, 1931.
H. Weil: *Joachim Murat, roi de Naples: la dernière année du règne,* Paris, 1909.

CHAPTER XV

Published Sources
Sir N. Campbell: *Napoleon at Fontainebleau and Elba,* London, 1869.
Grouchy: *Fragments Historiques,* Paris, 1829; *Mémoires,* Paris, 1873.
Sir F. Maitland: *Narrative of the Surrender of Buonaparte,* London, 1826.
Marie-Louise, Empress: *Private Diaries,* ed. F. Masson, London, 1922; *Lettres à la Comtesse de Colleredo et a Mlle. de Poutet,* Paris, 1887.
Marchand: *op. cit.*
J. H. Rose: *Napoleon's Last Voyages* (contemporary memoirs), London, 1906.
C. Shorter: *Napoleon and His Fellow-travellers* (contemporary memoirs), London, 1908.

Secondary Works
P. Bartel: *Napoléon à l'île de l'Elbe,* Paris, 1947.
A. F. Becke: *Napoleon and Waterloo,* revised ed., London, 1936.*
G. de Bertier de Sauvigny: *La Restauration,* Paris, 1955.
H. Houssaye: *1815,* Paris, 1893.
H. Kurtz: *The Trial of Marshal Ney,* London, 1957.
H. Lachouque: *Le Secret de Waterloo,* Paris, 1952.
E. Le Gallo: *Les Cent Jours,* Paris, 1924.
C. Manceron: *Which Way to Turn: Napoleon's Last Choice,* London, 1961.
J. Naylor: *Waterloo,* London, 1960.*
Young (Norwood): *Napoleon in Exile,* London, 1914.
The best detailed account of the Waterloo campaign is in Becke.

CHAPTER XVI

Published Sources
Mrs E. Abell (Elizabeth Balcombe): *Recollections of the Emperor Napoleon,* London, 1844.
Gourgaud: *Journal,* Paris, 1899.

W. Henry: *Events of a Military Life*, London, 1843.

E. Las Cases: *Memoirs of the Emperor Napoleon*, London, 1836.

Montholon: *History of the Captivity of Napoleon at St. Helena*, London, 1846; *Lettres du Comte et Comtesse Montholon*, ed. P. Gonnard, Paris, 1906.

B. O'Meara: *Napoleon in Exile*, London, 1822.

Lady Malcolm: *Diary of St. Helena*, London, 1899.

J. N. Santini: *An Appeal to the British Nation*, London, 1817.

W. Warden: *Letters written on board the 'Northumberland' and at St. Helena*, London, 1816; *Letters from the Cape of Good Hope, in reply to Mr Warden*, London, 1817.

See also Bertrand, Marchand, Shorter, *op. cit.*

Secondary Works

O. Aubry: *St. Helena*, London, 1937.

Brookes (Dame Mabel Balcombe): *St. Helena Story*, London, 1960.

F. Forshufvud: *Who Killed Napoleon?*, London, 1962.

W. Forsyth: *History of the Captivity of Napoleon at St. Helena*, London, 1853.

P. Ganière: *Le Dernier Voyage de l'Empereur*, Paris, 1956; *Napoléon a St. Hélène*, Paris, 1960.

R. Korngold: *The Last Years of Napoleon*, London, 1960.*

Rosebery, Earl of: *Napoleon, the Last Phase*, London, 1900.

E. de Veauce: *L'Affaire du Masque de Napoléon*, Lyon, 1957.*

Rosebery and Aubry remain classic accounts of Napoleon at St. Helena; but they now need to be supplemented by Ganière and Korngold, who take account of the recently published *Mémoires* of Marchand and *Cahiers* of Bertrand.

CHAPTER XVII

Published Sources

Dietrichstein: *Observations*, ed. J. de Bourgoing, *Revue des Études Napoléoniennes*, 1932.

Foresti: *Notes*, ed. J. de Bourgoing, *Revue des Études Napoléoniennes*, 1932.

Holland, Lord: *Foreign Reminiscences*, London, 1850.

Prokesch von Osten: *Mes Relations avec le Duc de Reichstadt*, ed. J. de Bourgoing, Paris, 1934.

Secondary Works

J. de Bourgoing: *Le Fils de Napoléon*, Paris, 1950.

A. Castelot: *Napoleon's Son*, London, 1960.*

J. Deschamps: *Sur la légende de Napoléon*, Paris, 1931.

P. Gonnard: *Les Origines de la légende napoléonienne*, Paris, 1906.*

A. Guérard: *Reflections on the Napoleonic Legend*, London, 1924.

J. Lucas-Dubreton: *Le Culte de Napoléon, 1815–1848*, Paris, 1960.

F. A. Simpson: *Rise of Louis Napoleon*, 3rd ed., London, 1950.

J. M. Thompson: *Louis Napoleon*, Oxford, 1954.

The best biography of the Duc de Reichstadt is Castelot, which takes account of the recently discovered Archives of Marie-Louise (see his Preface).

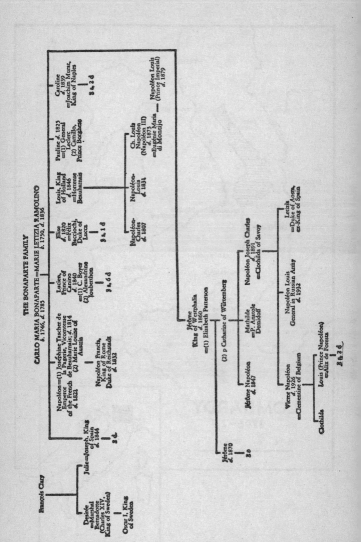

THE BONAPARTE FAMILY

CARLO MARIA BONAPARTE = MARIE LETIZIA RAMOLINO
b. 1746, d. 1785   b. 1750, d. 1836

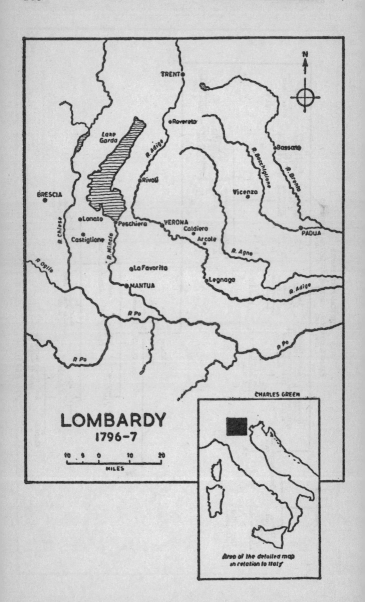

TRENT

Rovereto

Lake
Garda

R. Adige

Bassano

R. Bacchiglione

R. Brenta

Rivoli

BRESCIA

Vicenza

R. Chiese

Lonato

Peschiera

VERONA

Caldiero

PADUA

Castiglione

R. Mincio

Arcole

R. Agne

La Favorita

R. Oglio

Legnago

MANTUA

R. Adige

R. Po

R. Po

R. Po

CHARLES GREEN

LOMBARDY
1796–7

10   5   0   10   20

MILES

Area of the detailed map
in relation to Italy

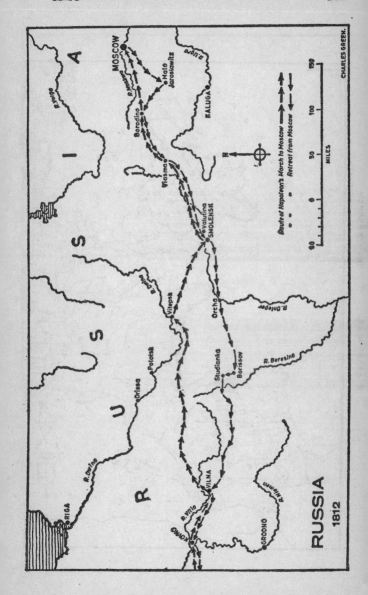

RUSSIA
1812

MOSCOW
Malo
Jaroslawitz
KALUGA
Borodino
R. Moscow
Vlasma
Valutina
SMOLENSK
Vitepsk
Orsha
Polotsk
Orisa
Studianka
Borissov
R. Beresina
VILNA
R. Vilia
KOVNO
GRODNO
RIGA
R. Dwina
R. Volga
R. Ugra
R. Dnieper
R. Dnieper
R. Niemen
N

Route of Napoleon's March to Moscow
Retreat from Moscow

MILES
50   0   50   100   150

CHARLES GREEN.

EUROPE
under
NAPOLEON · 1812

Empire of Napoleon (Direct rule)

Empire of Napoleon (Dependant States)

Allies of Napoleon

Independent States

100   50   0   100   200   300
MILES

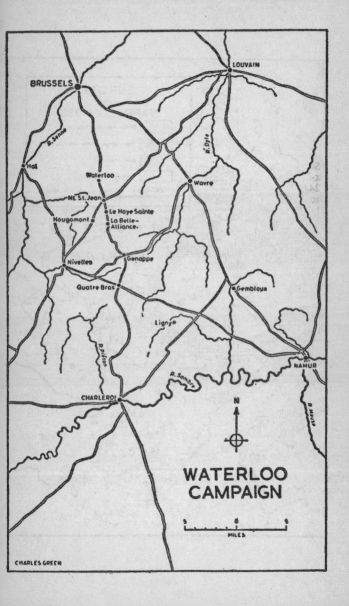

BRUSSELS
LOUVAIN
R. Senne
Hal
Waterloo
Mt. St. Jean
Wavre
R. Dyle
Le Haye Sainte
La Belle-
Hougomont
Alliance
Nivelles
Genappe
Quatre Bras
Gembloux
R. Piéton
Ligny
R. Sambre
NAMUR
R. Meuse
CHARLEROI

N

WATERLOO
CAMPAIGN

MILES

CHARLES GREEN

INDEX

Abensberg, 182
Abercromby, Sir Ralph, 90
Aboukir, 60, 63, 66, 67
Acre, Siege of, 65
Addington, Henry, Viscount Sidmouth, 90
Aix-la-Chapelle, Congress of, 244, 250
Ajaccio, 16, 17, 21, 22, 23, 68
Alba de Tormes, 69
Albitte, Antoine Louis, 27
Albuera, 169
Alessandria, 42, 86
Alexander I, Tsar: Character, 121; Relations with Prussia, 123, 124, 201, 208; France, 126, 128, 129, 167, 204, 214, 215; War in Russia, 186 ff., 200; Austria, 180; Sweden, 209; Opinion of the Bourbons, 215, 223; Congress of Vienna, 224, 228; Imprisonment of Napoleon, 245, 250
Alexandria, 59, 60, 61, 63, 66, 128
Alfieri, Vittorio, 175
Allemand, Zacharie, Comte, 115
Almeida, 168, 169
Alvinzy, Joseph, 46, 47, 48
America, see United States of America
Amiens, Peace of, 90, 94, 103, 105, 107, 108, 244
Ancona, 50, 151, 211
Andalusia, 169, 170
Anna, Grand Duchess, 186
Anspach, 123, 124
Antibes, 226
Antommarchi, Francesco: Physician, 251, 253, 257, 267; Death Mask, 254, 268, 269, 270
Antwerp, 209

Aosta, 84, 85
Aranjuez, 165
Arcis-sur-Aube, 213, 218
Arcola, 45, 47
Armed Neutrality, Second, 89, 90, 119
Arndt, Ernst Moritz, 175
Arnott, Doctor Archibald, 253, 270
Artois, Charles-Philippe Comte d', 110, 112, 223, 226
Ascension, 245
Aspern, 182, 183
Auditeurs, 98–9
Auerstädt, 126
Augereau, Pierre François Charles, Duke of Castiglione: and Napoleon, 33, 73, 74, 75, 135, 212; Italian Campaign, 47; Paris, 53, 71; Poland, 127
Austerlitz, 123, 124, 127, 129, 144, 162, 183, 191, 193
Austria: Economic Position, 161, 180; Relations with France, Alliances, 104, 155, 185, 190, 203; Peace Treaties, 49, 52, 53, 53–4, 83, 86, 89, 124, 183, 201–2, 204; War with, 24, 69, 158, 170, 180, 182, 205; War in Italy, 41–49, 70, 83–7, 89, 121; Relations with Russia, 70, 121, 122, 200; Piedmont, 41, 83
Auteuil, 89
Auxonne, 20
Avignon, 25, 153, 222

Babeuf, François, 44, 52
Bacciochi, Pascal, 145
Bacler de l'Albe, Louis-Albert-Ghislain, Baron, 136
Badajoz, 168, 170
Baden, 122, 124

Baden, Duke of, 111
Bagration, Prince, 190, 191, 192, 202
Balachov, General, 191
Balearic Islands, 125
Balcombe, Betsy, 242, 243
Balcombe, Jane, 242, 243
Balcombe, William, 242
Balmain, Alexandre, Comte de, 246
Bamberg, 126, 229
Bank of France, 80, 162
Barbé-Marbois, François, Marquis de, 162
Barclay de Tolly, Michel, Prince, 190, 191, 192
Bardo, 84
Barham, Lord, 115
Baring Bank, 162
Barras, Paul-F.-J.-Nicholas de, 25, 29, 30, 31-2, 52, 70, 73, 74, 161
Bartenstein, Convention of, 128
Barthélemy, François, 52, 53
Basle, Peace of, 32, 120
Bassano, 45, 46, 48
Bathurst, Earl, 244, 245, 246, 249, 250, 251, 253
Bautzen, 143, 204
Bavaria, 122, 124, 183, 207
Baylen, 166, 179, 124
Bayonne, 164, 165, 170, 171
Beauharnais, Eugène de: Relations with Napoleon, 31, 73, 121, 145, 186, 188; In Italy, 163, 174, 183; In Russia, 195, 196, 198; In Germany, 201, 203, 211, 212, 214
Beauharnais, Hortense de, 31, 73, 106, 109, 144, 145, 237
Beaulieu, Jeanne Pierre de, 41, 42, 45
Beethoven, Ludwig Van, 111
Belgium, 53, 89
Bellerophon, 138, 237, 238, 239
Bennigsen, Levin Auguste, Comte de, 127, 129
Berlier, Théophile, Comte, 96
Berlin, 127
Berlin Decree, 155, 156, 157
Bernadotte, Jean Baptiste Jules: Marriage, 30; Relations with

Napoleon, 69, 73, 74, 75, 89, 99, 133, 143; On Council of Five Hundred, 69, 72; In Germany, 122, 123, 127; Pontecorvo, 131; Conspiracy, 134; Prince Royal of Sweden, 188, 190, 206, 207, 208, 209
Bernaudet, Corporal, 141
Berthier, Louis Alexandre, Prince of Wagram: Chief of Staff, 40, 143; In Italy, 40, 42, 84; Minister of War, 80; The Reserve Army, 83; In Germany, 182, 211; In Russia, 192, 194, 196; Deserts Napoleon, 229
Berthollet, Claude Louis, 59, 62
Bertrand, Fanny, 240, 244, 257, 269
Bertrand, Henri-Gratien, Comte: In Elba, 221, 223; In St Helena, 241, 244, 247, 248, 250, 255; Diary, 251, 257, 258, 267, 269, 270
Bessières, Jean Baptiste, Duke of Istria, 143, 166, 189-90, 204
Blois, 225
Blücher, Gebhard Prince: In Germany, 203, 206, 207, 211, 212, 213; Charleroi, 230; Ligny, 230, 231; and Napoleon, 236
Bologna, 45, 50
Bombelles, Comte de, 221
Bonald, Louis, Vicomte de, 92
Bonaparte, Carlo, 17, 18
Bonaparte, Caroline, 17, 145, 146
Bonaparte, Charles Louis Napoleon (Napoleon III), 244, 264
Bonaparte, Charlotte, 165
Bonaparte, Elisa, 17, 22, 145, 165
Bonaparte, Jerome: 17, 113, 245; King of Westphalia, 129, 144; Marries American, 145; Silesia, 175; In Russia, 191; Pressure on Marie Louise, 218; Character, 263

Bonaparte, Joseph: 17; Marriage, 30; Lunéville, 89; Napoleon on, 109, 113, 168, 211, 237; Opposition to Napoleon, 133, 144; and Italy, 121; King of the Two Sicilies, 125; King of Naples, 135; King of Spain, 158, 165, 172, 190; Military Commander, 169, 170, 205, 214; Returns to Paris, 171, 213; Puts pressure on Marie Louise, 214, 218

Bonaparte, Letizia (Madame Mère): In Corsica, 16, 17, 18, 19, 20, 23; Misses Coronation, 113; Supports Lucien, 144–5; In Elba, 223, 225; Intervenes for Emperor, 245; St Helena, 251, 252; Grandson, 262; Death, 263; Character, 145

Bonaparte, Louis: 17, 48–5, 263; Son, 109; Refuses Thrones, 121, 165; King of Holland, 144; Marriage, 144

Bonaparte, Lucien, 17, 22–3, 133; Brumaire Crisis, 72, 73, 74, 75, 76; Minister of the Interior, 81, 82, 103; Relations with Napoleon, 113, 144, 146, 227; Hundred Days, 227, 228, 235; Exiled, 238; Character, 263

Bonaparte, Napoleon: Career of—Origins, 15, 16, 17; Education, 18, 19; In Corsica, 15, 20, 21, 23; At Toulon, 26; Arrested, 27; In Paris, 20, 21, 28, 57, 68; Vendémiaire Crisis, 29, 30; Marries Josephine, 31; In Italy, 20, 34, 39–54; In Egypt, 60–7; Brumaire Crisis, 71, 73–80; First Consul, 80–4, 88; Marengo Campaign, 83–7; Consul for Life, 101–2; Renews War with England, 108; Executes Enghien, 16, 110–2; Emperor, 113; Fails to invade England, 58, 114–6; Austerlitz Campaign, 123–4; Jena Campaign, 126; In Poland, 127 ff.; Tilsit,

129; In Spain, 166–72; In Austria, 180–4; Divorces Josephine, 185; Marries Archduchess Marie Louise, 186–8, 205; In Russia, 188–99; In Germany, 206–8; Campaign of France, 210–1; Abdicates, 153, 216; In Elba, 222–5; Returns to Paris, 226; Hundred Days, 217–35; Second Abdication, 235; On board *Bellerophon*, 138, 237; On board *Northumberland*, 240; Exile in St Helena, 241–54; Death, 253; Character, 20, 42, 55, 56, 78, 98, 101–2, 108, 133, 137, 139, 153–4, 222, 241; Opinions on: Administration, 62, 80, 82, 83, 98, 265; Economics, 161, 162; Education, 99, 147–9; England, 106, 107, 160; Europe, 56, 132, 174; Politics, 21, 27, 50, 52, 77, 79, 83, 97–8, 100, 132, 137, 149, 171, 173, 256; Press, 100, 106, 147; Religion, 62, 91–3, 258; Sea power, 58, 105, 118, 155; War, 27, 37, 39, 40, 46, 142, 183; Physique, 19, 136, 137, 138, 207, 221, 250–3, 267–8; Relations with: Children, 137, 242, 243; Family, 97, 144–6; Ministers, 153–4; Papacy, 50, 89, 90, 91, 131, 150–3; Servants, 140; Soldiers, 32, 42, 47, 99, 140–1, 141–2, 216, 224, 226, 236; Sovereigns, 132–3; Women, 30, 55, 97, 133, 137, 148; Will and apologia, 252, 253, 255, 256; Writings, 25, 55, 135

Bonaparte, Napoléon Charles, 109, 186

Bonaparte, Napoléon Francis Joseph Charles, King of Rome, Napoleon II, Duke of Reichstadt, 146, 174, 212, 215, 220, 221, 235, 259–63

Bonaparte, Napoléon-Louis, 74, 263

Bonaparte, Pauline, 17, 99, 145, 222, 225, 251

Bordeaux, 161, 171, 213
Borghese, Prince Camillo, 145
Borissov, 196
Bormida, 86
Borodino, 136, 193, 195
Boswell, James, 16
Boulay de la Meurthe, 215
Boulogne, 114, 115, 122
Boulton, Matthew, 160
Bourrienne, Fauvelet de, 75, 76, 136, 156
Braganza, 170
Brescia, 46
Brienne, 20, 211
Brittany, 91, 99
Brueys d'Aigalliers, François-Paul, 61
Bruix, Eustache, 67, 74, 83, 90
Brumaire Crisis, 71, 73, 78, 82, 133
Brumairian Party, 78, 79, 88
Brune, Guillaume, 70, 80, 81, 222
Brunswick, Duke of, 183
Buenos Aires, 128, 157, 158, 164
Bülow, Adam de, 126
Bülow, Friedrich Wilhelm, 207, 232, 234
Buonavita, Antonio, 250
Burghersh, Lord, 270
Burgos, 141, 166, 167, 170, 179
Burton, Doctor, 254, 269, 270
Busaco, 169

Cadiz, 115, 116, 166, 169
Cadoudal, Georges, 80, 81, 100, 109, 110, 111, 112, 113
Cairo, 61, 62, 63, 64, 66, 90
Calabria, 70, 125, 175
Calder, Sir Robert, 115
Caldiero, 47, 123
Cambacérès, Jean-Jacques, Prince of Parma, 80, 96, 111
Campbell, Sir Neil, 221, 222, 223, 238
Campo-Formio, Treaty of, 49, 53, 55, 68, 69, 83, 89
Canning, George, 106, 119, 128, 157, 166
Caprara, Cardinal, 150
Caprera, 22

Carnot, Lazare, 26, 28, 39, 52, 53, 70, 89, 101, 227
Cartagena, 67
Carteaux, Jean François, 25
Castanos, 166
Castiglione, 36, 45, 84, 183
Castlereagh, Robert Stewart, Viscount, 128, 171, 209, 212, 223, 224, 225, 239, 248
Catherine, Grand Duchess, 186
Catherine of Würtemburg, Princess, 145
Caulaincourt, Armand de, Duke of Vicenza: 132; Relations with Napoleon, 138, 140; In Russia, 186, 187, 188, 189, 194, 195, 196, 198, 204; Negotiator at Prague, 206; Foreign Minister, 208, 209, 212, 216, 217, 218
Cesari, General, 22
Ceva, 41, 42
Ceylon, 90
Chaboulon, Fleury de, 225
Champaubert, 212
Championnet, Jean Etienne, 69
Champollion, Jean-François, 64
Chandellier, Jacques, 251
Chaptal, Jean-Antoine, 38, 82, 103, 136, 154
Charles, Archduke, Commander-in-Chief, 180; In Italy, 45, 46, 48, 49, 122, 123; In Germany, 70, 89, 182, 183
Charles IV of Spain, 164, 165
Chateaubriand, François Auguste, Vicomte de, 92, 111, 138, 139, 154, 224, 225, 265
Châtillon, 212, 214
Chaumont, Treaty of, 213
Cherasco, 42
Chesapeake, 157
Choiseul, Etienne-François, Duc de, 35
Cintra, Convention of, 166
Cipriani, Franceschi, 250, 270
Cispadane Republic, 50, 51, 52, 53, 92, 104, 174
Ciudad Rodrigo, 168, 170
Clarke, H. J. G., Duke of Feltre, 44, 48, 177
Clary, Desirée, 30, 144

Clary, Julie, 30
Clausewitz, Karl von, 40, 193
Cockburn, Sir George, 240, 241, 244
Coignet, Captain, 183
Collingwood, Lord, 116
Colli-Rici, L. L. G., 42
Colombier, Caroline, 20
Committee of Public Safety, 38, 43, 72, 81, 102
Concordat, 51, 89, 92, 93, 101, 147, 150, 153, 245
Condé, Louis Joseph de Bourbon, 69
Conscription in France, 39, 142, 210, 229
Constant, Benjamin, 134, 227
Constantinople, 63, 65, 130, 187
Constitution of the Year VIII, 78–80, 95
Conté, Nicholas Jacques, 63
Continental System: Imposed, 103; Effects, 104, 144, 151, 155–63, 164, 174, 183, 186, 189, 190
Copenhagen, 90, 162
Coquebert de Montbret, 103
Corfu, 59, 125
Cornwallis, Marquis, 244
Corsica, 20, 21, 23, 28, 44, 68, 91
Corunna, 115, 167, 169
Corvisart, Jean, Baron, 135, 136, 268
Craonne, 213
Czartoryski, Prince, 121, 188

Dalmatia, 124, 146
Damas, Baron de, 152
Danzig, 128
Dardanelles, 128, 187
Daunou, Pierre C. F., 79, 88
Davout, Louis Nicholas, Prince of Eckmühl: In Germany, 126, 167; In Russia, 191, 192, 193, 196; Minister of War, 229; Capitulates, 233; Character, 143, 158
De La Touche, Mehée, 110, 111
Decaen, Comte, 105
Decrès, Denis, Duke, 115, 140, 153, 236

Dego, 28, 42
Delmas, Antoine-Guillaume, 94
Denmark, 118, 129, 157, 162
Dennewitz, 207
Desaix de Veygouz, L. C. A., 64–6, 85–6, 142, 233
Dietrichstein, Maurice, Count, 259, 260, 261
Dijon, 82, 83
Directory, 27, 51, 58, 68, 69, 70–1, 74–5, 81, 93, 94, 97, 132; Egyptian policy, 58, 67; Italian policy, 32, 33, 41, 43, 44, 45, 49, 50; Peace with Austria, 48, 49
Dolgorouki, Prince, 123, 133
Dommartin, Elzéard-Auguste, 25, 26
Dörnberg, Baron von, 183
Doveton, Sir William, 252
Dresden, 136, 205, 206, 207, 211
Drissa, 191, 192
Drouet, General, see Erlon
Drouot, Antoine, Comte, 190, 221, 225, 232, 233
Dubois-Crancé, E. L. Alexis, 80
Duchâtel, Madame, Elénore Denuelle, 237
Duckworth, Admiral, 128
Ducos, Roger, 71, 73, 74, 77
Dugommier, J. F., 26
Dumerbion, Pierre-Jadar, 28
Dumouriez, Charles François, 111
Dundas, Henry, Viscount Melville, 59, 115
Dupont, Pierre, Comte, 166, 224
Duroc, Michel, Duke of Friuli, 135, 143, 204, 251

East India Company, 241
Eblé, Jean-Baptiste, Comte d', 197
Eckmühl, 182
Egypt, 56, 57, 61, 67, 89, 105, 115, 128; Campaigns, 56, 60–7, 90; Institute of, 63, 64
Elba: Annexed to France, 104; Napoleon at, 216, 217, 219,

221, 222, 226; Return from, 141, 226
Emancipation Edict, 177
Embabeh, Battle of, 61
Embargo Act, 157
Enghien, Duc d', 16, 111–2, 121
England: Economic position, 90, 103, 155–61; Fleet, 52, 58, 59, 60, 61, 65, 66, 162; Superiority, 105, 108, 114, 117; Defence of West Indies, 114; Trafalgar, 115–7; Invasion of considered, 57, 58, 108, 114, 116; Peace with, 89, 90, 94, 103, 190, 209; Possession of Malta, 89, 105, 107; Relations with Prussia, 128; with Russia, 70, 84, 89, 105, 121, 122, 124, 125; War against France, 22, 92, 108, 121, 180
Erfurt, 167, 173, 186, 187
Erlon, Jean-Baptiste Drouet, Comte d', 230
Essling, 140, 143, 182, 183
Ettenheim, 111
Eylau, 127, 129, 143

Fain, Agathon, Baron, 99, 135, 204, 205
Ferdinand, King of Spain, 164, 165, 171, 172, 211, 257
Ferdinand, King of the Two Sicilies, 69, 122, 125, 190, 224
Ferrara, 45, 228
Ferrol, 115
Fichte, Johann Gottlieb, 175
Finkenstein, 128, 148
Finland, 187
First Coalition, 208
Five Hundred, Council of the, 72, 75, 76, 77
Fleurus, 37
Fontainebleau, 214, 221; Pope at, 153; Decree of, 158, 163; Treaty of, 217, 218, 219, 225, 228, 245
Fontanes, Louis, Marquis de, 92, 149, 150, 208
Foscolo, Ugo, 175
Fouché, Joseph, Duke of Otranto: Minister of Police, 74, 76,

146, 227; Enghien Affair, 100, 110–1; Dismissed, 154; Plots against Napoleon, 186; In Hundred Days, 235, 236, 258
Fourcroy, Antoine-François de, 148, 150
Fourès, Madame, 73
Fourier, François, 59
Fox, Charles James, 103, 106, 113, 124, 128
France: Constitutional changes, 18, 70, 71, 77, 78, 79, 101; Economic position, 71, 80, 161, 162; Education reform, 147–8; Fleet, 58, 59, 60–1, 65, 90, 105, 108–9, 114, 115, 116, 117; Law, 95–6; Local Government, 71, 80
Francis I, Emperor of Austria: Character, 180, 181; Changes title, 120–1; Marie Louise and son, 1, 218, 219, 259, 260, 262; Declares war, 121, 183, 203; Peace, 83, 89, 124, 202
Frankfort, Declaration of, 208, 209, 212
Frederick William III, King of Prussia: Neutrality of, 120, 124, 182; War with France, 124, 125, 127; Alliance with France, 128; and Stein, 176–7; Military Reorganization, 177, 178; Alliance with Russia, 200, 201
Friedland, 40, 129, 183, 191
Frochot, Nicholas, Comte, 133
Fructidor Coup, 44, 58, 69, 70, 71, 80
Fuentes D'Oñoro, 169

Ganteaume, Honoré, Comte, 68, 90, 114, 115
Gaudin, Martin Michel Charles, Duke of Gaeta, 80, 161
Gembloux, 232
Geneva, 84
Genoa, 16, 40, 43, 51, 84, 85, 121, 122
Gentz, Friedrich von, 180, 261
Gérard, Etienne-Maurice, Comte, 232

Germany, 27, 121, 175, 176, 205

Gneisenau, Augustus, Count, 177, 178, 232

Godoy, Manuel de, Prince, 162, 164, 165

Goethe, Johann von, 176

Gohier, Jerome, 71, 74

Gourgaud, Gaspard, Baron, 142, 241, 243, 250. 255; Journal, 257, 258

Goya, Francisco de, 164

Grenoble, 151, 226

Grenville, Lord, 157

Gribeauval, Jean-Baptiste de, 34, 35

Gross Beeren, 207

Grouchy, Emmanuel, Marquis de, 229, 231, 232, 233

Guibert, Jacques, Comte de, 37, 39

Hamburg, 207

Hanau, 207

Hanover: Occupation by France, 108, 121, 124, 146, 165; Offered to Prussia, 120, 122, 205; Occupied by Prussia, 128; Restored to England, 125

Hardenberg, Charles Augustus, Prince, 176, 177

Haugwitz, Christian, Count von, 123, 124

Hawkesbury, Lord, see Lord Liverpool

Heilsberg, 129

Hoche, Lazare, 52

Hohenlinden, 89

Hohenlohe, Prince, 126

Holland: Allied Forces in, 70, 89; Cape of Good Hope returned, 90; Evacuation of the French, 105; Louis, King of Holland, 144, 209; Direct rule by France, 146, 158; Export of wheat, 159; Fleet, 105

Hompesch, Ferdinand de, Baron, 60, 69

Hormayr, Joseph, Baron, 180

Hotham, Sir Henry, 237, 238

Hundred Days, 162, 217–25, 258

Hyde de Neuville, Jean Guillaume, Baron, 80, 88

Inconstant, 226

India, 57, 58, 59, 65, 89, 187

Invalides, 255

Ionian Islands, 125, 129

Istria, 123

Italy: and the Coalition, 122; Army of, 27, 28, 32, 39, 41–50, 53, 70, 73, 83, 84, 85; Invasion of by Russians, 66, 70; Kingdom of, 174; Occupation of, 44, 69; Religion in, 91, 150–1; Republic of, 104, 121, 257; Retreats from, 66

Ivrea, 84, 85

Jaffa, 65

Jamestown, 241, 242

Jefferson, President, 157

Jemappes, 34, 37

Jena, 40, 126, 129, 144, 156, 164, 178

John, Archduke, 182, 201

Jomini, Henri, Baron, 40, 206

Josephine, Empress, 30, 31, 43, 72, 187, 258

Jourdan, Jean Baptiste, Comte: In Germany, 44, 72; In Egypt, 66; Brumaire, 73, 74, 75, 80; Incompetence, 168

Junot, Jean Androche, Duke of Abrantès: Wife, 19, 30; Toulon, 26; Relations with Napoleon, 28, 56, 59, 143; Madame de Staël, 133; Army of Portugal, 165, 166; Russia, 191; Inadequacies, 143, 229

Kalisch, 201

Kaluga, 195

Katte, Friedrich Wilhelm von, 182

Katzbach, 207

Keith, Viscount, 138, 239

Kellerman, François Christophe, Duke of Valmy, 43, 86

King of Rome, see under Bonaparte

Kléber, Jean Baptiste, 61, 66, 67, 90
Koller, General von, 222
Krasnoi, 196
Kulm, 207
Kurakin, Alexandre, Prince, 190
Kutusov, Michael, Prince: At Ulm, 122, 123; In Russia, 193–6, 200

La Bedoyère, François, Comte de, 226, 227, 230
Laffitte, Jacques, 237
La Haye Sainte, 234
Laibach, 123
Lainé, Joseph, Vicomte, 208–9
Landshut, 181
Lallemand, Charles, Baron, 224, 240
Lanjuinais, Jean-Denis, Comte, 228
Lannes, Jean, Duke of Montebello: Relations with Napoleon, 143, 187; Italy, 201; Marengo, 85, 87; Austerlitz, 129; Essling, 182
Laon, 213
Laplace, Pierre-Simon, Marquis de, 38, 81
La Revellière-Lépeaux, Louis, 52, 91
La Rothière, 211
Las Cases, Emmanuel de, 255
Las Cases, Emmanuel-Joseph, Comte de: Negotiations with Bellerophon, 237; At St Helena, 241, 243, 247, 250; Publishes 'Mémorial de St Hélène,' 256, 261
Latouche-Tréville, Louis René, Comte de, 114
Lauderdale, Earl of, 125
La Vendée, 28, 80, 92, 161, 229, 237
Lavoisier, Antoine, 38
Leclerc, Victor Emmanuel, 99, 145
Lefebvre, François Joseph, Duke of Danzig, 131, 132, 216
Leghorn, 43, 44, 59
Legion of Honour, 94, 95

Leipzig, 176, 203, 207, 208, 210, 211
Lenoir, Richard, 104
Leoben, 49, 52, 53
Léon, Comte, 109, 186, 237
Ligny, 230, 231, 233
Ligurian Republic, 51
Lille, 107
Lisbon, 169
Lithuania, 192
Liverpool, Lord, 239
Loano, 32
Lobau, 181, 182
Locré, Jean-Guthrum, Baron, 82
Lodi, 42
Lombardy, 43, 50, 51, 84, 86
Lonato, 46
L'Orient, sinking of the, 63
Lorraine, 213
Louis XVI, 19, 21, 102
Louis XVIII: Declaration of Verona, 71; writes to Napoleon, 100; refuses Enghien enquiry, 112; Returns to France, 213, 216, 224, 235; and Talleyrand, 214; Accepts constitution, 215; Leaves Paris, 228
Louisiana, 104
Lowe, Sir Hudson: Relations with Napoleon, 244, 247, 248, 249, 252, 253, 254, 267, 269; Unpopularity, 255; Character, 245–6, 253
Luddite Riots, 159
Lunéville, 89, 104, 105, 121
Lützen, 143, 203, 204
Luxembourg, 89
Lyons, 24, 226, 227
Lyttelton, William Henry, Lord, 240

Macdonald, Etienne, Duke of Taranto, 199, 207, 216
Mack, Charles, Baron, 122
Maddalena, 22
Madison, President, 159
Madrid, 165, 167, 169, 170, 171, 172
Magallon, Consul, 57
Maida, 37, 125
Maistre, Joseph de, 113, 223

Maitland, Sir Frederick, 138, 237, 238, 239, 240, 241

Malcolm, Sir Pulteney, 245, 248

Malet, Claude-François de, 133, 198

Mallet du Pan, Jacques, 58

Malmaison, 108, 236

Malmesbury, Earl of, 52, 103

Malojaroslavetz, 195

Malta: Invasion of, 57, 58, 59, 60, 61, 125; Blockade, 83, 115; Capture by the English, 89, 90, 105, 106; Shipments through, 159; Possible internment of Napoleon, 241

Mamelukes, 57, 61, 63

Mantua, 45, 46, 47, 48, 86, 165

Marbeuf, Louis-Charles-René, Comte de, 16, 17, 18

Marbot, Antoine, Baron, 72

Marchand, Louis, Valet, 240, 250, 253, 255, 267, 268, 270

Marchand, Madame, 259

Marengo, 40, 85–6, 88, 89, 129, 233

Maret, Hugues-Bernard, Duke of Bassano, 83, 154, 198, 208, 225

Maria Carolina, Queen of the Two Sicilies, 125

Marie-Louise, Empress: Marriage to Napoleon, 217–8; Influence on, 133, 205; Regent, 203; Leaves for Rambouillet, 212, 218; Letters, 213, 217, 256; Remarries, 221; Referred to in Napoleon's Will, 257; Character, 221

Maria Louisa, Queen of Spain, 164

Markov, Arcadi-Ivanovitch, Count, 121

Marmont, Auguste F. L., Duke of Ragusa: Relations with Napoleon, 26, 28, 136, 141; Artillery Expert, 35; In Italy, 46; Marengo, 86, 87; Marshal, 143; Spain, 169, 170, 171; Germany, 182; Russia, 194; Hundred Days, 212, 213, 214, 216

Marseilles, 25, 161

Martinique, 114, 115

Masséna, André, Prince of Essling: Relations with Napoleon, 32, 137; In Italy, 42, 46, 83, 84, 85, 122, 125; Governorship of Rome, 69; Zürich, 70; Spain, 169; Austria, 183; Character, 143, 169

Mauritius, 65

Mazis de, Lieutenant, 19

Mediation, Act of, 104

Medina Del Rio Seco, 166

Mélas, Michael, Baron de, 83, 85, 86

Melito, Miot de, 49, 52, 77, 114, 168

Melzi D'Eril, François, Duke of Lodi, 121

Memel, 128

Méneval, Claude-François, Baron, 136, 138, 219, 259, 262

Menou, Jacques François, 62, 90

Merlin, Phillipe Antoine, 70

Metternich-Winneburg, Clement, Prince of: Relations with Napoleon, 139, 205, 265; Writings, 114, 163; Relations with Marie Louise, 218–21; Relations with King of Rome, 218–20, 259, 262; Austrian Ambassador, 154, 180; Prime Minister, 183, 185, 191; Congress of Vienna, 202, 224, 228; War with France, 203, 204, 205; Peace negotiations, 208, 209; Alliance with Murat, 211

Metz, 227

Mexico, 158, 162

Milan, 50, 70, 85, 92, 121; Decree of, 157, 159

Millesimo, 42

Minsk, 196

Mirabeau, Gabriel-Honoré Riquetti, Comte de, 21, 101, 102

Moghileff, 192

Molé, Louis Mathieu, Comte, 56, 227

Mollien, Nicholas, Comte, 162

Mombello, 49, 52, 56

Moncey, Adrien, Duke of Co-
negliano, 216
Mondovi, 41, 42
Monge, Gaspard, 17, 35, 38, 59,
62, 63
Montchenu, Marquis de, 243,
247
Montebello, 85
Montenotte, 42
Montereau, 211
Montesquiou, Madame de, 259
Montevideo, 157
Montholon, Charles Tristan,
Marquis de, 241, 249, 252,
254, 257
Montholon, Madame de, 250,
268
Mont St Jean, 231, 232, 233
Montmartre, 214
Montmirail, 40, 212
Moore, Sir John, 167
Moreau, Jean Victor: Relations
with Napoleon, 71, 89; In
Italy, 44, 45, 46, 49; Rhine,
84, 89; Exiled, 110, 206;
Death, 207; Character, 99
Mortier, E. A. C. J., Duke of
Treviso, 122, 195, 214, 233
Moscow, 192–94; Retreat from,
141
Moulins, Jean F., 71, 74
Mounier, Jean-Joseph, 81
Mount Tabor, 65
Murat, Joachim: Alliance with
Metternich, 211; Alliance with
Napoleon, 228, 229; Auster-
litz, 127, 129; Brumaire, 74,
76; Death, 248; Dress, 135;
Governor of Paris, 111; Italy,
175; Kingdom of the Two
Sicilies, 174, 224; Marengo,
87; Marriage, 145, 146; Rus-
sia, 192, 194, 195, 198, 199;
Spain, 166; Tuileries, 29;
Character, 143, 146

Naples, 43, 45, 69, 70, 90, 104,
116, 121, 125
Napoleon III, *see under* Bonaparte
Narbonne, Louis, Comte de,
141, 189, 204

Necker, Jacques, 133, 134
Neipperg, Albert, Count, 220,
257, 261
Nelson, Horatio, Viscount: Attack on Copenhagen, 90;
Death, 116; In Mediterrane-
an, 59, 60, 61, 63, 65, 69,
114, 115, 116, 120; Strategy,
117, 118, 119; Trafalgar vic-
tory, 115
Neuchâtel, 124
Ney, Michel, Prince of the Mos-
kowa: Austerlitz, 129; Death,
239; Germany, 203, 204, 207;
Hundred Days, 227, 229–31,
233, 234; Paris, 216; Rela-
tions with Louis XVIII, 223,
227; Russia, 192, 194, 196,
199; Spain, 167; Tactics, 37;
Character, 143, 227, 229
Nile, Battle of, 61, 64, 65, 69
Nogent, 211
Northumberland, 240
Norway, 190
Noverraz, footman, 268, 270
Novi, 70
Nuremberg, 126

Ocaña, 169
Oldenburg, 146, 158, 186, 188
O'Meara, Barry, 241, 251, 252,
256, 267
Oneglia, 27
Orcha, 196, 197
Orgon, 222
Orléans, Louis Phillipe, Duc d',
89, 235
Orthez, 171, 213
Osten, Prokesch von, 261, 262
Ostrovno, 192
Oubril, Count, 125
Oudinot, Charles-Nicolas, Duke
of Reggio, 197, 207
Ouvrard, Gabriel, 80, 162

Pacca, Cardinal, 152
Padua, 48
Paoli, Pascal, 16, 17, 20, 21, 22,
23, 106, 238, 266
Papacy, 45, 50, 104, 146, 150,
163
Papal States, 151, 153, 174, 264

Parma, 89, 104, 174, 217
Parthenopean Republic, 69, 70
Pasquier, Etienne, Duke, 151
Patterson, Elizabeth, 145
Paul I, Tsar, 69, 89, 112
Pavia, 44
Pellapra, Madame, 237
Peninsular War: 158; Duke of Wellington, 167, 169–71, 189; Tactics, 37, 125
Perceval, Spencer, 128
Permon, Laure, 19, 30
Permon, Madame, 30
Persia, 128
Peschiera, 45
Phélipeaux, 65
Phull, General von, 191
Piacenza, 174
Pichegru, Charles, 52, 110, 112
Piedmont: 104, 122, 209; Battles, 28, 40, 42, 83, 85; Peace with, 42, 43; Relations with Austria, 41
Pitt, William: Army in West Indies, 24; Assassination of Napoleon, 113; Death, 124; England economics, 90, 156, 160; Fails to invade, 84; Negotiation with France, 52; Organization of Third Coalition, 115, 121; Reinforces fleet, 59
Pius VI, Pope, 50, 51, 69, 92, 93, 112
Pius VII, Pope, 89, 91, 92, 93, 94, 150, 151, 152, 153, 185, 203, 245
Pius IX, Pope, 150
Planat, de la Faye, Colonel, 241
Poland, 27, 121, 127, 152, 175, 188, 192, 224, 228, 256, 257
Ponarskaia, 199
Poniatowski, Prince, 188
Pontécoulant, L. G. I. Doulcet de, 28
Portalis, Jean Etienne, 96, 150
Portland, Duke of, 128
Portugal, 59, 90, 158, 164, 167, 168, 209
Potsdam, 123
Pozzo di Borgo, Charles-André, Comte, 21

Prague, 204, 206
Pratzen, 123
Pressburg, Treaty of, 124
Prussia: 175; Alliance with Russia, 121, 123, 200–1, 205; Army in, 178; Neutrality, 32, 120, 122, 200; Reformation of, 176, 177, 179; Relations with England, 128, 204; Treaties with France, 124, 127–9, 190; War with France, 21, 124–6
Pultusk, 127
Pyramids, Battle of, *see* Embabeh

Quatre-Bras, 230, 231

Raab, 182
Rainer, Archduke, 260
Rambouillet, 212, 214, 219, 236
Rapp, Jean, Comte, 184
Rastadt, 53, 57
Réal, Pierre François, Comte, 209
Reichenbach, 205, 208
Reille, H. C., Comte, 231
Rémusat, Madame de, 31, 112, 133, 138
Reubell, Jean-François, 52, 70
Reynier, Jean, Comte, 125
Rheims, 213
Rhine, Army of, 44, 46, 48, 49, 83, 84, 99, 180
Rhine, Confederation of, 124, 204
Rhône Valley, 222
Ricketts, 252
Rivoli, 45, 47, 48, 50, 87
Robespierre, Augustin, 27, 32
Robespierre, Maximilien, 26, 27, 91, 102
Rochefort, 236
Roeder, Captain, 193
Roederer, Pierre-Louis, Comte, 72, 74, 109, 148
Rohan, Prince de, 57
Roman Republic, 69, 78, 91
Rome, 43, 51, 70, 146, 151, 153
Rostopchine, 194
Roumiantsov, Count, 186, 187

302							INDEX

Rousseau, Jean Jacques, 16, 20, 25, 56, 102, 139
Roustam, 135, 217
Rovereto, 46
Ruffo, Cardinal, 70
Rumelia, 130
Russia: Alliance with Austria, 70, 121, 122; Alliance with England, 70, 84, 89, 105–6, 112, 121, 122; Alliance with France, 89, 129, 155, 186, 187, 204; Alliance with Prussia, 121, 123, 200–1, 205; Declaration of War with France, 66, 69, 163, 188, 205; Battles with France outside Russia, 70, 123, 124, 127; Campaign, 185, 199; Economic position, 161; Protest on Enghien, 111; Turkey, 121, 128, 129, 130, 187, 188, 190

Sacken, F. G., Prince de, 212
St Aignan, Baron de, 208
St. André, Jean-Bon, 81
St Cloud, 74, 75, 77, 80
St Cyr, Laurent Gouvion de, 197, 207
St Germain, Claude-Louis, Comte, 18, 19, 35
St Helena, 225, 239–54
St John, Knights of, 57, 60, 69, 89
St Petersburg, 122, 190, 195
St Pierre, 57
St Priest, Guillaume-Emmanuel, Comte de, 213
St Raphaël, 68
Sainte-Croix, Charles Marie Robert, Comte de, 140
Salamanca, 167, 169, 170, 194
Saliceti, Christophe, 25, 27, 40, 43
Salzburg, 183
San Domingo, 99, 104, 105, 145
San Michele, 42
San Sebastian, 170
Santander, 170
Santarem, 169
Santini, Natale, 249
Saorgio, 27

Sardinia, 60
Savary, A. J. M., Duke of Rovigo: Ambassador to Russia, 186; Head of Gendarmerie, 110, 111; Minister of Police, 146, 210; Negotiations with Bellerophon, 237; Trial by French, 240; Character, 154
Savona, 152, 153
Saxony, 204, 224
Scharnhorst, Gerard David von, 176, 177, 178
Schérer, Barthélemy, 32, 41
Schill, Friedrich von, 182
Schlegel, August Wilhelm von, 175, 180
Schönbrunn, Treaty of, 124, 152, 183, 184
Schwarzenberg, Karl Philipp, Prince von, 197, 199, 200, 203, 206, 207, 212, 213, 216
Sebastiani, François, Comte, 74, 105, 121
Second Coalition against the Republic, 69, 70, 83, 89
September Massacres, 21
Serbelloni, Duke of, 51
Shortt, Dr Thomas, 253, 254
Sicily, 60, 115, 125, 174
Sieyès, Emmanuel Joseph, Comte: Brumaire, 74–82; In the Directory, 71, 72, 73; List of notabilities, 101; Plot against Napoleon, 88–9, 95; Character, 71
Smith, Sir William Sidney, 65, 66, 90
Smolensk, 40, 192, 193, 195, 196
Smorgoni, 198, 202
Soissons, 213
Soult, Nicolas Jean de Dieu, Duke of Dalmatia: Chief of Staff, 229, 230, 232; Germany, 213; In Spain, 167, 169, 170, 171; Character, 143
South America, 157, 158
Spain: 27; Fleet, 66, 67, 83, 105; Independence, 200, 257; Loss of, 200, 257; Louisiana sold to France, 104; Out of war, 32; Religious feeling,

152, 172; Resources, 164; Subsidy to French, 162; War in, 24, 119, 131, 163–72
Speranski, Michael, Count, 186
Stadion, Johann, Graf von, 180, 183
Staël, Auguste de, 134
Staël, Germaine de, 88, 100, 133, 134, 180
Staps, Frederick, 183
Stein, Friedrich, Freiherr vom und zum, 176–80, 200, 201, 208
Stendhal (Henri Beyle), 82, 98, 133, 154, 210
Stockach, 70
Stokoe, Dr John, 252, 267
Studianka, 197
Stürmer, Barthélemy, Baron, 246, 259
Stuart, Sir John, 125
Suchet, Louis Gabriel, Duke of Albufera, 170, 211, 229
Sulkowski, 47
Superb, 238
Sussex, Duke of, 239
Suvorov, Alexandre, Count, 70, 84
Sweden, 129, 187, 188, 190, 206
Switzerland, 69, 104, 105
Syria, 64, 65, 68

Talleyrand-Périgord, Charles Maurice de, Prince of Benevento: Brumaire, 73, 74, 76, 80; Congress of Vienna, 202, 214, 224; Enghien, 111; Erfurt, 187; Foreign Minister, 52, 57, 58, 63, 83, 104, 113; and Marie-Louise, 212, 214, 215; Negotiations with Austria, 123; Out of Office, 72; Peace settlement, 203; Relations with Napoleon, 106, 131, 154, 204, 264; Resigns, 154
Tallien, Madame, 30
Tarascon, 25
Taurroggen, 200
Tchitchagov, Paul, 197
Teil, Jean-Pierre, Baron du, 20
Thermidor Crisis, 27, 29

Thibaudeau, Antoine, Comte, 95–7, 101
Thiébault, Paul, Baron, 137
Third Coalition, 115, 121, 124
Tilsit, Treaty of, 129, 131, 153, 175, 186, 187
Tolentino, 50, 51, 91, 228
Torres Vedras, 169
Toulon, 20, 24, 66, 90, 114
Toulouse, 171
Trafalgar, 115, 119, 122, 155
Trent, 46
Trianon Decree, 158, 163
Tribunate, 146
Trinidad, 90
Turenne, 140, 218
Turkey: Friendship with France, 28; Napoleon sent to, 57; War with France, 57, 63, 64, 66, 68, 69, 90; Russia and, 121, 128, 129, 130, 187, 188, 190
Tuscany, 45, 174, 218
Tuscany, Grand Duke of, 89

Udine, 53
Ulm, 40, 122, 181
Undaunted, 222
United States of America: 156–9; War with England, 157; War of Independence, 117
Ushant, 115
Ussher, Sir Thomas, 222, 238
Uxbridge, Lord, 234

Valençay, Treaty of, 171, 203
Valence, 20, 21
Valencia, 170
Valetta, 60
Valmy, 20, 22, 34, 35, 111
Valutino, 192
Vandamme, Dominique-René, Comte, 207
Vauchamps, 212
Vendémiaire Crisis, 31
Venice, 53, 54, 56
Vercelli, Bishop of, 93
Verdun, 108
Verona, 53, 71
Viazma, 196
Victor, Claude Perrin, Duke of Belluno, 197
Vienna, 180, 181, 220, 264

Vienna, Congress of, 201, 202, 223, 224, 225, 228
Vignali, Angelo, 251, 253
Villeneuve, Pierre C. J. B., 114, 115, 116, 119
Vilna, 191, 192, 199
Vimiero, 166
Vincennes, 214
Visconti, 51
Vitebsk, 192
Vitrolles, Eugène, Baron de, 214
Vittoria, 180, 205
Voltri, 41
Vorarlberg, 124

Wagram, 140, 144, 151, 158, 169, 182, 183
Walcheren, 158, 182
Walewska, Marie, 186, 223, 237
Walewski, Alexandre, Comte, 186, 237
Warden, Dr William, 244
Warsaw, Grand Duchy of, 175, 183, 188, 204, 205
Waterloo: Napoleon and, 137, 162; Tactics, 37, 38, 40, 160, 233
Wavre, 231, 232, 233
Weapons, 34, 35, 38, 118

Wellington, Arthur Wellesley, Duke of: 16, 38, 65, 143, 158, 160; Final campaigns, 229–34, 242, 246; Opinion of Napoleon, 141, 169, 210–11, 245, 257; Peninsular War, 167, 169, 170, 171, 189
West Indies, 114, 225
Westphalia, 145
Wheeler, Private, 141
White Terror, 222
Whitworth, Earl, 105, 109
Windham, William, 113
Winkovo, 195
Wittgenstein, Prince, 197
Woronzoff, Alexander, Count, 121
Wrede, Karl Philipp, Prince von, 207, 213
Wright, Captain, 110
Wurmser, Dagobert, Count, 45, 46
Würtemberg, 122, 124

Yarmouth, Lord, 124, 125
Yorck, Ludwig, Count von, 179, 200
York, Duke of, 70

Zürich, 70